The media's watching Vault!
Here's a sampling of our coverage.

"For those hoping to climb the ladder of success, [Vault's] insights are priceless."
– *Money magazine*

"The best place on the Web to prepare for a job search."
– *Fortune*

"[Vault guides] make for excellent starting points for job hunters and should be purchased by academic libraries for their career sections [and] university career centers."
– *Library Journal*

"The granddaddy of worker sites."
– *U.S. News & World Report*

"A killer app."
– *The New York Times*

One of *Forbes'* 33 "Favorite Sites"
– *Forbes*

"To get the unvarnished scoop, check out Vault."
– *Smart Money Magazine*

"Vault has a wealth of information about major employers and job-searching strategies as well as comments from workers about their experiences at specific companies."
– *The Washington Post*

"A key reference for those who want to know what it takes to get hired by a law firm and what to expect once they get there."
– *New York Law Journal*

"Vault [provides] the skinny on working conditions at all kinds of companies from current and former employees."
– *USA Today*

VAULT
> the most trusted name in career information™

VAULT GUIDE TO THE
TOP PHARMA & BIOTECH EMPLOYERS

EDITED BY MICHAELA R. DRAPES & NICHOLAS R. LICHTENBERG

Library of Congress CIP Data is available.

ISBN 13: 978-1-58131-540-0

ISBN 10: 1-58131-540-6

Printed in the United States of America

ACKNOWLEDGMENTS

We are extremely grateful to Vault's entire staff—especially Ingrid Ahlgren, Todd Obolsky, Laurie Pasiuk, Mary Sotomayor and Marcy Lerner—for all their help in the editorial, production and marketing processes for this guide. Vault also would like to acknowledge the support of our investors, clients, employees, family and friends. Thank you!

To ensure that our research was thorough and accurate, we relied on a number of people within the companies that we profiled.

To the many employees who took the time to be interviewed or to complete our survey, we could never thank you enough. Your insights about life inside the top pharma and biotech employers were invaluable, and your willingness to speak candidly will help job seekers for years to come. We also thank the firms who were so helpful in completing this project.

Table of Contents

Introduction

Small molecules and large companies

Strictly speaking, the term "pharmaceuticals" refers to medicines composed of small, synthetically produced molecules, which are sold by large, fully integrated drug manufacturers. The largest of these players—companies like Pfizer, GlaxoSmithKline and Merck—as well as a handful of others are known as "Big Pharma" because they are huge research, development and manufacturing concerns with subsidiaries around the globe. Indeed, Big Pharma is where most of the industry's sales are generated. During 2006, the industry boasted about $643 billion in global sales, and prescription revenue increased about 8 percent in the United States.

A profitable business

According to the Kaiser Family Foundation, from 1995 to 2002, the pharmaceutical business was the most lucrative industry in America. Pharmaceutical manufacturers haven't fared as well in recent years, however. In 2003 the pharmaceutical industry ranked third, and in 2005 it ranked fifth. However, in 2006, the pharmaceutical industry ranked second in the country. Big pharmaceutical companies have struggled with the increased cost of developing new drugs that are more complex. Many firms have also faced lawsuits, pricing pressures and generic competition.

From aspirin to Herceptin: a brief history of the industry

Many of today's big pharmaceutical firms have roots that go back to the late 19th or early 20th century. Not all of these companies started out as drug manufacturers. For instance, Frederich Bayer founded Bayer in Germany in 1863 to make synthetic dyes. In the 1920s and 1930s, scientists discovered miracle drugs such as insulin and penicillin, and pharmaceutical companies began to market researchers' lifesaving inventions. During the 1950s and 1960s, companies started to mass produce and market new drugs such as blood-pressure medications, birth control pills and Valium. Pharmaceutical companies researched and developed new cancer treatments, including chemotherapy, in the 1970s. The modern biotech business was born when, in 1976, Herbert Boyer and Robert Swanson founded Genentech, which eventually made breast cancer biologic Herceptin. In the 1980s, drug companies faced new environmental and safety regulations and mounting economic pressures.

For Big Pharma, the 1990s was a time of turmoil; many large mergers and acquisitions drastically changed the industry's competitive landscape. In 1999, Pfizer made an unsolicited $82.4 billion offer for Warner Lambert just a few hours after the rival drug firm agreed to merge with American Home Products (now Wyeth). Pfizer's offer was significantly sweeter than AHP's, but it seemed Warner Lambert was not interested. Pfizer eventually won the battle for Warner Lambert, and the two companies merged in June 2000, creating a nearly $30 billion dollar company rivaled only by Merck. In 2000, SmithKline Beecham merged with GlaxoWellcome to become another gigantic company, GlaxoSmithKline. During the 1990s, Pharmaceutical companies also began to use contract research organizations for more of their R&D efforts.

Big Pharma

In 2006, large pharmaceutical companies launched several high-profile products including human papillomavirus vaccine Gardasil, oral diabetes drug Januvia and cancer treatment Sutent. Big Pharma is responsible for all those television commercials urging us to contact our doctors if we suspect we suffer from restless leg syndrome or social anxiety disorder or fibromyalgia. Yet despite lifesaving, cancer-fighting drugs and significant corporate philanthropy, Big Pharma's recent product recalls and concerns over drug safety have made it the industry many people love to hate. In late September 2004, Merck pulled Vioxx from the market after a long-term clinical trial revealed that some patients developed certain types of cardiovascular events (heart attacks and strokes) after taking the drug for extended periods. The FDA later concluded that all COX-2 inhibitors, like Vioxx, increased the risk of certain types of cardiovascular events with long-term use. After finding out about Vioxx's health risks, more than 30,000 people sued Merck. In 2007, GlaxoSmithKline's diabetes medication Avandia made headlines after researchers found it increased patients' risk of heart attack.

Before we help you chart a career in the industry, we should point out that both the scope of players and the types of products the industry produces are moving targets. This is because the pharmaceutical and biotech industries are gradually integrating into one industry.

Most of the largest Big Pharma players are gobbling up small biotechs through outright acquisitions or, alternatively, entering licensing agreements to co-develop new treatments. For example, in 2006, AstraZeneca acquired small biotech firm Cambridge Antibody Technology Group and Merck purchased GlycoFi and

Abmaxis. This trend is likely to continue throughout the rest of this decade, since it's increasingly difficult to find innovative new drugs through traditional science.

In fact, innovation is the industry's biggest current challenge. Companies are using acquisitions and alliances to round out their product pipelines and meet investor expectations. Big drug manufacturers can now claim to research, manufacture and sell both types of drugs: synthetic small molecules (or old chemistry), and injectable large molecules (or biologics).

What is biotechnology?

The biotechnology industry is unique because it is defined by the technology used to create its products—not by its products themselves. The United Nations Convention on Biological Diversity defines biotechnology as "any technological application that uses biological systems, living organisms, or derivatives thereof, to make or modify products or processes for specific use." In other words, biotechnology is any technology based on biology. Ancient practices, such as using microorganisms to ferment beverages or leaven bread, are a primitive form of biotechnology. So is farmers' alteration of fruits and vegetables through breeding them with other plants, or the creation of different breeds of livestock.

Today, four major industrial areas utilize biotechnology: crop production and agriculture, environmental uses, nonfood use of plants (such as biofuels) and health care. For the most part, when people hear the word "biotechnology"—or "biotech" for short—they think of its applications in medicine. Biotechnology companies have created new vaccines and therapies for diseases such as diabetes, cancer, autoimmune disorders and HIV/AIDS. However, nonmedical concerns, such as Diversa Corporation, customize enzymes for manufacturers in the industrial, and health and nutrition markets. Currently, the firm is applying its enzyme expertise to develop alternative fuels.

Modern biotech's beginnings

In 1973, Stanley Cohen of Stanford University and Herbert Boyer of UCSF created a new recombinant DNA technique. Together with venture capitalist Robert Swanson, in 1976 Boyer went on to found Genentech, which considers itself "the founder of the biotechnology industry." Today Genentech is one of the largest and most successful biotech companies. The firm's top-selling products include cancer treatments Rituxan, Avastin and Herceptin.

By the 1980s, small biotechnology firms were struggling to stay afloat. Some big pharmaceutical companies purchased smaller biotech companies. Other biotechs formed partnerships with "Big Pharma." The biotechnology industry has expanded rapidly since the 1990s. The Biotechnology Industry Organization (BIO) reports that there were 1,415 biotechnology companies in the United States in December 2005, an increase from about 1,300 in 1994. Of the more than 1,400 biotech companies in business today, 329 were publicly traded companies. The rest are private, discovery research-oriented firms. In 2005, the health care biotech industry's revenue topped $50 billion in the United States.

Small vs. big biotech

Most health care biotechnology firms are small, research-oriented companies dedicated to applying genetics to curing a multitude of diseases, from Alzheimer's to multiple sclerosis. A handful of companies—such as Amgen and Genentech—have broken through the rest of the pack to become "fully integrated" like their Big Pharma cousins. The term "fully integrated" means that they manufacture as well as sell their own products. The largest biotechs—dubbed "Big Biotech"—are actually much like midsized or large pharmaceutical companies, and are vertically integrated companies that research, develop and market their products. And like larger companies, Big Biotech sometimes has big profits. For instance, in 2006 Genentech's revenue topped $9 billion, and Biogen Idec brought in more than $2.6 billion.

Many smaller, younger biotech companies, on the other hand, have yet to see a profit. These firms are counting on drugs in the pipeline, which they hope will be big hits down the road. In recent years, to stay afloat, some small biotech companies have entered into partnerships with Big Pharma and Big Biotech. For example, California-headquartered Amylin, which has developed new medicines to treat of type 2 diabetes, has a collaboration agreement with Eli Lilly. Nuvelo—a small biotech business dedicated to discovering, developing and commercializing novel drugs—collaborated with larger, more established companies including Bayer and Amgen.

"Biologics": beyond experimental gene therapies

Biologic drugs go beyond experimental gene therapies. Anything used to treat, prevent or cure a disease that's also made from a living organism is a "biologic." Some medical products that have been around for decades fit into this category. Because vaccines are made from living organisms, they're considered biologics.

Insulin—created by extracting the gene for insulin from a human cell—is also considered a biologic drug. Novo Nordisk, which makes diabetes treatments including insulin, and competitor Lilly have said they oppose any FDA action that would approve the production and sale of generic insulin without clinical studies. The availability of generic insulin would put price pressure on branded insulin. The approval of generic insulin could also open the door to the development of generic versions of other biologics.

Therapeutics vs. diagnostics

Both synthetic and biologic drugs are directed toward the treatment of disease. The industry refers to this broad category as "therapeutics," since these drugs have a therapeutic effect on the disease condition. But the industry also has another category of products focused on helping medical scientists more accurately determine (or diagnose) what's wrong with a patient presenting multiple, often difficult-to-interpret symptoms. These products are called "diagnostics" and may come from biologic sources. Often, diagnostic agents (they are not called drugs) are used in conjunction with a medical device or instrument. A good example is the diagnostic imaging agent technetium 99m, which helps MRI machines create clearer cross-sections of the human body.

Organizational structures

Pharmaceutical companies are generally organized around the "blockbuster" model, i.e., they derive most of their sales and profits from a handful of broadly acting drugs. By industry consensus, a "blockbuster" is a drug whose annual revenue reaches or exceeds $1 billion. An example of a Big Pharma blockbuster is AstraZeneca's cholesterol-lowering Crestor, which had more than $2 billion in sales in 2006 and has been prescribed to more than six million people.

The biotech firms, on the other hand, tend to be organized around smaller franchises, i.e., their products are targeted to small patient populations with rare genetic diseases. Their biologics are sold by specialty sales representatives, who often have a relatively high degree of scientific knowledge. Because of this focus, biotech products are often referred to as specialty pharmaceuticals. To complicate matters, some biologics reach blockbuster status with respect to their revenue, since they are usually much more expensive than synthetics. Considering that some biologics cost $10,000 per patient per year, you would need a mere 100,000 patients to reach $1 billion in revenue. For example, Genzyme's biologic drug Cerezyme topped $1

Visit Vault at **www.vault.com** for insider company profiles, expert advice, career message boards, expert resume reviews, the Vault Job Board and more.

VAULT CAREER LIBRARY

5

billion in sales in 2006, but fewer than 5,000 people worldwide use the biologic meant to treat a rare genetic condition called Gaucher disease. However, Cerezyme costs more than $200,000 a year.

Introducing "biopharma"

The dividing line between the pharma and biotech industries will continue to fade. That leaves us with the problem of how to refer to the emerging industry. As discussed earlier, some biotech firms have grown so diverse that they're similar to large pharmaceutical companies. At the same time, pharmaceutical companies have been snapping up biotech businesses to beef up their pipelines. Some people refer to the emerging industry as "biopharma." In an April 2007 article in Science, writer Gunjan Sinha argued that the line between pharmaceutical and biotech companies is blurring. Sinha said that, as little as 15 years ago, the industries were distinct, but today the question of whether to work in biotech or pharmaceuticals may not matter. We'll be using the term "biopharma" to include both types of products.

The global pharmaceutical industry

Three major market segments dominate the global industry. North America is the largest and comprises more than 47 percent of the total market; Europe is second with some 30 percent. Japan comes in third, providing about 9 percent of 2006 sales. Although these combined markets account for nearly 87 percent of global sales, the remaining emerging market segments—other Asian countries, Africa, and Australia and Latin America—are growing rapidly. According to IMS Health, Inc., a health care research and information company, in 2006 sales in Asia, Africa and Australia were $52 billion, a 9.8 percent increase from 2005. The pharmaceutical industry is especially interested in China and India, both of which have growing middle classes. Global pharmaceutical sales in Latin America in 2006 were $27.5 billion, a 12.9 percent increase from the previous year.

Although a handful of super-large companies rake in most of the pharmaceutical industry's revenue, the global industry is actually highly fragmented. Over 2,000 pharmaceutical and biotech companies exist worldwide. In the top tier are the large, multinational companies that dominate the market, or Big Pharma. In the middle tier are the specialty companies. Many large companies tend to absorb second-tier companies before they can grow enough to pose a competitive threat. That trend has a contracting effect on the number of firms. The opposite happens on the third and lowest tier, which is composed of an ever-increasing group of startups mostly focused on discovery research.

According to IMS Health, Inc., as recently as 1999, the global pharmaceutical market was valued at $334 billion. By 2006, total global sales had nearly doubled to $643 billion, or more than half a trillion dollars! (IMS derived this figure from retail sales in major global markets.) This astonishing growth reflects the increasing role of pharmaceuticals as a first-line treatment option for many disease conditions in the developed world. The term "first-line" means that physicians opt to prescribe a pharmaceutical first in lieu of a more invasive procedure, such as surgery. In some cancers, physicians now have the option to recommend a tumor-shrinking drug, for example, before surgery to minimize the level of invasiveness to the body.

In the U.S.

The U.S. pharmaceutical industry is comprised of approximately 100 companies, according to the Pharmaceutical Research and Manufacturers of America (PhRMA), a leading industry trade and lobbying organization, with the top 10 companies referred to as Big Pharma.

The U.S. has not only the largest pharmaceutical market in the world, but also the only one without government price controls. This is a result of the privately owned system prevalent in the U.S. and a strong industry lobby, which has resisted government incursions into its market-based pricing. On the other hand, developed economies with universal health care access (European Union, U.K., Japan) exert stringent controls on the prices companies can charge. A big consequence is that, with thinner profit margins, the incentive for novelty is curbed, and former leaders, especially in the EU (German and French companies, in particular) lost the lead in innovation in the 1990s. Standard & Poor's expects the U.S. to continue to be the largest of the top-10 pharmaceutical markets for the near future, as well as the fastest growing.

Although pharmaceutical companies are scattered throughout the continental United States, the industry is geographically concentrated in the Mid-Atlantic states (New York, New Jersey and Pennsylvania) and on the West Coast in California. A handful of companies can also be found in Massachusetts, Illinois and North Carolina. New Jersey is the heart of the industry and has, by far, the largest number of companies within a single state. According to the California Healthcare Institute, roughly a quarter of U.S. biotech jobs are in sunny California.

Medicare change boosts drugs sales

Before January 1, 2006, Medicare, the federal health program for the disabled and elderly, didn't pay for outpatient prescription drugs. The Medicare Prescription Drug, Improvement and Modernization Act—known as Part D—gave Medicare beneficiaries the option to enroll in private drug plans. Due to the changes, Medicare became the country's largest public customer of prescription medications in 2006. The change to Medicare helped boost prescription sales in the United States in 2006, but the U.S. Department of Health and Human Services doesn't think it will have a huge impact on drug spending in the future.

Growth in generics

In 1984 the passage of the Drug Price Competition and Patent Term Restoration Act, also called the Hatch-Waxman Act, increased generic drug manufacturers' access to the marketplace. One recent trend in the industry has been a boom in generic drug sales. The biggest generic drug manufacturers—such as Israeli firm Teva and U.S.-based companies Mylan and Barr—have thousands of employees and generate a combined billion dollars in revenue. According to the Kaiser Family Foundation, in 2006 more than 60 percent of prescriptions dispensed and 20 percent of prescription drug sales were generics, and sales of generic drugs grew 22 percent from 2005 to 2006.

In the United States, managed health care has contributed to the rise in generic drugs. Managed care programs such as HMOs often ask their doctors to prescribe generic drugs in place of more expensive brand-name products. Recent changes to the Medicare program in the United States are also likely to lead to an increase in generic drug sales. Under Medicare Part D, through "multitiered pricing," plans can charge patients more for brand-name drugs than generics. In addition, plans can ask doctors to fill out prior authorization forms in order for patients to obtain branded drugs.

The expiration of patents on branded pharmaceuticals has also increased generic drug companies' revenue. As more brand-name drugs go off patent in coming years, generic drug manufacturers' profits are likely to increase. Big pharmaceutical companies that make brand-name drugs usually attempt to extend their drugs' exclusivity and prevent generic competition. They do this in various ways, including litigation. Some big pharmaceutical companies have responded to generic competition by entering into licensing agreements with generic drug manufacturers.

To complicate things further, not all pharmaceutical companies make just generics or only branded drugs. For example, Novartis has a generics division called Sandoz.

Due to strong growth and two major acquisitions in 2005, Sandoz is currently the second-largest generics company in the world based on sales after Teva. Some generic companies also sell branded pharmaceuticals. For instance, generic drug manufacturer Barr's subsidiary Duramed Pharmaceuticals develops, manufactures and sells the firm's proprietary pharmaceuticals, mostly female health care products like Seasonale and Seasonique oral contraceptives.

Battle over biogenerics

In May 2007, U.S. Presidential hopeful Hillary Rodham Clinton presented parts of her health care proposal. Among other things, Clinton suggested Americans could save money on health care through the creation of a regulatory pathway for approval of generic copies of biopharmaceuticals. Generic versions of biologic drugs are sometimes called "biogenerics" or "biosimilars," and they are quite controversial.

Typically, generic versions of conventional drugs hit the market shortly after patents have expired on brand-name pharmaceuticals. Generic drug companies simply need to show that the generic contains the same active ingredients, purity and quality as the brand-name version, and that the copycat version provides "bioequivalence" (the same level of the drug in the blood over time as the original). Biologics, however, are made from cultures of living material rather than from chemical recipes. Brand-name drug makers and many scientists have urged caution in the development of generic biologics. These individuals say biologic drugs are inherently variable and difficult to duplicate, and that patients could develop allergic reactions.

In spite of these concerns, generic drug companies are also branching out into generic versions of biologic drugs. In 2005, Barr Pharmaceuticals announced a deal to license Croatian pharmaceutical company Pliva's version of Neupogen, a white-blood-cell booster made by Amgen. In 2006, Barr and Iceland's Actavis Group battled for Pliva. Barr outbid Actavis, and—in a deal worth $2.5 billion—the company acquired Pliva. The Croatian company is working on a copycat version of Amgen's Epogen, a protein that boosts red blood cells. Barr has also broken ground on a $25 million biotech factory in Croatia.

A rise in CROs

Increasingly, pharmaceutical companies have outsourced drug research and development. As a result of this growth, contract research organizations (or CROs) have been on the rise. In 2005, a survey by Cambridge Healthtech Advisors found that 45 percent of pharmaceutical companies expected to outsource at least 60 percent of their clinical development work by 2008. Examples of CROs include New Jersey-based Covance and North Carolina's Quintiles Transnational Corporation. In 2006, Covance worked with more than 300 biopharmaceutical companies, ranging from small and startup organizations to the world's largest pharmaceutical companies. Quintiles helped develop or commercialize the world's 30 best-selling drugs. The use of CROs can benefit drug companies in several ways. First, they can help pharmaceutical companies reduce R&D costs. Outsourcing can also lower the amount of time it takes to develop a new drug and bring it to market. In addition, CROS can conduct trials in multiple geographic locations simultaneously.

WORKING IN THE INDUSTRY

According to the Bureau of Labor Statistics, about 29 percent of jobs in the pharmaceutical and medicine manufacturing industry are in professional and related occupations. Most of these positions are for science technicians and scientists. Some 12 percent of professionals in the industry work in office and administrative support, and three percent are employed in sales. About a quarter of jobs in the pharmaceutical and biotech business are in manufacturing and production.

Departments in a Pharmaceutical Company

The major departments of a conventional pharmaceutical and biotech companies include R&D, operations, quality control, clinical research, administration, business development and finance. Each department houses several functional groups, or specific, logically related areas of activity. The top-10 biotech companies are essentially mid-cap pharmaceutical companies. At generic drug companies, departments are similar as well. They might include administration, business development, finance, human resources, information technology, legal and intellectual property, manufacturing, marketing and sales. At most generic drug companies, researchers don't spend years trying to discover the next big thing. Instead, they reverse-engineer compounds that already exist to find bioequivalent compounds.

As you think about a career in the pharma and biotech industry, it's useful to identify the general area(s) where your primary interests and aptitudes lie. Let's take a look at the different departments.

Research and development

Because the pharmaceutical and biotech business is research-intensive, there are many jobs in R&D. In 2004, about 14 percent of medical researchers were employed in pharmaceutical and medical manufacturing. These researchers' median salary was $76,800.

The research and development (R&D) department is responsible for discovering promising drug candidates. The three major functions include discovery research, bioinformatics and animal sciences. The discovery research function is responsible for performing experiments that identify targets on the cell or potential drug candidates. The animal sciences function provides cell cultures, grows microorganisms, and manages the care of animals used in discovery research. The bioinformatics function analyzes extensive data generated from experiment, which in turn assists discovery research in identifying the most biologically active compounds.

At biotech companies such as Genentech, scientists participate in the drug research process from beginning to end. They often work in interdisciplinary teams. Biotechnology firms are always looking for talented researchers to fill their labs. The demand for researchers has increased, but supply hasn't. To have access to talented staff, some biotech firms have moved closer to places where these researchers live. For example, in 2005 Schering-Plough and Amgen announced plans to expand their R&D facilities in Cambridge, Mass., a major hub for biotech and pharmaceutical firms.

Clinical research

Once a drug candidate is identified as a potentially viable treatment in R&D, the clinical research department takes over and becomes responsible for shepherding the drug through the FDA approval process. The clinical research function sets up and manages the clinical trials needed to determine a drug's safety and effectiveness or "efficacy." The regulatory affairs function ensures that all FDA reporting requirements are completed and submitted in a timely manner. Finally, the medical affairs/drug information function is responsible for overseeing all the information related to a drug candidate.

Operations

The operations department is responsible for making commercial quantities of a candidate drug available. Once a promising drug candidate has been identified, the process/product development function determines how to "scale up" quantities of a product to make enough available for clinical trials, since laboratory-size quantities are usually very small. When a product successfully emerges from clinical trials, the manufacturing and production function creates the final product—complete with packaging and labeling—that we see on the shelves of pharmacies and drugstores. Also housed under the operations umbrella is the environmental health and safety function, which assesses the environmental impact of a potential product.

Quality

The FDA has strict safety regulations for factories that make pharmaceuticals and biologics. If the FDA suspects a flu vaccine or other drugs might be contaminated, the agency can close plants. Among other things, a pharma and biotech company's quality department makes sure the firm follows government regulations. The department has groups focusing on quality control, quality assurance and validation. These groups ensure that products are manufactured along rigorous, consistent standards of quality. This usually entails that well-defined and documented procedures are followed when producing a product either for clinical trials or as an end product.

Finance and administration

The finance and administration department contains these two functional areas as well as information systems and legal. All activities relating to the financial management of the company, its legal relationships to investors, creditors, employees and government regulators are housed in this department. The companywide computer systems—separate from computing specifically directed at analyzing research data—are also managed here.

Business development

The business development group is typically responsible for identifying prospective new alliance partners and managing existing alliances. The marketing function studies markets, identifies target customer bases, and sets pricing and promotion strategy. The sales function actually meets with potential customers in the field—usually specialist physicians in targeted areas of specialization (e.g., cardiologists, endocrinologists, urologists, etc.)

Project management

Finally, many pharma and biotech companies also have a separate project management department, which is responsible for ensuring that work requiring the collaboration of several internal departments is discharged smoothly and efficiently. This department oversees special projects that don't naturally fit into any of the traditional formal functions but that require cross-functional collaboration. Unlike general managers, who work on companies' overall operations, project managers tend to focus on specific projects. A project manager might help launch products, develop marketing programs, run annual sales meetings or manage clinical trials. Some universities and organizations—such as Massachusetts Biotechnology Council, the UC San Diego Extension and the University of Washington Extension—now offer certificate programs in biotech project management.

To lab or not to lab?

Given the breadth of choices in the pharmaceutical industry, you might well wonder how to focus your own career aspirations. You may be turned on enough by science while in college enough to earn a major in a scientific discipline but not be sure you want to make research your lifelong career. That's fine, as long as you have a sense of how to manage the critical early years of professional experience. To help you get a wide-angle view of the major career paths available, we have found it helpful to think in terms of two fundamental paths: laboratory research-oriented and non-laboratory research-oriented. Within each path are several different career tracks, discussed later.

Laboratory research-oriented career paths are found in the research and development (R&D) department. This area is also called "discovery research" because the work involves discovering new processes, drugs and technologies. These careers involve "bench work," referring to a laboratory bench, where scientists set up experiments generate data. In biotech research, two other areas—bioinformatics and animal sciences—are especially tightly integrated.

Non-research-oriented career paths include everything else. Several functions—operations, manufacturing and quality—have an engineering bent and are primarily focused on the applications of science. Others, like clinical research, include all the jobs needed to set up and manage clinical trials and oversee submissions to regulatory agencies. Note that the "clinical research" function includes all the jobs needed to set up and manage clinical trials. They are put here rather than in the research-oriented path since they require knowledge of medicine and occur in clinical settings—such as hospitals or clinics. Still others are business-oriented and include support functions, such as finance, administration, legal, IT, business development and sales/marketing. Finally many companies have a project management function that helps coordinate projects that overlap among several internal functions.

The common denominator is that careers in most of these functions require at least an undergraduate foundation in a life science. This includes the more generic business functions. Many careers require advanced training in science in addition to education in a functional area. For example, attorneys specializing in intellectual property often also have advanced degrees in the sciences. Business development people typically have either a bachelor's or a master's in a scientific area in addition to an MBA. The industry sets these educational prerequisites for employment outside the lab because business people need a thorough grounding in the vocabulary of genetics, an orientation to the basic concepts behind the products and a familiarity with the issues and challenges facing the industry. The bottom line is this: if you are up and coming in the educational system, you are joining a limited pool of qualified talent competing for the available jobs. That's good news if most of your career is still ahead of you.

LABORATORY RESEARCH CAREERS

Discovery research

At smaller companies, many jobs are in discovery research. Discovery researchers can range from protein chemists to geneticists to biochemists to many other disciplines in the life sciences. There are jobs at all levels. With a bachelor's, you can get an entry-level job as a research associate and work for several years, though you will need an advanced degree for more senior jobs. Most responsible positions, however, require a PhD. You can definitely break into the industry after undergraduate studies. Entry-level research positions will get your feet wet and give you a chance to experience the culture of research firsthand before committing yourself to advanced studies. The salary range for a research associate is from $40,000 to $70,000. The scientist job is the more senior researcher position in R&D. For the scientist track, the salary range is typically $60,000 to $130,000. Scientific managers can earn salaries in the range of $100,000 up to more than $175,000. As discussed earlier, many pharmaceutical companies have contracted out research to contract research organizations (CROs), so researchers also should consider working for CROs.

Animal science specialists

Instead of using chemicals the way traditional pharmaceutical chemists do, discovery research scientists use cells—obtained from animals—that are cultivated, separated and utilized in special facilities. Discovery researchers rely on veterinarians and other animal science specialists. They grow cultures, make and purify DNA, and help conduct the earliest phases of testing, when a drug's safety is determined via animal testing.

Bioinformatics

Since nearly all experimental setups are computerized and reams of data are generated with each experiment, the results of biotech experiments are analyzed by specialists who straddle the fence between the biological sciences and information technology. These data analysts are called bioinformatics professionals and comprise some of the most sought-after employees in the industry. They help discovery researchers identify those molecular structures that have the most favorable response profile, and thus the most promising drug candidates.

Bioinformatics has three realms of activity: you can create databases to store and manage large biological data sets, you can develop algorithms and statistics to determine the relationships among the components of these datasets, or you can use these tools to either analyze or interpret biological data—e.g., DNA, RNA or protein sequences, protein structures, gene expression profiles or biochemical pathways. The salary range for bioinformatics is from about $60,000 to $100,000.

Non-Laboratory Research Careers

Non-laboratory research careers encompass a large range of functions, including engineering, careers in medical and clinical settings, administrative/support functions and sales and marketing. Here we take a look at the medical and clinical settings positions.

When a product has been demonstrated to be safe in animals it's ready to be tested on a small sample of humans and be submitted as a candidate for a new drug to the FDA. These activities occur in clinical settings, involve interpretation of massive amounts of clinical data and require extensive documentation to the regulatory body. Two basic paths exist: clinical research and regulatory affairs. Jobs in these functions are usually grouped together in most companies.

Visit Vault at **www.vault.com** for insider company profiles, expert advice, career message boards, expert resume reviews, the Vault Job Board and more.

V/\ULT CAREER LIBRARY **15**

Clinical research

First, let's clarify the term "research" in clinical research. Clinical researchers are physicians, nurses and data management professionals who administer and interpret the reactions of patients who have been enrolled in clinical trials. Often, these patients suffer from the disease condition targeted and need to pass a set of qualification criteria set by specialist physicians, who must ensure that their overall health status is sufficiently stable to participate in testing the experimental drug. Once a drug is administered to an enrolled patient, the latter is carefully monitored for reactions to the drug. These include desired effects and other "adverse" or undesired effects. Both sets of data are captured both manually and electronically. Sometimes, manual data has to be transferred to electronic form. All data eventually becomes housed in computer databases, where physicians and database managers interpret the overall effects of the drug on the total population of patients enrolled in the study. These activities thus constitute research in a clinical setting using clinical data.

Medical knowledge at all levels is required for careers in clinical research—physicians identify prospective patients and interpret clinical data, nurses administer drug candidates and help monitor patient reactions, even database specialists need to have some understanding of the type of data the medical professionals generate to collaborate with physicians in interpreting it. With the hundreds of biotech drug candidates in the pipeline, clinical research jobs are expected to continue to be plentiful.

Regulatory affairs

Regulatory affairs is the other clinically oriented track. Jobs in this function involve dealing with all aspects of the regulatory environment surrounding drug approval, including submitting New Drug Applications (NDAs), preparing submissions to the FDA summarizing clinical trial results, keeping up with legislation affecting regulatory policy, ensuring the drug company meets new regulations and working with the marketing function to make sure the message sent to consumers is consistent with federal compliance requirements. Careers in this function often require extensive reading and writing skills, as well as enthusiasm toward activities that protect both the company and the consuming public.

Sales and Marketing

Most companies consider sales and marketing to be one function, but with two basic areas of activity. Within the sales function, you can typically find three career tracks: field sales, sales management and managed markets. A fourth track, sales training, is closely associated with sales and is distinct from the broader training and development function, which is usually associated with human resource departments. Sales training groups bridge the sales and marketing function: in some companies, they are considered part of marketing support, and hence part of the marketing function.

Within the marketing function are two main areas of activity: marketing management and marketing support. Marketing management is responsible for introducing products and managing product life cycles. Marketing support is an umbrella-like term that incorporates several distinct groups, some of which are quite large, but all of which serve essentially the same purpose: to provide support services for marketing managers. Depending on the size of the company, the distinction between the two areas may be either blurred or nonexistent. Typical marketing support groups include training and development, advertising and promotion, market analysis, customer call center, e-business, and commercialization and strategic planning.

Fully integrated Big Biotech companies have their own sales and marketing infrastructure and essentially the same job classifications with the same responsibilities. Unlike some of their Big Pharma cousins, biotech sales reps are specialty reps, who market products to specific and highly defined patients groups. For example, biotech sales reps promote specialty injectable protein products to specialist physicians (such as oncologists), who are treating a narrowly defined condition. This focus contrasts sharply with those Big Pharma reps promoting traditional pharmaceuticals to nonspecialist physicians (primary care doctors, internists) providing general medical care to the mass market.

Most companies require some experience in pharmaceutical sales before permitting someone to move into specialty sales. That's a significant factor in charting your career. Both Big Pharma companies as well as biotechs can have specialty products. The distinction is that biotech products are exclusively specialty products, whereas Big Pharma—which has a broader product offering—has products targeted at primary care physicians and products aimed at nonspecialists.

This is a good time to think about a career in biopharmaceutical sales and marketing, since more biotech-based drugs are moving through the development pipeline. In addition, roles in business development often require a foundation in sales (as well as experience in several other functions). Once hired, many companies encourage valued employees to gain such experience, and incorporate lateral moves in annual career development plans. This is important to know at the outset, since it will help you evaluate the opportunities available in sales and marketing.

Sales Positions: Field Sales, Sales Management and Managed Markets

Field sales

A position in field sales is the entry-level job in the sales function. The main purpose of the field sales force is to promote the company's products to customers—typically solo or small-practice groups of physicians—within an assigned geographic territory. Reps are carefully selected, trained rigorously, and equipped with detailed product information. They should know their products inside out and work hard to understand the medical science on which those products are based. Within field sales are two areas, territory sales and specialty sales.

The entry-level field sales positions are pharmaceutical sales representative and territory sales representative. The next rung is medical specialist or hospital specialist. Specialty sales representatives are the most experienced, often with several years of direct sales under their belt. This job exists in both Big Biotech and Big Pharma companies. The responsibilities of a pharmaceutical sales rep are well defined across the industry and fall into three distinct areas of activity. Selling is the main responsibility, and requires reps to sell the company's products within the assigned territory, make product presentations, arrange educational meetings for physicians and co-promote products (when the company has made co-marketing deals with another company).

Administrative responsibilities require reps to manage the selling process (i.e., prioritize their physician and pharmacy customer lists, take notes on call outcomes, prepare reports to district manager), attend company meetings, manage time effectively by working out optimal sales call schedules, work out territory logistics with team members, maintain expense logs, arrange for catering for lunchtime seminars with medical specialists, organize promotional materials and drug samples, and maintain the company car.

Professional development responsibilities require reps to learn features, benefits and basic medical science of assigned products; learn about competing products and their advantages or disadvantages relative to the company's own product; attend professional development training sessions; complete required online training programs; and master selling process and continually refine selling skills.

Generally speaking, cash compensation comprises salary plus bonuses. Total cash compensation for entry-level sales reps typically ranges from roughly $44K to $73K.

Marketing: Marketing Management, Marketing Support and Sales Training

Marketing management

Marketing management is where marketing strategy is formulated and implemented, new products are introduced and existing-product life cycles are managed. Until recently, the marketing function was vertically integrated, meaning that a single ladder existed for reaching senior positions. It was theoretically possible to begin a career as an entry-level marketing associate, and several decades later, achieve senior executive vice president of marketing. Some Big Pharma companies are still organized this way.

Yet with Big Pharma companies merging into mega-companies, some companies have opted to organize therapeutic areas and their associated products into separate business units, so that marketing management decisions get made with fewer layers of oversight and with closer contact with customer physicians and targeted patient groups. In this organizational model, therapeutic areas (i.e., oncology drugs, cardiovascular drugs, anti-hypertensives, etc.) and the products associated with them become wholly integrated business units. Most Big Biotech companies have opted to follow the second model, since their more-targeted products are best delivered via smaller organizations.

The main job title in marketing management (consistent throughout the industry) is product manager. A product manager's responsibilities fall into two main categories, management and administration. The product manager must develop and manage the short-term product strategy and marketing plans for assigned products, oversee development of business plans, specify the positioning of a product among its competitors, monitor those competitors' products, acquire both a quantitative and intuitive feel for customer needs, and act as an in-house champion for a product or brand. Administratively, product managers must develop budgets, maintain records of expenses, and manage and develop entry-level support staff (e.g., market research analysts, marketing associates, undergraduate interns and co-op students, etc.).

In companies where therapeutic areas and associated products are organized as business units, product managers effectively become mini-CEOs, involved in virtually every aspect of getting a product to market. Product managers should also have substantial communication and negotiation skills, as they are required to interact with professionals from every part of the organization. Total compensation for marketing product managers ranges from $62,000 to $109,000, depending on the manager's level of experience.

Interviewing at Pharmaceutical Companies

Regardless of their position and department, most employees at pharmaceutical companies say they endured several rounds of interviews. Typically, people have more interviews for higher-level positions than entry-level ones. Interviewers usually ask a combination of questions about applicants' backgrounds, interests and why they want to work at the company. Applicants for research jobs are sometimes asked to give a presentation of their past work. For some positions, applicants have tests in addition to interviews.

Most pharmaceutical company sources say interview questions tend to be straightforward. A contact at Bayer says the interview session included queries like "Why are you looking?" and "What can you do for Bayer?" One insider at Bristol Myers Squibb says, "The interview questions asked most are typical. What was your greatest achievement? What are your strengths and weaknesses? What do you like least about the company and what do you like the most? Where can you see yourself in five years?" Scenario-based questions are also common. For example, the contact at BMS was also asked to talk about handling a difficult situation. Another BMS insider says the most memorable question was "describe three features you like about yourself the most and the least." One scientist at J&J says, "Questions were about my personality, what were my qualities, examples of situations where I helped in the solution of problems, how I dealt with pressure and examples. Also there were questions about my education and experience: specific skills and knowledge."

If you're applying for a sales job, also be ready to talk about the company's products. One Amgen insider says, "I was asked what I thought I could contribute to the Amgen team, and what specific knowledge I had of Amgen products." Sometimes interviewers will also want to see you in action. One sales rep at Eli Lilly explains,

"It isn't uncommon for someone to pick up something off the desk and ask you to sell it to them."

The future of pharmaceuticals

Many pharmaceutical companies have downsized, especially in areas such as sales, during recent years. In late 2005, Merck announced a global restructuring program. Among other things, Merck planned to eliminate approximately 7,000 jobs by the end of 2008. According to a January 2006 article in Health Care News, the pharmaceutical industry lost at least 24,396 in the first 11 months of 2005. The publication added that this was a 150 percent increase from the same period in 2004, when the pharmaceutical industry announced 9,744 pharmaceutical job cuts. Downsizing has continued during the past two years. In early 2007, Pfizer CEO Jeffrey Kindler said the company was cutting 10,000 positions worldwide. A month later, AstraZeneca announced that it would cut that firm's global workforce by more than 4 percent. As discussed above, many pharmaceutical companies are outsourcing research and development to CROs, and this trend is likely to continue in coming years.

Overall, however, things bode well for people who are interested in working for pharmaceutical companies. The U.S. Department of Health and Human Services expects prescription drug spending to increase to $497.5 billion by 2016, a 148 percent increase from 2005, when prescription drug spending in the U.S. was about $200 billion. Moreover, the U.S. Bureau of Labor Statistics projects that the number of jobs in pharmaceutical and medicine manufacturing will increase by about 26 percent between 2004 and 2014. This makes it one of the fastest growing manufacturing industries. The bureau adds that, even if there's an economic downturn, the market for pharmaceuticals is likely to remain strong. The Bureau of Labor Statistics also projects that employment for medical researchers will grow much faster than other occupations.

Hiring in biotech

Because biotechnology applications exist across health care, agriculture, food processing and industry, virtually any college major in a scientific and life science is likely to find a biotech application. Biotech companies per se are most likely to have health care applications, and as previously noted, are essentially mid-cap pharmaceutical companies. Typical college majors among biotech professionals include chemistry, biology, physics, biochemistry, bioengineering, among many others. You can also get an undergraduate degree in bioinformatics. Potential employers span across government, private industry and academia. That pretty much covers most of the employment universe, so you may well feel bewildered about how to proceed.

Interconnected institutions

Universities are increasingly looking to leverage the intellectual capital of their researchers to land licensing deals with the private sector. Since much research is funded by the federal government (in other words, your taxpayer dollars), the feds have an incentive to see some of that money get recycled in the private sector economy through goods and services that can improve the lives and standards of living of ordinary Americans.

Thus, most universities have technology-licensing offices that help its scientists set up licensing and entrepreneurial deals with the private sector. The idea is to commercialize the science into products, devices, processes and products that are useful to consumers. This translates into increased revenue for private sector companies, which in turn increases the tax base for the federal government. From the private sector's perspective, venture capitalists are looking increasingly to late-stage research that's just about ready to be commercialized. That shortens their period of investment, which means they can cash out faster and invest limited partner dollars into the next promising project. Academic researchers whose work fits those criteria are attractive candidates. This is because someone else (the feds) picked up the tab for that early-stage phase when there is great uncertainty as to whether anything practical will come out of a research idea. Funding from private equity can now go right into creating the practical from the theoretical.

The upshot is that, whatever sector you choose to work in—government, private industry or academia—you are likely to forge links with colleagues in other sectors.

Interviewing at biotech firms

When interviewing for positions at a biotech firm, expect questions about the company and why you want to work there—as well as your background and work experience. One source, who now works at Amgen, says interviewers there asked questions such as "Why are you applying?" and "List some of your accomplishments in your current position." A former ImClone intern was asked "pretty general questions to get a feel for my overall background knowledge." A manager at Genentech says applicants there should expect panel interviews and a lot of behavioral interviewing. If you're interviewing for a sales or marketing job, be able to demonstrate that you know about the company's products.

The future of the biotech business

There are lots of jobs in the biotechnology field, especially for scientists, and things look like they're going to get better. The U.S. Bureau of Labor Statistics projects that biotech jobs will increase in the future. The bureau expects that biological technicians, a key biotechnology occupation, will grow by 19.4 percent between 2002 and 2012. The bureau also projects that the occupation of biological scientists will grow by 19 percent during this same period.

According to a December 2005 story published by *Genetic Engineering and Biotechnology News*, scientists whose skills are in hot demand include those with expertise in RNA interference, vaccines and molecular diagnostics. As the biotech industry matures, many companies are also adding manufacturing crews, sales people and other types of employees. When biotech firms begin to produce revenue through product sales, they'll also need employees with backgrounds in finance and administration.

The other good news is that, as competition rises for employees in the biotech industry, salaries are likely to increase, too. Already, the pay's not bad. An April 2006 study by Battelle Memorial Institute in Columbus, Ohio, found that the average biotech job pays $65,775 a year.

RECOMMENDED READING

Books

Angell, M. *The Truth About the Drug Companies: How They Deceive Us and What to Do About It*. Random House Trade Paperbacks, 2005.

Clayton, A. *Insight into a Career in Pharmaceutical Sales*. Pharmaceuticalsales.Com Inc, 2005.

Goozner, M. *The $800 Million Pill: The Truth behind the Cost of New Drugs*. University of California Press, 2004.

Hall, Linley A. *Careers in Biotechnology*. Rosen Publishing Group, 2007.

Hargittai, I. and Magdolna Hargittai. *Candid Science II: Conversations with Famous Biomedical Scientists.* World Scientific Publishing Company, 2002.

Hawthorne, F. *Inside the FDA: The Business and Politics Behind the Drugs We Take and the Food We Eat.* John Wiley & Sons, 2005.

Moynihan, R. *Selling Sickness: How the World's Biggest Pharmaceutical Companies Are Turning Us All into Patients.* Nation Books, 2005.

Prud'homme, A. *The Cell Game: Sam Waksal's Fast Money and False Promises— and the Fate of ImClone's Cancer Drug.* Harper Collins, 2004.

Ng, R. *Drugs-From Discovery to Approval.* Wiley-Liss, 2004.

Reidy, J. *Hard Sell: The Evolution of a Viagra Salesman.* Andrews McNeel Publishing, 2005.

Walsh, G. *Biopharmaceuticals: Biochemistry and Biotechnology.* John Wiley & Sons, 2003.

Werth, B. *The Billion Dollar Molecule: One Company's Quest for the Perfect Drug.* Simon & Schuster, 1995.

Periodicals and web sites

PhRMA—www.phrma.org
Biotechnology Industry Organization—www.bio.org
Pharmaceutical Executive—www.pharmexec.com
Gate2Biotech—www.gate2biotech.com
BIO.COM Jobs—www.bio.com/jobs
Genetic Engineering & Biotechnology News—www.genengnews.com

Pharmaceutical Manufacturing
Contract Pharma
Drug Discovery Today
Drug Discovery News
BioTechniques
Bio-IT World
Small Times
BioProcess International

Abbott Laboratories

100 Abbott Park Road
Abbott Park, IL 60064
Phone: (847) 937-6100
Fax: (847) 937-1511
www.abbott.com

LOCATIONS

Abbott Park, IL (HQ)
Alameda, CA
Altavista, VA
Barceloneta, PR
Casa Grande, AZ
Columbus, OH
Des Plaines, IL
Edison, NJ
Fairfield, CA
Irving, TX
North Chicago, IL
Redwood City, CA
San Juan, PR
Santa Clara, CA
South Pasadena, CA
Sturgis, MI
Temecula, CA
Whippany, NJ
Worcester, MA

Locations in more than 40
countries.

THE STATS

Employer Type: Public Company
Stock Symbol: ABT
Stock Exchange: NYSE
Chairman & CEO: Miles D. White
2006 Employees: 65,000
2006 Revenue ($mil.): $22,476
2006 Net Income ($mil.): $1,717

DEPARTMENTS

Accounting & Finance
Administrative Services
Clinical Research
Communications
Employee Health Services
Engineering
Ethics Compliance
Facility Services
Government Affairs/Legislative
 Affairs
Human Resources
Information Technology
Legal
Manufacturing & Operations
Marketing/Advertising
Pharmacovigilance
Public Affairs
Purchasing
Quality Assurance
Regulatory Affairs
Sales
Scientific Research & Development
Supply Chain/Materials Management
Tech Support
Training

KEY COMPETITORS

Merck
Roche
sanofi-aventis

EMPLOYMENT CONTACT

www.abbott.com/global/url/content/e
n_US/50:50/general_content/General
_Content_00013.htm

THE SCOOP

Abbott in a nutshell

Abbott, a name practically synonymous with pharmaceuticals for over 100 years, is currently a broad-based health services provider that discovers, develops, generates and markets a wide range of products. Headquartered in north suburban Chicago, the company serves clients in more than 130 countries, employing 65,000 people at more than 100 manufacturing, distribution, research and development, and other facilities around the world.

Hey, Abbott!

Dr. Wallace Calvin Abbott, a Chicago physician, founded Abbott for quite the elementary reason in 1888—he often prescribed alkaloids such as morphine and codeine in liquid form, and had recently heard that each could be manufactured as solids (which wouldn't spoil as fast). After these solids—in the shape of pills— became available in Chicago, Abbott was dissatisfied with them and struck out on his own. Other doctors soon joined his company, which was incorporated in 1900 as the Abbott Alkaloidal Company. By 1905, Abbott had a $200,000 per year enterprise on his hands ($4.7 billion in today's parlance).

Abbott (the firm) took on more drug manufacturing during World War I, as the German drug supply froze up. By the time of Wallace Abbott's death in 1921, the firm had opened up an R&D center in North Carolina and was starting to aggressively market new drugs. In 1929 the firm went public, listing on the Chicago Stock Exchange, expanding into Canada two years later. Many years later, in September 2007, Wallace Abbott's home was named a historic landmark by the City of Chicago.

The company's next great chief was DeWitt Clough, who ran the firm from 1933 to 1945. During the Great Depression he introduced a highly successful company magazine called *What's New?* and steered the firm into anesthetics, starting in 1936.

Shortly after Clough joined Abbott, in 1937, a University of Illinois scientist discovered a sugar substitute that came to be known as "cyclamate." The substance had tremendous potential for diabetics and Abbott eventually purchased the patent for it, bringing cyclamate to market in 1950. It soon wound up in beverages and foods and was one of the most widely used artificial sweeteners in the world by the 1960s. However, in 1968 the National Academy of Sciences reported to the FDA that further tests were required to ascertain cyclamate's potential health risks. The FDA duly banned the substance from all domestic sales in 1969. Abbott's annual sales fell from $17.9 million before the ruling to $3 million afterwards.

R&D in the 1980s

The company recovered in the 1980s under the leadership of its new chief, Robert Schoellhorn, who emphasized pharmaceutical R&D and improved the company's pipeline. Seven new drugs in 1982, for example, generated 17 percent of sales in 1985. Throughout the decade, Abbott's sales almost tripled and profits more than doubled as Abbott rose from 197th to 90th on the Fortune 500.

In the 1990s, Abbott was still plowing money into R&D. In 1994, for example, it reinvested 10 percent of annual sales back into R&D—a cool $1 billion. But Abbott didn't rest on its laurels; it actually feared being taken over by an acquisitive rival, and began to expand through its own purchases of other companies. In 1996 it bought MediSense (for $867 million), in 1997 certain branches of Sanofi Pharmaceuticals (for $200 million), in 1998 Murex Technologies (for $234 million), in 1999 Perclose (for $600 million), and so on.

Acquiring hands at work

In recent years, Abbott has continued in the acquisitive vein. In 2004 it bought TheraSense, Inc., which manufactures diabetes management technology. Combined with Abbott's existing diabetes monitoring business, it now makes up subsidiary Abbott Diabetes Care. The business crossed the billion-dollar threshold at the end of 2005 and established itself as a market leader in worldwide diabetes treatment. In 2004, Abbott also snapped up i-STAT Corp., which produces analyzers at the cutting-edge of point-of-care diagnostics allowing physicians to receive test results without leaving their patient's bedside. That year Abbott also acquired Spine Next S.A., a French technology company that developed a unique method of the emergent non-fusion segment of the spine market.

In December 2006, Abbott purchased Kos Pharmaceuticals for $3.7 billion, instantly making it the industry leader in the booming field of treatments that boost "good" HDL cholesterol. The major scores in the purchase, Niaspan and Advicor, are prescription forms of the nutrient niacin, an HDL booster. In April 2007, Abbott announced that it had received FDA approval for a new coated Niaspan tablet.

Visit Vault at **www.vault.com** for insider company profiles, expert advice, career message boards, expert resume reviews, the Vault Job Board and more.

VAULT CAREER LIBRARY   27

The firm acquired the vascular intervention and endovascular solutions businesses of Guidant Corporation in April of 2006.

Taking care of business

Abbott operates in four business segments: pharmaceutical products, medical products, nutritional products and vascular products. Abbott's diagnostic products segment had nearly $4 billion in sales in 2006, an increase over 2005 of nearly 6 percent. Products in diagnostics include the FreeStyle Lite, a blood glucose monitor that uses a very small blood sample size and returns an accurate reading within five seconds. The i-STAT handheld analyzer offers a broad menu of tests physicians can perform at a patient's bedside.

In January 2006, the FDA gave Abbott clearance to market the CHEM8+ cartridge, a metabolic test panel that enables doctors to obtain a quick snapshot of the function of important organs. The Abbott Prism, an analyzer designed for high-volume blood banks and centers, screens the blood supply in more than 30 countries. Abbott's FreeStyle Navigator, currently under FDA review, transmits glucose-level data every 60 seconds to diabetes patients, which would allow them to stay closely attuned to shifting blood-sugar levels.

Abbott also makes retail nutritional products, like Zone Perfect bars, Ensure, Pedialyte, PediaSure and Similac. In 2006, net sales in the company's nutrionals segment were $4.3 billion, an increase from around $4 billion in 2005. Abbott hopes to strengthen its international reach in growing markets such as Latin America and Asia, and the firm created Abbott Nutrition International in 2006.

The company's vascular products segment sells endovascular, coronary and vessel closure devices for the treatment of vascular disease. Abbott Vascular sells products that include Perclose ProGlide, which helps surgeons quickly close the femoral artery after coronary intervention. In April 2006, Abbott acquired Guidant's vascular business, and the company is now the third-largest player in the vascular care market.

Fun with pharma

Abbott's pharmaceuticals division focuses on the areas of anesthesia, anti-infectives, cardiovascular, immunology, metabolics, neuroscience, oncology, pain care, renal care and virology. For the fiscal year 2006, Abbott's pharmaceutical products segment had $12.4 billion in sales, a drop from $13.7 billion in 2005.

Humira, Abbott's treatment for rheumatoid arthritis (RA), surpassed expectations in 2005 with worldwide sales of $1.4 billion. When Abbott expanded indications for Humira beyond RA, the drug surpassed $2 billion in annual sales in 2006, making it the firm's leading pharmaceutical product. In 2006 the company launched Humira for anklyosing spondylitis, a type of arthritis that affects the spine. Abbott began selling Humira to treat Crohn's disease in early 2007, and the firm expects to submit a new drug application for Humira for psoriasis treatment.

In April 2007, Abbott opened a new biotechnology manufacturing facility in Barceloneta, Puerto Rico, to support the long-term supply of Humira and future biologics. In June 2007, CFO Thomas Freymann announced that that company was targeting sales of more than $2.8 billion for the drug, an increase from the $2.7 billion previously estimated. In September, the drug won the 2007 Galen Prize—a French award in its first year reviewing American drugs—for excellence in pharmaceutical research.

Kaletra, Abbott's HIV medication, continued its reign as the world's No. 1 HIV protease inhibitor, bolstered by data showing that HIV patients new to the treatment exhibit no viral resistance after six years. A majority of these Kaletra patients also maintained an undetectable amount of HIV in the blood. During 2005, a new Kaletra indication was approved, allowing some patients to take the medication once daily. The company also introduced Aluvia, a new version of Kaletra that doesn't require refrigeration.

Synthroid, a half-century old medication prescribed for thyroid therapy, faces generic competition. In 2006, sales of Synthroid totaled $470 million, a drop from $498 million in 2005. TriCor, Abbott's leading cholesterol treatment, continued to perform well in 2005—sales increased 20 percent to more than $900 million. Sales of TriCor continued to be strong in 2006. In the first quarter of 2007, the drug sold $223 million, an increase of 8.7 percent versus the first quarter of 2006.

Sour grapes

In September 2006, after Boston Scientific purchased Guidant, Johnson & Johnson sued Abbott in connection with its acquisition of Guidant's stent and vascular products division. J&J's suit, for $5.5 billion in damages, contended that Abbott and Boston had illegally shared information in their purchase of Guidant.

Johnson & Johnson stated that Boston Scientific would have faced a long antitrust review of uncertain outcome had it not been able to sell Guidant's stent and vascular products to Abbott. Furthermore, J&J asserted that Guidant violated a clause that prevented solicitation of competing offers and that Boston Scientific should not have shared information with Abbott. Naturally, both Abbott and Boston Scientific responded that the suit was without merit.

To GE or not to GE?

In January 2007, Abbott had announced a deal to sell its diagnostic units to General Electric for $8.1 billion. The units—two labs in Illinois and New Jersey—accounted for over $2 billion in sales in 2006, and looked like a perfect fit with GE's diagnostic machines business, which makes such things as CAT scanners and MRI equipment. But by July the deal was off for no apparent reason; the firms mutually failed to agree on final terms. A week later, Abbott was slapped with a lawsuit from a disgruntled shareholder, claiming compensatory damages as a result of the scuttled agreement.

Thailand troubles

Big pharmaceutical companies, including Abbott, hope to expand into developing nations, but breaking into these new markets is proving to be tough. In January 2007, the Thai government sent Abbott a letter warning that it was preparing to break Abbott's patent on AIDS medicine Kaletra to produce or import cheaper copies of the drug.

Abbott initially said it would revoke plans to bring new drugs to Thailand, which only aroused criticism from groups such as Doctors Without Borders. The company later said that it was willing to sell new versions of Kaletra in Thailand at deep discounts, on the condition that the Thai government respects its patent. Abbott faced a similar battle in Brazil in 2005. Brazil withdrew its threat to revoke the patent when Abbott agreed to reduce the price of Kaletra by almost half.

Leading to troubles everywhere else

In April 2007 Abbott moved to disarm its international critics, announcing that it would slash the prices of its AIDS drugs by more than half in over 40 countries worldwide. In particular, its star product Kaletra would be offered at a price of $1,000 per year—far below its American status—to every country defined by the World Bank as having low and low-middle income.

Abbott handled its international critics in quite a different way the very next month—suing the French AIDS activist group Act Up Paris for launching a cyber attack on Abbott's web site. Act Up Paris had taken issue with Abbott's blacklisting of

Thailand in particular, and, although moderate AIDS activism groups don't support cyber attacks, Abbott has received widespread criticism for its legal action.

Up next

In 2007, the company expects to file for FDA approval of Simcor, a combination therapy for both HDL and LDL cholesterol. In addition, a number of drugs are currently in phase III development. These include a controlled release version of pain medication Vicodin as well as Crestor and TriCor. In 2008, Abbott hopes to launch Xience V, a next-generation drug-eluting stent. The company is also developing bioabsorbable stents, which are designed to be naturally absorbed by the body. Abbott believes this breakthrough technology represents the future of the vascular market.

In February 2007, Abbott confirmed plans to cut about 200 drug research jobs in the Chicago area and to eliminate hundreds of drug sales reps. Abbott is reducing duplication in sales of cholesterol drugs following its 2006 acquisition of Kos Pharmaceuticals.

GETTING HIRED

Joining the team

The company's corporate web site (https://jobs.brassring.com/EN/ASP/TG/cim_home.asp ?sec=1&partnerid=281&siteid=50) includes a searchable database of jobs in locations across America in more than 20 job categories, including accounting and finance, administrative services, clinical research, communications, employee health services, engineering, ethics compliance, facility services, government affairs/legislative affairs, human resources, information technology, legal, manufacturing and operations, marketing/advertising, pharmacovigilance, public affairs, purchasing, quality assurance, regulatory affairs, sales, scientific research and development, supply chain/materials management, tech support and training. Go to the company's BrassRing service to search current openings or upload a resume.

Abbott also offers a summer internship program, as well as professional development programs for recent college graduates in departments including engineering, environmental, health and safety, finance, information technology, manufacturing and quality assurance. Interested applicants can find additional information about internships

Visit Vault at **www.vault.com** for insider company profiles, expert advice, career message boards, expert resume reviews, the Vault Job Board and more.

VAULT CAREER LIBRARY   **31**

at www.abbott.com/global/url/content/en_US/50.60.10:10/general_content/General_Content_00166.htm

Multiple meetings

Abbott Laboratory insiders say it's typical to meet with multiple people during the interview process. One source reports meeting with two different people. Another says, "I had one round of interviewing with four people. I interviewed with the department manager and three project managers in the department." The respondent doesn't remember "specific interview questions other than the usual," but adds, "I do remember discussing with the department manager the opportunities for growth within the company."

Find an in through internships

A former finance intern says that the company's internship is a good way to get a job offer, adding "The experience is great, heavily focused in accounting. They throw you in as if you were a full-time employee." The former intern says there are "two rounds of interviews one phone call and an on-campus/ or on-site interview." The source says, "They told us that they only took 250 of over 12,000 applicants, so they are highly selective," adding that interns are the "future prospects" for the company's PDP Program, "a two-year rotational program, which again is very selective."

Praise Abbott

In 2005, *Fortune* magazine listed Abbott among the 50 Best Companies for Minorities and 100 Most Desirable MBA Employers. The following year, the firm made it onto *The Scientist*'s Best Places to Work in Industry list and *Working Mother*'s 100 Best Companies to Work For list. Abbott was also one of *Fortune*'s Most Admired Companies in 2006. In September 2007, the firm made *BusinessWeek*'s 50 Best Places to Launch a Career list for the second straight year.

OUR SURVEY SAYS

Diagnosis on perks and pay

An Abbott insider says, "The company offers diversity, solid training and is diligent in the hiring process." One sales rep, however, feels "Training is a bit of a joke."

Raises at Abbott "are determined for all employees in March of each year" and are "awarded based on performance. In addition to salaries, some employees at Abbott are eligible bonuses, which are "based on company profits and personal performance." One project coordinator says, "There are no stock options, but there is a retirement pension fund. You are fully vested after five years of employment, and it is fully funded by the company."

Abbott also has "a 401(k) program, 15 days of vacation, plus two personal days. Sick days are not limited, but if you have to be out for more than 40 consecutive hours then you have to request a short-term medical leave." The source says medical leave can be up to six months in duration, "and you get full pay and full benefits while you are on leave."

Overall, sources say, the company's outlook is "decent" and "there is high job security." An insider who works in Abbott's Alameda offices adds, "Abbott Diabetes Care is a growing company in the diabetes management field. Anyone interested in working in the medical device field would be wise to consider this company." Another source says, "there is a good chance to move up, but once you put your time in. Seniority rules all in such a big corporation." The insider adds, "If you have a long career with Abbott, plan on being moved many times between different departments and offices."

Visit Vault at www.vault.com for insider company profiles, expert advice, career message boards, expert resume reviews, the Vault Job Board and more.

VAULT CAREER LIBRARY   33

Acambis PLC

Peterhouse Technology Park
100 Fulbourn Road
Cambridge CB1 9PT
United Kingdom
Phone: +44-12-2327-5300
Fax: +44-12-2341-6300
www.acambis.com

LOCATIONS

Cambridge, UK (HQ)
Cambridge, MA
Canton, MA
Rockville, MD

THE STATS

Employer Type: Public Company
Stock Symbol: ACM
Stock Exchange: LSE
CEO: Ian Garland
2006 Employees: 263
2006 Revenue ($mil.): $62
2006 Net Income ($mil.): $31.9

DEPARTMENTS

Communications & Investor Relations
Financial Management
Marketing, Policy & Strategy
Operations
Regulatory Affairs & Quality Systems
Research & Development

KEY COMPETITORS

Baxter
GlaxoSmithKline
Merck

EMPLOYMENT CONTACT

www.acambis.com/default.asp?id=
941

THE SCOOP

The house of vaccines

Acambis aims to save lives by developing new vaccines to prevent infectious diseases. The company boasts a pipeline of vaccine candidates targeting diseases, which includes C. difficile, an antibiotic-resistant bacteria found in institutions such as hospitals, and West Nile virus. In addition, Acambis has established a smallpox vaccine franchise, and the firm has contracts with governments around the world to supply smallpox vaccines. In September 2006, the company sold its travel vaccines business, BPC, to another vaccine company, Crucell, for $17 million.

All about the Cambridges

Acambis is a Cambridge, U.K.-based company, although all of its research and development occurs in Cambridge, Mass. The firm originated out of some intellectual property that had begun at Cambridge University and entered the business world in 1992 as Peptide Therapeutics. The company floated on the London Stock Exchange in November 1995, and it gained its foothold in Massachusetts with a 1999 acquisition. In 2000, the company changed its name to Acambis to reflect its merger of operations in the two countries.

The firm with the pox moxie

In September 2000, the U.S. Centers for Disease Control and Prevention awarded Acambis the first of a number of contracts to manufacture and supply an investigational smallpox vaccine. Soon after the September 11 terrorist attacks, anthrax-laced letters appeared in the mail. The U.S. government, worried that bioterrorism could spread smallpox (all but extinct since 1980), announced its decision to procure a smallpox vaccine stockpile adequate to provide a dose for every man, woman and child in the country.

The government accelerated and expanded Acambis' existing smallpox contract, and awarded the company a second contract worth $428 million. After this, other governments around the world also gave Acambis contracts to supply smallpox vaccines. In 2003, the U.S. government awarded Acambis another contract, this time to develop Modified Vaccinia Ankara (MVA), a weaker smallpox vaccine, citing MVA as a "safer" smallpox vaccine.

Vaccination litigation

In February 2006, Denmark's Bavarian Nordic, which was also trying to land government contracts for a smallpox vaccine, filed action against Acambis in an Austrian court. Bavarian Nordic alleged that Acambis' MVA3000 infringed on its MVA patents. In September, an administrative law judge with the U.S. International Trade Commission (ITC) ruled that Acambis was infringing on two of Bavarian Nordic's patents but determined that those patents were invalid.

The firm got bad news in November 2006 when the U.S. Department of Health and Human Services decided not to award Acambis a contract for MVA3000. In 2007, the District Court of Delaware dismissed Bavarian Nordics' claims of unfair competition and trade acts related to Acambis' use of a smallpox virus sample. Another case is ongoing in the commercial court in Vienna.

However, the U.S. government's decision not to award Acambis the contract means that MVA3000 is no longer part of Acambis' strategic focus, and the three legal cases related to the smallpox vaccine are now largely immaterial to the company's business goals. By mid-2007 Acambis had settled the lawsuit with Bavarian Nordic.

In September 2006, Novartis agreed to pay Acambis $19 million in cash to settle a dispute related to Arilvax, a vaccine for yellow fever. The Novartis settlement strengthened the company's financial position during an otherwise challenging year.

Reducing reliance on biodefense ... and American employees

To deal with its income and contract losses, Acambis sacked its chief in March 2007, ousting CEO Gordon Cameron and announcing a restructuring program designed to cut costs by about 20 percent. The restructuring efforts include plans to reduce employee headcount by approximately 15 percent across the organization. Many jobs will be cut in the United States.

The company's board appointed Ian Garland as the firm's new CEO in May 2007. The firm's main priority in biodefense is to finalize a manufacturing contract for ACAM2000, which would give the company sustainable revenue for several years. In May 2007, the FDA Advisory Committee backed Acambis' ACAM2000 smallpox vaccine. The FDA granted licensure of ACAM2000 in August 2007. Analysts expect that the so-called "warm-base manufacturing" contract (to produce the vaccine in the U.S.) will earn around $30 million of annual revenue.

What say you, Dr. Watson?

The company's strategy for the future is to use money from biodefense contracts to expand its R&D portfolio, which would, in turn, reduce the company's reliance on biodefense contracts. New R&D boss Dr. Michael Watson should help matters—he came aboard with new CEO Garland and has a long history in both vaccines and development, working for sanofi pasteur (the vaccines arm of sanofi-aventis) for the last 10 years and serving as European project leader for Merck and sanofi's HPV vaccine Gardasil.

To build its pipeline into an increasingly valuable portfolio, the firm aims to drive key projects through licensure as quickly as possible. These projects include the vaccines for C. difficile and West Nile virus, as well as vaccines for influenza and Japanese encephalitis. The company's vaccine candidate against Japanese encephalitis has completed phase III clinical testing, its investigational vaccine against West Nile virus is in phase II trials in target population and its vaccine candidate against dengue (Chimer-Vax-Dengue) has completed phase II trials.

Acambis plans to seek out partners to help the firm develop and commercialize current products. Already, the company has established partnerships with Dr. Watson's old employer Sanofi Pasteur and Bharat Biotech to license and commercialize ChimeriVaxTM-JE, a single dose vaccine against Japanese encephalitis. ChimeriVax-Dengue has been out-licensed to sanofi pasteur during phase I trials. In addition, the company is keen on expanding its portfolio by acquiring new products or companies.

GETTING HIRED

Acambis aims to attract employees who are "talented, motivated and interested in working at a company where they can make a useful contribution." The employment section of the firm's web site (www.acambis.com/default.asp?id=941) allows prospective employees to view vacancies in the company's Cambridge, U.K., headquarters as well as in Cambridge, Mass., Canton, Mass., and Rockville, Md.

Departments at Acambis include communications and investor relations, business development, financial management, marketing, policy and strategy, operations, regulatory affairs and quality systems, research and development and manufacturing. In the United States, the firm also has an internship program.

Allergan, Inc.

2525 Dupont Drive
Irvine, CA 92612
Phone: (714) 246-4500
Fax: (714) 246-6987
www.allergan.com

LOCATIONS

Irvine, CA (HQ)
Anasco, PR • Ann Arbor, MI •
Baltimore, MD • Boston, MA •
Charlotte, NC • Chicago, MI •
Cleveland, CA • Costa Mesa, CA •
Dallas, TX • Detroit, MI • Grand
Rapids, MI • Hato Rey, PR •
Houston, TX • Kansas City, KS •
Louisville, KY • New York, NY •
Pittsburgh, PA • Phoenix, AZ •
Sacramento, CA • San Antonio, TX
• San Jose, CA • Santa Barbara,
CA • Salt Lake City, UT • Tampa,
FL • Waco, TX • West Palm Beach,
FL

37 international locations in 32
countries.

THE STATS

Employer Type: Public Company
Stock Symbol: AGN
Stock Exchange: NYSE
Chairman & CEO: David E.I. Pyott
President: F. Michael Ball
2006 Employees: 6,500
2006 Revenue ($mil.): $3,063
2006 Net Income ($mil.): -$127

DEPARTMENTS

Corporate Communications
Corporate Development
Distribution
Facilities
Field Sales
Finance
General & Administration
Human Resources
Information Systems
Legal Affairs
Manufacturing
Marketing/Development
Manufacturing QA
Research & Development
Research Compliance
Sales Support

KEY COMPETITORS

Bausch & Lomb
Bristol-Myers Squibb
CIBA Vision
Hoffman-La Roche
Johnson & Johnson
Pfizer

EMPLOYMENT CONTACT

www.allergan.com/site/careers/

THE SCOOP

Eyeing Allergan

Allergan, Inc. is a technology- and research-driven global health care company offering specialty pharmaceutical products. Headquartered in Irvine, Calif., Allergan develops and markets products in ophthalmology, neurosciences, medical dermatology, medical aesthetics and other specialty markets, and has global sales and marketing capabilities with a presence in more than 100 countries.

With more than 6,500 employees and three high-tech manufacturing plants, the company boasted total sales of over $2 billion for the first time in its history in 2004, driven by revenue from its pharmaceuticals line, which grew by 16 percent. In 2005, pharmaceutical sales rose by 17 percent to $2.3 billion, and sales hit $3 billion in 2006.

In 2006, Allergan was No.644 on *Fortune*'s annual ranking of America's largest corporations, up from its previous rank of 734.

The house that Botox built

A large part of Allergan's record growth can be attributed to the sales of its product Botox, which brought in $705 million in 2004, about a 25 percent increase over 2003's figures. By 2006, Botox global sales totaled $1.5 billion. Allergan was seen as a small ophthalmic company that made prescription eye therapies and contact lens care products, initially marketing Botox in 1991 as a treatment for muscle spasms, and especially for rare eye disorders that concern misalignment (i.e., crossed eyes) and uncontrolled blinking.

Although some people still use Botox to treat muscle spasms, it has become world-famous for its ability to get rid of facial aging signs. Throughout the 1990s in Hollywood, Botox became a popular off-label prescription for frown lines and the like and Botox's sales skyrocketed. Allergan sought and gained official FDA approval for its cosmetic use and in 2002, Botox was rebranded as a beauty product. By 2005, Botox had become the most popular doctor-administered "aesthetic procedure" in America, with some 3.3 million occurrences.

The company continues researching additional uses for Botox, including migraine treatments, overactive bladder and post-stroke spasticity. In October 2005, for instance, an Allergan-sponsored study suggested that repeated Botox injection over the year after a patient suffers a stroke can improve muscle tone and decrease pain in the arms and legs, making daily activities easier for stroke victims.

And Botox's sales show no signs of slowing down. In 2005, Allergan signed a long-term deal with GlaxoSmithKline to develop and promote Botox in Japan and China; in return, the company picked up rights to co-promote two of GSK's migraine remedies as part of its plans to diversify into the neurology market.

The Allergan era

Allergan's business has been developing for a very long time—since 1948, to be exact. That year, a Los Angelenian drugstore owner named Gavin Herbert started a small ophthalmic business above one of his pharmacies, and it was there that amateur chemist Stanley Bly invented its first product, an anti-allergy nose drop called Allergan. In 1953, the company was grossing around $25,000 per year (about $188,000 in 2006 dollars) when Bly suddenly died, leaving behind few directions to his chemical creations.

The company soon looked set to close when Herbert was injured in a car crash and his son was drafted into the Navy for the Korean War, but a young associate professor at the University of Southern California's School of Pharmacy took an interest and saved it. Later in the 1950s, the company moved into a larger, more professional space in the city and hired a former SmithKline salesman, Jack Browning. By 1960, the company was earning $1 million annually.

The company's ophthalmic focus aided it in the 1960s, with the advent of contact lenses. Quickly becoming adept at contact lens solution, the company enjoyed a steady growth rate of 20 to 25 percent through the 1960s, and brought in over $10 million in revenue in 1970. Allergan went public the next year, and was led by founder Gavin Herbert until his death in 1978, when he was succeeded by his son, Gavin Herbert Jr.

A 1980s interlude and a new business model

SmithKline Beckman Corporation purchased Allergan for $236 million in 1980, but this would by no means mark the end of its impact on the marketplace. In fact, new parent company SmithKline empowered Allergan's R&D efforts, and the division continued to produce advances in contact lenses throughout the 1980s, as the market for them grew to surpass $500 million by 1987. At the start of the decade, Allergan was pulling in $100 million; this total grew to $800 million by 1989.

SmithKline merged with Beecham Corporation in 1989 and spun off Allergan to its shareholders, just as the eye care market started to slow down. Within a year, the company's stock price fell from $25 to $15, and President and CEO William Shepherd steered the company in a new direction. He reduced the workforce by 10 percent, consolidated manufacturing operations and began concentrating the company's pipeline on specialty pharmaceuticals.

The first glint of Botox

The firm acquired its future star product with the 1991 purchase of Oculinum, Inc., which was then the only outfit marketing Type A botulinum toxin, a safe and effective treatment of neuromascular disorders. It soon gained the market name Botox. In 1992 and 1993, the company got out of the contact lens business for good, divesting all of its holdings in that field.

The overnight success of Botox would not occur for almost another decade, and even though Allergan surpassed the $1 billion-in-sales mark in 1995, it went through numerous restructurings through the rest of the 1990s. It attempted to merge with Pharmacia & Upjohn in 1996, but gave up the attempt after Pharmacia's minor shareholder, AB Volvo, blocked the deal; Allergan cut about 450 jobs, for a charge of $75 million, later that year.

Two years later, a new executive leadership instituted the closure of five of Allergan's 10 plants and reduced employee headcount by 9 percent (550 people). Although the company incurred losses of over $90 million that year, it bounced back in 1999 with the hiring of 300 new scientists and professionals, as well as a $70 million expansion of the R&D campus at headquarters in Irvine, Calif. After the turn of the 21st century, the company must have been pleased with the success of Botox in a totally unexpected market sector.

Keeping growth alive

Despite Botox's astronomical success, Allergan's eye care business still accounted for $1.53 billion in 2006, about 50 percent of overall sales. Allergan's original therapeutic dry eye product, Restasis ophthalmic emulsion, the first FDA-approved eyedrop for increasing tear production, reached $100 million in sales in 2004, its first full year on the market. In 2006 Restasis had $270 million in sales, a 42 percent increase over 2005. Lumigan ophthalmic solution, an intraocular pressure reduction agent, took in $327 million in 2006 sales, increasing 22 percent from 2005.

Skin deep

Allergan's dermatology unit (not to be confused with the neuromodulators unit that handles Botox) suffered several setbacks in 2004. The FDA slapped a "non-approvable" sticker on Allergan's application for tazarotene oral, despite company claims that the compound achieved its primary efficacy goals in treating moderate-to-severe psoriasis. Sales of Allergan's in-line dermatology products slipped by 5 percent, mainly due to excess inventory of Tazorac cream and gel at the retail pharmacy level.

In January 2005, Allergan released Prevage MD, a cream containing idebenone, an antioxidant the company claims reduces the appearance of fine lines and wrinkles and protects skin from future damage from environmental stressors. Although Prevage MD is not a drug and requires no prescription, it is only available through doctors' offices. At $115 for each one-ounce-sized container of the cream, Prevage MD has taken on a certain cachet among its customers.

During fall 2004, intrigued by articles in fashion and beauty magazines, clients began calling dermatologists for the ultra-rare, one-ounce vials. In May 2005, Allergan entered into an exclusive co-marketing agreement with Elizabeth Arden, Inc. to sell new formulation of Prevage in department stores and other cosmetic retailers. In 2006, sales for the company's skin care line looked to be recovering and increased by 5 percent from 2005, to $126 million, with Tazorac strengthening its position as a treatment for psoriasis and acne (not to be confused with tazarotene, which the FDA rejected for approval two years previous, Tazorac has been approved since 1997).

Next up

The company's R&D strategy is "to develop innovative products to address unmet medical needs." In 2006, the company spent more than $1 billion on R&D, an increase over $388.3 million in 2005 and $342.9 million in 2004. Some 1,200 employees work on Allergan's R&D efforts. During the third quarter of 2005, Allergan announced several future products. In August, the company confirmed it had obtained written approval from the FDA to market Alphagan P 0.1%, a drug that lowers intraocular pressure in patients with open-angle glaucoma or ocular hypertension. Allergan launched Alphagan P 0.1% in early 2006.

In September 2005, Allergan announced that it received positive opinions for Combigan, the company's Alphagan/timolol combination product for glaucoma, from each of the 21 Concerned Member States included in the Combigan Mutual

Recognition Procedure for the European Union. In late 2006, the company got an approvable letter from the FDA for Combigan.

Aesthetically ambitious

In March 2006, Allergan purchased Inamed for approximately $3.4 billion, and in January 2007, in a deal worth roughly $220 million, completed a follow-on acquisition of Groupe Cornéal Laboratories in France. The acquisition of Inamed signals Allergan's future direction, as it brings with it Juvéderm, a line of dermal fillers that fill in unwanted mouth creases, and the Lap-Band, an adjustable, stomach-shrinking device. Perhaps most significantly, the FDA and Health Canada approved Allergan's Inamed line of silicone gel-filled breast implants in 2006.

All of these offerings reflect Allergan's new strategy, which has largely been created by the accidental Hollywood success of Botox—the creation of a leading aesthetic franchise focused on "breast aesthetics, facial aesthetics and devices to treat obesity."

But regardless of Allergan's aesthetic aspirations, it still has its eye on growth prospects, however unattractive they may sound. Take overactive bladders, for example. Allergan is currently testing Botox for effectiveness in this field, and in September 2007 it acquired Esprit Pharma, Inc., maker of the $40 million bladder drug Sanctura. Allergan will have patent protection for Sanctura for three years, which should coincide perfectly with Botox's expected approval for this purpose in 2009. Allergan values the overactive bladder market as worth $1.7 billion a year, and predicts that its offerings can bring in around $300 to $400 million annually fairly soon. That should help recoup the cost of buying Esprit, which set Allergan back $370 million in cash.

GETTING HIRED

Getting in

The careers section (www.allergan.com/site/careers) has an advanced search function for applicants to sort opportunities by job type. Categories include corporate communications, corporate development, distribution, facilities, field sales, finance, general and administration, human resources, information systems, legal affairs, manufacturing, manufacturing QA, marketing/development, research and development, research compliance and sales support. The company only accepts resumes submitted for specific current open positions listed on their employment opportunities search site, except the following areas where it has ongoing needs: biopharmaceutical sciences, biostatistics, clinical research, medical writing, pathology, regulatory affairs and toxicology. Allergan also accepts internship applications through the site.

Amgen, Inc.

One Amgen Center Drive
Thousand Oaks, CA 91320
Phone: (805) 447-1000
Fax: (805) 447-1010
www.amgen.com

LOCATIONS

Thousand Oaks, CA (HQ)
Bothell, WA • Boulder, CO •
Cambridge, MA • Fremont, CA •
Juncos, PR • Longmont, CO •
Louisville, KY • San Francisco, CA •
Seattle, WA • Washington, DC •
West Greenwich, RI • Auckland •
Barcelona • Breda, The Netherlands •
Brussels • Budapest • Burnaby,
Canada • Cambridge • Cork • Dublin
• Espoo, Finland • Hawthorn,
Australia • Hellerup, Denmark • Milan
• Mississauga, Canada • Munich •
North Ryde, Australia • Paris • Porto
Salvo, Portugal • Prague •
Regensburg, German • Saitama,
Japan • Solna, Sweden • Tokyo •
Vienna • Vika, Norway • Warsaw •
Zug, Switzerland

THE STATS

Employer Type: Public Company
Stock Symbol: AMGN
Stock Exchange: Nasdaq
Chairman, President & CEO: Kevin
 W. Sharer
2006 Employees: 20,100
2006 Revenue ($mil.): $14,268
2006 Net Income ($mil.): $2,950

DEPARTMENTS

Administrative
Clinical Development
Engineering/Operations
Finance/Law
Human Resources
Information Systems
Logistics
Manufacturing
Medical Affairs
Postdoctoral
Preclinical Development
Process Development
Public Relations
Quality
Regulatory
Research
Sales & Marketing

KEY COMPETITORS

Abbott Labs
Bristol-Myers Squibb
Genentech

EMPLOYMENT CONTACT

wwwext.amgen.com/careers

THE SCOOP

The nuts and bolts

Based in Thousand Oaks, California, Amgen is one of the world's largest biotech companies with sales of more than $14 billion in 2006. The company rose to industry dominance primarily with three superstar drugs: the anti-anemia medications Epogen and Aranesp, which together account for roughly half of the company's sales, and rheumatoid arthritis drug Enbrel.

A pioneer at birth

Amgen got its start with a slightly longer version of the same moniker—Applied Molecular Genetics. A diverse mix of scientists and venture capitalists looking to create health care products based on molecular biology founded the company in 1980, concentrating on manufacturing a few potentially lucrative projects.

But the fledgling Applied Molecular Genetics neared bankruptcy until company scientist Fu-Kuen Lin cloned the human protein erythropoietin (EPO) in 1983. Armed with the breakthrough, which stimulates red blood cell production, Amgen went public and formed a partnership with Japanese beermeisters and biotechnology hobbyists Kirin Brewery to develop and market EPO (brand name Epogen) in 1984.

The two firms also teamed up to create recombinant human granulocyte colony stimulating factor (G-GSF, later redubbed Neupogen), a protein that stimulates the immune system. Amgen joined Ortho Pharmaceutical, a subsidiary of future nemesis Johnson & Johnson, in a star-crossed marketing alliance in 1985 and forged a tie with Roche in 1988. Amgen's prosperity skyrocketed after 1989, as the FDA approved Epogen and, soon after, the Epogen-related Neupogen, both blockbuster drugs.

The empire that Epogen and Neupogen built

Amgen introduced Epogen, one of the first biologically derived human therapeutics, to the U.S. market in 1989, for patients with end-stage renal disease who cannot produce adequate amounts of erythropoietin and thus suffer from anemia symptoms. Anemia becomes a significant problem for people with chronic kidney disease on dialysis, and the only treatments for it before Epogen included potentially dangerous blood transfusions and testosterone-based therapies often causing strong side effects. Amgen's first product in nine years of business, the drug racked up $17 million in sales by the end of its first month on the market.

Neupogen, introduced in 1991, is a recombinant version of a human protein that selectively stimulates production of infection-fighting white blood cells, neutrophils, in bone marrow. By the time of Neupogen's release, a long-running lawsuit between Amgen and Genetics Institute was wrapping up, and it favored Amgen, giving it a near monopoly over the EPO market. Neupogen sold over $260 million in its first year on the market and Amgen skyrocketed to the head of the biotech industry. In 1992, Amgen was the first biotech firm to exceed $1 billion in sales. The next year, Neupogen was selling over $700 million annually.

Neupogen's sister drug, Neulasta, approved in 2002, calls for only one injection per cycle. Neulasta sales rose to $2.7 billion in 2006, an increase from about $2.3 billion the year before. In 2000, Amgen continued to battle to keep its monopoly on the Epogen market. The company sued Transkaryotic Therapies and Aventis for alleged patent violations in both the U.S. and the U.K. Although initially victorious in the U.K., the verdict was overturned in 2002, leaving Amgen vulnerable to generic competitors when Epogen's patents expired in 2004.

Amgen comes of age

Amgen hired MCI-veteran Kevin Sharer as president in 1992 to solidify the company's status as industry leader. In 1993 Amgen became the first American biotech firm to gain a foothold in China when it formed an alliance with Kirin Pharmaceuticals to sell Neupogen (under the moniker Gran) and Epogen there.

By this point, Amgen was the world's largest biotech company, and it made a splash with the biggest deal in industry history—acquiring the industry's third-largest company, Seattle-based Immunex Corporation, for $17.8 billion. The deal bolstered Amgen's presence in the inflammation field, a key new therapeutic area; gave it significant research abilities and new pipeline drugs; and, most importantly, added Enbrel, a groundbreaking new anti-inflammation agent, to Amgen's drug roster.

The upstart

In 2001, Amgen introduced Aranesp. Like Epogen, Aranesp is a recombinant erythropoietic protein (EPO) stimulating the production of oxygen-carrying red blood cells, with greater biological activity and a longer half-life (approximately three times longer) than its older sibling. The drug treats anemia associated with chronic renal failure in patients both on dialysis and not.

Visit Vault at **www.vault.com** for insider company profiles, expert advice, career message boards, expert resume reviews, the Vault Job Board and more.

VAULT CAREER LIBRARY   **47**

In 2002, regulatory agencies in the U.S. and Europe approved Aranesp for chemotherapy-related anemia. Additionally, Amgen created TREAT (Trial to Reduce Cardiovascular Events with Aranesp Therapy), an international, multiyear trial to determine whether treating anemia in patients with chronic kidney disease and type 2 diabetes may lower their risk for death or cardiovascular events. It seeks to avoid such health problems as stroke, heart attack or heart failure (cardiovascular events being the most common cause of patient death for those suffering from chronic kidney disease).

From rheumatoid arthritis to psoriasis

Enbrel, Amgen's rheumatoid arthritis remedy, has emerged as one of the company's biggest sellers. Since its approval in 1998, physicians have prescribed Enbrel as a treatment for rheumatoid arthritis and other inflammatory conditions. However, it was the FDA approval in 2004 for use in chronic moderate to severe plaque psoriasis that has driven its huge success.

Some 1.5 million Americans suffer from moderate-to-severe psoriasis. Before Enbrel, they had only topical creams and phototherapy to relieve the cracked, bleeding and itchy skin that characterizes the condition. In one study, three out of four psoriasis sufferers taking Enbrel experienced dramatic results within a month's time. Sales of Enbrel increased from $2.6 billion in 2005 to nearly $2.9 billion in 2006

Going head-to-head with J&J

When Amgen joined a marketing partnership with Johnson & Johnson subsidiary Ortho Pharmaceutical in 1985, it also signed a licensing deal that would come back to haunt it more than a decade later. The two companies started feuding because Amgen—then a fledgling, cash-stricken company—licensed Procrit to J&J. In 1998, a dispute over Amgen's licensing agreement ended with an arbiter's decision to award $200 million to its rival, but later that year, Amgen emerged successful from a legal conflict over the rights to a promising new anemia drug that would eventually become Aranesp.

Bad news on Epogen and Aranesp

In early 2007, safety questions emerged about two of Amgen's top-selling drugs, Epogen and Aranesp, as various studies suggested that the two products might actually be harming patients. (Epogen and Aranesp accounted for almost half of the company's sales in 2006.) Then, in March 2007, the FDA put new black-box warnings on the drugs and other anemia medications. The warning urged doctors to use the lowest possible dose of the drugs.

In early May, the FDA released a staff scientist report that suggested cancer patients might need to stop using these medications. Amgen reacted to the uncertainty of future sales of the drugs by delaying the opening of a new factory in Ireland and implementing a hiring slowdown. Later that month, shareholders sued Amgen over Epogen and Aranesp, contending that the company misrepresented clinical studies of the two drugs. The suit also alleges insider trading by CEO Sharer and other Amgen executives.

The news for Amgen would eventually get better, but only after it got a little bit worse. In July, the Centers for Medicare and Medicaid Services (CMMS) enacted stricter reimbursement rules for Aranesp, significantly cutting into the success of Amgen's top-selling drug in 2006 (it brought in $4.12 billion).

Amgen, though, had doubled its spending on lobbyists from the year before, up to $10.2 million in 2007. After major lobbying, the U.S. Senate passed a resolution in September—sponsored by Republican Arlen Specter and Democrat Frank Lautenberg—to reconsider the decision. The American Society of Clinical Oncology also came out in support of Amgen, arguing that reimbursement restrictions will harm the anemia treatments. But no one knows how CMMS will respond. The Aranesp battle looks bound to continue.

How many patents?

Amgen is battling over Aranesp and Epogen in another area—over patent protection. Through a quirk of the patent process, Amgen and its founding researcher, Dr. Lin, only received one patent for erythropoietin research in Europe, but received seven in the United States. This could potentially expand these blockbuster drugs' shelf-life far beyond the 20 years usual for patent law—the patents should have expired in 2004.

Other firms are itching to take Amgen on in this respect, including Roche, which is trying to bring its peg-EPO product, Mircera, to market. In October 2007 Amgen won a resounding victory over Roche in court, prevailing in an injunction effort to block Mircera. The judge in the case also upheld several of Amgen's seven patents. For now, Epogen remains without significant competition stateside, although Roche gained approval to sell Mircera in the EU in 2007.

Visit Vault at **www.vault.com** for insider company profiles, expert advice, career message boards, expert resume reviews, the Vault Job Board and more.

VAULT CAREER LIBRARY

49

Some M&A and R&D

The company has responded to the prospect of competition from other companies by entering into strategic acquisitions and partnerships, as well as ramping up R&D. In April 2006, Amgen acquired Abgenix for approximately $2.1 billion. The acquisition of Abgenix brought the full ownership of Vectibix, Amgen's first cancer therapeutic.

Vectibix nix?

In March 2007, Amgen stopped a study of Vectibix after finding poor survival in patients who received the drug in addition to Genentech's drug Avastin, plus chemotherapy, for the treatment of colorectal cancer in advanced patients. Amgen said it still hopes to expand Vectibix's label to treat early stages of colon cancer, and the company is testing the drug as a single biologic added to chemotherapy.

The company ran into more governmental opposition—this time from across the pond. In May 2007, a European regulator (CHMP, the European Committee for Medicinal Products) said the drug's benefits didn't outweigh its risks and advised against approving Vectibix. The CHMP flip-flopped after an Amgen appeal, however, and allowed the drug onto the market for a limited population of patients in September 2007.

Looking forward

Amgen's research efforts have roughly tripled since 2002, and in 2006 the firm raised R&D spending to $3.2 billion, an increase of nearly 40 percent from 2005. Analysts have pointed out that the company's pipeline is uncertain in spite of big investments in R&D, but Amgen continues to pour money into research. At the end of 2006, the company also entered into a partnership with Cytokinetics to discover, develop and commercialize a cardiovascular treatment. During 2007, the firm plans to increase R&D investments to support clinical trials for late-stage programs and advance a number of molecules into phase II trials. Amgen hopes to launch a new osteoporosis drug called Denosumab by the end of 2009.

The firm also announced a number of job cuts in 2007. In August, CEO Sharer revealed plans to trim the company's 20,000-strong headcount by as much as 13 percent, hopefully saving more than $1 billion in the process. About 700 employees had accepted buyouts within a month's time, and the company then released the rest of its layoff figures. By November, it slashed 675 jobs at its Thousand Oaks, Calif.

headquarters and 450 at its manufacturing facility in Greenwich, Rhode Island. The rest of the 1,500 job cuts will come at other sites worldwide.

GETTING HIRED

The way in

Go to the careers section of the company's web site (wwwext.amgen.com/careers) for more information on open opportunities at Amgen. The site offers a searchable database of employment openings in numerous job categories, including administrative, clinical development, engineering/operations, finance/law, human resources, information systems, logistics, manufacturing, medical affairs, postdoctoral, preclinical development, process development, public relations, quality, regulatory, research, and sales and marketing. Amgen also offers internship opportunities and cooperative education programs for college students. All applications are made online.

Amgen has won its share of accolades, and with good reason. The firm gives workers benefits that include generous vacation time (it's in the top 10 percent of all U.S. companies in all industries for paid time off); comprehensive, affordable health care coverage; a stock purchase plan; a retirement plan with company matching, and more.

In 2006, Amgen won first place in *Pharmaceutical Executive*'s Industry Audit, an analysis of the financial performance for 16 publicly traded pharmaceutical and biotechnology companies. And that's not all: the company has recently been named one of the best places to work by several sources. In 2006 Amgen placed fourth in a ranking of biopharma employers by *Science* magazine and 41st on the *Sunday Times'* London list, in addition to appearing on the 100 Best Workplaces in Europe rundown in the *Financial Times*. To top it all off, Amgen won the 40th place spot on *Fortune*'s coveted 100 Best Companies to Work For list in 2007.

Lots of interviews and a few tricky questions

The interview process at Amgen usually involves a phone interview followed by "an all-day interview." One insider says that during the initial phone interview, the HR recruiter "asked several behavioral-based questions." During the on-site interview, the individual met with "four associate directors, a senior manager and a director," and the job seeker "also had to give a one-hour presentation to about 15 department staff." A second interviewee reports meeting with "three different groups after an initial phone interview." Another says that the follow-up interview included 30-minute meetings "with about 8 people/groups of people, including potential peers as well as colleagues."

One person says questions were "mostly behavioral-based." However, the interviewee shares, "some questions were tricky and very creative." An example? "Using the first five letters of your first name, give me a word that begins with each of those letters that describes your personality." Also, the source says, "The last interviewer asked me to go down the list of each of the interviewers I met with and recap what I learned from each one."

OUR SURVEY SAYS

Company culture is a mixed bag

Staff members at Amgen say the people are "helpful" and "very smart," but insiders also describe the company's culture as "stressful and demanding." One source in Thousand Oaks says, "Opportunities for advancement are high. In particular, one can change departments relatively easily."

Another says Amgen, although it is a large company, tries to have a "small company feel." The contact explains, "The yearly/semiyearly, multi-department events (Christmas parties, seminars, conferences, etc.) help take employees' minds off their work and the stresses of staying competitive in such a complicated and crowded market." Some insiders say hours are "very reasonable," but others warn you should "expect to work long hours."

Solid pay, handsome benefits, pricey locale

Respondents say salaries tend to be "above market," although they point out that the cost of living in Thousand Oaks is high. One insider says, "Amgen takes employee morale very seriously, and one feels, when working here, that the company truly is taking care of its employees." A senior associate in Thousand Oaks says, "Vacation time and days off are among the best in the industry."

In addition to loads of vacations days, holidays and sick days, there are two weeks when the office closes, "one week at Christmas and one week for the Fourth of July." The insider adds, "Education reimbursement is a great perk." Another employee mentions that benefits include "stock options, health benefits that started immediately, [and a] 401(k) with automatic 5 percent of pay put in whether or not I want to contribute myself (company contributes for you)." Sources also say Amgen has a "casual" dress code.

Diversity issues and other inequalities

Insiders say the company is still working toward becoming more diverse and inclusive. One source says, "diversity is encouraged, but in my opinion is still not fully accepted." Another feels that "diversity is not embraced by Thousand Oaks," and adds that "employees at the home office in Thousand Oaks have many more benefits and privileges" than staff at Amgen's other offices. Also, "Employees at Thousand Oaks have a far better chance for advancement due to their ability to network." Sources say managers are not always good, and favoritism can be a problem. One adds that there is "a feeling of an in-crowd and an out-crowd" at Amgen.

Confronting challenges

For the most part, Amgen insiders think the company will continue to do well in the future. One source says, "The near future looks bright for the company." A manager comments, "This company is very successful and will be around for a long time." Respondents are concerned with expiring patents and possible competition from Roche. However, a source says, "I believe we have a realistic sense of the challenges we have in the next few years, and have plans for how to meet them aggressively."

Visit Vault at **www.vault.com** for insider company profiles, expert advice, career message boards, expert resume reviews, the Vault Job Board and more.

VAULT CAREER LIBRARY   53

Amylin Pharmaceuticals, Inc.

9360 Towne Centre Drive
San Diego, CA 92121
Phone: (858) 552-2200
Fax: (858) 552-2212
www.amylin.com

LOCATIONS

San Diego, CA (HQ)
Beachwood, OH
Boulder, CO
Brentwood, TN
Doylestown, PA
Mandeville, LA
Washington, DC

THE STATS

Employer Type: Public Company
Stock Symbol: AMLN
Stock Exchange: Nasdaq
President & CEO: Daniel M. Bradbury
2006 Employees: 1,550
2006 Revenue ($mil.): $511
2006 Net Income ($mil.): -$218

KEY COMPETITORS

Eli Lilly
Novo Nordisk
sanofi-aventis

EMPLOYMENT CONTACT

www.amylin.com/careers

DEPARTMENTS

Administration • Analytical Research & Development • Bioanalytical Chemistry • Biometrics • Business Continuity Planning • Business Development • Business Information • Clinical • Clinical Operations • Clinical Research • Clinical Science • Clinical Services • Commercial Services • Comparative Medicine • Corporate Affairs • Corporate Development • Corporate Learning • Customer Service • Data Management • Depreciation • Discovery Biology • Engineering & Commercial Product Development • Facilities Planning & Services • Finance • Global Safety • Government Affairs • Human Resources • In Vivo Pharmacology • Information Services • Information Technology • Investigational Supplies • Lab Quality Ops • Legal • Manufacturing • Market Research • Marketing Administration • Medical Affairs • Medical Writing • National Accounts • New Product Planning • Nonclinical Drug Safety • Operations Administration • Pharmaceutical Sciences • Pharmacology • Product Development • Product Development Administration • Project Management • Quality Assurance—Auditing • Quality Assurance/Regulatory • Research Administration • Research Chemistry • Sales • Sales Administration • Sales Training • Statistical Programming • Statistics • Strategy & Technical Planning • Supply & Logistics • Validation

THE SCOOP

People with type 1 diabetes are unable to produce two particular hormones: insulin and amylin. And individuals with type 2 diabetes have insufficient insulin production, as well as impaired secretion of amylin. In 1987, researchers at Oxford University in the U.K. discovered the cellular composition of—what else?—amylin. Researchers near the other Cambridge, in Massachusetts, formed a company the same year to begin researching a drug replicating the hormone's function and decided to call it—naturally—Amylin Pharmaceuticals.

The company is still focused on discovering, developing and selling medicines primarily for the treatment of diabetes and obesity. The company has gained FDA approval for its products Byetta and Symlin. In 2006, Amylin's first full year as a commercial organization, its revenue hit nearly $511 million.

Help from the Red Cross company

In the two decades between its formation and commercial debut, Amylin went public in 1992 and slogged through a number of unprofitable years as it set about bringing its Symlin drug (which basically stands for simulated amylin) to market. In 1995 Amylin entered into a worldwide collaboration agreement with Johnson & Johnson's subsidiary LifeScan Inc., which brought a much greater amount of financial support to Amylin's R&D efforts. In 1996 alone, J&J floated Amylin $22 million, a significant amount for a company then earning $35.8 million in annual revenue.

In the next two years, J&J invested more than $170 million in Amylin and decided to end its funding in 1998, just as Symlin's commercialization was nearing. Amylin hired a new CEO that year, 28-year Eli Lilly veteran Joseph Cook, and the new boss reduced costs by slashing 75 percent of the company's headcount. Financial analysts approved, as company stock rose 1,568 percent over the course of 1999. Flush with this investment, all that remained was to finally bring Symlin to market.

Smiling about Symlin

Amylin presented its Symlin product to the FDA's Endrinologic and Metabolic Drugs and Advisory Committee (EMDAC) in July 2001, and early reviews were bad. In late July, the EMDAC panel voted against authorizing Symlin for type 1 diabetes 8-1 and for type 2 by 6-3. But the following October, the FDA approved the drug against these recommendations. With this development, Symlin became the first and only approved drug in a new class of compounds called amylinomimetics.

Visit Vault at **www.vault.com** for insider company profiles, expert advice, career message boards, expert resume reviews, the Vault Job Board and more.

VAULT CAREER LIBRARY   **55**

Symlin works with insulin to give patients more stable blood glucose levels throughout the day and after meals. The drug also leads to weight loss in most patients. Because it works with insulin to control blood sugar, patients often need less insulin to achieve desired blood sugar levels after eating. It's not a perfect solution, though—the FDA rejected Symlin for use with some kinds of insulin in October 2007. The drug generated $40 million in sales in 2006.

Fun with Eli & Lilly

CEO Cook acted to secure more investment for the company in 2002, entering into a collaborative agreement with his old employer, Eli Lilly & Co., which is still in effect today. The deal was worth an initial investment of $80 million, and potentially $300 million over the long run. Cook stepped down in 2003, replaced by Ginger Graham, another former Eli Lilly man. The next drug in Amylin's pipeline focused on the hormone exenatide. It eventually earned the brand name "Byetta" and surpassed Symlin as the firm's top-selling drug, with $430 million in sales in 2006.

Betting on Byetta

Byetta has somewhat unusual origins, for which it has earned the nicknames "Lizzy" and "Gilly." Back in the 1990s, Dr. John Eng at New York's Bronx Veterans Affairs Medical Center noticed that the Gila monster, a lizard found in the Southwestern U.S., might be able to help diabetics. The lizard can, for example, eat 50 percent of its body weight at once and go months without eating afterwards, with no effect on its blood sugar. Eng found that the secret ingredient behind this biology is the Gila's saliva, which contains the exenatide hormone. Dr. Eng presented his findings to the American Diabetes Association, and Amylin licensed rights to the drug back in 1996.

This treatment is the first and only approved drug in a new class of compounds called incretin mimetics. The FDA approved twice-daily formulation of the diabetes treatment in 2005, and Amylin started selling the medicine in the U.S. in June 2005. The drug's active ingredient, exenatide, mimics the effects of GLP-1, a human hormone that is normally released after eating, and Byetta stimulates digestion and insulin production.

In late 2006, the FDA approved the use of Byetta in combination with a category of medicines called TZDs. Amylin estimates that, as a result of the FDA's approval, about three million new patients could be treated with Byetta. In February 2007, the company announced FDA approval of more convenient storage instructions for

Byetta—patients previously had to refrigerate the drug after first use, but now they can now store it at room temperatures below 77 degrees Fahrenheit.

In the pipeline

In spite of Amylin's two promising and profitable drugs, the company reported year-end losses of $219 million in 2006. Amylin attributed the losses to increased expenses related to expanded support for its drugs as well as the cost of ongoing R&D investments. It's not a new development—Amylin has been unprofitable for the past several years.

One product in the pipeline is a long-acting release, once-weekly formulation of Byetta, which the firm has been working on since signing an agreement with Alkermes in May 2000. Alkermes is a firm that focuses on developing products based on proprietary drug delivery technologies, and the deal called for Alkermes to give Amylin an exclusive, worldwide license to Medisorb, a technology for injectable sustained-release formulations of exenatide and related compounds. In exchange, Amylin agreed to provide Alkermes with R&D funding, as well as possible future milestone payments and royalties on any future product sales.

Looking forward

Amylin is currently studying a new formulation of exenatide for nasal delivery and has four clinical trials ongoing to evaluate compounds in development for the treatment of obesity. The company also expects to expand the market for its existing drugs, anticipating the launch of Byetta in various European countries in 2008.

Also in 2007, Amylin received a bout of press attention for a management shake-up and the great potential success of its products. Effective as of March, the company named Daniel Bradbury its new CEO. Bradbury has been the company's COO since 2003 and began work at the company in 1994. In September, Bradbury celebrated the results of a study suggesting Byetta was more effective for type 2 diabetes than rival Lantus, a sanofi-aventis product. Also in September, Bradbury released a number of statements denying that Amylin was the subject of any merger or acquisition talks. Industry pundits have identified Eli Lilly—which already has over 40 successful diabetes drugs—as a natural suitor. That firm already has a 50 percent stake in Byetta's success, due to its collaboration agreement with Amylin.

Visit Vault at **www.vault.com** for insider company profiles, expert advice, career message boards, expert resume reviews, the Vault Job Board and more.

VAULT CAREER LIBRARY   57

GETTING HIRED

Smilin' Amylin

Job seekers can check out opportunities at Amylin's careers site, at www.amylin.com/careers. At press time, opportunities were listed in every department from finance to medical affairs to project management to quality assurance, and the company has dozens of other departments listed on the site. If you want to drop the company a line, you can upload a resume and cover letter and send them right along. The site will also try to match a job to the skill-set on your resume.

Amylin offers full-time a range of benefits. These include medical, dental and a voluntary vision plan, domestic partner coverage, a 401(k) disability, an employee stock purchase plan, life and accidental death and dismemberment insurance, flexible spending accounts and education assistance. Heck, the company even offers discounted gym memberships.

Amylin also offers a summer internship program for students interested in exploring a career at Amylin or in the biotech industry. Summer internships are usually 10 to 12 weeks long and begin in May or June and end in August or September. Typically, the company accepts resumes from prospective interns starting in January. The firm offers internships in both scientific and non-scientific areas. More information about Amylin's internships and how to apply for them is online at careers.amylin.com/internships.asp.

National and local publications have recognized Amylin as a great place to work. In 2007, *The Scientist* ranked the company No. 7 on its list of the Top 15 Small Companies. The same year, the *San Diego Business Journal* listed Amylin as one of the Best Employers in its large business category (500-plus employees). In September 2006, *San Diego* magazine also honored Amylin, listing the biopharmaceutical company as one of the Best Companies with 500 or more employees.

Applera Corporation

301 Merritt 7
P.O. Box 5435
Norwalk, CT 06856
Phone: (203) 840-200
Fax: (203) 840-2312
www.applera.com

LOCATIONS

Norwalk, CT (HQ)
Alameda, CA
Foster City, CA
Rockville, MD

THE STATS

Employer Type: Public Company
Stock Symbol: ABI (Applied
Biosystems Group); CRA (Celera
Group)
Stock Exchange: NYSE
Chairman, President & CEO: Tony L.
White
2007 Employees: 5,530
2007 Revenue ($mil.): $2,132
2007 Net Income ($mil): $159

DEPARTMENTS

Accounting & Finance • Administrative
• Bioanalysis • Biochemistry •
BioEngineering • Biology • Business •
Business Development • Chemical
Engineering • Chemistry • Clinical
Development • Corporate Communi-
cations/Investor Relations • Customer
Service • Diagnostics • Drug Discovery
• Education, Training & Library •
Engineering • Environmental Health &
Safety • Facilities • Financial
Operations • Financial Services •
Formulation • Genetics • Human
Resources • Immunology • Informatics
• Information Technology • Legal •
Library Scientist • Management
Consulting • Manufacturing •
Marketing • Materials • Metabolism •
Oncology • Operations • Pharma-
ceutical Sciences • Pharmokinetics •
Pharmacology • Physics • Process
Development • Product Development •
Project Management • Proteomics •
Purchasing • Quality Assurance •
Quality Control • Regulatory Affairs •
Research • Sales • Statistics •
Strategic Planning • Supply Chain •
Toxicology • Training • Validation

KEY COMPETITORS

Affymetrix • Beckman Coulter • Bio-
Rad Labs

EMPLOYMENT CONTACT

www.applera.com/applera/appleraho
me.nsf/sectionhome/careers-section

Visit Vault at **www.vault.com** for insider company profiles, expert advice,
career message boards, expert resume reviews, the Vault Job Board and more.

VAULT CAREER LIBRARY

59

THE SCOOP

The name game

Applera Corporation is actually the successor company to the Perkin-Elmer Corporation, which was founded as an optical technology firm in 1937 and was involved in building the Hubble Telescope in the 1970s and 1980s. By the 1990s, Perkin-Elmer consisted of three major divisions—life sciences, organic sciences and inorganic sciences.

The company decided to shake up this unwieldy combination in 1999, recapitalizing to focus on its life sciences unit, which has since developed into a large biotechnology firm. Perkin-Elmer changed its name to Applera Corporation and exchanged Perkin-Elmer's stock for two new "tracking" stocks now known as Applera Corporation-Applied Biosystems group common stock and Applera Corporation-Celera Genomics group common stock. Applera Corp. functions as a sort of holding company (there is no single security called "Applera") and these two classes of stock are listed on the New York Stock Exchange.

To make matters more confusing, EG&G, which bought Perkin-Elmer's Analytical Instruments division, has since adopted the name PerkinElmer, and operates independently and separately from Applera Corp.

One company, two sides

Currently, Applera oversees two operating groups: Applied Biosystems Group and the Celera Group. The Applied Biosystems Group focuses on the life science industry and research community by developing and marketing instrument-based systems, software and services. These tools are used by the company's customers to analyze nucleic acids (DNA and RNA), small molecules and proteins for making scientific discoveries and developing new pharmaceuticals. Applied Biosystems also sells its products to some markets outside of life science research, such as the fields of human identity testing (forensic and paternity testing), biosecurity and quality and safety testing. Based in Foster City, Calif., Applied Biosystems pulled in reported sales of $2.1 billion in the 2007 fiscal year, up from $1.9 billion in 2006.

Celera is a diagnostics business delivering personalized disease management solutions through a combination of tests and services based on proprietary genetics discovery platforms. The business operates from four facilities, with two located in Alameda, Calif., South San Francisco, Calif., and Rockville, Md. The business employs about 540 people and recently acquired Berkeley HeartLab, gaining a CLIA-certified laboratory with corresponding sales force. Celera develops diagnostic products that predict disease risk and optimize therapy selection, monitoring and patient outcome. It has a strategic and profit-sharing alliance with Abbott Laboratories, through which the companies sell and support molecular diagnostic products. Celera's discovery platforms are the basis for multiple discovery and therapeutic product development collaborations. However, the division is tiny compared to Applied Biosystems, with $43 million in 2007 revenue.

Diagnosis: Spin-off

Based in Alameda, Calif., Celera Diagnostics was created in 2001 as a 50/50 joint venture between Celera and Applied Biosystems. One of the fledgling company's first projects came in October 2002, when drug powerhouse Bristol-Myers Squibb signed on with Celera to develop treatments and tests for heart disease and diabetes, with BMS gaining rights to medicines based on research, and Celera getting the rights to market the products.

That December, Celera Diagnostics released its first product for market, Viroseq Genotyping System, a gene-based test that helps physicians decide the best course of treatment for patients with the HIV virus. In January 2006, Celera acquired Applied Biosystems' 50 percent share of Celera Diagnostics. Now as one company, Celera focuses on advancing the field of targeted medicine and personalized disease management, where genomic and proteomic discoveries can enable the prevention and earlier detection of disease, ensure the right therapy at the optimal dosage for each patient, and lead to better and more cost-effective health care.

Applera made two strategic acquisitions in 2006. In March, Applied Biosystems acquired the research products division of Ambion, Inc., an Austin, Tex.,-based developer and supplier of products to study RNA. Then, in summer 2006, Applied Biosystems purchased Agencourt Personal Genomics to the tune of $120 million. This Beverly, Mass., startup company is developing ultra high-throughput, low-cost genetic analysis technology. Applied Biosystems expects the technology will expand the research market by allowing studies that require low-cost processing of large numbers of samples. In October 2007, Applied Biosystems launched its next-generation DNA sequencing platform based on the Agencourt technology, called SOLiD™.

Visit Vault at **www.vault.com** for insider company profiles, expert advice, career message boards, expert resume reviews, the Vault Job Board and more.

VAULT CAREER LIBRARY

61

Cutting costs

Applied Biosystems cut 3.3 percent of its workforce, roughly 145 workers, in July 2004 as part of a restructuring plan, which realigned the company into four divisions: molecular biology, proteomics, applied markets and service. Then, Celera Genomics reduced its workforce by some 240 positions—primarily in small molecule drug discovery and development—over the course of 2006. This reduction was due to the sale and termination of Celera's small molecule programs as well as the integration of Celera Diagnostics into Celera Genomics.

Science at the forefront

Celera's industrial-scale, high-throughput proteomics discovery platform has been highly productive in identifying and validating new targets for drug development in cancer. This platform has allowed identification and measures of the level of hundreds of proteins that are over-expressed on the surface of cancer cells and not on normal cells. These cell surface proteins could be promising targets in therapeutic antibody and small molecule drug development, as well as diagnostics, building potential long-term value for Celera.

To date, the company has fully validated 51 cancer targets and selected an additional 184 potential targets for validation studies for discoveries from pancreatic, colon, breast, gastric, renal and lung cancer specimens. Celera currently collaborates with Abbott and Seattle Genetics—focusing on converting discoveries into new, targeted anticancer therapies.

Applied Biosystems may be best known for providing instruments for DNA analysis to life science researchers in universities and research institutions. A notable example of AB's technology leadership in DNA analysis is the 96-capillary ABI PRISM 3700 DNA Analyzer, introduced in 1998, which allowed Celera Genomics and the Human Genome Project to complete the human genome sequence draft years ahead of schedule. Outside of DNA analysis, Applied Biosystems' technologies are used in many applications, including DNA and gene expression analysis, genotyping, proteomics and small molecule analysis.

Moving forward

After 2007, Applied Biosystems anticipates that growth will be driven by core markets in basic and clinical research, forensic analysis and other non-research uses of the company's technologies, not to mention emerging markets including China and India. The company has entered into a hopefully profitable alliance with the food-testing unit of DuPont. Applied Biosystems expects the alliance with DuPont will expand the firm's participation in quality and safety testing. Celera Genomics Group would like a larger share of the $2 billion molecular diagnostics industry. Celera plans to continue to expand its diagnostic business by introducing new products.

The company's diagnostics should receive a boost soon from an acquisition—the October 2007 purchase of Berkeley HeartLab for about $195 million. True to its name, the HeartLab focuses on cardiovascular research and testing. In literal terms, the acquisition brings Applera a 40,000-square-foot clinical testing facility in Alameda, Calif., with other offices spread out around the state, and about 300 employees. Applera stated that it would operate the company as a business unit of Celera, and announced no immediate plans to cut any jobs.

GETTING HIRED

Apply yourself

Applera's corporate web site (www.applera.com/applera/applerahome.nsf/sectionhome/careers-section) allows job searches for the company's separate businesses: Applied Biosystems in Foster City, Calif. and Celera in Alameda, Calif., and Rockville, Md.—as well as positions at the parent company. As each business expands, it offers new scientific, engineering and marketing opportunities. Applied Biosystems and Celera are independently managed and positions for professional development can be found in research, development, manufacturing, quality assurance, regulatory, marketing, sales, legal and support posts.

Visit Vault at **www.vault.com** for insider company profiles, expert advice, career message boards, expert resume reviews, the Vault Job Board and more.

VAULT CAREER LIBRARY   63

AstraZeneca PLC

15 Stanhope Gate
London, W1K 1LN
United Kingdom
Phone: +44-20-7304-5000
Fax: +44-20-7304-5151

US Headquarters:
P.O. Box 15437
Wilmington, DE 19850-5437
Phone: (302)-886-3000
Fax: (302)-886-2972
www.astrazeneca.com

LOCATIONS

London (HQ)
Hato Rey, PR • Irving, TX • Los
Angeles, CA • Newark, DE • Palo
Alto, CA • Schaumberg, IL •
Tampa, FL • Torrance, CA •
Waltham, MA • Washington, DC •
Wayne, PA • Westborough, MA •
Wilmington, DE • Woodland Hills,
CA

Locations in over 100 countries.

THE STATS

Employer Type: Public Company
Stock Symbol: AZN
Stock Exchange: NYSE
CEO: David Brennan
President & CEO, AstraZeneca US:
 Tony Zook
2006 Employees: 66,000
2006 Revenue ($mil.): $ 26,475
2006 Net Income ($mil.): $4,392

DEPARTMENTS

Administrative
Business Development & Licensing
Clinical Development
Corporate Communications/Public
 Relations
Customer Service & Call Center
Drug Safety/Pharmacovigilance
External Scientific Affairs
Finance
Government Affairs & Public Policy
Human Resources
Information Services
Installation, Maintenance & Repair
Legal
Manufacturing & Production
Marketing & Analytics
Operations
Purchasing
Quality Assurance
Regulatory Affairs
Research & Non-Clinical
Development
Sales

KEY COMPETITORS

GlaxoSmithKline
Merck
Novartis

EMPLOYMENT CONTACT

www.astrazeneca-us.com/content/
aboutAZ/astrazeneca-careers.asp

THE SCOOP

England's healing touch

One of the world's top pharmaceutical firms, London-based AstraZeneca specializes in treatments for gastrointestinal, cardiovascular and oncology therapeutic areas, with products in respiratory and inflammation, infection and neuroscience as well. Though the company makes medications for a variety of ailments, its best-selling drugs include acid reflux stopper Nexium, schizophrenia treatment Seroquel and the cholesterol reducer Crestor.

In addition to its core pharmaceutical business, AstraZeneca also owns subsidiary companies that operate in health-related markets. Aptium Oncology, formerly Salick Health Care, develops and manages outpatient cancer treatment clinics, mostly in the United States. The company's AstraTech subsidiary manufactures medical equipment.

From Z to AZ

AstraZeneca traces the main line of its ancestry back to 1926. That year, four British chemical companies—Nobel Industries, United Alkali, British Dyestuffs and Brunner, Mond & Co.—merged to form a new company called Imperial Chemical Industries (ICI). The newly formed ICI focused on research, recruiting chemists, engineers and managers, and forming a funneling system with leading universities. Between 1933 and 1935, at least 87 new products rolled off the shelves, including polyethylene.

Fortunes declined in the aftermath of World War II as competition increased worldwide. In 1982, ICI shifted from bulk chemicals to high-margin specialty chemicals such as pharmaceuticals and pesticides. That business became Zeneca, which spun off from ICI in 1993. Good fortune shone upon Zeneca in 1995, when Glaxo was driven to sell a migraine drug candidate to complete its merger with Wellcome. Zeneca snapped up the then-unproven drug (Zomig) and enjoyed great success when the pill earned FDA approval two years later. In 1999 Zeneca completed its purchase of Sweden's Astra to form AstraZeneca.

Ulcer pain is AstraZeneca's gain

AstraZeneca's drug portfolio concentrates on five major treatment areas: gastrointestinal, oncology, cardiovascular, neuroscience, and respiratory and

Visit Vault at **www.vault.com** for insider company profiles, expert advice, career message boards, expert resume reviews, the Vault Job Board and more.

VAULT CAREER LIBRARY

65

inflammation. The company's main gastrointestinal (GI) drugs are Nexium and Prilosec/Losec. Prilosec, introduced in 1989, was the first proton pump inhibitor (PPI) approved for the treatment of ulcers. The drug set sales records and became, at one point, the best-selling pharmaceutical in the world. AstraZeneca has sold more than 840 million Prilosec doses since the drug's launch.

No reflux for Nexium

2004 was the year of Nexium for AstraZeneca. Sales of the purple pill reached $3.9 billion, up 15 percent over the year before. Nexium is used to remedy a wide range of acid-related disorders, including heartburn and gastroesophageal reflux disease (GERD). First launched in Sweden in 2000, the drug is now available in approximately 75 markets, including the United States, Canada and major European countries.

Nexium arrived just in time for AstraZeneca, as it lost patent protection for its previous acid-reflux medication Prilosec and stood to lose its No. 1 position in gastrointestinal therapeutic products. As patients opted for Nexium or generic forms, U.S. sales of Prilosec plummeted 58 percent in 2004, to $366 million. In 2006 Prilosec had $1.4 billion in sales, while Nexium generated $5.2 billion in the same period.

Sequel to Nexium—Seroquel

Seroquel, AstraZeneca's second best-selling drug behind Nexium, is an antipsychotic drug used to treat schizophrenia and acute manic disorders in bipolar disorder. In 2006, Seroquel sales increased 24 percent from 2005, to $3.4 billion. The drug is indicated for bipolar mania in 73 markets and for schizophrenia in 87 markets. In the United States, the drug has the additional indication for bipolar depression. Seroquel has also been found effective in the treatment of agitation associated with dementia in elderly patients living in long-term care facilities.

Heartbeat of the company

In 2006, AstraZeneca's cardiovascular sales grew by 15 percent to $6.1 billion. The company's third best-selling drug is Crestor, a member of a class of drugs called statins. Sales of Crestor grew by 59 percent in 2006, rising from $1.3 billion in 2005 to more than $2 billion in 2006. Crestor has been approved in more than 90 countries on five continents.

Despite widespread approval from regulatory agencies, Crestor came under fire during 2004, as a consumer advocacy group called Public Citizen filed a Citizen's Petition demanding the FDA withdraw it from the market. AstraZeneca stood by Crestor and launched a web site in September 2004 that contained a database of pre- and post-approval clinical trials and post-marketing observation of patients treated with Crestor since its launch in 2003.

Though the safety allegations affected Crestor's sales, particularly in the United States, sales still totaled $908 million in 2004. More negative news came in May 2005 when the American Heart Association journal *Circulation* reported that Crestor is significantly more likely than other statins to cause muscle deterioration that can lead to kidney disease.

In March 2007, a new clinical trial showed that Crestor slowed (but didn't reverse) progression of atherosclerosis in people with early signs of the disease. However, the study also found the overall frequency of renal adverse events was similar in the group who took Crestor and people who were given a placebo.

Seloken/Toprol-XL is AstraZeneca's other cardiovascular megastar with $1.8 billion in total sales in 2006. The once-daily tablet controls blood pressure and is used to treat heart failure and angina. In early 2006, a U.S. district court invalidated AstraZeneca's patent protection for Toprol-XL. The company appealed the decision unsuccessfully, as an appeal court ruled against AstraZeneca again in July 2007.

Cancer drug setbacks and successes

In May 2003, AstraZeneca launched lung cancer drug Iressa to much fanfare. The drug was a new type of anticancer agent intended to block signals for cancer cell growth and survival. Despite early positive clinical trials, two publications appeared in 2004 explaining that patients who had reacted favorably to Iressa had a genetic alteration within the tumor cells and that Iressa probably didn't extend the lives of cancer patients.

In 2005 AstraZeneca pulled the drug from the approval process in Europe. In the U.S. and Canada, regulatory authorities restricted use of the drug to patients who were already benefiting from it. Iressa took another hit when a study sponsored by the National Cancer Institute found that it had no significant effect on breast cancer survival rates. In 2006 Iressa's sales were only $237 million, a 30 percent decline from 2005.

One oncology drug that AstraZeneca has had success with is Arimidex. The drug is the leading hormonal breast cancer therapy in the United States, Japan and France. Arimidex's sales grew 29 percent in 2006 to $1.5 billion. Casodex, AstraZeneca's second-best-selling cancer treatment, is used to treat early and advanced prostate cancer. In 2006, Casodex had global sales of more than $1.2 billion.

Government crackdowns and investigations

As competition among pharmaceutical companies to lock up lucrative markets has increased over the past few years, drugmakers have resorted to ever-more aggressive marketing efforts to get physicians to notice their products. In a case involving AstraZeneca, however, those tactics crossed the line from enthusiastic promotion to fraud.

To increase sales of its prostate drug Zoladex, the company courted urologists with free samples and other perks. Doctors who were in on the scheme gave these free samples of the drug to their patients, charged Medicare or Medicaid for the cost—as much as $300 per dose—and pocket the reimbursement from the government. What's more, AstraZeneca was accused of recruiting doctors by bribing them with free travel, entertainment and speaking fees. Government prosecutors estimated total losses to the health care system at both the federal and state levels at more than $40 million.

When investigators were able to uncover proof that AstraZeneca was aware of the fraud, the company pleaded guilty in June 2003 to conspiracy to violate a federal prescription drug marketing law. As part of the settlement, AstraZeneca agreed to pay $355 million in penalties and restitution. It was the second-largest prescription fraud settlement ever— topped only by a similar case in 2001 involving Boston-based drug manufacturer TAP Pharmaceuticals.

Developments in 2007 have revealed that AstraZeneca's legal troubles may be far from over. In February 2007, the U.K.'s Serious Fraud Office launched an investigation into whether companies, including AstraZeneca, had paid bribes to Saddam Hussein's regime in Iraq. The firm has denied allegations of unethical behavior in its trading relationships with Iraq.

The following June, a U.S. federal judge ruled against the company as part of a class-action lawsuit related to its earlier practice of secretly inflating the "average wholesale price" of its drugs and encouraging doctors to claim full reimbursement from Medicare. AstraZeneca's monetary damages from this lawsuit have yet to be determined.

Good news, lukewarm predictions

AstraZeneca shareholders got some great news in January 2007 when the company's fiscal 2006 financials came in. The numbers showed that drug sales had raked in $26.48 billion in revenue before taxes ($8.54 billion in profit, a 28 percent increase from 2005). However, AstraZeneca also announced in January that it would be cutting 3,000 jobs over the course of 2007 to cut costs and increase profits, a goal investors feared it might not reach.

Another method that AZ hopes will pay off in 2007: buying up new drugs from outside labs. As part of that plan, which AZ considers key to long-term growth, the firm made a $1 billion deal to distribute Bristol-Myers Squibb's diabetes meds in December 2006 and bought up antiviral drug firm Arrow Therapeutics for $150 million a month later.

Innovation anticipation

AstraZeneca is buying up new drugs from other companies such as Arrow and Bristol-Myers Squibb, but it's also buying other businesses. In April 2007, the company announced that it was acquiring MedImmune, a U.S. biotechnology company, for $15.2 billion. Through the purchase, AstraZeneca will gain Synagis, a treatment for infant respiratory infections, as well as flu vaccines.

The acquisition, however, led AstraZeneca to more than double its budgeted number of job cuts for 2007, increasing the number from the already whopping 3,000 to the tremendous total of 7,600, or 11 percent of the workforce. The following September, the company was buying again, bringing in Atlantis Components for $71 million, a Cambridge, Mass.-based designer and maker of dental implants.

In addition, the firm is ramping up its in-house R&D efforts. Worldwide, AstraZeneca has 16 research and development centers. In total, AstraZeneca's R&D organization is comprised of about 12,000 people located in eight countries including Canada, France, India, Japan, Sweden, the United Kingdom and the United States.

The company is also building a new innovation center in China. In January 2007, AstraZeneca announced a $100 million research investment to boost research in the infectious disease area and to continue cancer research at the company's R&D center near Boston. The expansion, scheduled to be completed by mid-2009, will accommodate up to 100 additional researchers.

GETTING HIRED

Joining the team

Applicants can search a list of available positions on AstraZeneca's web site at www.astrazeneca-us.com/content/aboutAZ/astrazeneca-careers.asp. The site offers a searchable job database containing openings in a number of areas, including: business development and licensing, clinical development, corporate communications and public relations, customer service and call center, drug safety and pharmacovigilance, external scientific affairs, finance, government affairs and public policy, human resources, information services, legal, manufacturing and production, marketing and analytics, operations, purchasing, quality assurance, regulatory affairs, research and nonclinical development and sales.

Employee benefits

AstraZeneca's compensation package includes a base salary plus the opportunity to earn performance-based incentive bonuses in the form of cash or company stock. The company offers a choice of medical plans as well as prescription drug, dental, vision, disability and life insurance coverage. For retirement benefits, AstraZeneca provides both a defined contribution plan and 75 percent matching funds for employees' individual 401(k) savings accounts.

Additional benefits include on-site child care and fitness facilities for employees at the Wilmington headquarters, up to $5,000 in adoption assistance, tuition reimbursement and, at some locations, health screenings and on-site health services. AstraZeneca also sponsors activities such as "Take a Child to Work Day," an annual company picnic and discount tickets to museums, theaters and other cultural attractions.

AstraZeneca has been named to both *Fortune*'s 100 Best Companies to Work For list and *Working Mother* magazine's 100 Best Companies for Working Mothers list since 2003; *Fortune* ranked the company 71st in 2007, while *Working Mother* placed it fifth in 2006. With perks like CEO breakfasts, flexible work schedules and the transparency of town-hall style meetings, it's easy to see why voluntary turnover is at a low 7 percent.

Major departments and locations

London-based AstraZeneca employs more than 58,000 people worldwide—11,000 of them in the United States. The company's U.S. headquarters is located in Wilmington, Del. AstraZeneca's jobs are categorized into the several areas listed above. The firm has two major U.S. research labs: one in Wilmington and another in Waltham, Mass. (suburban Boston).

Supply and manufacturing facilities are located in Newark, Del., and Westborough, Mass. Finally, field sales positions are based at six U.S. regional business centers located in or near Boston, Dallas, Los Angeles, Chicago, Tampa and Philadelphia. AstraZeneca's web site lists all open positions and offers the option of creating a personalized user profile.

OUR SURVEY SAYS

Corporate culture

Sources say that AstraZeneca's "British" corporate culture includes a "strong" work ethic, "solid" job security, and "generous" benefits. Some of our contacts say that their distance from the British headquarters can be "frustrating," but they are "optimistic" about AstraZeneca's current effort to transform itself into "a truly global corporation." AstraZeneca's recent success in developing cancer medication, moreover, has enabled its insiders to boast about "improving the quality of life for people everywhere."

Visit Vault at **www.vault.com** for insider company profiles, expert advice, career message boards, expert resume reviews, the Vault Job Board and more.

VAULT CAREER LIBRARY 71

Barr Pharmaceuticals, Inc.

Corporate Headquarters:
223 Quaker Road
Pomona, NY 10970
Phone: (845) 362-1100
Fax: (845) 362-2774

Executive Offices:
400 Chestnut Ridge Road
Woodcliff Lake, NJ 07677
Phone: (201) 930-3300
Fax: (201) 930-3330
www.barrlabs.com

LOCATIONS

Pomona, NY (HQ)
Bala Cynwyd, PA
Buffalo, NY
Cincinnati, OH
East Hanover, NJ
Forest, VA
North Towanda, NY
Northvale, NJ
Washington, DC
Woodcliff Lake, NJ

THE STATS

Employer Type: Public Company
Stock Symbol: BRL
Stock Exchange: NYSE
Chairman, President & CEO: Bruce
  L. Downey
2006 Employees: 8,000
2006 Revenue ($mil.): $1,315
2006 Net Income ($mil.): $336

DEPARTMENTS

Accounting & Finance •
Administration • Biostatistics •
Clinical Operations •
Communications • Health & Safety •
Human Resources • Information
Technology • Legal • Maintenance &
Engineering • Manufacturing •
Packaging • Process Development •
Production Management • Production
Planning • Project Management •
Purchasing • Quality Assurance •
Quality Control • Regulatory Affairs •
Regulatory Compliance • Research &
Development • Sales • Scientific
Affairs • Security • Technical Affairs
• Training • Validation • Warehouse
& Distribution

KEY COMPETITORS

McNeil Pharmaceutical
Mylan Laboratories
Ortho-Watson Pharmaceuticals

EMPLOYMENT CONTACT

www.barrlabs.com/careers

THE SCOOP

Barr basics

Barr Pharmaceuticals, a primary holding company, has three main subsidiaries: Barr Laboratories, Duramed Pharmaceuticals and Pliva. The Barr Laboratories division develops, manufactures and markets generic pharmaceutical products, currently producing 75 generic pharmaceutical products, including 22 oral contraceptive products that accounted for about 48 percent of total generic sales during 2006.

Meanwhile, Duramed Pharmaceuticals develops, makes and sells the firm's proprietary products. It currently manufactures and distributes 19 proprietary pharmaceuticals, mostly female health care products such as Seasonale and Seasonique extended-cycle oral contraceptives. Lastly, the Croatia-based Pliva focuses on biopharmaceuticals and other value-added generics. Barr Pharmaceutical's revenue topped $1.3 billion in its 2006 fiscal year, a 25 percent increase from 2005.

Fed up with the FDA

Barr Laboratories, founded in 1970, was among the first generic pharmaceutical firms in the United States. Its fortunes looked sure to improve in 1984, with the passage of the Drug Price Competition and Patent Restoration Act—often called the Hatch-Waxman Act. The act loosened generic reproductions of major brand pharmaceutical products, and the industry exploded with activity.

By 1987, however, Barr co-founder, Chairman and CEO Edwin Cohen began to take issue with the Food and Drug Administration (FDA) and its treatment of rival generic drugmakers. That year, he approached the FDA with concerns about its approval process. After hearing nothing back, he testified for a House Subcommittee on Oversight 1989 investigation into generic drugs. His allegations? That generic drug makers were bribing the FDA for product approval.

The following year, the FDA responded by filing suit against Barr, seeking to shut it down for "fundamentally flawed" manufacturing processes. *The New York Times* profiled the lawsuit in 1992, and quoted an analyst with Furman Selz, who called the FDA's approach "unprecedented." The *Times* also noted that Barr had laid off 25 percent of its workforce to fight the lawsuit. The lawsuit wrapped up in 1995, but not until Barr co-founder Cohen stepped down, as president in 1993 and as chairman and CEO in 1994.

Barr gets a lift from Downey

The new chairman, president and CEO was Bruce Downey, who had been Barr's lead attorney in the FDA case since 1991. His legal background—he was also a former partner at Winston & Strawn—served him well, as he imbued Barr with a litigious strategy, challenging major drug firms' patents to bring more and more generics to market. By 2001, he had successfully challenged eight major patents, including Eli Lilly's Prozac, Glaxo Wellcome's AIDS medication AZT and Dupont Merck's Coumadin (Barr's generic version of Coumadin collected $15 million in sales during its first month alone).

Revenue swelled accordingly, rising from $58 million during the FDA lawsuit in 1993 to $109 million in 1994 and $232 million in 1996. It more than doubled that mark in 2001, bringing in $593 million and it more than doubled again the next year, breaking into a new stratosphere with $1.18 billion in sales. Downey's growth strategy had obviously paid off by now, but he had also started producing brand drugs and delving into the mergers and acquisitions market. His first major move was the 1999 purchase of rival Duramed Pharmaceuticals for $571 million—now a distinct subsidiary.

Branching out into biotechs

It appears that CEO Downey has his ear to the ground for other pursuits, as well, such as generic biopharmaceuticals. Downey sent a Barr executive to scout businesses with biotech expertise in 2003 and the search ended in Croatia, home of pharmaceutical company Pliva. The firm, established in 1921, is a leading pharmaceutical in Central and Eastern Europe that specializes in developing, producing and distributing generic pharmaceutical products, including biological drugs.

In 2005, Barr announced a deal to license Pliva's version of Neupogen, a white-blood-cell booster made by Amgen. Things heated up in 2006, when Barr and Iceland's Actavis Group battled for Pliva. Barr outbid Actavis, and that October—in a deal worth $2.5 billion—Barr won out. Downey sent a senior vice president from the company's New Jersey headquarters to Zagreb to oversee Barr's biotech initiative.

In a glass-and-steel research center a few miles from Croatia's capital of Zagreb, Pliva is now working on a copycat version of Amgen's Epogen, a protein that boosts red blood cells, and other new pharmaceuticals. Barr has also broken ground on a

$25 million biotech factory in Croatia. The new laboratories, located about 30 minutes from Zagreb, are scheduled to be finished in 2009.

Pliva's continuing integration into Barr took a minor hit in September 2007, when Paul Bisano—Barr president and COO since 1999, and in charge of the Pliva acquisition—left for the president and CEO position at Watson Pharmaceuticals. CEO Downey took the president job back on an interim basis and released a statement anticipating no difficulty over the management shuffle.

Looking forward

Barr Pharmaceuticals continues to move beyond generic drug replications, as it invested $140 million in new products in 2006. In generics, the company plans to continue to pursue drug delivery methods—such as creams and ointments, patches, injectable medicines and nasal sprays—that are outside of Barr's traditional strengths in solid oral dosages.

As the company's proprietary products business grows, the firm hopes to explore new areas in women's health care. For example, several products in early stages of development are based on the company's vaginal ring drug-delivery system. In 2006, the company acquired FEI women's health and its ParaGuard Intrauterine Device, which expanded the firm's proprietary contraceptive portfolio into nonhormonal contraception, a first for Barr. The company would also like to explore additional therapeutic areas beyond women's health care.

Plan B victory and controversy

One of Barr's more notable (and controversial) women's health care drugs is Plan B, also known as the "morning-after" pill. In August 2006, the FDA allowed for women 18 years or older to obtain Plan B without a prescription, provided they show identification proving their age. Women under age 18 would still need a prescription to get Plan B.

Reproductive-rights groups welcomed this decision, but added that the age restriction was unnecessary. Antiabortion groups were angry, though, and argued that the decision wouldn't prevent younger teenagers from getting the drug. Barr and the FDA agreed to take steps to try to enforce the age restriction, and Barr said Plan B would be sold only in stores or clinics with a medical professional. The company also agreed to send "anonymous shoppers" to confirm that pharmacies were sticking to the rules.

Barr started distributing Plan B to pharmacies in November 2006. The following month, *USA Today* reported that some independently owned pharmacies were not stocking the drug because of perceived lack of demand or pharmacists' moral objection. Major pharmacies, such as Walgreens and CVS, carry Plan B and have made promises to ensure that customers will be able to buy it. Now that Plan B is available without a prescription, the company expects use of the drug to increase.

GETTING HIRED

Applicants can search for openings through the careers section of the company's web site (www.barrlabs.com/careers). Job categories include accounting and finance, administration, biostatistics, clinical operations, communications, health and safety, human resources, information technology, legal, maintenance and engineering, manufacturing, packaging, process development, production management, production planning, project management, purchasing, quality assurance, quality control, regulatory affairs, regulatory compliance, research and development, sales, scientific affairs, security, technical affairs, training, validation, and warehouse and distribution. The company also offers internships.

Benefits at Barr include a 401(k) plan, a cafeteria plan, medical and dental insurance, supplemental life insurance, a travel assistance program and a legal reference program.

Bayer AG

Corporate Headquarters:
Bayerwerk
Gebäude W11, Kaiser-Wilhelm-Allee
51368 Leverkusen
Germany
Phone: +49-214-30-1
Fax: +49-214-30-66328
www.bayer.com

Bayer Corporation Headquarters:
100 Bayer Road
Pittsburgh, PA 15205
Phone: (412) 777-2000
Fax: (412) 777-2034

LOCATIONS

Leverkusen, Germany (HQ)
Pittsburgh, PA (US HQ)

THE STATS

Employer Type: Public Company
Chairman & CEO: Werner Wenning
2006 Employees: 106,200
2006 Revenue (€mil.): €28,956
2006 Net Income (€mil.): €1,683

DEPARTMENTS

Accounting & Financial •
Administrative • Business
Development • Clinical •
Communications • Customer Service
• Data Management • Engineering •
Health & Safety • Human Resources
• Information Technology • Legal •
Logistics • Manufacturing • Medical
• Procurement • Production • Quality
Assurance • Research &
Development • Sales & Marketing •
Supple Chain • Training & Education
• Transportation

KEY COMPETITORS

BASF AG
Johnson & Johnson
Schering-Plough

EMPLOYMENT CONTACT

www.bayerjobs.com

THE SCOOP

Can you Bayer it?

Bayer AG, the German drug and consumer materials juggernaut, is a force to be reckoned with in the pharmaceutical industry. The firm has three subgroups (HealthCare, CropScience and MaterialScience) supported by three service companies (business services, technology services and industry services).

Its U.S. subsidiary, Bayer Corporation, on its own is comprised of the same divisions—HealthCare, CropScience and MaterialScience—and an internal services division. Bayer HealthCare produces pharmaceuticals and over-the-counter (OTC) medicine. This unit also includes animal health and diabetes care. The MaterialScience unit produces plastics, coatings and polyurethanes. The CropScience division makes herbicides, fungicides and insecticides. Bayer employs about 106,200 people across 18 U.S. states and all over the world.

A past in dyes

On August 1, 1863, a merchant named Friedrich Bayer and a master dyer named Johann Friedrich Weskott set up a small dyestuffs factory in Barmen, now a district of the city of Wuppertal, Germany. On July 1, 1881, the sons and sons-in-law of Bayer and Weskott founded a joint-stock company under the name Farbenfabriken vorm. Friedr. Bayer & Co., with an initial capital of 5.4 million marks. Two years later, the company's shares were listed on the Berlin Stock Exchange. The company had first expanded operations into the U.S. back in 1865, when it bought a stake in an Albany, N.Y.-based coal-tar dye plant.

In 1884 the company hired a chemist by the name of Carl Duisberg. In 1888 Duisberg set up a "pharmaceutical department" and soon after designed Bayer's central scientific laboratory. These two institutions were the scene of many pioneering discoveries. In 1891 Bayer purchased from Carl Leverkus a factory for manufacturing alizarin red dyes as well as another site in what is now the city of Leverkusen. The first plants there were built at the turn of the century, and company headquarters was transferred to Leverkusen in 1912.

From dyes to chemicals

As Bayer became a world leader in dyestuffs, it employed a number of chemists to test its products for resistance to bacteria, lasting color and other considerations.

Soon, they made a number of historical breakthroughs, such as Antinonin (the first synthetic pesticide) in 1892, aspirin in 1899 and synthetic rubber in 1915.

By the 1920s, Germany possessed a leading pharmaceutical industry, with a number of incredibly powerful firms, including Bayer. In 1925 Duisberg, then Bayer's president, organized a merger of major German chemical companies, creating the immensely powerful I.G. Farbenindustrie AG. In the deal, Bayer became part of I.G. Farbenindustrie's Lower Rhine consortium. In 1934, the Bayer cross became the sole trademark for all pharmaceutical products marketed by I.G. Farbenindustrie.

A bunch of Bayers

At the end of World War II, the Allies confiscated and later split up I.G. Farbenindustrie. Bayer was re-established as Farbenfabriken Bayer Aktiengesellschaft in 1951, and the company changed its name to Bayer AG in 1972. Bayer had lost its American arm during World War I, when it was seized by the American government and sold to Sterling Drug.

The U.S. government also stripped Bayer of its trademark rights. In the postwar United States, Bayer's aspirin brand became a household name, but Sterling profited from it, not Bayer AG. The company regained partial rights from Sterling to the Bayer aspirin and brand in the U.S. in 1986. Eight years later, Sterling's parent company Eastman Kodak sold Sterling to SmithKline Beecham in 1994; weeks later SmithKline turned around and sold the full Bayer naming rights (and Sterling's $366 million OTC business) to Bayer AG for $1 billion. Bayer named its new North American arm the Bayer Corporation.

Another big buy

In 2006, Bayer acquired Germany-based pharmaceutical company Schering AG— not to be confused with Schering-Plough Corp.—for about €17 billion (more than $22 billion), the largest acquisition in Bayer's history. It was one of the largest in world history, too, as it created a global health care company ranked among the top 12 in the world.

After the Schering purchase, Bayer announced that it would cut approximately 6,100 jobs worldwide, to reduce overlap. The firm said it planned to eliminate 3,150 jobs in Europe, 1,000 jobs in the U.S., 750 jobs in the Asia Pacific region and 1,200 jobs in Latin America and Canada.

The bulk of the business

Bayer HealthCare develops products for primary care, women's health, specialized therapeutics, hematology/cardiology and dermatology. Before Bayer's purchase of Schering, the firm's prescription medications included drugs used for the cardiovascular system (angina treatment Adalat), anti-infectives (Avelox and Cipro), erectile dysfunction (Levitra), diabetes (Precose) and cancer treatment (advanced prostate cancer treatment Vaidur).

In 2006, after Bayer acquired Schering AG, the company's pharmaceutical sales soared 83.9 percent to about €7.5 billion ($9.9 billion). Bayer's best-selling pharmaceutical products in 2006 included Betaferon, a drug used to modify the course of MS, and oral contraceptives Yasmin/YAZ (both acquired from Schering), as well as hemophilia drug Kogenate, angina treatment Adalat, antibiotic Cipro, anti-infective Avalox and impotence drug Levitra.

Caring for people and the animals that love them

The company's largest business division, Bayer HealthCare, hauled in roughly 40 percent of overall sales in 2006. Bayer HealthCare's mission is "to research, develop, manufacture and market innovative products that improve the health of people and animals throughout the world." The HealthCare division is subdivided into four categories: Bayer Schering Pharma (discussed above), animal health, consumer care and diabetes care.

Bayer's animal health division dates back to 1919. About 3 percent of the division's 2006 revenue came from medicine, pesticide and vaccine sales for farm animals, including cattle, sheep, pigs, poultry and bees, as well as companion animals like dogs and cats. In 2006, the animal health division's sales hit €905 million (about $1.3 billion), an increase of 5.7 percent from 2005. This increase was mostly due to the strong performance of the Advantage flea-control line as well as the continued market introduction of Profender, an antiparasitic treatment for cats.

Tender loving consumer care

Around the time that Bayer acquired Schering AG, it was also reshuffling its other divisions. Since the 1980s, when Bayer had regained a foothold in the North American OTC drugs market, the company has become a dominant player in the sector. It became one of the top-three OTC consumer health organizations in the world in January 2005, when its acquisition of Roche Consumer Health brought its already successful consumer care division into more than 100 countries.

Among the consumer care division's best-known drugs are cough and cold medicine Alka-Seltzer Plus, aspirin and Aleve, gastrointestinal medicines Talcid, Rennie and Alka-Seltzer, and topical products like Bepanthol and Canestan. It also sells multivitamins and dietary supplements including One-A-Day, Berocca and Vital 50 Plus, and CardioAspirin, which helps to prevent heart problems. The consumer care division employs 6,600 people worldwide.

In June 2004, Bayer reshuffled more of its divisions, splitting its diagnostics division into the Bayer HealthCare Diagnostics Division and the HealthCare Diabetes Care Division. The diabetes care division offers blood monitor systems directly to consumers and is headquartered in Elkhart, Indiana. Sales in the diabetes care division improved by 12.8 percent in 2006, primarily due to strong performance from the new Ascensia Contour blood glucose monitoring system. Also in 2006, the company agreed to sell Bayer Diagnostics to Siemens Medical Solutions in a deal worth €4.3 billion (about $5.7 billion); it was finalized in January 2007.

From fungicides to insecticides

Back in 1914, a Bayer chemist discovered that fungal pathogens could be controlled by chlorophenol mercury without harming a seed's ability to germinate. The product hit the market that year under the name Uspulun, and at the end of the 1920s it was followed by Ceresan powder, which was safer to apply and contained a lower mercury content. These seed treatment products thrived until they were replaced at the end of the 1970s by mercury-free products. The flagship treatment since 1980 has been the systemically active Baytan (triadimenol), which penetrates seeds as they germinate, dispensing the substance throughout the nascent plant.

Bayer's CropScience division also produces insecticidal seed treatments and has been an industry leader since the 1985 discovery of imidacloprid. The company considers imidacloprid, on the market since 1991, to be one of its most important active substances, particularly in the form of seed treatment Gaucho, which prompted a new era in crop protection.

Bayer's CropScience division accounted for about 19 percent of the company's total revenue in 2006, clocking in at €5.7 billion (more than $7.5 billion). The division's headquarters are located in Monheim, Germany, with the American head at Research Triangle Park, North Carolina.

Visit Vault at **www.vault.com** for insider company profiles, expert advice, career message boards, expert resume reviews, the Vault Job Board and more.

VAULT CAREER LIBRARY

81

Living in a material world

The MaterialScience department brought in about 35 percent of Bayer's total 2006 revenue. And MaterialScience's business grew during the fiscal period, with sales advancing 7.6 percent to roughly €10.2 billion (more than $13.4 billion).

The department is subdivided into five individual business units, the first of which is coatings, adhesives and sealants. The second unit holds polycarbonates, including one of Bayer's most cherished discoveries, Makrolon. Next come polyurethanes, which produce the raw material for all varieties of foam. The fourth division, thermoplastic polyurethanes, comprises the manufacturing of products that make up rubber and thermoplastic materials. Finally, the inorganic basic chemicals unit is the worldwide chlorine supplier for Bayer MaterialScience.

In January 2005 Bayer spun off Lanxess AG, which houses its chemicals activities and parts of the polymers business. The new company immediately became an industry leader in rubber, rubber chemicals, styrenics, semi-crystalline products, Dorlastan fibers, the polymer additives of Rhein Chemie and numerous specialty chemical goods. The U.S. headquarters for Lanxess Corporation is located in Pittsburgh.

Investing in the future

During 2006, Bayer invested over €2.2 billion (roughly $3 billion) in R&D. As a result of the Schering acquisition, R&D will be consolidated into three major R&D sites: Berkeley, Calif., Wuppertal, Germany, and Berlin. By 2008, the company plans to close its research sites in West Haven, Conn., and Richmond, Calif., which will affect about 600 employees in R&D.

Bayer Biological Products, headquartered in Berkeley, Calif. since 1903, uses cutting-edge technologies for discovering, developing and manufacturing protein therapeutics and gene therapy. Bayer BP claims discoveries, such as a next-generation recombinant factor for making hemostasis products for blood coagulation, more efficient drug delivery methods and does research into removing pathogenic prion proteins from the manufacturing processes. Eventually, Bayer could add jobs at the Berkeley lab.

One product Bayer recently developed and brought to the market is Vasovist, a blood-pool contrast agent used to diagnose vascular disease. A promising drug candidate for the future is Rivaroxaban, an anticoagulant for the prevention and treatment of conditions such as pulmonary embolism and stroke; it is currently in clinical trials.

The firm launched a new initiative, "Triple-i: Inspirations, Ideas, Innovation" in 2006. The initiative encourages all Bayer AG employees to submit ideas for possible new products. In the first eight months of "Triple-i," employees submitted more than 1,900 ideas.

Later in 2007 the firm unveiled a new growth strategy: cutting back on ink spilled from accounting paperwork. In September, the firm announced that it was delisting shares from the New York Stock Exchange, citing the costs and time necessary to file reports with the Securities and Exchange Commission. The firm expects to save close to $21 million annually with the decision.

GETTING HIRED

Bayer-ing up

Bayer maintains a career database at www.bayerjobs.com, which lists positions in various Bayer departments in the U.S., including CropScience, MaterialScience, corporate and business services, and HealthCare. Through the site, job hunters can search for available job opportunities or submit a general resume to the database. The web site notes that your odds of getting hired increase if you apply for a specific position. Bayer keeps applicants' information active for one year.

Student recruitment

Bayer also visits university campuses for recruitment activities. Entry-level positions can be found in engineering, information technology, procurement, research and development, finance and administration, and marketing and sales. Applicants should click on the appropriate online links for job descriptions and requirements.

In addition, the company has a co-op program for college students. The program is made up of three rotations, each of which is considered a semester. To apply, students should have completed at least their freshman year in college and be pursuing an engineering degree. Bayer requires a GPA of 3.0 or above for the program.

The firm also offers college internships in engineering, marketing and sales, research and development, information technology, procurement and finance, and administration. Again, applicants should have a GPA of at least 3.0 and should have completed their freshman year in college.

Visit Vault at **www.vault.com** for insider company profiles, expert advice, career message boards, expert resume reviews, the Vault Job Board and more.

VAULT CAREER LIBRARY   **83**

OUR SURVEY SAYS

A conservative-progressive atmosphere

"Bayer defines itself as a 'leading integrated chemical-pharmaceutical enterprise.'" Although insiders report that "Bayer takes a basically conservative approach to its business practices," they describe their co-workers and office atmosphere as progressive. Bayer's size "can be somewhat bureaucratic at times," but the company stresses "individual innovation" and "widespread participation in quality control efforts."

Employees throughout Bayer comment that the interactive environment fosters "camaraderie," even though some recent hires are disappointed by the "poor quality" of the communication between lower and upper management. Some feel that "Bayer's internal politics have interfered with quality decision-making." At Bayer, "to be 'successful' you need to be political."

One insider feels that communications are "getting better," as the company is "using feedback via Internet surveys." However, one 30-year Bayer veteran advises those interested in Bayer to "get in, get experience, and then get out." Another respondent corroborates this, citing "slow [career] growth potential."

Bayer benefits

Bayer's benefits seem to please most U.S. employees. As one insider puts it, "The company does a very good job of taking care of its people." "Bayer benefits are the best in the industry," giving employees "12 plans to choose from," raves another. Insiders say the company pays "90 percent of the premiums for your medical and dental insurance."

As far as the pay scale, "Bayer is not bad," having "good benefits, proper salary and a 401(k) that beats any around." Perks include a "company store on premises with dry cleaning pickup and delivery," "photo processing" and a "credit union office and ATM on site." Of course, Bayer is an enormous company with outposts all over the world, and its benefits vary from location to location. Even within the U.S., where it employs over 15,000 people, benefits vary depending on the department.

International relations

Many agree that Bayer takes serious steps to diversify its workforce, yet some insiders note, "in terms of diversity, more needs to be done." "As with many major corporations, there are 'glass ceilings' that affect gender and race," some warn, reporting "there are some instances where the glass ceiling has prevented people from advancement."

The company is evidently aware of these problems: "The diversity issue has been championed from the very highest levels in management and is an ongoing program," says an insider. "Each year we go through one or two programs that encourage us to open our minds to those of different origins and cultures."

Another company veteran states that Bayer has a "very diverse workforce" and is "working hard to promote diversity." International culture is inherent to the company. "As Bayer is a German company, there are a lot of foreign workers here," and an "influx of German culture since Bayer AG is our parent company. This can be good or bad depending on your perspective."

Dress code

While details such as dress code and scheduling flexibility vary by department and location, in general "plant locations are usually business casual and corporate is business attire—suits, dresses." From May until the end of September, the dress code for "corporate is business casual." Work hours vary considerably based on location, but "in general, offices are open from 8 to 5."

Visit Vault at **www.vault.com** for insider company profiles, expert advice, career message boards, expert resume reviews, the Vault Job Board and more.

VAULT CAREER LIBRARY

85

Becton, Dickinson and Company

1 Becton Drive
Franklin Lakes, NJ 07417
Phone: (201) 847-6800
Fax: (201) 847-6475
www.bd.com

LOCATIONS

Franklin Lakes, NJ (HQ)
Bedford, MA • Billerica, MA • Boston, MA • Bridgeport, NJ • Broken Bow, NE • Canaan, CT • Chino, CA • Columbus, NE • Detroit, MI • Durham, NC • Franklin, WI • Grayson, GA • Hancock, NY • Holdrege, NE • Indianapolis, IN • Lynn, MA • Madison, WI • Mansfield, MA • Nogales, AZ • Ocean Side, CA • Research Triangle Park, NC • Rockville, MD • Sandy, UT • San Diego, CA • San Jose, CA • Sarasota, FL • Seneca, SC • Sparks, MD • St. Louis, MO • Sumter, SC • Teterboro, NJ • Waltham, MA • Wheat Ridge, CO • Woburn, MA

International locations in over 40 countries worldwide.

THE STATS

Employer Type: Public Company
Stock Symbol: BDX
Stock Exchange: NYSE
Chairman, President & CEO: Edward J. Ludwig
2007 Employees: 28,018
2007 Revenue ($mil.): $6,359
2007 Net Income ($mil): $890

DEPARTMENTS

Accounting/Finance
Business Development
Clerical/Administration
Communications/Advertising/Public Relations
Customer Service
Engineering
Environmental/Health/Safety
General Management
Human Resources
Information Technology
Legal/Ethics
Life Sciences
Marketing
Medical Affairs
Operations
Quality
Regulatory Affairs
Research & Development
Sales, Sales Support & Services
Supply Chain & Logistics

KEY COMPETITORS

Abbott Laboratories
Boston Scientific
Johnson & Johnson

EMPLOYMENT CONTACT

www.bd.com/us/careers

THE SCOOP

In a nutshell

With $6.4 billion in 2007 revenue and more than half of its sales in the international market, Becton, Dickinson and Company (BD) is a leading medical device, instrumented systems and reagent manufacturer and provider. The company is divided into three major business segments: BD Medical, BD Diagnostics and BD Biosciences.

BD Medical is one of the world's leading suppliers of medical devices, including needles, syringes and intravenous catheters for delivering medication; insulin injection devices; prefillable drug delivery devices; surgical blades and anesthesia needles; critical care monitoring devices; ophthalmic surgery devices; sharps disposal containers; and home health care products, such as ACE brand elastic bandages.

The BD Diagnostic unit provides products for the safe collection and transport of diagnostics specimens and instrumentation for quick, accurate analysis for a broad range of microbiology and infectious disease testing, including the growing problem of health care-associated infections. The segment also offers molecular testing systems for sexually transmitted diseases, microorganism identification and drug susceptibility systems, and rapid manual testing products. The BD Biosciences segment focuses on supplying research and clinical tools to life scientists and clinicians. Principal products include florescence-activated cell sorters and analyzers, cellular imaging systems, monoclonal antibodies and kits, reagent systems for life sciences research, labware and tools to aid in drug discovery and growth of tissue and cells, and diagnostics assays.

Headquartered in Franklin Lakes, N.J., BD employed 28,018 people worldwide in 2007. In 2005, 2006 and 2007 *Fortune* named BD one of America's Most Admired Companies. In 2007 the firm ranked second on *Fortune*'s list of most admired medical products and equipment companies, trailing only St. Jude Medical.

BD Beginnings

Maxwell W. Becton and Fairleigh S. Dickinson met as two salesmen in a railway dining room in Texarkana, Texas in 1897. Months later they came together to form a business, which they dubbed Becton, Dickinson and Company. In October of the same year, Becton made BD's first sale—a Luer all-glass syringe that sold for $2.50. (The company later purchased half of the patent rights to the Luer product.)

In 1904 the company made its first acquisition, the Philadelphia Surgical Company, enabling it to manufacture its own metal surgical products. Two years later, BD incorporated in New Jersey and built the U.S.'s first facility specifically for manufacturing thermometers, hypodermic needles and syringes. The company produced its first all-cotton elastic bandage in 1913; later named the BD ACE bandage, it proved one of the company's most famous products.

Onward and upward with the medical arts

BD continued its upward trajectory in the following years, often in lock-step with advancements in syringes and other medical technology for the treatment of blood. In the 1920s, for example, the company developed the first syringe specifically for insulin injection (1924) and the soon-standard Yale Luer-Lok syringe (1925); it also began working with Andrew "Doc" Fleischer in 1921—the inventor of the blood pressure machine the mercurial sphygmomanometer.

By the mid-20th century, the firm's continued innovation allowed it to survive the move into the era of disposable medical devices. It introduced its first disposable blood collection set in 1950, later selling it to the American Red Cross; the company then produced the first disposable syringe in 1954. Its increasing focus on disposable products led BD to introduce the BD Pastipak in 1961 after 10 years of development; the company went public the next year to raise more funds.

Along the way, the company had gone international, purchasing its Toronto-based distributor in 1951, a Mexican company in 1952, then opening a Brazilian location in 1956 and a French arm in 1958. Its new products also fed into growth, as it opened facilities purely for their manufacture—a Canaan, Conn., facility for the Plastipak in 1961, and a Plymouth, England, plant for the Vacutainer in 1981, to name a few.

In 1970, BD cracked *Fortune*'s 500-largest American companies' list for the first time. By 1981 the company had surpassed $1 billion in sales. The company gained an early foothold in the two important Asian markets of China and India, opening ventures in both in 1995.

On the safe side

The BD Medical segment still manufactures devices for working with blood: injections and infusion-based drug delivery. It is still also the largest BD business segment, reporting $3.4 billion in 2007 revenue, a jump of 10 percent over 2006.

The division's major products include the BD Vacutainer Push Button Collection Set, which helps minimize the possibility of potential needle injuries for nurses and other health care workers, and the BD Integra Syringe with Retracting BD PrecisionGlide Needle, designed to provide a detachable needle, low "waste space" and dosing accuracy.

BD Medical also provides safety products beyond the syringe- and needle-set. The BD Bard-Parker Protected Blade System—which offers a reusable stainless-steel surgical handle with a clear, locking plastic sliding shield—helps protect surgeons against scalpel wounds. Products like BD's Nexiva Closed IV Catheter System provide benefits to patients, by reducing the risk of infection by minimizing the potential for fluid contamination. BD is also a leading provider of surgical hand antiseptic products with such products as the BD E-Z Care Rinseless, Brushless Antiseptic.

Not just for the professionals

Though known within the industry for products used by hospitals and health care centers, BD also has a home health care and consumer goods market. The company produces a variety of goods for preventing and treating athletic problems, including BD ACE bandages, hot and cold compress treatments, elbow, wrist and rib braces, and at-home digital thermometers, including thermometers featuring cartoon characters from *Dora the Explorer* and *Spongebob Squarepants*, in a partnership with the Nickelodeon Network.

Diagnosis: growth

In 2007, BD's diagnostic systems unit brought in solid worldwide sales of the molecular BD ProbeTec ET and the BD Viper systems. The preanalytical systems unit saw strong sales of safety engineered products. All told, the diagnostics segment's revenue grew in 2007 by 11 percent over 2006 to $1.9 billion.

Visit Vault at **www.vault.com** for insider company profiles, expert advice, career message boards, expert resume reviews, the Vault Job Board and more.

VAULT CAREER LIBRARY

89

Treating HIV/AIDS

BD's diagnostic products play an important part in the areas of HIV/AIDS and developing world health care. One of BD's most heralded products is the BD FACSCanto system, introduced in 2004, which enables researchers to better understand HIV/AIDS.

Products such as the BD SoloShot VX and BD SoloMed syringes are critical in treatment, particularly in light of World Health Organization estimates that 40 percent of all injections in poor countries are administered with used needles, leading to an estimated 260,000 HIV/AIDS infections annually caused by reused devices.

And the company utilizes each of its three sectors in fighting HIV/AIDS. BD FastImmune reagents are used alongside flow cytometers produced by BD Biosciences to help HIV vaccine researchers assess immune response. Advanced protection devices from BD Medical help prevent device reuse and help safeguard health care workers from transmitting HIV and other diseases through accidental injuries caused by contaminated needles. BD Diagnostics technologies include the BD BACTEC MGIT 960, a diagnostic tool that reduces the time required for the detection and susceptibility testing of tuberculosis, a leading killer of AIDS patients worldwide.

BioSuccesses

BD BioSciences revenue increased by 13 percent to $1 billion in 2007, thanks in part to strong sales of instruments and flow cytometry reagents (which the firm cited in previous years for similar rates of growth in the sector). Increased demand for research and clinical analyzers drove sales of these products.

Preparing for the flu

The flu vaccine shortage at the beginning of 2005 brought an unexpected flurry of activity for BD, which experienced a boom in sales of its dose-sparing syringes, needles with a special plunger that allows health care workers to maximize the available vaccine supply, unlike regular syringes—the BD syringes allow an extra half-millimeter dose from each vial to be used.

"The demand for the product immediately began to go up as people learned about the flu vaccine shortage," explained BD Medical President Gary Cohen, who added that manufacturing plants went into production around the clock. The company also announced plans for a new vaccine system to inject medicine into the top layers of skin instead of deep into muscle tissue, making for a less painful administration as well as a faster dispersal throughout the body.

In late September 2005, the FDA granted 510(k) clearance for BD's Directigen EZ Flu A+B Test. In 15 minutes or less, this two-step influenza check can differentiate between influenza A and influenza B, helping health care providers in selecting the appropriate treatment, such as administering antivirals to certain patient populations. Studies have shown that the test is able to detect avian influenza H5N1 isolates, a valuable consideration in light of heightened concerns about a possible avian flu pandemic.

Texarkana hold-em

Messrs. Becton and Dickinson formulated the germ of the BD idea in Texarkana over 100 years ago, and the company has returned to the scene over the past few years under less auspicious circumstances—in court. Rival medical manufacturer Retractable Technologies took BD to court after a 2002 *New York Times* article profiled BD's close (and perhaps inappropriate) financial relationship with Novation, a national buying group that purchases syringes and such for hospitals in bulk. The *Times* article revealed two payments of "special marketing fees" to Novation in 2000 that totaled more than $1 million.

Retractable Technologies filed an antitrust lawsuit against BD, Novation and others in Texarkana's federal court, alleging irreparable financial damage. It was a David vs. Goliath battle—BD's revenue in 2003 was $4.5 billion and Retractable's was $19 billion. Nevertheless, BD agreed in July 2004 to settle the case ahead of trial for $100 million. The Texarkana legal skirmishes look all but over; Retractable filed a patent infringement case against BD in June 2007 and BD filed its own against Retractable the following September. Both lawsuits' venue is—you guessed it—Texarkana.

Becton, Dickinson gets more company

BD got even bigger in 2006. The company purchased GeneOhm Sciences, Inc. in February 2006. GeneOhm develops molecular diagnostic testing for the quick detection of bacterial organisms. BD hopes to continue to grow in molecular diagnostics. The company would also like to become a leader in preventing health care-associated infections.

In December 2006, the firm acquired TriPath Imaging, which develops, manufactures, markets, and sells products to improve the clinical management of cancer. BD hopes the TriPath purchase will increase and advance the company's position in cancer diagnostics.

Continuing ed

To continually expand upon the capabilities of its employees, the company offers BD University (BDU), a training program based on the BD business strategy and meant to help BD associates on a global basis develop and hone leadership and professional skills. Under BDU's Leaders as Teachers program, hundreds of BD leaders teach courses, including coaching for performance improvement, selection interviewing, ethics, diversity, career development, lean manufacturing, Six Sigma, program management, sales excellence and leadership.

GETTING HIRED

They help you "make it"

The careers section of BD's web site (www.bd.com/us/careers) includes a searchable database of available positions in fields such as accounting/finance, business development, clerical/administration, communications/advertising/public relations, customer service, engineering, environmental/health/safety, general management, human resources, information technology, legal/ethics, life sciences, marketing, medical affairs, operations, quality, regulatory affairs, research and development, sales, sales support and services, and supply chain and logistics.

BD also offers summer internships to undergraduates who have completed their junior year, as well as to graduate students with one year of graduate course work under their belt. More information on these programs can be found at www.bd.com/us/careers/internships.

BD believes in its employees' growth and progress. Each associate is the primary driver of his or her own career, with "leaders" as "development coaches" aiding in career development, in addition to professional development courses provided through BD University. On top of competitive base salaries, BD offers supplementary cash and stock-based rewards programs based on individual and company performance, and an employee benefits package, including a matching

401(k) program, a pension program, and a host of health and personal welfare benefits, including educational assistance, financial planning, wellness initiatives, health screenings and more.

A long process

One source in the firm's Franklin Lakes headquarters says starting out in a temporary job "is the best way to obtain a position within the company." The insider adds, "Most lower-level employees are usually temporary employees who must apply for positions that they already may be doing."

Even temporary employees go through what employees describe as a long, slow hiring process. A senior scientist reports that BD has a "fairly challenging interview process." The scientist reports that there was a "telephone screening interview, a second telephone technical interview with the manager, and then an invitation to the site for six or more interviews with associates and managers, HR and even a vice president."

Another source began with an hourlong phone interview with a hiring manager. About a month later, the respondent was invited for an on-site interview. The insider returned two weeks after that for an interview with a VP and again "six weeks later for in-house interviews with a group of about five managers." A couple of contacts say it took about a month after their last interview to find out if they had the job or not. One adds, "In total the process took about five months, which is longer than I expected."

One BD insider warns that recruiters "are not very responsive" and that "interviewers run late." According to another source, "questions are basically behavioral in nature, as they seem to want to have cohesiveness on teams." The source adds that there were also "some elements of a stress interview, where an interviewer basically tries to go off script to see if you will stay composed and professional."

OUR SURVEY SAYS

BD, good and bad

A manager describes staff members at BD as "dedicated and hardworking," and sources say BD is a nice place to work. One insider who until recently worked at the firm's Franklin Lakes office says, "I had work/life balance, good benefits and

Visit Vault at **www.vault.com** for insider company profiles, expert advice, career message boards, expert resume reviews, the Vault Job Board and more.

VAULT CAREER LIBRARY

93

wonderful associates with whom to work." The source adds the there is "room for advancement, provided you are the 'right candidate.'" Another Franklin Lakes insider adds that BD's benefits include "good medical plans" and "great on-site services." Some examples are "fitness centers, cafeterias, bank, dry cleaning service and health centers including chair massages."

BD's buildings are "aesthetically pleasing," and "there are many nonbusiness activities that go on throughout the week, such as diversity fairs, which give you an opportunity to meet others in a different environment." An insider says employees start with three weeks of vacation, "but are not eligible for an additional week until 10 years of service."

One source believes the company's "overall business outlook is good," adding that "core product lines generally fair well against competitors" and that "leadership has resolved to improve the quality as well as seek opportunity in new areas." There are, however, some negative things about BD. One respondent says BD is a "huge bureaucracy" where "actions are slow moving and conservative." The contact also feels that "reorganization occurs too frequently." Another source adds, "if you are not on the right list of the right people, you will not be able to move within the company even if your position is being eliminated."

Biogen Idec Inc.

14 Cambridge Center
Cambridge, MA 02142
Phone: (617) 679-2000
Fax: (617) 679-2617
www.biogenidec.com

LOCATIONS

Cambridge, MA (HQ)
Research Triangle Park, NC
San Diego, CA
Waltham, MA
Washington, DC
Wellesley, MA

International locations in Australia, Austria, Belgium, Canada, Denmark, Finland, France, Germany, Ireland, Italy, Japan, the Netherlands, New Zealand, Norway, Portugal, Spain, Sweden, Switzerland and the UK

THE STATS

Employer Type: Public Company
Stock Symbol: BIIB
Stock Exchange: Nasdaq
Chairman: Bruce R. Ross
President & CEO: James C. Mullen
2006 Employees: 3,750
2006 Revenue ($mil.): $2,683
2006 Net Income ($mil.): $217

DEPARTMENTS

Biopharmaceutical Sciences
Commercial Operations
Corporate
Engineering & Facilities
Finance
General & Administrative
Human Resources
Information Technology
Legal
Medical Affairs
Medical Research
Quality
Regulatory
Research & Preclinical Development
Sales & Marketing

KEY COMPETITORS

Genentech
GlaxoSmithKline
Amgen

EMPLOYMENT CONTACT

www.biogenidec.com/site/001.html

THE SCOOP

Biogen Idec's identity

Biogen Idec develops, manufactures and sells therapies in the areas of neurology, oncology and immunology. Patients in more than 90 countries use the firm's drugs, and Biogen Idec has two blockbusters: Rituxan and Avonex. Rituxan, for the treatment of certain B-cell non-Hodgkin's lymphomas, is also indicated for the treatment of moderate-to-severe rheumatoid arthritis. Avonex, used to treat patients with relapsing forms of multiple sclerosis, is the most prescribed MS product in the world.

The company's other products are Tysabri, Zevalin and Fumaderm. In 2006, Biogen Idec's total revenue was about $2.7 billion, an increase of about 11 percent from approximately $2.4 billion in 2005.

The Biogen and Idec story

Biogen was founded in Cambridge, Mass., in 1978 by the venture capital firm T.A. Associates, which recruited a group of notable biologists, led by Nobel Prize winner and Harvard Professor Walter Gilbert. At that point, biotechnology was in its infancy and pioneering firms like Biogen (others from the same period include Genentech, Genex and Centocor) hit pay dirt in the 1980s when the Supreme Court ruled that genetically engineered bioproducts could be patented. Around that point, in 1985, a small biotech firm started up in San Francisco, known as Idec Pharmaceuticals.

The two firms were of very different sizes, but shared a few traits in common, such as going public. Biogen went public in 1983, five years after its formation; Idec pulled the trick in 1991, after six years of existence. Both were also unprofitable. By 1984, Biogen had racked up over $100 million in losses and Idec did not record a profit until 1998, 13 years after its founding.

Both companies turned things around with new executives, more financing and (finally) some hit products, although their fortunes rose and dipped at different times. Biogen had a great year in 1992, with $123.8 million revenue and profits of $38.3 million (a 500 percent increase on the year before). In the later 1990s and turn of the 21st century, Idec hit with what became the leading non-Hodgkin's lymphoma drug, Rituxan, and then with the cancer drug Zevalin.

The problem and the merger

The problem with Idec's success was that Genentech was reaping most of the benefits of Rituxan and Zevalin's blockbuster status. Back in 1995, when Idec had been on the verge of going under, Genentech bailed it out financially in return for the lion's share of its drugs' future profits. When Rituxan pulled in $1.47 billion in 2002, Idec only earned $370 million from it.

In the meantime, Biogen had enjoyed a profitable streak under the leadership of President James Tobin in the 1990s. Although the firm weathered a rough patch in 1994, cancelling plans for its much-anticipated Hirulog drug, the launch of Avonex in 1996 brought the company's revenue and profit margins to all-time highs. Tobin was promoted to CEO the next year, and the firm won the National Medal of Technology in 1998. All appeared well, but Tobin suddenly quit in 1999.

Even though the firm reached the record sales figure of $557.6 million in 1999, more than 70 percent of that total had been derived from Avonex, which brought in $394 million all by itself. The company needed another dependable product, as Avonex's orphan drug (i.e., exclusive) status would expire in 2003.

Tobin's replacement as CEO, Jim Mullen, soon found a solution in one of his newfound friends: William Rastetter, the CEO of Idec Pharmaceuticals. By November 2003, the two outfits merged in a deal valued at $6.5 billion. It was the largest biotechnology merger ever and created the world's third-largest biotech concern.

Idec's new identity

Deals that are called mergers in business are often acquisitions, but the deal that united Biogen and Idec truly seemed to be complementary. Technically, Idec was the purchaser in the deal, with 50.5 percent of the new entity's shares (Biogen had the other 49.5 percent), but Biogen brought sales figures and a number of employees roughly three times the size of its new partner. Also, new company headquarters were located in Biogen's traditional base of Cambridge, Mass., with Jim Mullen taking the helm and William Rastetter becoming the executive chairman.

Biogen Idec Inc., as the firm was now known, started settling in the next year. It moved operations into a brand new six-building, $400 million campus, on which Idec had begun working in 2001. The firm also exceeded analysts' $1.5 billion expectations, pulling in $2.21 billion for the 2004 fiscal year.

Visit Vault at **www.vault.com** for insider company profiles, expert advice, career message boards, expert resume reviews, the Vault Job Board and more.

VAULT CAREER LIBRARY

97

The new biotech power soon started throwing its weight around, purchasing Conforma Therapeutics in May 2006. The deal expanded its oncology pipeline and research capabilities. Then, in June 2006, the company acquired Fumapharm AG and the oral psoriasis therapy Fumaderm along with it (the product sold $9.5 million in 2006). At the same time, Biogen Idec shed its psoriasis product Amevive and sold several other assets.

Tysabri troubles

Biogen Idec and Elan Corporation have collaborated on the marketing and distribution of MS treatment Tysabri since 2004. But in February 2005, the two firms announced a voluntary suspension in sales of the drug, citing reports of serious adverse events in some patients in clinical trials. During the trials, a small number of patients treated with Tysabri in combination with Avonex developed a rare and frequently fatal brain infection known as progressive multifocal leukoencephalopathy.

After the drug suspension news, Biogen Idec's stock lost more than 40 percent of its value. And shareholders, who accused the company of not disclosing potential health risk of Tysabri before withdrawing the drug from the market, filed a class-action lawsuit against the company.

One could almost hear the corporate sigh of relief when a March 2006 federal advisory panel recommended Tysabri's return to the marketplace. About two dozen people with multiple sclerosis testified at the panel's meeting that they were willing to accept Tysabri's risks because they viewed the drug as the best hope for slowing the progression of their illness. In June 2006, the FDA allowed the reintroduction of Tysabri for the treatment of relapsing forms of MS. Now doctors must closely monitor patients who are taking Tysabri, available only through authorized infusion centers.

In 2005, Biogen Idec's net revenue associated with sales of Tysabri was $4.7 million. This consisted of $15.1 million from sales before the company suspended sales of the drug, offset by sales returns of $10.4 million related to product returns. In 2006, the company's revenue on sales of Tysabri in the U.S. and Europe were $11.9 million and $10.0 million respectively.

Old standbys

Luckily, the company's top-selling standbys, Avonex and Rituxan, did well in 2006. Avonex racked up $1.7 billion for the year, an 11 percent increase from 2005. And

Rituxan, which now treats large B-cell lymphoma as well as moderate-to-severe rheumatoid arthritis, in addition to non-Hodgkin's lymphoma, brought in $811 million, a 14 percent increase from 2005.

On the horizon

Biogen Idec recognizes that it can't depend on its two blockbusters forever. To reduce the costs and risks associated with drug development, the firm plans to continue acquiring promising products and companies that make them. In January 2007, it acquired Syntonix, a privately held biopharmaceutical firm. Syntonix is focused on discovering and developing therapeutic products for chronic diseases, and it has multiple preclinical programs in hemophilia, including FIX:Fc, a product for the treatment of hemophilia B.

Biogen Idec currently has more than 20 products in clinical development, such as Galiximab for the treatment of non-Hodgkin's lymphoma and Luxmiliximab for chronic lymphocytic leukemia. The company is also investigating how its core products might be used for other indications. For example, the firm is exploring the use of Tysabri for the treatment of Crohn's disease.

Also, the firm is looking at new markets for the company's products. Launches of Tysabri are continuing in other countries in 2007. In addition, the company intends to pursue the expansion of Avonex into emerging markets. Between 2007 and 2010, it plans to introduce the drug in the Czech Republic, Slovenia, Slovakia, Brazil, Mexico, Argentina, India and China.

Biogen goes a-courting

Finally, Biogen Idec might not be independent for much longer, as it has been looking into potential sales since October 2007. At that point, investor Carl Icahn reportedly owned about 3 percent of the company's shares and started actively urging the company to look for a buyer among the ranks of big pharmaceutical firms. He even informally offered to head up a group to buy the company for between $70 and $80 per share (about $20 billion). So, in October, Biogen issued a statement that it was considering "potential strategic interest on the part of major pharmaceutical companies."

By December 2007, however, Biogen hadn't found any willing buyers. In fact, a Biogen spokeswoman stated that the company had approached Icahn about a formal bid and he declined. After the news, the company's stock fell by over $20 in one day of trading on the NYSE. Ironically, this could lower the company's selling price enough to interest another investor.

GETTING HIRED

Throw your hat in the ring

Prospective applicants can search jobs and submit a resume through the company's BrassRing site (www.biogenidec.com/careers). Job categories include biopharmaceutical sciences, commercial operations, corporate, engineering and facilities, finance, general and administrative, human resources, IT, legal, medical affairs, medical research, quality, regulatory, research and preclinical development, and sales and marketing.

Biogen Idec offers comprehensive benefits to employees. These include a 401(k) plan with company match; medical, prescription, dental and vision coverage, commuter benefits, a company gym in some locations, tuition reimbursement, life insurance and stock options. The firm's core values are courageous innovation; quality, integrity and honesty; the team as a source of strength; commitment to the people the company serves; and growth, transformation and renewal.

The firm also has a summer internship program. Internships are aimed at students in life science disciplines as well as in fields such as marketing and finance. The company seeks "students who are interested in building a long-term relationship with Biogen Idec." Students must be at least 18 years old to apply, and must be able to work for 10 to 12 weeks starting in June. More information about the company's internships and how to apply is available online at www.biogenidec.com/site/internships.html. Applicants for internships need to submit resumes by mid-April.

In 2006, *Science* named Biogen Idec a 2006 Top Employer in the magazine's 2006 Top Biotech and Pharma Employers survey. The company ranked No. 698 on *Fortune*'s 2007 ranking of America's largest corporations, up from No. 706 in 2006.

Boehringer Ingelheim Corporation

Binger Strasse 173
55216 Ingelheim
Germany
Phone: +49-6132-770
Fax: +49-6132-720

US Headquarters:
900 Ridgebury Road
Ridgefield, CT 06877
Phone: (203) 798-9988
Fax: (203) 791-6234
www.boehringer-ingelheim.com

LOCATIONS

Ingelheim, Germany (HQ)
Bedford, OH
Columbus, OH
Petersburg, VA
Ridgefield, CT
St. Joseph, MO

Affiliates in 45 countries around the world.

THE STATS

Employer Type: Private Company
Chairman & CEO: Alessandro Banchi
2006 Employees: 38,428
2006 Revenue ($mil.): $13,961
2006 Net Income ($mil.): $3,373

DEPARTMENTS

Accounting & Finance • Administrative & Support Services • Advertising/Marketing/PR • Arts/Entertainment & Media • Biotechnology & Pharmaceuticals • Customer Service & Call Center • Education/Training & Library • Engineering • Environmental Health & Safety • Government & Policy • Healthcare • Human Resources • Information Technology • Installation/Maintenance & Repair • Internet/E-Commerce • Law Enforcement & Security • Legal • Manufacturing & Production • Market & Outcomes Research • Sales • Science/Research & Development • Telecommunications • Transportation & Warehousing

KEY COMPETITORS

Eli Lilly
Merck
Pfizer

EMPLOYMENT CONTACT

International: www.boehringer-ingelheim.com/corporate/career

U.S.: us.boehringer-ingelheim.com/career

Visit Vault at **www.vault.com** for insider company profiles, expert advice, career message boards, expert resume reviews, the Vault Job Board and more.

VAULT CAREER LIBRARY   101

THE SCOOP

Boehringer, the private pharmaceutical powerhouse

Family-owned Boehringer Ingelheim, headquartered in Germany, has grown from a company of about 20 people into a giant firm with over 38,000 employees. It is the world's largest privately held pharmaceutical company and one of the largest drug firms in Germany.

Boehringer Ingelheim focuses on the development of chemicals, human pharmaceuticals, biopharmaceuticals and animal health products. The firm's top-five prescription products are chronic obstructive pulmonary disease (COPD) drugs Sprivia and Combivent, hypertension treatment Micardis, urology drug Flomax and arthritis medication Mobic.

The company also makes consumer health products such as Dulcolax, the No. 1 laxative worldwide. In 2006, the business successfully acquired heartburn medication Zantac.

In 2006, 96 percent of the firm's sales were in human pharmaceuticals and 4 percent were in animal health. The company's 2006 revenue was nearly $14 billion, an 11 percent increase from 2005.

Family-owned factory to pharma giant

In 1885, Dr. Albert Boehringer founded a chemical factory in Ingelheim, Germany. The factory initially made tartaric acid and employed about 20 people. Pharmacies and dyeing works used the product and demand soon surged as baking powder and fizzy lemonade became popular. In the 1890s, Dr. Boehringer discovered that he could use bacteria to produce lactic acid in commercial quantities, and the company slowly started to transform into a "biotech" firm, just as the idea of biotechnology started to emerge.

At the turn of the 20th century, the firm began manufacturing morphine and codeine (through the extraction of alkaloids from plants), and soon it was selling its compositions in pharmacies. Its earlier experience with alkaloids led to the formulation of cough medicines in the 1920s and afterwards. Albert Boehringer died in 1939, by which time the company was employing 1,500 people.

After Boehringer's death, his two sons took over the business. But World War II derailed any growth until the 1950s, when the company resumed manufacturing organic materials. In the late 1950s, the firm introduced new drugs to treat respiratory, gastrointestinal and cardiovascular diseases. During the coming decades, Boehringer Ingelheim continued to grow and expanded into overseas markets.

Patent battle resolved

In May 2005, Astellas Pharma and Boehringer Ingelheim filed a patent infringement lawsuit against Ranaxby. The firm had submitted an abbreviated new drug application for a generic version of Flomax, one of Boehringer Ingelheim's top-five prescription products with 2006 sales over $1.2 billion. In February 2007, Astellas and Boehringer won the patent infringement lawsuit. Ranaxby won't be allowed to make a copycat version of Flomax until the drug's patent expires in 2009.

U.S.A. operations

Boehringer's American operations employ over 8,000 people and boast its largest subsidiary (Boehringer Ingelheim Pharmaceuticals) and a U.S. market leader (Ben Venue Laboratories, leading in sterile injectable drugs). These two units are located in Ridgefield, Conn., and Bedford, Ohio, respectively. Boehringer has three other American units: B.I. Chemicals in Petersburg, Va., B.I. Vetmedica in St. Joseph, Miss., and Roxane Laboratories in Columbus, Ohio.

Vetmedica is aptly named—it provides veterinary drugs and vaccinations, primarily for livestock. Roxane Labs serves as Boehringer's main American R&D and drug manufacturing facility. B.I. Chemicals deals with more complex chemical substances; it even has a U.S. governmental clearance to deal with controlled substances.

Boehringer is good to its American children, too, as it keeps pouring significant funds into its facilities. For instance, its Vetmedica campus in Missouri added a $125 million expansion at the turn of the century, with a new manufacturing facility, an R&D complex and a centralized warehousing building.

The chemicals division has won a number of major investment funds in recent years, in no small part due to former Virginia Governor Mark Warner, who often flew to Germany to lobby on behalf of the city of Petersburg, home of B.I. Chemicals. In 2000, Warner was able to announce 104 new jobs and investment funds of $52 million in the city. Just three years later, the job count had grown to 165 and the funds had increased to $260 million—Boehringer had committed them to the city until 2011, the largest investment in Petersburg history.

Looking forward

Boehringer Ingelheim's product pipeline focuses on virology, respiratory and cardiovascular diseases, central nervous system, immunology, metabolic disease and oncology. The firm currently has three oncology drugs in phase II clinical development. In 2006, the company invested about €1.5 billion (more than $2 billion) in research and development, an increase of about 16 percent from the previous year. More than 6,000 people work in R&D at Boehringer Ingelheim. In addition to developing drugs in-house, the company also enters into strategic alliances.

In March 2007, CEO Alessandro Banchi said the company was not planning any major acquisitions. Rather, he said, the company planned to focus on partnerships and smaller acquisitions in the near future. Banchi also said that the company expects revenue to surpass €12 billion in 2008, compared to €10.57 billion (about $13.96 billion) in 2006. (He also is projecting the firm to out-earn main German rival Bayer in 2008.)

GETTING HIRED

Get roped in to Boehringer

In the United States, applicants can search and apply for jobs at us.boehringer-ingelheim.com/career. Job categories in the U.S. include accounting/auditing, administrative and support services, advertising/marketing/ public relations, biotechnology and pharmaceuticals, customer service and call center, engineering, environmental health and safety, finance/economics, financial services, government and policy, human resources, information technology, legal, manufacturing and production, sales, and science/research and development.

Benefits at Boeringer Ingelheim include health coverage (medical, dental, vision and prescription drug), flexible spending accounts, domestic partner benefits, life and disability insurance, 401(k) retirement plan (matched up to 5 percent of pay), subsidized cafeterias, tuition assistance, a scholarship program and free company products. At the firm's campus in Ridgefield, Conn., employees can take advantage of an on-site child development center and an on-site fitness center.

Making the collegiate rounds

Boehringer Ingelheim recruits at graduate and undergraduate students at campuses across the United States, including Yale University, the University of Connecticut, the University of California, Columbia, Dartmouth, Wellesley College and the University of Rhode Island.

The company also has a summer internship program for college students who are sophomores, juniors, seniors and graduate students. Internships are offered in research and development, marketing, information technology and medical. Applicants must have at least a 3.2 GPA and need to show proof of eligibility to work in the United States. More information about Boehringer's internship program is located at us.boehringer-ingelheim.com/career/internships.html.

Visit Vault at **www.vault.com** for insider company profiles, expert advice, career message boards, expert resume reviews, the Vault Job Board and more.

VAULT CAREER LIBRARY

105

Bristol-Myers Squibb Company

345 Park Avenue
New York, NY 10154-0037
Princeton, NJ 08543
Phone: (212) 546-4000
Fax: (212) 546-4020
www.bms.com

LOCATIONS

New York, NY (HQ)
Barceloneta, PR • Billerica, MA •
Evansville, IN • Greensboro, NC •
Hopewell, NJ • Humaco, PR •
Lawrenceville, NJ • Manati, PR •
Mayaquez, PR • Mt. Vernon, IN •
Nassau Park, NJ • New Brunswick,
NJ • Plainsboro, NJ • Princeton, NJ
• Skillman, NJ • Syracuse, NY •
Wallingford, CT • Zeeland, MI

International locations in Argentina,
Australia, Austria, Brazil, Canada, the
Czech Republic, Denmark, Finland,
France, Germany, Hungary, Ireland,
Italy, Japan, The Netherlands,
Norway, Spain, South Korea,
Sweden, Switzerland, Taiwan,
Turkey, the UK and Venezuela.

THE STATS

Employer Type: Public Company
Stock Symbol: BMY
Stock Exchange: NYSE
Chairman: James D. Robinson III
CEO: James M. Cornelius
2006 Employees: 43,000
2006 Revenue ($mil.): $17,914
2006 Net Income ($mil.): $1,585

DEPARTMENTS

Accounting • Auditing •
Administrative Support • Advertising
& Marketing Services • Aviation •
Communications • Compliance •
Customer Service • Distribution •
Engineering • Environment, Health &
Safety • Facilities • Finance •
General Management • Human
Resources • Information
Management • Information
Management/System • Learning &
Development • Legal •
Manufacturing & Production • Market
Research • Marketing • Medical
Development • Medical Science •
Operations Management • Planning &
Development • Product Management
• Purchasing • Quality • Research &
Development • Resource
Management • Sales • Security •
Supply Chain/Logistics • WW
Business Intelligence

KEY COMPETITORS

Amgen
GlaxoSmithKline
Merck
Novartis
Pfizer

EMPLOYMENT CONTACT

www.bms.com/career

THE SCOOP

An industry heavyweight

Bristol-Myers Squibb, a New York City-headquartered pharmaceutical titan founded in the 1800s, is currently one of the largest drug companies in the world and leads in medicines to battle cancer, cardiovascular and metabolic disorders, infectious diseases—including HIV/AIDS—and serious mental disorders. The company also sells nutritional and cardiovascular imaging products. BMS reported $17.9 billion in 2006 revenue, a decrease from $19.2 billion in 2005.

Merging into a giant

Dr. Edward Squibb founded his eponymous firm in New York City in 1858, where he developed techniques for making pure ether and chloroform, turning the business over to his sons in 1891. The company supplied penicillin and morphine to soldiers during World War II and formed a split venture with Denmark's Novo (now Novo Nordisk) to sell insulin in 1982.

In 1887, William McLaren Bristol and John Ripley Myers purchased drug manufacturing firm Clinton Pharmaceutical Company and renamed it Bristol, Myers in 1898 and hyphenated the name after Myers's death in 1899.

By the end of World War II, BM had recognized the potential financial windfall presented by penicillin and other antibiotics, and used proceeds from those products to acquire a number of companies, growing into a large, diversified and successful firm. In 1989, BM merged with Squibb, instantly becoming a global leader in the health care field and the world's second-largest pharmaceutical company.

In an effort to streamline operations, Bristol-Meyers Squibb restructured in September 2005, unifying United States and international pharmaceutical operations under a new division called worldwide pharmaceuticals. BMS' health care group is made up of the company's non-pharma businesses—Mead Johnson Nutritionals, ConvaTec and BMS Medical Imaging. These health care companies have provided stability to BMS during what the firm describes as a "transitional time" for the company's pharmaceutical business.

Visit Vault at **www.vault.com** for insider company profiles, expert advice, career message boards, expert resume reviews, the Vault Job Board and more.

VAULT CAREER LIBRARY   **107**

A firm in transition

Bristol-Myers Squibb is just emerging from operating under a deferred prosecution agreement (DPA) with the federal government, signed in June 2005. The U.S. government began its investigation in 2002. Apparently, BMS was inflating sales results by courting wholesalers with questionable incentives, all while keeping such activity secret from the company's board.

In 2003, CEO Peter Dolan hired Frederick Lacey, an esteemed private attorney and former federal judge, to guide the company's legal affairs. Lacey first became the company's "monitor" in 2004, after a separate settlement with the Securities and Exchange Commission; he then brokered the federal DPA in June 2005, which called for an $800 million charge against the company, the demotion of Dolan as chairman of Bristol's board and Lacey's own installation as official "federal monitor" of the company's affairs until (at least) 2007. He would be heard from again.

Narrowing its horizons

CEO Dolan also reshuffled the company's business model in 2003, shifting its focus from being spread thinly over 35 disease categories to building drug franchises in 10 major areas. The board defined these areas as serious diseases with then-unmet needs. Alongside diabetes and rheumatoid arthritis, the categories included HIV/AIDS, Alzheimer's disease, atherosclerosis and thrombosis, cancer, hepatitis, obesity, psychiatric disorders and solid organ transplant.

Dolan announced in April 2005 that BMS' profit growth was not likely to pick up again until 2007 and the company continued losing sales from its Glucovance diabetes treatment, Cefzil antibiotic and Paraplatin cancer treatment. Then Dolan started slimming the company down, selling off properties that included its oncology medicine-distribution business, its consumer products assets and the North American rights to its over-the-counter lines. Novartis acquired these last items for $660 million in July 2005, gaining the Keri line of skin products and Excedrin headache medicine in the process.

An innovation setback

In October 2005, BMS suffered another blow when the FDA raised questions about Pargluva, its oral treatment for diabetes, which has been in development for years and was expected to become a blockbuster drug. The type 2 diabetes treatment would have been the first of a new class of treatments intended to regulate blood sugar while lowering levels of triglycerides, raising levels of "good cholesterol" and increasing the effectiveness of insulin.

In May 2006, BMS decided to halt development work on Pargluva, which hurt the firm's sales, already down due to generic competition for Glucophage and Glucovance, its current diabetes lines. BMS responded in January 2007 by starting collaborations with AstraZeneca to develop and commercialize two compounds for the treatment of type 2 diabetes. The following April, BMS and Pfizer announced a collaboration to develop metabolic compounds for the treatment of metabolic disorders, including diabetes and obesity, as well as apixiban, an anticoagulant.

The Plavix affair

Meanwhile, Bristol-Myers and its collaborative partner, sanofi-aventis, were conducting a civil lawsuit concerning the patent for Plavix—one of the world's best-selling drugs, with $3.3 billion in sales for 2004. Sanofi had all but invented Plavix, working with BMS largely for marketing purposes. The lawsuit was aiming to stop the Canadian pharmaceutical company Apotex from releasing a generic version of Plavix statewide before the patent's expiration. In April 2006, however, the FDA approved Apotex's application to market its generic version of Plavix in the United States.

In March 2006, sanofi-aventis and Bristol-Myers Squibb reached a tentative settlement with Apotex; but the U.S. government didn't approve its antitrust measures and the firms went back to the drawing board. As it turned out, the companies couldn't come up with anything amicable, as the following July, BMS and sanofi-aventis announced that the Plavix patent infringement litigation with sanofi-aventis would continue.

But Apotex launched its generic version of Plavix in the United States the very next month. A judge issued a preliminary injunction halting its further distribution just weeks later, on August 13, but Apotex's product managed to grab a massive share of the market in its short time on sale—BMS estimated that Apotex's actions reduced its Plavix sales in 2006 by around $1.3 billion.

Dolan spells Waterloo "P-L-A-V-I-X"

One month later, in September 2006, BMS' "federal monitor," Frederick Lacey, re-emerged with a bombshell that has set Wall Street shaking to this day. Due to alleged irregularities in settlement negotiations with Apotex, he demanded the company fire

Peter Dolan as CEO, although he insisted that this request had nothing to do with any financial wrongdoing on Dolan's part. The BMS board agreed, and Dolan stepped down as CEO the very next morning, on September 12, 2006.

Of the entire affair, *The New York Times* wrote that "Mr. Lacey appears to have exercised unprecedented power in prompting Mr. Dolan's ouster. And the episode has set off a debate whether Mr. Lacey represents a tougher-style monitor who may put new teeth into that role in corporate America—as some admirers hope—or whether, in the view of some critics, he has overstepped his authority at Bristol-Myers." *The Wall Street Journal* also weighed in, noting that Lacey and his crew submitted their own 400- to 500-page quarterly reports to BMS' board. Its conclusion: "Good work if you can get it."

As a sort of afterthought, the rest of the Apotex saga concluded in 2007, as Bristol-Myers and its marketing partner, sanofi-aventis, each pleaded guilty to irregularities in settlement discussions with Apotex, and each paid $1 million fines to the federal government. The kicker? A judge ruled in October 2007 that BMS and sanofi's patent was totally valid and ordered Apotex to pay damages, so there was never any need for former CEO Dolan to engage in the settlement dealings that led to his departure. There was a financial component, too—the settlement stipulated that Apotex wouldn't have to pay the treble damages customary with patent infringement, which were estimated at between $500 and $600 million in this case.

The aftermath

Months later, in December 2006, BMS agreed in principle to a $499 million settlement with the U.S. Department of Justice over an investigation into illegal sales and marketing activities that had taken place between 1994 and 2005. The company finalized the settlement in September 2007, by which point the monetary penalties had accumulated interest, clocking in at $515 million. As part of the settlement, the firm also entered into a corporate integrity agreement with the U.S. Department of Health and Human Services.

In April 2007, BMS announced that the company had named interim CEO James Cornelius as the company's permanent leader for the next two years. Cornelius' former positions include CFO at Eli Lilly and interim chief of Guidant. His appointment set off speculation that Bristol-Myers might be a takeover target, since Cornelius had helped set up Boston Scientific's purchase of Guidant in a similar situation, but the new CEO has repeatedly refused to comment upon any acquisition rumors.

The company achieved a measure of closure in June 2007, when a federal judge in a New York court upheld sanofi and Bristol-Myers' patent on Plavix. The judge in the patent case disallowed future generic versions of Plavix until the patent's expiration, prohibiting Apotex from selling additional supplies of its generic version of the anticlotting drug. The judge also ordered a future hearing to determine the amount of damages Apotex should pay to sanofi-aventis and Bristol-Myers.

Also that month, Bristol-Myers' deferred prosecution agreement with the federal government expired. The company issued a press release, stating that it had "complied with the letter and spirit of the DPA and (that) the company believes its business operations are stronger today as a result of having embraced a culture of compliance." Upon the news of the DPA ending and the favorable lawsuit outcome, both Bristol-Myers and sanofi's stocks gained dramatically.

A friend to those in need

Despite its myriad legal issues, BMS has remained one of several big pharmaceuticals to provide prescription drugs to those who need them but are unable to afford them. These charity programs target patients whose incomes teeter just above the poverty line but make too much to qualify for Medicaid. Now, many of these grateful recipients have been forced to consider other alternatives.

The new Medicare program, which went into effect in 2005, has had an unintended effect on the pharmaceutical industry's charity drug programs, as the companies see that older recipients are now eligible for Medicare drug coverage and thus are re-evaluating their programs. In response, Bristol-Myers Squibb provided free drugs worth more than $400 million to over half a million people in the United States over the course of 2006. Together with the firm's foundation, BMS also contributed $87 million to education, health and community projects around the globe.

The company leads in charitable HIV/AIDS treatment, research and charitable work abroad, as well. In October 2005, for example, BMS signed a contract with the Maryland-based International Partnership for Microbicides, to provide an infection-preventing gel to women at risk of AIDS in poor countries.

In addition, BMS and the Baylor College of Medicine have established medical centers in Africa that are dedicated to caring for HIV/AIDS-infected infants, children and their families. There are currently centers in Lesotho, Botswana and Swaziland, and centers in Uganda and Burkina Faso are scheduled to open in 2008.

Visit Vault at **www.vault.com** for insider company profiles, expert advice, career message boards, expert resume reviews, the Vault Job Board and more.

VAULT CAREER LIBRARY   **111**

Three-in-one

In July 2006, the FDA approved the use of a pill manufactured by Bristol-Myers Squibb and Gilead Sciences that contains a combination of three antiretroviral drugs for the treatment of HIV. The pill is made up of one drug manufactured by Bristol-Myers and two made by Gilead, and is intended to simplify the complex drug regimen that HIV patients must follow in order to control the disease.

In addition to Atriplia for HIV/AIDS, BMS launched products in 2006 that included Orencia for rheumatoid arthritis, Sprycel for chronic myelogenous leukemia and EMSAM, a transdermal patch to treat serious depression.

Eyes on the future

Due to generic competition for many of its drugs, Bristol-Myers Squibb is investing heavily in research and development to come up with new products. The company spent over $3 billion on R&D in 2006, a 12 percent increase over 2005. In addition, the firm says it has a "pipeline within a product" approach to R&D, which involves exploring a range of potential uses for preexisting medicines, like Sprycel and Orencia.

Bristol-Myers Squibb has also pursued strategic partnerships with biotech and other pharmaceutical companies, such as AstraZeneca and Pfizer, to strengthen its product portfolio and sustain BMS' pipeline. It's likely that BMS will enter into more such partnerships in the future.

Bio-friendly firm happenings

Biologics are of growing importance to the firm. In 2007, the company is beginning construction of a new biologics facility in Devens, Mass. Bristol-Myers Squibb is also expanding existing facilities in Manati, Puerto Rico and Syracuse, N.Y. Perhaps the biggest sign yet that biologics could be major new direction for the company was its September 2007 announcement that it was buying biologics firm Adnexus Therapeutics for $430 million.

The deal brings aboard one major drug currently in phase I clinical trials— Angiocept, a biologic for cancer treatment. More importantly, Adnexus has a reputedly impressive pipeline that will significantly boost Bristol-Myers' in-house R&D. This kind of move is quite en vogue for major pharmaceutical firms, including two of BMS' main partners; Pfizer issued a statement the same month that it would focus on in-house biologic R&D and AstraZeneca acquired biologic firm MedImmune in April 2007.

Reducing the size of BMS

In December 2007, BMS announced a massive restructuring that will reduce its workforce by more than 10 percent and its 27 worldwide manufacturing sites by nearly half. It will particularly affect North American employees, as the firm will close its medical imaging unit in North Billerica, Mass., and move its headquarters from New York City to nearby New Jersey. BMS will probably retain use of one floor at 345 Park Avenue in Manhattan; a decade previously, it had occupied 550,000 square feet in the building.

Bristol-Myers stated that 1,300 employees were put on notice in December 2007 and that another 3,500 jobs would be eliminated by the end of 2008. The most affected divisions will be in human resources, information technology, finance and back-office operations. Even more BMS units could also make way in 2008, as the firm also announced in December that it was weighing "strategic alternatives" for Mead Johnson Nutritionals, its Evansville, Ind.-based baby formula business, and ConvaTec, its Skillman, N.J.-based maker of wound care products and related items.

Bristol-Myers is evolving into a more R&D-heavy, specialty-treatment firm (as evidenced by its many recent partnerships with biotechnology firms), and these moves should bring the company's shape more in line with that identity. In December 2007, when *The New York Times* surveyed this restructuring, it pointed out that BMS has "shifted away from high-volume, low-cost drugs to lower-volume, higher-priced products," and as a result, the volume of products it sold in 2007 was 70 percent below the volume of its 2001 sales. But the company has, until now, retained 2001's level of manufacturing sites and employees over the same period. The times, they are-a-changin' for Bristol-Myers Squibb.

GETTING HIRED

Working at BMS

The BMS corporate web site offers a database of job openings in numerous departments, including marketing, research and development, sales, finance, information management and systems, manufacturing and operations, human resources and administrative support. Job seekers can view listings and descriptions online at www.bms.com/career.

BMS offers its employees a savings and investment program that matches employee contributions at 75 cents on the dollar (up to the first 6 percent of pay), as well as medical, dental and life insurance policies. Under pharmacy benefits coverage, most BMS branded prescriptions are filled at no cost. BMS offers full health benefits as well as dental and a savings plan.

Other benefits include short- and long-term disability coverage, travel accident coverage, dependent care reimbursement accounts and a financial counseling service. Work/life benefits include adoption assistance, flexible work options, and prenatal and infant formula programs. Additional on-site resources, which vary by location, may include physical fitness centers, child development centers, employee credit unions, on-site medical treatment, hair salons, dry cleaning, photo processing and video rental.

BMS interviewing basics

A project coordinator says BMS has outsourced hiring to a company called Experion, "which has [been] chosen to save money." The source explains, "Experion will call the admin, obtain availability of the manager interviewing, and schedule the interview. Second rounds are likely if they are interested." The insider says that a typical interview included questioning like "What was your greatest achievement?" as well as "What are your strengths and weaknesses?" and "Where can you see yourself in five years?" The source was also asked "How do you handle a difficult situation?" and "How would you describe your working style?"

A boon for maternity and diversity

In 2006, for the ninth consecutive year, *Working Mother* named BMS a Top 100 Company for working mothers. In 2007, the National Association of Female Executives selected BMS as one of the top-30 companies for executive women for the sixth year in a row. The company was also chosen as a Top Organization for Multicultural Business Opportunities for 2006 through an online poll sponsored by DiversityBusiness.com.

OUR SURVEY SAYS

A good pipeline, but not all is well

One source at BMS describes the company's culture as "highly diverse" and "very political." The insider adds that it can be difficult to advance at the company. Another feels, "Squibb was a very good company to work for, until Bristol took over." Respondents say BMS has high turnover rate and that people are "constantly posting around within and outside the company."

Although BMS has a "good drug pipeline," one insider says employees are "very stressed and overloaded." The contact also feels the firm's salaries are "not competitive with other companies in the area." In spite of BMS' drawbacks, the insider says the company can be a good place for someone "looking to gain some knowledge and find a better opportunity."

Visit Vault at **www.vault.com** for insider company profiles, expert advice,
career message boards, expert resume reviews, the Vault Job Board and more.

VAULT CAREER LIBRARY   115

Celgene Corporation

86 Morris Avenue
Summit, NJ 07901
Phone: (908) 673-9000
Fax: (908) 673-9001
www.celgene.com

LOCATIONS

Summit, NJ (HQ)
Baton Rouge, LA • Cedar Knolls, NJ
• San Diego, CA • Warren, NJ •
Wilmington, DE • London • Madrid •
Melbourne • Milan • Munich •
Oakville, Canada • Paris • Porto
Salvo, Portugal • Tokyo • Uxbridge,
UK • Utrecht • Vienna • Zürich

THE STATS

Employer Type: Public Company
Stock Symbol: CELG
Stock Exchange: NASDAQ
Chairman & CEO: Sol J. Barer
President: Robert J. Hugin
2006 Employees: 1,287
2006 Revenue ($mil.): $898.9
2006 Net Income ($mil.): $69

DEPARTMENTS

Accounting • Analytical Research &
Development • Clinical Operations •
Clinical R&D • Compliance
Management • Corporate
Communications • Development
Quality • Drug Metabolism &
Pharmokinetics • Drug Safety • Early
Drug Development • Human
Resources • Inside Sales •
Information Technology • Legal •
Lifebank (Placenta-Cord Banking
Service) • Manufacturing • Marketing
• Medical Information • Metrology •
Oncology Research • Patient
Services • Pre-Clinical Development •
Project Management • Purchasing •
Quality Assurance • Quality Control •
Regulatory Affairs • Research &
Development—Cellular Therapeutics
• Sales • Technical Operations •
Treasury • Key Competitors • Amgen
• Bristol-Myers Squibb • Genentech

EMPLOYMENT CONTACT

www.celgene.com/Careers.aspx

THE SCOOP

It's in their genes

Celgene Corporation is an integrated biopharmaceutical company headquartered in Summit, New Jersey. The firm focuses on discovering, developing and commercializing innovative therapies to treat inflammation and cancer through gene and protein regulation. Lifebank, a placenta-cord banking service, is a Celgene subsidiary. In 2006, the company, which has more than 1,200 employees, posted about $899 million in revenue, roughly a 67 percent increase from 2005.

Thal me all about it

Celgene started out in 1980 as a unit of the Celanese Corporation (a European chemicals firm founded in 1912). Celgene spun off to independence in 1986, following a merger of Celanese Corporation and American Hoechst Corporation. Over a decade later, the FDA gave the company approval to market Thalomid—a modified version of thalidomide—for the treatment of a complication of leprosy. Some doctors also prescribed the drug off-label for treatment of a blood cancer called multiple myeloma and other cancers.

Thalomid's price has risen from $4,000 a year to more than $35,000 in the years since 1998—boasting nearly $433 million in sales in 2006, a more than 11 percent increase from 2005. In May 2006, the FDA approved the drug, in combination with dexamethasone, for the treatment of patients with newly diagnosed multiple myeloma.

The pharmaceutical phoenix

For many years, Celgene's fate was directly tied to its Thalomid product, which was problematic given the drug's reputation in the 1950s and 1960s for causing extreme birth defects (phocomelia, which causes limbs resemble "flippers"). In the late 1970s, the Celanese Research Corp. hired a scientist named Sol Barer to expand its R&D efforts; Barer soon headed up the R&D at Celanese's new Celgene division and proved instrumental in its 1986 spin-off.

By the early 1990s, Barer and his then-senior scientist David Stirling had researched a potential new use for Thalomid: preventing or affecting the formation of blood vessels in diseased limbs, for ailments such as leprosy, cancer or even AIDS. Celgene had a new mission—to rehabilitate what Barer himself once described as "the most reviled drug in history." Barer became Celgene's president in 1993, and, with the help of CEO John Jackson (a pharmaceutical veteran), the company geared all of its fund raising and R&D efforts towards the drug for the rest of the decade.

The FDA granted a limited approval of the drug in 1998 (with a big boost from AIDS activists), but Celgene's work was by no means finished. The FDA placed such limits on any use of the drug that Celgene had to create a dramatically restricted distribution system—the System for Thalidomide Education and Prescribing Safety (S.T.E.P.S.), which became a model for subsequent restricted medications.

As the drug has proven useful, Celgene's fortunes have improved, not to mention those of Barer. As of January 2007, the company reported market capitalization of $14 billion and ranked as the fifth-largest biotechnology concern worldwide. Sol Barer became CEO in May 2006 and chairman of the company's board in January 2007.

Other stuff Celgene sells

Beyond Thalomid, the company has also entered into agreements with other companies and acquired other firms to expand its product line. In April 2000, Celgene reached an agreement with Novartis Pharma to license d-MPH, a version of Ritalin. The FDA subsequently granted approval to market the drug, sold as Focalin, in November 2001.

Celgene completed a merger with Signal Pharmaceuticals in August 2000. Signal, a privately held biopharmaceutical company, focused on discovering and developing drugs to regulate disease-related genes. In December 2002, Celgene acquired another private firm—Anthrogenesis, which developed processes for the recovery of stem cells from human placental tissue for use in stem cell transplantation, cancer, autoimmune diseases, regenerative medicine and biomaterials for organ and wound repair. In October 2004, the company acquired Penn T, a worldwide supplier of Thalomid.

Celgene's second best-selling drug is Revlimid. In December 2005, Celgene won the FDA's approval to sell Revlimid for the treatment of patients with certain types of transfusion-dependent anemia. Revlimid generated more than $320 million in its first year of sales.

One of a kind

Celgene's 2002 acquisition of Anthrogenesis brought the LifeBankUSA business into the fold. Since 1998, LifeBank has served as one of the few American organizations committed to storing umbilical cords and similar genetic information. It is accredited by the AABB (American Association of Blood Banks) and has garnered praise from corners far and wide.

Baseball Hall-of-Famer Rod Carew has spoken out for the importance of such placenta banks, as he tragically lost his daughter in 1996 for lack of a bone marrow transplant donor. On the LifeBank web site, he says, "I wish cord blood banking was available when my daughter was born." Perhaps the future of Celgene lies in politics, as this division is now researching stem cells derived from the umbilical cord as well as from placental tissues after childbirth—a medical approach that should entirely defuse the stem cell controversy in Congress.

Looking for the next big thing

Although Celgene's therapies are selling well, the company is actively engaged in researching new drugs. Products in the pipeline include CC-10004, currently in phase II trials for the treatment of psoriasis, psoriatic arthritis and rheumatoid arthritis. CC-2025, for the treatment of inflammatory disease, is in phase I trials. Celgene is also developing a variety of products for the treatment of cancer, fibrotic diseases and more. The firm continues to study new uses for its tried-and-true treatments. For example, ADHD drug Focalin is in phase II trials for the treatment of cancer fatigue.

Going global

One of Celgene's objectives is to accelerate the transformation of the firm into a global biopharmaceutical company. The company recently established international headquarters in Neuchâtel, Switzerland. Celgene would like to extend its global market presence. As a result, the firm says it would like to reinforce "global culture," and it is firmly headed down this path with its planned $2.9 billion acquisition of Pharmion, a U.S.-based company with strong ties to the European market. In fact, Pharmion markets Celgene's thalidomide treatments in Europe, and Celegene hopes it will soon be selling Revlimid on the continent as well.

Visit Vault at **www.vault.com** for insider company profiles, expert advice, career message boards, expert resume reviews, the Vault Job Board and more.

VAULT CAREER LIBRARY   119

GETTING HIRED

They've got good genes!

Current job openings are posted at www.celgene.com/Careers_JobList.aspx. Resumes should be submitted electronically, and applicants need to send a resume for each position in which they are interested.

Job categories include accounting, analytical research and development, clinical operations, clinical R&D, compliance management, corporate communications, development quality, drug metabolism and pharmokinetics, drug safety, early drug development, human resources, inside sales, IT, legal, Lifebank (placenta-cord banking service), manufacturing, marketing, medical information, metrology, oncology research, patient services, preclinical development, project management, purchasing, quality assurance, quality control, regulatory affairs, research and development—cellular therapeutics, sales, technical operations and treasury.

Benefits at Celgene include medical, dental and vision coverage, health care flexible spending account,; life insurance, accidental death and dismemberment insurance, disability plans, education assistance and more.

In the United States, the company strives to create a diverse workforce. Among Celgene's North American employees, approximately half are women, and one out of three Celgene employees is a person of color.

Cephalon, Inc.

41 Moores Road
Frazer, PA 19355
Phone: (610) 344-0200
Fax: (610) 738-6590
www.cephalon.com

LOCATIONS

Frazer, PA (HQ)
Eden Prairie, MN
Salt Lake City, UT
Maisons-Alfort, France

Sales offices across the US and in
Germany, Italy, Spain and the UK.

THE STATS

Employer Type: Public Company
Stock Symbol: CEPH
Stock Exchange: NASDAQ
Chairman & CEO: Frank Baldino Jr.
2006 Employees: 2,895
2006 Revenue ($mil.): $1,720
2006 Net Income ($mil.): $145

DEPARTMENTS

Accounting/Finance
Corporate & Public Affairs
Facilities
Information Technology
Legal
Manufacturing
Manufacturing & Engineering
Quality Assurance
Research & Development

KEY COMPETITORS

Johnson & Johnson
Novartis
Pfizer

EMPLOYMENT CONTACT

www.cephalon.com/careers

Visit Vault at **www.vault.com** for insider company profiles, expert advice,
career message boards, expert resume reviews, the Vault Job Board and more.

VAULT CAREER LIBRARY 121

THE SCOOP

Get a load of Cephalon!

Cephalon, Inc., based in Pennsylvania, is dedicated to discovering, developing and selling innovative products to treat human diseases. The company focuses its efforts in four therapeutic areas: central nervous system disorders, pain, cancer and addiction. Cephalon's 2006 revenue was nearly $1.8 billion, an increase of almost 50 percent from 2005.

The firm makes five primary products: Provigil, a wakefulness-promoting agent for patients with certain sleep disorders; Actiq, a drug to treat pain in opioid-tolerant cancer patients; epilepsy drug Gabitril; cancer treatment Trisonex; and Vivitrol, a medication to treat alcohol dependence. Provigil tablets, Cephalon's most significant product, accounted for approximately 46 percent of net sales in 2006. The company's second-best selling drug is Actiq, which comprised some 34 percent of 2006 net sales.

In 2006, *The Scientist* ranked Cephalon among the top 40 companies in magazine's Best Places to Work in Industry survey. In the United Kingdom, Cephalon UK was on the *Sunday Times'* Best Small Companies to Work For list. In 2007, the company appeared on *Fortune*'s annual ranking of America's largest companies for the first time, squeaking in at No. 930.

A brief history

In 1987, Dr. Frank Baldino Jr.—a pharmacologist and former research biologist— and a small group of young researchers launched Cephalon. They had $3 million, a promising compound and a vision for an integrated biotechnology company with a presence in major markets worldwide. After teaming with Schering-Plough to research Alzheimer's drugs in the late 1980s, the firm went public in 1991, raising $55 million. In the 20 years since, the firm has grown into an international biopharmaceutical company with nearly 3,000 employees.

Cephalon has acquired products as well as other companies. The firm purchased Anesta, a company that developed and marketed products to manage cancer pain, in October 2000 for about $340 million. Cephalon also gained Actiq, currently the company's second-best selling drug, in the Anesta acquisition. In December 2001, the firm acquired France's Group Lafon, and with it the worldwide rights to Provigil, its current leading drug. In August 2004, Cephalon acquired CIMA Labs, a drug delivery company that makes fast-dissolving tablets.

The "Awake Pill"

In February 2007, ABC's *20/20* produced a story centered around Cephalon's sleep drug Provigil; the drug racked up sales of $735 million in 2006. The *20/20* story was critical: the FDA approved it to treat three sleep disorders, but a large percentage of the drug's sales are for off-label use. The *20/20* story also revealed that studies favoring Provigil in medical journals have been written by paid consultants to Cephalon. Finally, *20/20* unearthed an independent study by the U.S. Army's sleep labs, finding that the amount of caffeine in a large cup of coffee worked just as well as Provigil on a group of sleep-deprived soldiers.

Cephalon released statements that the news program was inaccurate, and insisted Provigil was intended for sleep disorders only, implicitly denying any off-the-label use. The firm did admit to supporting "independent, accredited, continuing medical education programs," but insisted that "we [Cephalon] do not control their content."

Investigations

The government is also taking a closer look at Cephalon. In the fall of 2004, Cephalon announced that it had received subpoenas from the U.S. Attorney's Office in Philadelphia as well as a voluntary request for information from the Office of the Connecticut Attorney General. The subpoenas and the request for information focused on the firm's sales and promotional practices in regards to Provigil, Actiq and Gabitril, including the extent of off-label prescriptions of these products. Cephalon is providing documents and other information to both offices in response to these requests, and the company is involved in ongoing discussions with both parties.

In March 2007, Rep. Henry A. Waxman asked Cephalon for documents as part of an investigation into product safety and marketing practices. He also sought information from Boston Scientific, Johnson & Johnson, Eli Lilly and AstraZeneca about some of their products. Waxman's letter to Cephalon asked the firm for information about narcotic painkillers Fentora and Actiq.

New drugs ... same concerns

In 2006, the FDA approved two new products: Fentora and Vivitrol. But later that year, in September, Barr Laboratories released a generic version of Actiq onto the U.S. market. Generic sales significantly eroded Cephalon's sales of Actiq in late 2006, and the company expects this erosion to continue in 2007.

Visit Vault at **www.vault.com** for insider company profiles, expert advice, career message boards, expert resume reviews, the Vault Job Board and more.

V/\ULT CAREER LIBRARY   **123**

Cephalon suffered a major blow from its new product Fentora in September 2007, when the FDA released a warning of the medication's potentially fatal side effects after reports of several deaths. The deaths, however, were mostly attributable to that old bugbear—off-label use. In its own report to the FDA, Cephalon blamed inappropriate prescribing for the deaths, as the casualties were mostly people with migraine headaches who had taken the drug against medical advice.

I want a new drug

Together, Provigil and Actiq account for around 80 percent of the company's sales, but Cephalon recognizes that it can't rely on these two drugs forever. One drug the firm has been developing is Nuvigil, the next generation of flagship product Provigil. In June 2007 it won FDA approval, perhaps setting it up to successfully replace its predecessor. CEO Baldino issued a statement that the approval would allow Cephalon "to preserve [its] current leadership position in the area of wakefulness." Cephalon is looking into gaining approval for the drug as a treatment for other conditions: bipolar depression, schizophrenia, Parkinson's disease and cancer fatigue, to name a few.

The company reinvests more than 25 percent of its revenue in research and development. In 2006, the company's research and development expenses increased $48.5 million, or 14 percent, as compared to 2005. Drugs in phase III trials include Lestaurtinib for acute myeloid leukemia and Treanda for indolent non-Hodgkin's lymphoma. But Cephalon is not done shopping for outside resources; it closed a $100 million deal for North American rights to the muscle relief drug Amrix in August 2007.

GETTING HIRED

Applicants can apply for positions through the company's career web site (www.cephalon.com/careers). Departments include information technology, manufacturing, engineering, quality assurance and research.

Cephalon offers comprehensive benefits to full-time employees, including a health care plan with medical, prescription and dental coverage, life insurance, long- and short-term disability coverage, health care and dependent care reimbursement accounts, education reimbursement, adoption assistance, employee referral bonuses and charitable giving matching. As soon as employees join the company, they can enroll in the 401(k) plan and receive a company matching contribution to their plan.

Charles River Laboratories International, Inc.

251 Ballardvale Street
Wilmington, MA 01887
Phone: (978) 658-6000
Fax: (978) 658-7132
www.criver.com

LOCATIONS

Wilmington, MA (HQ)
Baltimore, MD
Bethesda, MD
Cincinnati, OH
Reno/Sparks, NV
Shrewsbury, MA
Tacoma, WA

Additional US locations in Arkansas, California, Connecticut, Michigan, New York, North Carolina, Pennsylvania, South Carolina and TexasInternational locations in 17 countries.

THE STATS

Employer Type: Public Company
Stock Symbol: CRL
Stock Exchange: NYSE
Chairman, President & CEO: James C. Foster
2006 Employees: 8,000
2006 Revenue ($mil.): $1,058
2006 Net Income ($mil.): -$55

DEPARTMENTS

Administrative • Animal Welfare & Enrichment • Clinical Research • Customer/Client Service • Environmental Health & Safety • Engineering • Facilities/Maintenance/ Security • Finance & Accounting • Histology • Human Resources • Information Technology • Laboratory • Legal/Business Corporate Development • Management • Marketing • Operations • Pathology • Poultry Management • Preclinical Research • Purchasing • Quality Assurance/Regulatory Affairs • Research & Development • Sales • Scientific • Surgical Services • Technical Writer • Technicians— Animal Care • Technicians— Laboratory • Training • Veterinary Services

KEY COMPETITORS

Covance Inc.
Invitrogen Corporation
MDS Inc.

EMPLOYMENT CONTACT

www.criver.com/about_charles_river/ careers

Visit Vault at **www.vault.com** for insider company profiles, expert advice, career message boards, expert resume reviews, the Vault Job Board and more.

VAULT CAREER LIBRARY   125

THE SCOOP

Charles River Laboratories, which has been operating since 1947, describes itself as "a leading global provider of solutions that advance the drug discovery and development process." In unscientific terms, the Boston-area firm provides researchers with animals (mice, rats, rabbits) to use in R&D for new drugs, devices and therapies. The company has offered new, disease-specific rats since 2001, which are used to find treatments for diabetes, obesity and cardiovascular and kidney disease.

The company's customers include biotechnology and pharmaceutical companies, government agencies, and hospitals and academic institutions. In addition to providing research animals, Charles River also offers preclinical services and sometimes runs trials for biotechnology companies, which have increasingly outsourced preclinical trials in recent years. In 2006, Charles River's net sales were $1.06 billion, a 6.55 percent increase from 2005.

A company that knows the rat-race all too well

In 1947, veterinarian Henry Foster founded Charles River Laboratories in Cambridge, Mass. The company moved to a larger space in Wilmington, Mass., in the mid-1950s and went public on the Nasdaq exchange in 1968. The company's early success was assured by Henry Foster's commitment to medical needs—he pioneered the technique that ensured totally germ-free rats for research purposes and equipped his workers with sterile coveralls, gloves, caps and surgical masks. (Workers without their necessary equipment could be fired on the spot.) These germ-free animals were worth the risk, as one unclean specimen could throw off an experiment, and researchers paid Charles River top-dollar for its laboratory creatures.

Charles River became the industry leader, reaching $5.5 million in sales by 1970 and seeing off attempts to enter the market by major firms such as Becton Dickinson and Ralston Purina. The company had first expanded internationally in the 1950s, and now had international locations in Canada, France, Italy and the U.K. The firm's profits exceeded $1 million for the first time in 1973.

Fun with parent companies

In 1984, when Bausch & Lomb was restructuring its operations a bit, it acquired Charles River Labs for the tune of $130 million. That year, Charles River had grossed over $35 million and was a consistently profitable enterprise. In 1992, James

Foster succeeded his father as the firm's CEO, who was retiring at the age of 67 to enjoy the city of Boston (he was named chairman of the board for Boston's Museum of Fine Arts in 1991). But it wasn't all smooth sailing for the founder's son and parent company Bausch & Lomb, as the younger Foster told *Forbes* in 2002: "They treated us like a bank. I would go to … meetings and talk about contact lenses." Foster told the magazine that he came close to quitting and the magazine put it this way: "He endured his personal hell with one goal in mind: to liberate Charles River one day."

That day came in 1999, when Bausch & Lomb changed executive leadership and looked to unload Charles River, still a profitable asset. That year, James Foster led a $470 leveraged management buyout, taking the company private. However, Foster's new investment partners, the private equity firm Donaldson, Lufkin & Partners, saddled the company with $393 million worth of buyout-related loans. That year, the company's revenue was $230 million, so Foster had some catching up to do. With that in mind, Charles River went public again in 2000, raising $224 million. With some more hard work, James Foster started to pay off the company's debt and looked ahead to meeting the company's targeted growth goals.

The river overfloweth with business deals

By 2002, Charles River pulled down $554 million in annual revenue, and recorded its first billion-dollar year in 2005 with $1.1 billion in sales. A number of acquisitions helped the firm along the way, as it acquired a number of preclinical testing and drug testing firms in the new millennium. In 1999, Charles River purchased drug tester Sierra Biomedical for $22.3 million and in 2001 and 2002 the firm acquired the testing outfits Primedica Corp., Pathology Associates International, BioLabs and Springborn Laboratories for a combined cost of $141 million. Charles River added to its assets in October 2006, acquiring the Tacoma-based Northwest Kinetics, an early phase clinical pharmacology unit with expertise in branded drug studies.

The biggest purchase in Charles River's history, for roughly $1.5 billion, was that of North Carolina-based Inveresk Research Group in 2004. A leading provider of drug development services to companies in the pharmaceutical and biotechnology industries, Inveresk strengthened Charles River's position as a leading global provider of preclinical and clinical drug development services and products. The acquisition also expanded Charles River's business into testing drugs in humans.

Visit Vault at **www.vault.com** for insider company profiles, expert advice, career message boards, expert resume reviews, the Vault Job Board and more.

VAULT CAREER LIBRARY

127

Charles River Labs sold its company's phase II-IV clinical services business to Kendle International in August 2006. As part of the divestiture, Charles River changed its business reporting segments. The company's two business segments are now research models and services (RMS), which produces and sells research animals, and pre-clinical services, which conducts phase I clinical services. In 2006, the research model and services segment accounted for 49 percent of Charles River's total net sales and the pre-clinical Services segment represented the other 51 percent.

An advocate for animal welfare?

Charles River Laboratories chooses not to ignore the controversy over animal testing that naturally comes with its business model. Rather, the firm has launched a "Humane Care Initiative," committed to good treatment of the critters it produces for researchers and uses in research activities. Charles River's animal welfare and training group—comprised of professionals trained in laboratory animal medicine and science, training, and education and ethics—heads up the Humane Care Initiative.

This isn't to say that Charles River hasn't sometimes been the focus of animal rights activists. The company has largely attracted criticism for its dealings with monkeys, which it has handled since 1972 and now account for roughly 5 percent of Charles Rivers' animal testing business.

In the early 1990s, the company's primate import facility in the Florida Keys started aggravating local authorities, which complained about, well, monkey business. Apparently, some rogue rebus monkeys escaped from a Charles River facility and were eating the leaves of state-protected red mangrove trees, contaminating local water supplies with their fecal matter and generally wandering around and creating havoc in the community. The state of Florida soon succeeded in evicting Charles River Labs.

A few years later, Charles River was forced to relocate a primate imports facility from upstate New York to Texas. The reason for the move? New York's government had begun to worry that the imported animals were carrying the Ebola virus and enacted some tough laws against importing them. The primate business didn't fare much better after moving to Texas. In 1991, Texan animal rights activists waged "gorilla" warfare against Charles Rivers' new primate imports facility. Members of the group, some of whom wore gorilla suits, staged a demonstration in opposition to the importation of animals to Houston. After two chimpanzees in the firm's care died in

2002, local authorities filed animal cruelty charges against Charles River in 2004. However, a state judge in New Mexico dismissed the charges in 2005.

Forging forward

Charles River Labs plans to continue broadening the scope of its products and services, both through internal development and through focused acquisitions and alliances. In 2006 the firm invested heavily in expanding its facilities capacity during 2006 and in March 2007, it opened a new, 450,000-square-foot preclinical services facility in Shrewsbury, Mass.

The firm is also expanding its global reach. In March 2007, Charles River announced that the company was increasing its footprint in Asia as part of its strategy to support pharmaceutical and biotechnology companies' research and development efforts there. The first phase of this expansion includes a joint venture agreement with Shanghai BioExplorer Co. Ltd., a China-based preclinical services provider. As part of the agreement, Charles River is building a 50,000-square-foot facility in Shanghai, scheduled to open in the second half of 2008. Also in 2008, Charles River will open facilities in Nevada and Maryland, and throughout the year it will be working on a new 300,000 square foot preclinical services facility in Sherbrooke, Quebec, which isn't scheduled to open until at least 2010.

GETTING HIRED

Take me to Charles River

One of the more unusual job categories at Charles River is poultry management. Job seekers can check out the company's other categories at its careers site, at www.criver.com/about_charles_river/careers. At press time, the most recent open position were technologist in molecular diagnostics, report writer in clinical testing and senior quality assurance auditor. The firm's benefits include medical/dental insurance, domestic partner benefits, long and short-term disability, supplemental life insurance, a 401(k) plan, a stock purchase plan, vacation, sick and holiday pay and an employee assistance program. In 2006, the *Boston Business Journal* named Charles River its Company of the Year.

Visit Vault at **www.vault.com** for insider company profiles, expert advice, career message boards, expert resume reviews, the Vault Job Board and more.

VAULT CAREER LIBRARY   129

Covance Inc.

210 Carnegie Center
Princeton, NJ 08540
Phone: (609) 452-4440
Fax: (609) 452-9375
www.covance.com

LOCATIONS

Princeton, NJ (HQ)
Alice, TX • Austin, TX • Berkeley,
CA • Boise, ID • Chantilly, VA •
Cumberland, VA • Dallas, TX •
Daytona Beach, FL • Dedham, MA •
Denver, PA • Evansville, IN •
Gainesville, FL • Gaithersburg, MD •
Honolulu, HI • Indianapolis, IN •
Kalamazoo, MI • Madison, WI •
Nashville, TN • Portland, OR •
Reno, NV • San Diego, CA • Spring
Mill, PA • Vienna, VA

International locations in Argentina,
Australia, Belgium, Canada, China,
the Czech Republic, France,
Germany, Hungary, Italy, Japan,
The Netherlands, Poland, Singapore,
South Africa, Spain, Sweden,
Switzerland and the U.K.

THE STATS

Employer Type: Public Company
Stock Symbol: CVD
Stock Exchange: NYSE
Chairman & CEO: Joseph Herring
2006 Employees: 8,100
2006 Revenue ($mil.): $1,340
2006 Net Income ($mil.): $144.9

DEPARTMENTS

Administration
Biotechnology/Pharmaceutical
Clinical Research
Facilities/Maintenance
Finance/Accounting
Healthcare
Human Resources
Information Technology
Lab Services/Technicians
Legal
Medical Technologist
Purchasing/Procurement
Quality
Regulatory Affairs
Sales/Marketing
Senior Management/Exec.
Technician—Animal Care
Toxicology
Veterinarian

KEY COMPETITORS

Charles River Laboratories
MDS, Inc.
Pharmaceutical Product Development

EMPLOYMENT CONTACT

www.covance.com/careers

THE SCOOP

The Covance way

Princeton, N.J.-based Covance is a contract research organization (CRO), providing a variety of early-stage and late-stage product development services for the pharmaceutical, biotechnology and medical device industries. Covance describes itself as "one of the world's largest and most comprehensive drug development services companies."

In addition, the company offers services such as laboratory testing to the agrochemical, chemical and food industries and its Covance Research Products unit provides laboratory animals to the biomedical community. Covance employs approximately 8,100 people in 20 countries throughout Europe, Asia, North America and Australia. In 2006, Covance served more than 300 companies, ranging from small and startup organizations to the world's largest pharmaceutical companies. The firm's revenue that year was more than $1.3 billion, a 12.3 percent increase from 2005.

A development services company develops

Before Covance existed, it was the health and sciences division of the upstate New York leading glass firm Corning Glass Works (later Corning Incorporated). Corning consolidated this division into one entity in 1977 and then began to add to it through acquisitions, bringing in numerous drug development companies through the late 1980s and 1990s. Some of them, such as Hazleton Laboratories and G.H. Besselaar Associates, dated back much farther, even to the 1940s. Corning then spun them all off in 1997, creating the publicly traded company, Covance Inc.

The firm acquired the Netherlands-based Virtual Central Labs in October 2002. In recent years, the firm has acquired a number of firms to bolster its phase I and phase II testing operations. In August 2005, Covance purchased GFI Clinical Services, expanding its phase I clinical capacity. In April 2006, the company acquired eight early-phase clinical pharmacology sites from Radiant Research for more than $66 million. Besides its testing benefits, this purchase also gave Covance access to specialized patient populations. In May 2006, the firm expanded its offerings in monoclonal antibodies when it paid $9.1 million for the Dedham, Mass., company Signet, a leading producer of the antibodies used in the research of cancer, neurodegenerative and infectious diseases.

The company opened a $30 million expansion in Harrogate, United Kingdom, in 2006. In addition, the firm increased the square footage of its Munster, Germany, toxicology facility, completed an expansion in Madison, Wisc., and expanded clinical development capabilities with new offices in Bulgaria, Romania and Russia. Covance plans to open a lab in Shanghai, China, in late 2007.

Primate problems

Covance has faced controversy over its animal laboratory business in the United States and Europe. In Germany, an undercover journalist alleged that the firm's Munster facility was abusing monkeys and other primates. Local authorities ruled that the company install video cameras to monitor the staff working with primates, but Covance appealed the decision, claiming to do so would infringe on the rights of its staff. Authorities ultimately cleared Covance of all charges, and a German court prohibited further distribution of the footage.

In the United States, People for the Ethical Treatment of Animals (PETA) sent an undercover operative to investigate the company, and reported primate abuse in the company's Vienna, Va., lab. Covance brought a lawsuit against PETA and the two parties settled in October 2005—PETA agreed not to conduct any undercover investigation of Covance for five years and Lisa Leitten, who collected video recordings for PETA at Covance's Virginia site, accepted a three-year ban on infiltrating commercial animal research facilities worldwide.

The settlement also required PETA and Leitten to provide video footage and written notes taken from its Covance investigation. In 2006, the company announced that the FDA had completed an inspection of the Virginia facility. The FDA cited some minor issues, but found nothing to substantiate PETA's claims against the facility.

PETA and CAC have a bone to pick

PETA Europe successfully went public with the video footage, however. A British judge ruled against Covance's request for an injunction in June 2005, which would have barred PETA from airing the video footage. Two years later, PETA still isn't leaving Covance alone, as some of its members protested the planned construction of a new Covance laboratory in Chandler, Ariz., as recently as July 2007.

In fact, ever since Covance announced the opening of its Chandler facility in 2005, it has been facing resistance from the local community. A number of protest groups formed after the announcement, including Citizens Against Covance (CAC), which broke some distressing news in December 2006. The group had made a public records request and found one report that five monkeys at the company's Wisconsin facility had tested positive for tuberculosis in June 2006. The company confirmed the report in December 2006, claiming in a written statement that it was the first case of tuberculosis in 12 years of testing animals.

Other activist groups have joined the anti-Covance movement. The Physicians Committee for Responsible Medicine, a doctor-led nonprofit organization, joined seven local Chandler residents in filing a lawsuit against Covance in October 2007, alleging that the company had secretly met with city officials to negotiate the opening of the laboratory. The company officially broke ground on its Chandler facility the previous month, in September 2007.

Poised for growth

Like other contract research organizations, Covance is likely to grow. Biotech and pharmaceutical companies have increasingly turned to CROs to help them develop new products. Currently, pharmaceutical and biotech firms outsource about $15 billion in drug development to CROs, but Covance estimates this amount will double in coming years.

The company is trying to become more attractive to clients by increasing geographic coverage and scale in areas such as Central and Eastern Europe, Asia and Latin America. Covance has already signed big, dedicated-capacity agreements with five of the world's largest pharmaceutical and biotech companies, and the firm expects more contracts like this in 2007.

GETTING HIRED

Go Covance and you won't go back

The careers section of Covance's website (www.covance.com/careers) includes a searchable database of available positions. Job categories include administration, biotechnology/pharmaceutical, clinical research, facilities/maintenance, finance/accounting, healthcare, human resources, information technology, lab services/technicians, legal, medical technologist, purchasing/procurement, quality, regulatory affairs, sales/marketing, senior management/executive, animal care technician, toxicology and veterinarian.

Visit Vault at **www.vault.com** for insider company profiles, expert advice, career message boards, expert resume reviews, the Vault Job Board and more.

VAULT CAREER LIBRARY **133**

Applicants can submit resumes online or by mail. The company keeps resumes in a database for approximately six months. If an applicant is a good match for a position, a representative from Covance contacts the applicant. Next, a Covance representative conducts a job-related screening, which might involve a questionnaire, phone interview or face-to-face meeting. The company then schedules interviews with the most qualified applicants.

Covance views talented people as a key to the company's success. In 2006, the firm hired more than 800 employees and promoted approximately 1,400 people within the organization. Employee benefits include medical, dental, vision, life insurance, short- and long-term disability coverage, a 401(k) with company match, tuition reimbursement and more.

CSL Limited

45 Poplar Road
Parkville, Victoria 3052
Australia
Phone: +61-3-9389-1911
Fax: +61-3-9389-1434
www.csl.com.au

LOCATIONS

Melbourne (HQ)
King of Prussia, PA (US HQ)
Boca Raton, FL
Indianapolis, IN
Kankakee, IL
Knoxville, TN

International locations in Argentina, Australia, Belgium, Brazil, Canada, China, Denmark, France, Germany, Greece, Italy, Japan, Mexico, New Zealand, Portugal, Spain, Switzerland, Sweden and the UK.

THE STATS

Employer Type: Public Company
Stock Symbol: CSL
Stock Exchange: Australian Stock
 Exchange
Chairwoman: Elizabeth Alexander
2007 Employees: 9,000
2007 Revenue ($mil.): $2,956
2007 Net Income ($mil.): $481

DEPARTMENTS

Accounting/Finance • Administrative/Clerical • Business Development • Clinical R&D/Trials • Customer Service • Distribution/Warehousing • Engineering • Facilities Services • Healthcare • Human Resources • Information Technology • Laboratory Services • Legal • Management • Manufacturing • Marketing • Medical Affairs • Nursing • Procurement/Purchasing • Public Relations • Quality • Regulatory Affairs • Research • Sales • Security • Supply Chain • Technical Operations

KEY COMPETITORS

Baxter
Bayer
Cytomedix, Inc.
GlaxoSmithKline
MedImmune Inc.
Novartis AG
sanofi-aventis
Talecris

EMPLOYMENT CONTACT

www.cslbehring.com/careers
www.csl.com.au/Careers.asp

Visit Vault at **www.vault.com** for insider company profiles, expert advice, career message boards, expert resume reviews, the Vault Job Board and more.

VAULT CAREER LIBRARY   135

THE SCOOP

CSL's deal

CSL Ltd., headquarted in Melbourne, Australia, is a specialty biopharmaceutical company that develops, manufactures and markets products to prevent and treat serious human medical conditions. The firm makes plasma products, pharmaceuticals and vaccines. CSL is the only influenza vaccine manufacturer in the Southern hemisphere.

The company employs over 9,000 people in roughly two dozen countries and is in excellent financial shape, raking in about $2.9 billion in 2007—a major jump from its 2006 revenue of $2.1 billion. CSL's subsidiaries include CSL Behring, CSL Bioplasma and CSL Biotherapies, along with a global research and development operation.

Rising up from Down Under

In 1916, when World War I led to a shortage of certain pharmaceuticals in Australia, the country's government established Commonwealth Serum Laboratories (CSL) to produce sera, vaccines and other products. The company started producing insulin in 1923 and made a number of products in the following decades, including penicillin, the BCG vaccine for the prevention of tuberculosis, the tetanus vaccine and the Salk polio vaccine. The company also manufactured anti-venoms against Australia's poisonous snakes, jellyfish and spiders.

CSL was incorporated as a public company in April 1991. In September 1994, CSL acquired U.S. cell culture company JRH Biosciences Inc. The same year, CSL also acquired a majority interest in Iscotec, a Swedish company with global rights to commercialize a novel adjuvant, which enhanced the response to vaccines. In June 2000 CSL acquired ZLB, the world's fifth-largest manufacturer of plasma products.

In 2004, the firm purchased Aventis Behring to create ZLB Behring, a global leader in plasma therapeutics. In 2007, the company changed its name to CSL Behring, to more closely align with its parent. Also in 2004, CSL sold its animal health division to Pfizer so that it could focus on human medical conditions. In early 2005, CSL sold JHR Biosciences, its cell culture division, to Sigma-Aldrich Corporation. The company acquired Zenyth Therapeutics, a company that develops therapies for cancer and inflammation, in November 2006.

Gardasil gains

CSL played a key role in developing Gardasil, a vaccine against human papilloma virus that gained FDA approval in June 2006. Merck has exclusive global rights for the vaccine, but CSL has the distribution rights for New Zealand and Australia. CSL will also receive royalties from global sales of Gardasil. (For additional information about Gardasil, read Vault's profile of Merck.)

In 2006, the FDA also approved Vivaglobin, a subcutaneous immunoglobin. Vivaglobin is a treatment for people with primary immunodeficiency, an inherited condition in which a person's immune system doesn't work properly. Vivaglobin was the first product of its kind launched in the United States.

Everything you can do, I Kankakee better!

CSL has two American subsidiaries, CSL Behring and CSL Biotherapies, both based out of King of Prussia, Penn. In recent years, CSL Behring's Kankakee, Ill., manufacturing facility has been getting a lot of attention. In April 2006 the FDA licensed the production of Zemairia, a treatment for the asthma-like lung disease Alpha 1. A little over a year later, CSL poured more money into the Kankakee plant, already 113,000 square feet. The company poured $15 million into the facility for a new, high-speed syringe filling line, which should dovetail nicely with its new flu vaccine (more on that below).

Flu news

In February 2006, CSL announced plans to introduce a seasonal flu vaccine to the U.S. market through its subsidiary, CSL Biotherapies The firm—which leads the southern hemisphere in providing seasonal flu vaccine—launched its influenza vaccine in the U.S. for the 2007-2008 winter season. The company is investing $60 million to double its production capacity in Australia. On October 1, 2007, CSL Biotherapies announced that the FDA had approved the vaccine, which is known as Afluria in the U.S. In addition, CSL is testing and producing an experimental vaccine against the H5N1 bird flu.

The company's future R&D focus is on new protein-based medicines that can be purified from human plasma, produced using recombinant biotechnology or made from traditional sources (as with influenza vaccines). The firm is working with academic and corporate partners, such as the University of Queensland, Merck, Chiron Corporation and the Ludwig Institute for cancer research, to develop new medical marvels. Products in clinical development include vaccines to treat diseases that include melanoma, HPV and hepatitis C. CSL is also working on treatments for heart disease and stroke as well as a topical drug for age-related macular degeneration.

GETTING HIRED

See what CSL's got

CSL's main careers web site is at www.csl.com.au/Careers.asp. However, the careers page notes that only people who are eligible to work in Australia should apply for jobs listed on the site. Other applicants should e-mail careers@csl.com.au.

In addition, the company's two largest presences in the U.S., CSL Behring and CSL Biotherapies, each host career web sites. CSL Behring, a global leader in the plasma protein biotherapeutics industry, is headquartered in King of Prussia, Pa. Its ZLB Plasma subsidiary runs more than 60 plasma collection centers across the United States and eight in Germany.

Behring brings good employment tidings

Applicants can search for career opportunities with CSL Berhring at www.cslbehring.com/s1/cs/enco/1153191062783/page/1151517262830/JobSearch.htm. Job categories include accounting/finance, administrative/clerical, business development, clinical R&D/trials, customer service, distribution/warehousing, engineering, facilities services, health care, human resources, information technology, laboratory services, legal, management, manufacturing, marketing, medical affairs, nursing, procurement/purchasing, public relations, quality, regulatory affairs, research, sales, security, supply chain and technical operations.

Applicants can search for opportunities at ZLB Plasma by location at www.zlbplasmahiring.org/bylocation.asp. Positions at plasma collection centers include medical reception, phlebotomists, nurses, paramedics, physicians, compliance/quality specialist and various levels of management. Through a management training program, ZLB Plasma makes sure current or new employees understand the business.

ZLB Plasma also looks for medical laboratory technicians, laboratory technologists, laboratory assistants, lab supervisors, managers and people to work in its warehouses. In its corporate offices, there are opportunities in fields such as information technology, finance and accounting, marketing, human resources, regulatory, quality, document control, planning and materials management.

CSL Biotherapies, the other main U.S.-located branch, has no job site of its own. For opportunities, seekers can check the main listings at www.csl.com.au/Careers.asp, which featured four Australia-located positions at press time. The firm is also based regionally out of King of Prussia, Penn., so one could contact the company there.

Visit Vault at **www.vault.com** for insider company profiles, expert advice,
career message boards, expert resume reviews, the Vault Job Board and more.

VAULT CAREER LIBRARY   139

Eli Lilly and Company

Lilly Corporate Center
Indianapolis, Indiana 46285
Phone: (317) 276-2000
Fax: (317) 277-6579
www.lilly.com

LOCATIONS

Indianapolis, IN (HQ)
Bothell, WA (Icos)
Clinton, IN
Lafayette, IN
San Diego, CA (Applied Molecular Evolution)

Sales locations across the US; R&D and manufacturing facilities worldwide.

THE STATS

Employer Type: Public Company
Stock Symbol: LLY
Stock Exchange: NYSE
Chairman & CEO: Sidney Taurel
President & COO: John C. Lechleiter, PhD
2006 Employees: 41,500
2006 Revenue ($mil.): $15,691
2006 Net Income ($mil.): $2,662

DEPARTMENTS

Administrative/Assistants • Clinical Research • Drug Information Residency • E-business • Elanco Animal Health—R&D • Elanco Animal Health—Sales/Marketing • Engineering • Finance • General • Human Resources • Information Technology • Legal • Manufacturing • Marketing • Medical Information • Physicians • Post-Doctoral Program • Procurement • Public Relations/Government Affairs • Quality • Regulatory • Sales—Lilly • Science • Statistical Science • Visiting Scientist Program

KEY COMPETITORS

GlaxoSmithKline
Novartis
Pfizer

EMPLOYMENT CONTACT

www.lilly.com/careers

THE SCOOP

Where the Lillys grow

Eli Lilly and Company, founded in 1876 and headquartered in Indianapolis, wants to make patients happy and keep them calm. The company is best known for making antidepressant Prozac, schizophrenia treatment Zyprexa (its No. 1 seller) and Strattera, the first non-stimulant ADHD drug.

Other top products include cancer treatment Gemzar, osteoporosis medication Evista, Humalog insulin, diabetes drug Actos and erectile dysfunction treatment Cialis. Along with its neurological, oncological and diabetes drugs, Eli Lilly also manufactures antibiotics, growth hormones, antiulcer agents, cardiovascular treatments and animal health products.

All told, in 2006 the company raked in roughly $15.7 billion sales in 143 countries, an increase from $14.7 billion in 2005. Eli Lilly and Company has R&D facilities in nine countries and manufacturing plants in 13 countries, with some 41,500 employees on the payroll.

From one colonel, a corporate giant is sown

Civil war pharmacist and Union officer Colonel Eli Lilly founded his eponymous company in 1876 with $1,300. He created gelatin-coated pills, which led to sales of almost $82,000 by 1881 ($1.6 billion in 2006 dollars) and to his development of gelatin capsules, a technique the company uses to this day.

Eli Lilly died in 1898, and his sons and grandsons ran the company until 1953. Eli Lilly and Company began mining insulin from hog and cattle pancreases in 1923. Other breakthroughs from the 1920s and 1930s included the antiseptic Merthiolate, the sedative Seconal and treatments for pernicious anemia and heart disease. Eli Lilly started selling diethylstilbestrol (DES), a drug to prevent miscarriages, in 1947, and in the 1950s, it was a major supplier of the Salk polio vaccine.

In 1971, the company owned a 70 percent share of the DES market, when researchers noticed a rare form of cervical cancer in the daughters of women who had used DES. Eli Lilly found itself mired in a bog of pioneering product-liability lawsuits that stretched into the 1990s.

Top of the pile

Zyprexa, Eli Lilly's schizophrenia and bipolar disorder treatment, is now the company's best-selling drug, surpassing its previous star, Prozac. Zyprexa accounted for nearly one-third of overall sales in 2006, with $4.4 billion, an increase from $4.2 billion in 2005.

The company breathed a sigh of relief in April 2005 when a federal judge turned away claims of generic drug manufacturers looking to overturn a patent for Zyprexa. The three Companies—Zenith Goldline Pharmaceuticals, Dr. Reddy's Laboratories of India and the U.S. sector of Israeli-based Teva Pharmaceuticals Industries—challenged a 1993 patent granting Lilly exclusive U.S. rights to the drug until 2011.

In late 2006, a series of articles in *The New York Times* suggested that Eli Lilly had engaged in inappropriate sales and marketing techniques in regards to Zyprexa. Multiple states have also sued Lilly for its marketing of that the drug, each claiming that the firm promoted Zyprexa for unapproved uses and hid side effects of the medication. Eli Lilly, which denies the allegations, has said it behaved legally and appropriately.

Lilly has also faced a large number of American lawsuits involving Zyprexa from individuals with product liability claims. The company has reached two primary settlements with approximately 28,500 claimants, who said the drug caused or contributed to diabetes or high blood-glucose levels. Approximately 1,300 claims remain. Eli Lilly has paid over $1 billion to settle these lawsuits so far.

The firm's second-best-selling drug is Cymbalta, used to treat major depressive disorder and diabetic peripheral neuropathic pain. In 2006, Cymbalta had $1.3 billion in sales, nearly double the drug's 2005 sales.

Up-and-comers

One new drug that's doing well for Eli Lilly is Byetta, a biotechnology product to treat type 2 diabetes that was produced in collaboration with Amylin Pharmaceuticals. Patients who take Byetta, unlike those using insulin, usually lose weight. By the end of 2006, the drug's first full year of sales, Byetta ranked fourth in new prescriptions among branded products for type 2 diabetes in the United States. Eli Lilly plans to launch it in 60 international markets by December 2008.

Another drug Lilly is excited about is an experimental anticlotting drug called prasugrel, which Lilly is teaming with Daiichi Sankyo Co. to create. An October 2005, study showed that the drug outperformed the current anticlotter Plavix in three head-to-head tests on healthy volunteers. These early-stage studies suggested that prasugrel successfully stopped blood platelet clumping in all of the recipients, while Plavix did not prompt a response in 22 to 43 percent of study's participants.

Lilly and Daiichi Sankyo recently received mixed, but positive results from a phase III study pitting prasugrel against Plavix. In November 2007, the firms reported that prasugrel reduced heart attacks in target patients by 24 percent, compared with Plavix, although the drug is more likely than Plavix to increase severe bleeding. The study was sufficiently positive that the firms will submit the drug for FDA approval as soon as the end of 2007.

Arousing results and a promising pickup

Lilly released impotence drug Cialis in 2003 with joint venture partner Icos, a biotech firm located in Bothell, Washington, and today sells the product in over 100 countries. In 2006 Cialis saw worldwide sales of $971 million, a 30 percent increase over 2005. Cialis is the impotence drug leader in France and Brazil.

In October 2005, promising results were seen in a study testing Cialis as a treatment for men experiencing urinary problems from benign enlargement of the prostate. The findings could provide Lilly with a foothold into a major market, as more than half of men over 50 years of age have urinary problems caused by prostate enlargement, and more than six million men in the U.S. and Europe take prescription medication for the problem. Lilly and Icos are also looking at Cialis as a potential hypertension treatment.

Lilly assumed full ownership of the impotence treatment Cialis with its $2.3 billion acquisition of Icos in October 2006. Sidney Taurel, Lilly chairman and CEO, said the move would make the Cialis brand more efficient by reducing employment redundancies in development, marketing and sales. In January 2007, Taurel proved true to his word, as Lilly cut 570 of Icos' 700 jobs.

Preparing for the future

Eli Lilly is getting ready for expiration of patents on older products beginning in 2011. The company invested approximately 20 percent of sales into research and development in 2006. The firm also entered into an agreement with OSI Pharmaceuticals in January 2007. Under the agreement, Lilly will acquire the rights to PSN010, a compound for potential treatment of type-2 diabetes.

Mining new markets

In addition to looking for new drugs, Eli Lilly is also looking for new markets. Lilly is looking to China as its new big growth area, both due to a burgeoning population and capitalist marketplace. But many of America's drugmakers are wary about investing in China, where counterfeiting and patent fraud are common. CEO Taurel has taken annual trips to Asia, and in August 2005, he focused his visit to Beijing on encouraging the government to ramp up efforts to halt the production of counterfeit drugs. Eli Lilly hopes to boost sales in China to $600 million a year by 2015, up from $100 million in 2004.

The company has a long history in the Chinese market, first selling medicine there in 1918 and opening its first Chinese office in 1928. It left during the Communist Revolution in 1949 but returned in 1993, the same year the Chinese government began allowing patents on drug compounds. But patent enforcement is still an issue. Pfizer's Viagra served a valuable lesson to American pharmaceutical companies, as six months after the drug was launched in the Chinese market in 2000, reports surfaced that 90 percent of Viagra pills sold in Shanghai—China's largest city—were counterfeit. But pressure from visits such as Taurel's now appear to be paying off. Thus far, he said, Lilly has won or expects to win all of the six patent challenges it has faced in the Chinese judicial system.

In late 2004, Lilly also opened a research center outside Shanghai operated by the Chinese company ChemExplorer, which researches exclusively for Eli Lilly and employs 230 Chinese-educated scientists and technical staff. With salaries in China a third of what they are in Indianapolis, basic research in China is significantly less expensive. Lilly conducts a significant portion of the company's research in foreign laboratories, and 20 percent of its scientists are based in the China research center. In 2006, the firm also added 100 sales representatives to Lilly's diabetes business in China to respond to "enormous unmet need."

In August 2007, Lilly kept pouring resources into China, inking a $29 million drug discovery and development deal with Hutchison China Meditech. It's just part of a bigger plan, as the company's president and COO, John Lechleiter, outlaid plans in June 2007 to invest $100 million in China until 2011.

Moving with a Lech-leiter step

John Lechleiter will soon have a much larger say in Lilly's boardroom, as the company announced in December 2007 that he will become chairman and CEO by the end of 2008. Lechleiter stated that he plans "to be an agent of change," but industry analysts see the move as preserving Lilly's status quo—Lechleiter is a 28-year Lilly veteran and has been a clear-cut successor figure since becoming president and COO in 2005. Lechleiter also holds a degree in organic chemistry, which differentiates him from current CEO Sidney Taurel, who rose through the ranks of Lilly's marketing department. Taurel is expected to retire as CEO in March 2008 and as chairman later in the year.

GETTING HIRED

Put Lilly in your life

Eli Lilly's site (jobs.lilly.com) has a searchable database of job opportunities in areas including administrative/assistants, clinical research, drug information residency, e-business, Elanco Animal Health, engineering; finance, human resources, information technology, legal, manufacturing, marketing, medical information, physicians, procurement, public relations, government affairs, quality, regulatory affairs, sales, science and statistical science.

Eli Lilly also offers internships for college students. Eli Lilly offers a 401(k) savings plan, retirement planning, extended disability leave, life insurance and flexible spending accounts. Health benefits include health insurance, domestic partner benefits, prescription drug benefits, on-site care of minor illnesses, dental insurance and long-term care insurance.

Visit Vault at **www.vault.com** for insider company profiles, expert advice, career message boards, expert resume reviews, the Vault Job Board and more.

VAULT CAREER LIBRARY   **145**

Exelixis, Inc.

170 Harbor Way
South San Francisco, CA 94083
Phone: (650) 837-7000
Fax: (650) 837-8300
www.exelixis.com

LOCATIONS

South San Francisco, CA (HQ)
Portland, OR
San Diego, CA
Köln, Germany

THE STATS

Employer Type: Public Company
Stock Symbol: EXEL
Stock Exchange: Nasdaq
Chairman: Stelios Papadopoulos
President & CEO: George A. Scangos
2006 Employees: 651
2006 Revenue ($mil.): $99
2006 Net Income ($mil.): -$102

DEPARTMENTS

Biology • Biostatistics & Clinical Data
Management • Chemistry •
Chemistry, Manufacturing Control •
Clinical Development • Clinical
Operations • Corporate
Communications • Corporate
Services • EPS Metabolic Engineering
• Finance & Administration •
Genome Biochemistry • Human
Resources • Information Technology
• Lead Discovery • Licensing •
Medicinal Chemistry • Molecular &
Cellular Pharmacology • New Lead
Discovery • Non-Clinical
Development • Patents •
Pharmacology • Pharmacy • Program
Management • Purchasing • R&D
Informatics • Regulatory Affairs •
Strategic Marketing • Translational
Medicine

KEY COMPETITORS

AstraZeneca
Celera Group
Novartis Corporation

EMPLOYMENT CONTACT

www.exelixis.com/careers.shtml

THE SCOOP

I like Exelixis!

Exelixis is an integrated drug discovery and development company, committed more to developing drugs than bringing them to market. Whereas many similar, small biotech companies tend to focus on one or two drugs, Exelixis has taken a different approach. To date, Exelixis has filed 11 investigational new drug applications.

The company also serves as a sort of drug farm for bigger pharmaceutical firms, as it has almost as many ongoing collaborative relationships as applications for new products. Its research partners include such major firms as Bristol-Myers & Squibb, GlaxoSmithKline and Wyeth. These large research partners also underwrite much of Exelixis' activity, as the firm has not turned a profit in a number of years.

Exelixis has a pipeline of compounds that will potentially treat cancer, various metabolic and cardiovascular disorders and renal disease. In October 2006, Exelixis successfully completed a public offering of common stock that raised net proceeds of $90.5 million. The company had $98.67 million in revenue in 2006 (a nearly 30 percent increase from 2005), although it accrued net losses of $101 million during the fiscal period.

An Exel-ent beginning

Two research scientists with roots in venture capital, Stelios Papadopoulos (Exelixis' current chairman) and Corey Goodman (just named Pfizer's head of research in the bay area in October 2007) co-founded Exelixis in Cambridge, Mass., in 1994. The biotech startup moved its headquarters to South San Francisco in 1997 and immediately began to establish various partnerships and collaborations with other pharmaceutical companies.

That year, Exelixis purchased a partial stake in Artemis Pharmaceuticals, a privately held German company that focused on the use of vertebrate model genetic systems such as zebra fish and mice as tools for drug discovery. In July 1999 Exelixis purchased MetaXen—a subsidiary of London-based Xenova—taking a major step towards becoming an integrated pharmaceutical drug discovery company.

In April 2000, Exelixis completed a successful initial public offering (IPO), at which point co-founder Goodman left to start up Renovis Inc., another biotech firm. The

Visit Vault at www.vault.com for insider company profiles, expert advice, career message boards, expert resume reviews, the Vault Job Board and more.

VAULT CAREER LIBRARY   147

next year, Exelixis acquired the remaining assets of Artemis in May 2001, taking the firm further down the drug discovery road.

Working with the big guys

During recent years, Exelixis has ramped up its familiar method of strategic partnerships and collaborations, as bigger pharmaceutical companies and biotech firms noticed the research capacities of this new kid on the biotech block. Major pharmaceutical players such as Bristol-Myers Squibb, Wyeth and GlaxoSmithKline all ponied up to work with Exelixis, mostly focusing on drugs for metabolic disorders.

In 1999, the company first established a research collaboration with Bristol-Myers Squibb (BMS), to identify the mechanism of action of key molecular targets. The two partnered again in 2001 and 2005, to discover novel cancer targets and cardiovascular and metabolic disorders, respectively. And the two firms will continue to make sweet music together until at least 2009 thanks to a new deal reached in 2005, with BMS kicking in $7.5 million more in funding.

The company formed a "broad alliance" with GlaxoSmithKline in October 2002. The two companies will try to discover, develop and commercialize novel therapeutics in the research areas of inflammatory disease, vascular biology and oncology.

In June 2005, Exelixis entered into collaboration with Genentech to discover and develop therapeutics to target cancer, inflammatory diseases, and tissue growth and repair. That December, Exelixis and Wyeth entered into a license agreement related to compounds targeting FXR, a nuclear hormone receptor implicated in a variety of liver and metabolic disorders.

Exelixis—so popular!

The partnerships keep on coming. In March 2006, Exelixis established a new collaboration agreement with Sankyo Company—a subsidiary of Daiichi Sankyo Company—to discover, develop and commercialize novel therapies targeted against a nuclear hormone receptor (NHR) implicated in a variety of cardiovascular and metabolic diseases. Genentech signed onto a new project with Exelixis in January 2007, developing the XL518, a type of small-molecule inhibitor.

The firm undertook perhaps its most unusual collaboration in August 2007. Exelixis entered into business with Dow Chemical Co. through each firm's mutual subsidiaries, Dow Agrosciences and Exelixis Plant Services. As part of the deal, Dow will purchase "certain intellectual property and physical assets used for crop trait discovery" from Exelixis, and the two companies will enter into a contract research agreement for "the development of new tools for gene discovery and validation of novel crop traits."

Apparently, Dow will be able to take this technology into directions that Exelixis couldn't, or wouldn't. As Exelixis CEO Scangos stated in a press release at the time: "This deal … will ensure that the assets that have been developed at Exelixis Plant Sciences are developed in a way in which they receive the critical mass of agricultural expertise and resources they deserve."

Because Exelixis has so many partnerships, the company's pipeline is filling up nicely. However, at least one analyst has expressed concern that—should the drugs eventually win approval—Exelixis' many partnerships could cut into revenue.

Trial troubles

In November 2006, Exelixis suspended enrollment of new patients in the XL999 clinical trial program. Although a preliminary review of patient data showed signs that XL999 had beneficial potential for patients with acute myelogenous leukemia and lung cancer, the company's internal safety monitoring board was worried about the frequency of cardiovascular events among patients in the program.

Exelixis worked closely with the FDA to reinitiate the clinical development of the drug. In April 2007 the FDA agreed that Exelixis could reinitiate the clinical trial of XL999 in patients with non-small cell lung cancer.

More bad news greeted the firm in October 2007, when kidney disease candidate XL784 failed a mid-stage study. Exelixis has many other drugs in the pipeline, though, and expects other treatments, notably XL880, to report positive data from testing, so Exelixis' clinical frustrations should not be overstated.

Analysts actually suggested that such negative results could attract more investors. Eric Schmidt, an analyst at Cowen and Co.—the venture capital firm where Exelixis co-founder Papadopoulos had once been vice chairman—told CNN that he expected Exelixis to outperform its rivals in bringing its 13 cancer drug candidates to market.

In the pipeline and down the line

In addition to XL999, Exelixis has an array of drugs in clinical development. The company has presented promising data from phase I trials of XL999, XL880, XL820, XL647 and XL184 at oncology conferences such as the 2006 annual meeting of the American Society of Clinical Oncology. In early 2007, the firm filed investigational new drug applications (INDs) for two compounds for treating cancer, XL418 and XL147. Exelixis expects to file two additional INDs by the end of 2007.

The company is also planning to continue to pursue strategic partnerships to expand its pipeline, advance promising drug candidates and fund the firm's proprietary programs. Exelixis has incurred net losses each year since the company's inception, including a net loss of $101.5 million in 2006. The firm expects to continue to incur net losses for the foreseeable future.

Exelixis and its research partners will have more space very soon. In September 2007, the firm signed a lease for approximately 66,000 square feet of office space in a building under construction directly adjacent to its current headquarters in South San Francisco. It should be starting operations there in May 2008. The news coincided almost directly with a further issuance of company stock on September 10, 2007, which raised about $72 million.

GETTING HIRED

Do you like Exelixis?

The careers section of Exelix's web site (www.exelixis.com/careers.shtml) states Exelixis looks for and encourages innovation in its employees. In 2006, the company had about 650 full-time employees; of these, nearly a third held PhD and/or MD degrees. Most of the employees with MD and/or PhD degrees worked in full-time research and development activities.

Job categories at Exelixis are even more numerous than the number of compounds that company has in development. Categories include biology, biostatistics and clinical data management, chemistry, chemistry/manufacturing control, clinical development, clinical operations, corporate communications, corporate services, EPS metabolic engineering; finance and administration, genome biochemistry, human resources, information technology, lead discovery, licensing, medicinal chemistry, molecular and cellular pharmacology, new lead discovery, nonclinical development, patents, pharmacology; pharmacy, program management, purchasing, R&D informatics, regulatory affairs, strategic marketing and translational medicine.

Both local and national publications have recognized Exelixis as a good place to work. In September 2005, SF Chronicle Jobs and HR.com ranked Exelixis as the No.1 Mid-Size Company to work for in the Bay Area. In April 2006, the *San Francisco Business Times* recognized the company as one of the 20 Best Places to Work in the Bay Area. In both 2006 and 2007, *The Scientist*'s readers ranked Exelixis among the top 10 places for life scientists to work in the industry.

Benefits at Exelixis include medical, dental and vision insurance, domestic partner benefits, health and dependent care flexible spending accounts, a 401(k) plan with an employer match, a group legal plan, adoption assistance, an infertility assistance program, stock options, a subsidized cafeteria, free gourmet coffee, subsidized gym memberships and more.

Forest Laboratories, Inc.

909 Third Avenue
New York, NY 10022
Phone: (212) 421-7850
Fax: (212) 750-9152
www.frx.com

LOCATIONS

New York, NY (HQ)
Cincinnati, OH
Commack, NY
Farmingdale, NY
Hauppauge, NY
Inwood, NY
Jersey City, NJ
St. Louis, MO
Dublin
Kent, UK

THE STATS

Employer Type: Public Company
Stock Symbol: FRX
Stock Exchange: NYSE
Chairman & CEO: Howard Solomon
President & Chief Operating Officer:
 Lawrence S. Olanoff
2007 Employees: 5,126
2007 Revenue ($mil.): $3,183
2007 Net Income ($mil.): $454

DEPARTMENTS

Administrative & Support • Business
Development • Clinical Operations •
Clinical Operations & Biometrics •
Clinical Research • Clinical Systems •
Compliance • Data Management •
Facilities • Finance/Accounting •
Health Economics • Human
Resources • Information Systems •
Legal • Licensing • Managed Care •
Manufacturing & Distribution—
Engineering • Manufacturing &
Distribution—Production • Market
Research • Marketing • Marketing
Services • Medical • Medical Affairs
• Quality Assurance • Quality Control
• Regulatory Affairs • Research &
Development • SAP • Sales & Sales
Management • Training &
Development

KEY COMPETITORS

Eli Lilly
GlaxoSmithKline
Pfizer

EMPLOYMENT CONTACT

www.frx.com/careers

THE SCOOP

Prescription for success

Forest Laboratories, a New York City-based research facility founded in 1954, looks to find potential treatments that fulfill unmet medical needs or that improve on what's currently available on the market. The company conducts preclinical and clinical submission studies, manages regulatory approval processes and markets products to physicians, in addition to co-promoting products with companies.

Forest boosted profits by more than 65 percent over three years at the turn of the 21st century, from $537.8 million in 1999 to $2 billion in 2002. The company pulled in revenue of about $3 billion in 2006, a slight decrease from $3.1 billion for the fiscal year 2005. The firm's net income for its 2006 fiscal year was $708.5 million, down from about $839 million in 2005.

Forest's broad product line includes Lexapro, the fastest growing selective serotonin reuptake inhibitor (SSRI) antidepressant in the U.S.; Benicar, a well-used treatment for hypertension; and Namenda, the first approved therapy in the U.S. for those with moderate to severe Alzheimer's disease.

Award-winning history

Since 2000, Forest has earned a spot on a variety of "best" lists, including The Best Companies to Sell For (*Selling Power*), Top 50 Manufacturing Companies (*Industry Week*) and Best Performers of the S&P 500 (*BusinessWeek*). In September 2006, *Pharmaceutical Executive* ranked Forest third in its fifth annual industry audit, which analyzes financial performance of the top publicly traded pharmaceutical and biotech companies.

The company also ranked No. 27, up from No. 29, on *Pharmaceutical Executive*'s May 2006 list of the top 50 pharmaceutical companies. In 2007, *Forbes* ranked Forest Laboratories 655th on its annual ranking of America's largest companies.

Cat of three lives

But the firm has not always sold branded drugs—in fact, it has been through three distinct incarnations. First, the company served as exactly what its name described for two decades after its formation—providing laboratory services to other corporations in the research and manufacturing of drugs.

The company went public in 1967 and around the same period created Synchron, a technology which allows for the slow release of a drug into the body of its host. In 1977, the company entered its second phase of life as the company's chairman and CEO resigned and its new chief took the firm into the high-margin sector of generic drugs, utilizing Forest's manufacturing technology while bypassing heavy R&D investment.

In 1984, Forest purchased O'Neal, Jones & Feldman, a discredited firm that had sold deadly drugs without FDA approval. The purchase brought a sales force to Forest, along with the strategy of purchasing branded drugs that had not been sold with much fervor by other companies.

Forest's branded and generic business flourished side by side, and by 1990 the firm had surpassed $100 million in sales. It only continued to grow in the 1990s, clocking in $348 million revenue in 1993 and $461 million in 1996. Also in 1996, Forest licensed the drug that would, more than any other, carry it into the next decade with explosive growth, the antidepressant Celexa.

Celexa-bration

The FDA approved Celexa in 1998, and by the next year the drug was pulling in $91 million all by itself—and $427 million in 2000! By 2004, generic replication hurt Celexa's sales, although Forest launched its own generic version of the drug the next year. During the 2006 fiscal year, sales of branded and generic Celexa brought Forest about $19 million, but branded Celexa accounted for less than 1 percent of the company's sales over the same period, down from and 21.6 percent in 2005 and 41 percent in 2004.

One of the company's best-selling drugs is antidepressant Lexapro, which accounted for 67 percent of Forest's 2006 sales, an increase from about 52 percent in 2005 and 41 percent in 2004. In July 2006, the company's stock soared after a federal judge upheld a patent for Lexapro (the ruling also held up on appeal in September 2007). The antidepressant's patent expires in 2012.

Safety first

In September 2004, Forest announced it was teaming up with then-New York Attorney General Eliot Spitzer to create an online registry containing result summaries for all company-sponsored clinical trials for drugs conducted after January 1, 2000. The announcement came after Spitzer began investigating whether pharmaceutical companies had suppressed data about the safety and efficacy of a number of drugs.

Forest had hoped that an experimental compound, neramexane, could team with other medications and help Alzheimer's patients maintain cognition and functionality better than other drugs alone. But, that same September, the company announced that its clinical tests revealed the compound to be ineffective, signaling a return to the drawing board. Forest will study the drug further in future clinical trials.

Meanwhile, Forest's Namenda, an Alzheimer's drug the company hoped would be aided by neramexane, continued to grow in sales. In 2006, Alzheimer's treatment Namenda accounted for about 18 percent of the firm's sales, up from about 11 percent in 2005 and 1.7 percent in 2004.

Ready, set, launch!

In January 2005, Forest launched Campral Delayed-Release Tablets to physicians, patients and pharmacies nationwide, after the FDA approved Campral to help maintain alcohol abstinence in patients with alcohol dependency. The drug was the first new treatment for alcoholism in 10 years. During the 2006 fiscal year, sales of Campral were nearly $23 million.

Also in 2005, Forest began selling Combunox, which combines oxycodone (considered 10 times more potent than codeine) with ibuprofen to treat moderate to severe pain. In 2006, sales of Combunex reached more than $8 million, an increase from $4 million in 2005.

Ready, set, partner!

Historically, Forest Labs has not been able to afford to develop its own drugs, so the firm has relied on acquiring pharmaceuticals from other companies. This trend has continued in recent years. During the period between November 2005 and April 2006, Forest completed five major partnership transactions.

Two of these transactions were with Hungarian pharmaceutical company Gedeon Richter. In November 2005, Forest acquired two drugs from Gedeon Richter: a product for neuropathic pain, and a compound for treatment of anxiety and possibly depression. Then, in January 2006, Forest entered into an agreement with Mylan Laboratories for hypertension drug nebivolol.

The following month, Forest entered into an agreement with Replidyen for faropenem, a novel antibiotic for skin and respiratory infections. In April 2006, the company concluded a deal with Spanish pharmaceutical company Almirall Prodesfarma for LAS-34272, a treatment for chronic obstructive pulmonary disease. In September 2007, Forest was at it again, floating $70 million to Microbia for rights to Linaclotide, a drug for the treatment of IBS (irritable bowel syndrome).

Breaking blood down and building up the pipeline

Forest also has several drugs in its own research pipeline, one of the newest medications being desmoteplase. It treats blood clots using a crucial ingredient from vampire bat saliva that breaks down the fibrin in blood, which creates clots. The drug is in phase IIb/III trails, and the company expects to have results from the study in 2008. The FDA has granted desmoteplase fast-track status. Other drugs Forest is developing include milnacipran for fibromyalgia, oglemilast for COPD and asthma, and RGH-188 for schizophrenia.

In January 2007, Forest's pipeline grew when the firm acquired Cerexa Inc., an innovation-driven biopharmaceutical company that focuses on developing novel anti-infective therapies. Through the $480 million deal, plus a potential $100 million milestone payment, Forest gained development and marketing rights to Ceftaroline, a novel antibiotic that will enter phase III clinical trials in 2007, as well as ME1036, an antibiotic in preclinical development. In addition, the company obtained an option to a third early-stage antibiotic.

GETTING HIRED

Walk into the Forest

Working at Forest Labs requires "commitment, creativity and teamwork," and the company looks for motivated staff to fill open positions. Interested applicants can find a list of available openings on the company's web site at www.frx.com/careers. Applicants can search positions by location, job title and key words. Along with the usual employee benefits (like health insurance, a 401(k) and profit sharing), Forest also offers more in-depth perks such as vision and hearing care, fertility assistance and well-woman and well-child care. Potential employees should submit a resume online at www.frx.com/careers/resumeform.aspx.

Job categories at Forest include administrative and support, business development, clinical operations, clinical research, clinical systems, compliance, data management, facilities, finance/accounting, health economics, human resources, information systems, legal, licensing, managed care, manufacturing and distribution, market research, marketing, medical, medical affairs, quality assurance, quality control, regulatory affairs, research and development, sales and sales management, and training and development. The company also lists internship opportunities on its careers web site.

Forest offers employees a bonanza of benefits. A few of these benefits are medical and dental insurance that begin on an employee's first day of work, a 401(k) plan with company match, flexible spending accounts, short- and long-term disability insurance, a commuter benefit program (for employees in New York, New Jersey and Long Island), and flex-time and summer hours at some locations.

Genentech, Inc.

1 DNA Way
South San Francisco, CA 94080
Phone: (650) 225-1000
Fax: (650) 225-6000
www.gene.com

LOCATIONS

South San Francisco, CA (HQ)
Cambridge, MA
Hillsboro, OR
Louisville, KY
Oceanside, CA
Redwood City, CA
Vacaville, CA

THE STATS

Employer Type: Public Company
Stock Symbol: DNA
Stock Exchange: NYSE
Chairman & CEO: Arthur D. Levinson
2006 Employees: 10,533
2006 Revenue ($mil.): $9,284
2006 Net Income ($mil.): $2,113

DEPARTMENTS

Accounting & Finance • Administration • Business Development • Commercial Operations/Customer Care • Corporate & Investor Relations • Drug Development Sciences • Engineering/Facilities/Security • Environmental Health & Safety • Human Resources • Information Technology • Legal • Managed Care • Manufacturing • Marketing • Process Development • Procurement • Product Development • Quality • Regulatory Affairs & Compliance • Research & Discovery • Sales • Supply Chain • Training

KEY COMPETITORS

Amgen
Biogen Idec
Genzyme

EMPLOYMENT CONTACT

www.gene.com/gene/careers

THE SCOOP

Genentech-nically speaking

Since its founding, Genentech has called South San Francisco, Calif., its home base. From its humble beginnings in a rented building with a two-person staff, the company's South San Francisco campus now contains 38 buildings and some 8,200 employees. Unlike many of its competitors, Genentech eschews a diversified group of drugs, focusing on—and dominating—a few specific areas, notably including oncology treatments.

Genentech also makes cardiovascular therapies, human growth hormone Nutropin, cystic fibrosis drug Pulmozyme and asthma treatment Xolair. Genentech—about 56 percent of which is owned by Roche—finished fiscal 2006 with sales of $9.28 billion, an increase of 40 percent over the year before. Considered one of the founders of the biotechnology industry, it is one of the two or three biggest biotechnology companies in the world at any given time.

Genentech's genetics

In 1976, venture capitalist Robert Swanson joined molecular biologist Herbert Boyer to turn Boyer's patented gene-splicing technology into mass-produced genetically engineered substances, naming the project Genentech. The company went public in 1980 and its first product hit the market two years later. A bioengineered version of human insulin, it was purchased by Eli Lilly and marketed as Humulin. Genentech sold marketing rights for royalties to maintain its focus on research.

The first product to keep the Genentech name was the human growth hormone Protropin, approved by the FDA in 1985. Roche bought 60 percent of Genentech in 1990 for $2.1 billion, including some $500 million to preserve its long-term research pipeline. In 1995, Genentech's CEO Kirk Raab got the boot after an attempt to secure a $2 million personal loan from Roche and was replaced by scientist Arthur Levinson, a move seen by industry analysts as a symbol of the company's commitment to research and development.

Contributing to cancer cures

Cancer treatments are critical to Genentech's current financial success. The company currently manufactures four oncology treatments, which accounted for about 69 percent of total product sales in 2006. Genentech's best-selling drug is Rituxan, with sales of $2 billion in 2006, up from $1.8 billion the year prior. Approved by the FDA in 1997, Rituxan is a chimeric monoclonal antibody used for treating non-Hodgkin's lymphoma.

Relative newcomer Avastin, approved by the FDA in February 2004, is Genentech's second-best seller with 2006 sales of more than $1.8 billion, a 54 percent increase over 2005. Avastin is designed to be used in combination with intravenous chemotherapy as treatment for first-line metastatic colorectal cancer and is also approved for treatment of metastatic non-squamous non-small cell lung cancer.

Herceptin, an anti-HER2 antibody for metastatic breast cancer developed in conjunction with ImmunoGen, boasted more than $1.2 billion in total sales in 2006, up 65 percent from 2005. Genentech's other oncology treatment is Tarceva, a tumor growth factor inhibitor approved by the FDA in November 2004. It registered $402 million in sales during 2006, a 43 percent increase from 2005.

Not afraid of commitment

Genentech's research department, and the company's pride and joy, employs over 900 scientists and channels its capital into three disease categories: oncology, immunology and disorders of tissue growth and repair. The firm charges steep prices for these drugs. For instance, a year's supply of cancer treatment Avastin is about $55,000. However, the firm uses profits to pay for big R&D investments, as when it reinvested approximately 19 percent of its operating revenue in R&D in 2006.

Genentech funnels a great deal of its R&D budget towards its oncology product line, with departments that include molecular oncology, molecular biology, protein engineering, protein chemistry, physiology, pathology, bioorganic chemistry and bioinformatics. Genentech also has an immunology research team and a vascular biology squad.

Genentech of the west

Genentech conducts research at its South San Francisco headquarters, one of its three California work sites. Genentech's Vacaville site is located on 100 acres in Solano County, 50 miles northeast of San Francisco. Acquired in 1994, the facility houses more than 900 employees, who work in manufacturing operations and quality and administrative service. Currently under expansion, the Vacaville outfit will be the largest biotechnology manufacturing plant of its kind in the world when completed in 2009.

Located on 60 acres 35 miles north of San Diego, the Oceanside site (bought in June 2005) is a state-of-the-art biologics manufacturing plant. After receiving FDA licensure in April of 2007, the Oceanside operations added 90,000 liters of capacity dedicated to producing Avastin bulk drug substance.

In September 2006, Genentech acquired land west of Portland, in Hillsboro, Oregon. Construction of a new plant there is expected to be completed in 2008. The new site should be licensed and operational by 2010 and will employ approximately 300 employees by 2015.

In December 2006, the company sold a facility in Porriño, Spain, to Lonza. However, Lonza plans to continue manufacturing Avastin for Genentech through 2009. Genentech has an agreement under which the company can opt to purchase a Lonza manufacturing facility that's currently under construction in Singapore.

License to thrive

Genentech earned almost $1.4 billion in royalties in 2006, cashing in on patented practices used by other drug manufacturers. But in late September 2005 a potential threat emerged to a Genentech patent, covering techniques for making monoclonal antibodies. The patent was scheduled to expire in 2018 but in February 2007, the Patent and Trademark Office issued an office action in a re-examination that rejected the patentability of the claims. The government's decision on the patent could cost Genentech hundreds of millions of dollars over the coming decade. Genentech filed a petition for continued re-examination and the re-examination proceedings are ongoing.

Genentech vs. Genentech

In 2006, Genentech was set to debut Lucentis for the treatment of an eye disease that causes blindness in the elderly (wet macular degeneration). However, physicians say another, equally effective drug is already on the market, and at one-tenth the price— Avastin, another Genentech product. Although Avastin has achieved great success as a blockbuster colorectal cancer treatment, specialists have begun using it off-label as a treatment for the eye condition.

Lucentis and Avastin both bind to the same protein (VEGF) but Lucentis is designed and manufactured specifically for use in the eye. Probably aware of the potential overlap, Genentech stated concerns about the off-label use of Avastin, and has no

Visit Vault at **www.vault.com** for insider company profiles, expert advice, career message boards, expert resume reviews, the Vault Job Board and more.

VAULT CAREER LIBRARY   **161**

plans to officially study the drug for inter-ocular use. The two medications are scheduled for a head-to-head study in 2008, sponsored by the National Eye Institute.

High praise

In April 2007, the *San Francisco Business Times* ranked Genentech No. 1 on its list of Best Places to Work in the Bay Area. The company has been on *Fortune*'s Top 20 list of Most Admired Companies for the past four years and in 2007, *Fortune* placed Genentech in second place on its 2007 list of the 100 Best Places to Work. There's good reason for the accolades: the company's employees are incredibly loyal. With six-week paid sabbaticals available every six years, as well as a reputation for being a haven for scientists, Genentech retains some of the best researchers around.

Looking ahead

In somewhat of a departure for the traditionally pipeline-focused Genentech, the company acquired rival biotech firm Tanox for $919 million in August 2007. Indeed, the deal is Genentech's first-ever acquisition.

Tanox's main attraction is the asthma drug Xolair, which Genentech has been selling and paying royalties to Tanox for since its development in 1996. Genentech stated it would review Tanox's infrastructure to determine how to place its employees, although industry pundits hinted that layoffs could be imminent.

The firm received some bad news in December 2007, when an FDA panel narrowly voted—by a count of five to four—not to recommend approval of Avastin as an advanced breast cancer treatment. Genentech had reason to believe it would win the panel's favor, as, based on the same trials the FDA reviewed, Avastin has been approved for this purpose in Europe. Also, it is probably being prescribed for breast cancer off-label in America. The trials showed a notable delay in cancerous tumors worsening—11.3 months with Avastin instead of about six months without—but none of the test subjects lived longer as a result, the reason the FDA cited for recommending against the treatment. If the FDA votes to approve Avastin anyways, analysts estimate that would mean another $1 billion in sales for the drug.

GETTING HIRED

In good company

Want to work at Genentech? Better start studying. Of the company's approximately 10,500 employees, more than 80 percent have college degrees and more than 20 percent hold advanced degrees, including PhDs and MDs.

Candidates can find job openings on Genentech's corporate web site for jobs (www.gene.com/gene/careers); at press time openings were listed in many departments, including administration, business development, commercial operations/customer care, corporate and investor relations, drug development sciences, engineering/facilities/security, environmental health and safety, finance and accounting, human resources, information technology, legal, managed care, manufacturing, marketing, process development, procurement, product development, quality, regulatory affairs and compliance, research and discovery, sales, supply chain and training.

Great benefits

Genentech employees rave about "one of the best benefit packages in the country." "You will be hard-pressed to find a better benefit package around," says one satisfied insider, listing "medical, dental, vision, long-term disability, employee stock program, 401(k)." Employees get about 10 holidays plus three weeks vacation. After six years, regular full-time Genentech employees are rewarded with a six-week sabbatical. Other than that, though, one respondent claims there is "no increase in rewards or benefits with length of service."

There's also an "education reimbursement program so that you can take courses relative to your field, pursue a Master's or PhD and get reimbursed." Campus perks include "subsidized cafeterias, a credit union, travel department, medical services and an ATM." Health care coverage extends to the entire family of Genentech employees, including same-sex partners.

Educated and well regarded

Genentech's research division offers a postdoctoral program to recent PhD graduates. It pairs young researchers with Genentech's experienced scientists for a fellowship of approximately three years. Check out www.gene.com/gene/research/postdoctoral for information on how to apply.

OUR SURVEY SAYS

Still in school?

Genentech insiders indicate the firm has a distinctly collegiate air: "Basically my description in a nutshell would be that it's like a university atmosphere," says one. "It is more like a college campus than a company," says another. "The corporate culture closely mirrors the campus atmosphere of academia." Employees enjoy a "laid-back culture," with "no policy manuals." Those in research and development appreciate an atmosphere that is "encouraging of freedom." "The company understands that its future is new products and so tries to establish an environment conducive to creativity." This apparently extends to extracurricular projects: "Our scientists are allowed to work on their own projects several times a month."

Dust off those Birkenstocks

College campuses are, of course, usually devoid of suits. "Most people wear jeans and sneakers," says one source. Another agrees: "You will find the majority of employees in T-shirts, jeans, shorts, tennis shoes, Birks—oh—and lab coats, too." And what would college be without a little partying? "Genentech is a very social environment. On Friday, the company has 'Ho-Hos'—gatherings to mingle with co-workers and friends," reports one contact. These get-togethers, usually on campus between 5 and 7, are well loved by Genentech employees. One insider noted the presence of many "Genencouples."

In keeping with the theme, Genentech employees also enjoy "Date Night," a company-sponsored event that allows workers with children some free time with their spouse/significant other. The company day care center (dubbed 2nd Generation) stays open until 10 p.m. once every three months, babysitting in a "slumber-party" atmosphere. Genentech parents get a rare night alone. There is a fee ($20 for the first child, $16 for each additional sibling), but Genentech winds up picking up half the tab.

Student budgets

Unfortunately, Genentech insiders sometimes sound like starving graduate students. Some chalk it up to living in San Francisco. "Pay is decent but the Bay Area is really expensive." Others blame the company: "You might find better pay at one of the smaller biotech companies that seem to be popping up all over the Bay Area."

"Genentech pays slightly below the industry standard," says another, "but the human resources group is supposed to implement an adjustment based on the industry standard."

Not everyone is so optimistic: "The compensation is measly." A longtime employee believes that worker/manager relations are "worsening," claiming that the "pay gap has become too large." The environment is also somewhat reminiscent of college dorms, according to one insider, who states that office space is "often cramped and nonexistent at lower levels." However, the insider continues, "Management just built themselves new luxury offices."

Hardworking but happy

Sources report working "hard," "fast-paced" and "sometimes long hours." One says there is a minimum expected number of work hours (40) and "no limit as to how many hours you want to put in." However, respondents at the company appreciate flexible hours for non-shift workers: "there are no strict starting or quitting times." "People are very dedicated to science and hard work," comments one insider. "I have been with Genentech for nine years and have no plans of moving on," reports another, "even though in my position I have been offered several attractive opportunities with other biotech organizations."

Visit Vault at **www.vault.com** for insider company profiles, expert advice, career message boards, expert resume reviews, the Vault Job Board and more.

VAULT CAREER LIBRARY

165

Genzyme Corporation

500 Kendall Street
Cambridge, MA 02142
Phone: (617) 252-7500
Fax: (617) 252-7600
www.genzyme.com

LOCATIONS

Cambridge, MA (HQ)
Allston, MA • Exton, PA •
Framingham, MA • Los Angeles, CA •
Middleton, WI • Monrovia, CA • New
York, NY • North Miami Beach, FL •
Oklahoma City, OK • Orange, CA •
Philadelphia, PA • Phoenix, AZ • San
Antonio, TX • San Diego, CA • Santa
Fe, NM • Tampa, FL • Vienna, VA •
Waltham, MA • Washington, DC •
Westborough, MA • Yonkers, NY

International locations in:
Argentina • Australia • Austria •
Belgium • Brazil • Bulgaria • Canada •
Chile • China • Colombia • Croatia •
the Czech Republic • Denmark •
Finland • France • Germany • Greece
• Hong Kong • Hungary • Ireland •
Israel • Italy • Japan • Malaysia •
Mexico • Norway • The Netherlands •
Poland • Portugal • Romania • Russia
• Singapore • South Africa • South
Korea • Spain • Sweden •
Switzerland • Taiwan • Turkey • UK •
United Arab Emirates • Venezuela.

THE STATS

Employer Type: Public Company
Stock Symbol: GENZ
Stock Exchange: Nasdaq
CEO: Henri A. Termeer
2006 Employees: 9,000
2006 Revenue ($mil.): $3,187
2006 Net Income ($mil.): -$16.8

DEPARTMENTS

Accounting/Finance • Administrative •
Biomedical Operations/Biostatistics •
Business/Program Management •
Clinical Research • Competitive
Intelligence • Corporate
Communications • Customer Service •
Distribution/Logistics • Engineering •
Environmental Health & Safety •
Facilities Engineering • Genetic
Counseling • Human Resources •
Information Technology • Investor
Relations • Laboratory Technology •
Legal • Management • Manufacturing
& Development • Marketing • Materials
Management • Medical • Multimedia
Technology • Office Services •
Purchasing • Quality • Regulatory
Affairs • Reimbursement • Research &
Development • Sales •
Telecommunications

KEY COMPETITORS

Abbott Labs • Amgen • Chiron •
Genentech • Johnson & Johnson •
Quest Diagnostics

EMPLOYMENT CONTACT

www.genzyme.com/corp/careers

THE SCOOP

The broad view

Cambridge, Mass.-based Genzyme Corp. is a leading biotechnology company specializing in enzyme therapies for rare genetic diseases. Since its founding, Genzyme has evolved into a diversified global company with an annual revenue exceeding $3 billion, more than 25 products serving patients in nearly 90 countries, and employing over 9,000 people in more than 30 countries around the globe.

Genzyme's various businesses focus on six broad areas of medicine: lysosomal storage disorders, renal disease, orthopedics, transplant and immune diseases, oncology and genetics/diagnostics. The company is also committed to research and development, focusing some $565 million, or more than 17 percent of its revenue, on new treatments for genetic diseases, immune system disorders, cardiovascular disease and oncology.

From startup to prime time

Tufts University professor Henry Blair teamed with Sherman Snyder and Oak Ventures Partners to found the company in 1981. Genzyme became profitable in 1984 and went public two years later, then focused on diversifying through acquisitions, adding operations in fine chemicals, diagnostics and biotherapeutics.

In 1992, the company began constructing a state-of-the-art biopharmaceutical manufacturing facility in Allston, Mass., for making Cerezyme, a treatment in testing at the time. That same year, the company began work in gene therapy, focusing initially on cystic fibrosis. Genzyme began cancer research collaborations in 1997, and in 1998 received FDA approval for four drugs.

In October 2005, Genzyme announced a major real estate plan in three Massachusetts locations, including the expansion of the Allston facility, a new research center in Waltham and the construction of a new 177,000-square-foot research facility in Framingham. The Framingham site will have a six-story, glass-walled building that the company hopes will be the first research lab in America to win a "green building" certification.

Visit Vault at **www.vault.com** for insider company profiles, expert advice, career message boards, expert resume reviews, the Vault Job Board and more.

VAULT CAREER LIBRARY   **167**

No poor orphans here

Genzyme owes its success to treating so-called "orphan" diseases—afflictions with a patient population so small that other drugmakers would not deem research worth the effort. In 1984, Genzyme began clinical trials on a recombinant second-generation product called Cerezyme (imiglucerase for injection) that would become, two decades later, the company's unequivocal superstar with $1 billion in revenue in 2006, about 35 percent of the company's consolidated product revenue.

Cerezyme—which was introduced in 1991 and is manufactured at the company's plant in Allston, Mass.—is an intravenous drug that restores enzymes in lacking cells of patients suffering from Gaucher's disease. Fewer than 5,000 people worldwide use the drug, one of the world's most expensive at some $200,000 annually per patient. Gaucher's disease is a rare genetic condition in which patients are incapable of breaking down certain varieties of fats, which then build up in the body and can cause enlarged organs and weakened bones.

Finding its niche

The company continued to explore the lucrative nature of the niche drug market with Fabrazyme (agalsidase beta). Introduced in Europe in 2001 and two years later in the U.S., the drug is used to treat a genetic disorder called Fabry disease and costs about $200,000 a year. More than 1,900 patients in about 45 countries use the drug. Fabrazyme accounted for $359 million in sales in 2006, an 18 percent increase from 2005.

In July 2005, Genzyme filed an application with the FDA asking for priority approval of Myozyme, which would become the world's first treatment for Pompe disease, a genetic disease with fewer than 10,000 sufferers worldwide. The drug appeared to significantly improve survival for infants born with Pompe; these infants lack an enzyme responsible for clearing waste out of cells, leading to floppy muscles and severely enlarged hearts, seldom surviving their first year. In April 2006, the FDA approved Myozyme therapy for Pompe disease.

Buy, buy baby

With income provided by the continued success of Cerezyme, Genzyme has acquired a wide assortment of drugs and products developed by smaller firms, which are increasingly unlike its customary rare disease products. Genzyme bought Biomatrix in 2000, bringing in the artificial knee fluid product Synvisc. That same year,

Genzyme bought Geltex and with it control of Renagel, which reduces phosphate buildup in kidney-dialysis patients.

Genzyme's $1 billion purchase of Ilex Oncology in December 2004 strengthened its capacity in cancer products, research and development. And the May 2005 acquisition of Middleton, Wisc.-based Bone Care International boosted Genzyme's kidney disease product line with vitamin D substitute Hectorol, the second-highest-selling vitamin D substitute in the country, which is patent-protected until 2021.

Love thy neighbor, but build a fence

In January 2005, Genzyme sued Shire (well, the dispute began with Transkarotic Therapies Inc., but Shire bought that firm) in an Israeli court, alleging that Shire's method of distilling a treatment for Gaucher's disease infringed upon its proprietary technology. Shire claimed that Genzyme was looking for court permission to confiscate and demolish its experimental treatment, then being used in an Israeli clinical trial.

Genzyme argued that the disputed process was essential to its ability to produce Cerezyme. The suit did not represent the first time Genzyme and Shire had butted heads: in October 2003, the two rivals had settled disputes over two drugs and agreed to partner in developing another of Shire's drug candidates. During the lawsuit the two continued to partner in the development of Shire's I2S—an experimental treatment for Hunter's disease. (Basically, Hunter's disease is another rare genetic disorder that renders patients unable to process carbohydrates, leading to disfiguration and death.)

Ongoing oncology

With the acquisition of San Antonio's Ilex Oncology in January 2005, Genzyme drastically extended its cancer treatment line. Ilex brought with it two cancer treatments, Campath (for B-cell chronic lymphocytic leukemia) and Clolar (for children with lymphoblastic leukemia); both fit snugly into Genzyme's tradition of treating rare diseases, as only 2,900 patients in the U.S. qualify for Clolar, for example. Industry analysts noted that the demand for treatments of individual forms of cancer by Clolar and Campath closely resemble the rare genetic diseases on which Genzyme has traditionally focused.

In May 2007, Genzyme said it planned on buying out business partner Bioenvision Inc. for $345 million. Bioenvision had been sharing rights with Ilex (and thus,

Genzyme) in the cancer medication Clolar, and this deal would consolidate Genzyme's ownership of the drug. A certain Bioenvision shareholder then complained the bid was too low, but Genzyme stated in October 2007 that it had made its final offer.

Both companies wouldn't take shareholders' "no" for an answer, and petitioned a Delaware court judge to hold a revote on the merger, claiming that a JPMorgan shareholder missed the voting period by about 45 minutes, and that its votes would have won the day for the merger. Some of Bioenvision's shareholders have stated they've never seen companies go to such lengths to ensure a deal's survival. After holding the revote on October 23, 2007, shareholders voted in favor of the acquisition, and the purchase became effective on October 24, 2007.

You catch more flies with honey

In August 2006, Genzyme attempted to expand its oncological interests with a tender offer for AnorMED, a company specializing in drugs for hematology, oncology and HIV. Genzyme had its eye on AnorMED's Mozobil, a drug for hematopoietic stem cell transplantation (HSCT), for some time, believing that the company lacked the funding and expertise to fully exploit the value of the treatment. Genzyme's bid was $380 million in cash, a 70 percent premium over the value of AnorMED's outstanding shares. AnorMED, however, rejected these overtures, stating that the offer undervalued their company, leading Genzyme to take the offer directly to AnorMED's shareholders. But the hostile takeover strategy failed: the following month, AnorMED accepted a friendly offer of $515 million—a sweet premium of 40 percent over Genzyme's initial price—from Millennium Pharmaceuticals.

In October 2006, Genzyme sweetened the deal by offering approximately $580 million for AnorMED. The company completed its purchase of AnorMED for some $584 million in November 2006. Genzyme expects to apply for FDA approval of Mozobil in early 2008. Two other drugs in late stage clinical trials are alemtuzumab, for multiple sclerosis, and Tolevamer. If approved, Tolevamer could be the first nonantibiotic treatment for Clostridium difficile-associated diarrhea, which primarily affects patients in nursing homes and hospitals. In 2007, Genzyme also plans to apply for approval of next-generation versions of products Synvic and Renagel.

Sweet home Massachusetts

The firm is spreading money around internally, as well, announcing plans to expand its Allston Landing, Mass., facility with a $150 million investment in September 2007.

Within two years, it will add 90 new employees to the 400 already working at the plant. The expansion will also add more space for "manufacturing support functions," doubling the size of the building by nearly two-thirds to 300,000 square feet.

Executives and Massachusetts governmental officials have described the plan as a demonstration of the firm's commitment to the state. It also demonstrates a commitment to Massachusetts' famously liberal politics, as construction will seek environmental standard approval from the U.S. Green Building Council's LEED (Leadership in Energy and Environmental Design) rating system.

GETTING HIRED

Put Genzyme in your coconut

Genzyme's corporate web site includes a searchable database of job opportunities at www.genzyme.com/corp/careers. These are organized into categories such as accounting/finance, administrative, biomedical operations/biostatistics, business management, clinical research, competitive intelligence, corporate communications, customer service, distribution/logistics, engineering, environmental health and safety, facilities engineering, genetic counseling, human resources, information technology, investor relations, laboratory technology, legal, management, manufacturing and development, marketing, materials management; medical, multimedia technology, office services, purchasing, quality, regulatory affairs, reimbursement, research and development, sales and telecommunications.

In addition, the company has a college internship program. The firm offers an internship/co-op program for students in all life science disciplines, plus non-science opportunities such as marketing, finance, engineering, IT and operations. In addition, Genzyme offers internships for graduate and MBA students. Typically, internships run from May or June through August. More information about the company's internships and how to apply for them is online at www.genzyme.com/corp/careers/intern_positions.asp.

In the United States, all employees who work at least 20 hours per week are eligible for medical and dental insurance. Genzyme contributes approximately 80 percent toward the cost of medical and dental plan coverage. Other benefits include short- and long-term disability coverage, life insurance, a 401(k) plan with company matching, commuter assistance and a stock-purchase plan.

Visit Vault at **www.vault.com** for insider company profiles, expert advice, career message boards, expert resume reviews, the Vault Job Board and more.

VAULT CAREER LIBRARY

171

It can take time with Genzyme

Employees say applicants should expect multiple rounds of interviews with long wait times between." Another source, who describes the company's hiring process as "very comfortable," says, "I was hired after two phone interviews and an all-day interview session on site with a number of people." One insider adds, "HR moves at a snail's pace, and so do the business units. Skills are stressed."

For the fifth consecutive year, *Science* magazine named Genzyme a "Top Employer" in its annual 2007 survey for scientists in the biotechnology and pharmaceutical industries. In 2006 and 2007, *Fortune* selected Genzyme as one of the 100 Best Companies to Work for in the United States and the *Financial Times* listed it as one of the 100 Best Workplaces in Europe.

OUR SURVEY SAYS

Great benefits, low raises

Most insiders agree that Genzyme's benefits are good. An employee in the company's Cambridge office says Genzyme has "great benefits for health care, tuition reimbursement and 401(k)." Another employee mentions that there are "stock option grants every year that are immediately fully vested" and a "401(k) match up to 6 percent that is immediately fully vested." Employees can also buy discounted stock. Sources say leave time is generous, too. Their first five years at Genzyme, employees have three weeks of vacation per year, which goes up to four weeks of vacation after that. In addition, people have holidays, plus seven days of sick leave. There is also a "small company-paid life insurance policy on the employees."

Overall, employees say Genzyme pays okay, although they think raises could be higher. An administrative assistant warns, "expect only 2 to 5 percent per year." One source in New Mexico, who says the "average raise" is 3.5 percent, feels wages could be higher, too. The insider says, "Santa Fe is an expensive place to live, and the salaries are mediocre ... A number of our employees live in Albuquerque and commute 60 miles because the cost of living is cheaper. The company does maintain a fleet of three commuter vans for the benefit of the Albuquerque employees."

Problems with morale

At Genzyme, "there are plenty of bright people and the work environment is good." However, some employees say morale at the company has been declining. One insider feels that, since Genzyme acquired Impath, "the workplace has gone sharply downhill." The source adds, for two years we have been under a mandatory global overtime policy." Another feels that company is "top heavy with management," adding that Genzyme tends to be "bureaucratic" and sometime "slow moving." A source in the company's Cambridge office says, "While we are proud about the patients we help and the work we do, the lack of management is really hurting the organization."

Most people think the firm will continue to do well in spite of these problems. One respondent says, "The company has some good products on the market and in the pipeline." The source adds, "I worry a little that they are too slow-moving in the small molecule arena and overly used to the biologics side." Another insider feels that "Genzyme will have continued success" but thinks the company "will need to some big changes if it wants to retain good people."

Gilead Sciences, Inc.

333 Lakeside Drive
Foster City, CA 94404
Phone: (650) 574-3000
Fax: (650) 578-9264
www.gilead.com

LOCATIONS

Foster City, CA (HQ)
Durham, NC • San Dimas, CA •
Seattle, WA • Westminster, CO •
Alberta • Athens • Cambridge •
Cork • Dublin • Istanbul • Lisbon •
Madrid • Melbourne • Milan •
Munich • Ontario • Paris • Uxbridge,
UK • Vienna

THE STATS

Employer Type: Public Company
Stock Symbol: GILD
Stock Exchange: Nasdaq
President & CEO: John C. Martin
2006 Employees: 2,500
2006 Revenue ($mil.): $ 3,026
2006 Net Income ($mil.): -$1,190

KEY COMPETITORS

Bristol-Myers Squibb
GlaxoSmithKline
Merck
Roche

EMPLOYMENT CONTACT

www.gilead.com/wt/sec/careers

THE SCOOP

There is a biotechnological balm in Gilead

For over two decades, California-headquartered Gilead Sciences has focused on discovering, developing and commercializing small molecule therapeutics. This biotech firm's products treat patients with a wide range of life-threatening diseases, including HIV, systemic fungal infections and chronic hepatitis B. Gilead also receives royalties from other products, including Tamiflu for influenza and Macugen for age-related macular degeneration, an eye disease in the elderly.

The firm's revenue surpassed $3 billion in 2006, an increase of nearly 50 percent from 2005, when total revenue was about $2 billion.

Balmy beginnings

Gilead, mentioned in the Bible, was known for plants that produced a resin used in medicine—the famous Balm of Gilead. The company known as Gilead has a logo featuring a leaf, which symbolizes the healing power of science to treat life-threatening illnesses.

In 1987, a young doctor—with a background in venture financing—named Michael Riordan founded Gilead. For most of the next decade, Riordan secured funding while researching and developing drugs for viral diseases, mostly STDs and notably HIV. Riordan took the firm public in 1992, raising $86.25 million. The investment was crucial, as the company would not launch its first commercial product—Vistide, a drug for the treatment of AIDS-related eye infections—until 1996. Riordan stepped down as chairman of the firm in 1997, vacating the position in favor of board member Donald Rumsfeld. (Rumsfeld stepped down in 2001, when President George W. Bush appointed him secretary of defense.)

Acquiring minds want to know ...

Rumsfeld steered Gilead into some big buys, most notably that of the much larger NeXstar in 1999. Gilead had been negotiating with NeXstar—a Colorado-based drug discovery firm that had grossed three times the sale of its purchaser in 1998—since April 1997, almost immediately after Rumsfeld had taken over as chairman.

Over the course of 1999, the company moved to transform itself into a biopharmaceutical company with a global presence focused on infectious disease, picking up two major products: fungal treatment AmBisone and anticancer agent DaunoXome. Then, in 2003, Gilead bought Triangle Pharmaceuticals and announced its first full year of profitability—a proud accomplishment for a company digesting so many purchases. In the coming years, the firm launched several products, including Truvada and Atripla.

Treating HIV/AIDS

Despite its rapid growth, Gilead's main focus is still HIV drugs, the same subject it studied without cease during the latter half of the 1980s. The company's HIV franchise generated $2 billion in sales (82 percent of the company's revenue) in 2006. Its top-selling drug is HIV treatment Truvada, which moved nearly $1.2 billion in 2006, more than twice its 2005 figures. The company's second-best selling drug is Viread, another antiretroviral drug, which had about $689 million in sales in 2006, a slight drop from approximately $779 million in 2005.

In May 2006, two AIDS advocacy groups in India asked the country's authorities to stop Gilead from patenting Viread, available in India as a generic drug. The groups argued that if Viread was patented and the cheaper versions became illegal, the drug would become too expensive for patients in India and other parts of the developing world.

Gilead responded that it would not block access to Gilead's HIV medication in India or in other developing countries affected by the AIDS epidemic. By the end of 2006, the company had completed regulatory submissions for Viread in nearly 97 resource-limited nations. The company also reached nonexclusive license agreements with 11 Indian generic drugmakers to manufacture and distribute generic versions of the medication in developing countries. Gilead also makes the company's drugs available to low-income patients in the United States through its Advancing Access program.

Glad to be Gilead

In recent years, the company has begun tackling other illnesses besides HIV and AIDS, both through acquisitions and in-house development. In August 2006, Gilead acquired Corus Pharma, a company committed to developing and commercializing products for respiratory diseases. Through this $415.5 million purchase, Gilead gained aztreonam lysine, a phase III drug candidate for the potential treatment of lung infections in cystic fibrosis patients.

Then, in November 2006, Gilead purchased Myogen for about $2.5 billion. In doing so, Gilead gained ownership of Ambrisentan, a potential treatment for pulmonary arterial hypertension. The drug was in late-stage clinical trials when Gilead acquired Myogen and was approved by the FDA in June 2007. Through the acquisition, Gilead also grabbed up darusentan, a promising candidate for the treatment of resistant hypertension, and Flolan, a therapeutic indicated for the treatment of primary pulmonary hypertension.

Looking forward

In terms of in-house development, Gilead's 2006 R&D expenses represented a dramatic leap forward from previous years, clocking in at $384 million, compared to $278 million for 2005 and $224 million for 2004. One product the firm is working on is GS 9190, a novel compound to treat hepatitis C. GS 9190 is currently in early clinical development.

The firm has an HIV drug in the pipeline as well: GS 9137, a once-a-day integrase inhibitor. The company is currently testing the drug, licensed from Japan Tobacco. Unlike other medications that are currently marketed for HIV, integrase inhibitors target a different stage in the virus' replication cycle. Combined with other anti-retrovirals, they may effectively prevent the replication of the virus, particularly a drug-resistant form of HIV, in the body. However, Gilead's drug is 18 months to two years behind Merck's new integrase inhibitor, raltegravir.

GETTING HIRED

Getting in with Gilead

Interested applicants can apply online for positions through Gilead's career web site at sh.webhire.com/servlet/resp/grf?acctid=273. Job seekers can also search specific job categories, which include administrative, biology, chemistry, clinical/regulatory/drug safety, commercial operations (sales), business development, facilities/EH&S, finance/investor relations, HR, IT, legal, medical affairs/communications, pharmacology, project management, public affairs, QA/QC/manufacturing, sales administration, toxicology/metabolism and marketing.

In addition, Gilead offers a variety of internships. In Foster City, Calif., the company has paid MBA internships in marketing, finance and corporate development.

Students must be currently enrolled in a full-time MBA program to apply. The company also offers paid scientific internships in Foster City. Students should be in their junior year and need a B average or better to apply. For scientific internships, they also need to have completed at least one lab course. Internships are posted online, and students can apply by visiting the current opportunities section of Gilead's career web site.

Some 60 percent of Gilead's staff works in research and development functions. Another 23 percent is in sales and marketing and 17 percent of Gilead's employees are in general and administrative positions.

In 2007, Gilead Sciences appeared on *Forbes'* 400 Best Big Companies list for the second time. Benefits at Gilead include a medical plan with several coverage options, dental care, vision care, life insurance, long- and short-term disability coverage, a stock-option plan, tuition reimbursement for job-related courses and a company-matched 401(k) retirement plan.

GlaxoSmithKline PLC

980 Great West Road, Brentford
London, TW8 9GS
United Kingdom
Phone: +44-20-8047-5000
Fax: +44-20-8047-7807
www.gsk.com

LOCATIONS

London (HQ)
Aiken, SC • Bristol, TN • Clifton, NJ
• Collegeville, PA • Conshohocken,
PA • Durham, NC • Hamilton, MT •
King of Prussia, PA • Marietta, PA •
Memphis, TN • Parsippany, NJ •
Piscataway, PA • Pittsburgh, PA •
Philadelphia, PA • Raleigh, NC • St.
Louis, MO • Upper Merion, PA •
Upper Providence, PA • Zebulon, NC

International locations in 39
countries worldwide.

THE STATS

Employer Type: Public Company
Stock Symbol: GSK
Stock Exchange: NYSE, LSE
Chairman: Sir Christopher Charles
 (Chris) Gent
President & CEO: Andrew Witty
2006 Employees: 100,000
2006 Revenue ($mil.): $45,500
2006 Net Income ($mil.): $10,557

DEPARTMENTS

Administrative
Business Development
Clinical
Corporate/Public Affairs
Engineering
Environmental Health & Safety
Facilities
Finance
Human Resources
Information Technology
Legal
Logistics
Managed Care
Manufacturing
Marketing
Procurement
Project Management
Quality & Validation
Regulatory Affairs
Sales
Scientific

KEY COMPETITORS

Novartis AG
Pfizer Inc.
sanofi-aventis

EMPLOYMENT CONTACT

www.gsk.com/careers

Visit Vault at **www.vault.com** for insider company profiles, expert advice,
career message boards, expert resume reviews, the Vault Job Board and more.

VAULT CAREER LIBRARY   179

THE SCOOP

Gargantuan Glaxo

Forged from four sizeable and formerly independent pharmaceutical companies, GlaxoSmithKline is one of the industry's giants. Company revenue totaled more than $45 billion in 2006. In addition to prescription medications, Glaxo also manufactures vaccines, over-the-counter (OTC) drugs, oral care products and nutrition drinks, marketing more than 1,200 different brands in more than 140 countries worldwide.

Glaxo is Europe's largest pharmaceutical company, and the world's second-largest in terms of sales; and its massive proportions are reflected throughout the organization. The company's massive $5 billion annual research and development budget is among the largest in the industry—it spends roughly $14 million per day (or $562,000 per hour!) on its studies. And Glaxo has a lot of resources for selling its drugs, too—a 40,000-strong sales force keeps products moving out of the warehouses and into the market. The result of these expenditures? Glaxo's annual pharmaceutical sales make up about 7 percent of the global market.

Glaxo, headquartered in the U.K., also has facilities in 39 countries, including a highly significant presence in the U.S. Overall, the company employs over 100,000 people, and its sales and marketing force, which totals more than 40,000 workers, is the largest in the industry. About 15,000 more employees work in the company's 24 research and development laboratories.

A tale of many mergers—and baby food

One would never guess it from this firm's ultra-modern sounding "Glaxo" name, but this company has roots stretching back to the era of industrial revolution and maritime commerce—the 19th century. In 1873, an England-born New Zealander named Joseph Nathan started a company for the importing and exporting of all sorts of goods, including medicines. He eventually retired to London, leaving his business—Joseph Nathan & Co.—to be run by his sons.

In the process of running the family business, one of Nathan's sons discovered a process of drying milk. The Nathans were soon making and selling this product as Glaxo Baby Food, with the memorable slogan, "Builds Bonnie Babies." By World War I, the business was based out of the U.K. and highly profitable. Baby food offerings led the firm into vitamins in the 1920s and into a fitting combination of its two pursuits in the 1930s—a top-selling vitamin-enriched milk, called "Ostremilk."

It was during World War II that Joseph Nathan & Co. ceased existence and Glaxo emerged as a pharmaceutical force, initially to peddle huge amounts of penicillin. The company truly came of scientific age in the postwar period, when it isolated vitamin B12 —essential for treating anaemia—at virtually the same exact time as Merck did, across the ocean.

By the 1970s, Glaxo (in collaboration with Hoffman-Laroche, now Roche) had produced its own antiulcer drug, Zantac. The drug was taking in one quarter of the prescriptions market by 1984, and soon began selling stateside. The next year, Glaxo underwent its first major merger, joining with the even older firm Wellcome.

Wilkommen Wellcome! And SmithKline and Beecham, too!

Wellcome was founded in London in the 1870s by a young man named Silas Burroughs, fresh out of the Philadelphia College of Pharmacy. He entered into business with Henry Wellcome in 1880, retitling the firm Burroughs Wellcome & Co. After Burroughs' death in 1895, Henry Wellcome managed the company for 30 more years, handing it off to the British government during World War I.

The next aged pharmaceutical firm to join the Glaxo family was SmithKline Beecham, founded in 1830 by Philadelphia druggist John K. Smith (bookkeeper Mahlon Kline joined in 1865). The firm acquired French, Richards & Co. in 1891, expanding both its repertoire (with perfumes, cough medicines and home remedies) and its name (to Smith, Kline & French). The firm soon became one of the first in America to expand its trade south of the border.

Smith, Kline & French's major 20th century drugs included Thorazine, released in the 1950s, and Tagamet, released in 1976 and becoming the world's first drug to earn $1 billion per year in 1989. The company underwent a number of major mergers that affected its masthead, starting in 1982 with Allergan and Beckman Instruments, changing the firm's name to SmithKline Beckman. In 1989, SmithKline traded a "Beckman" for a "Beecham," merging with the Beecham Group to form SmithKline Beecham.

Thomas Beecham had formed his eponymous company in 1842, selling a laxative called Beecham's Pills. In 1895, the company founded the world's first medicine factory in St. Helens, England, churning out treatments in bulk. In the 20th century,

Beecham discovered the penicillin nucleus (in 1959), which enabled mass generic reproduction; the group also discovered amoxicillin in 1972, now one of the world's most-prescribed substances.

These varied and proud companies merged together in 2000, when Glaxo Wellcome and SmithKline Beecham joined forces to become Glaxo SmithKline. At the time, it was the world's largest pharmaceutical company.

Inside Glaxo's medicine cabinet

Today, Glaxo has an extensive line of prescription drugs, with successes in anti-infection, central nervous system (CNS), respiratory and anti-viral medications. Among the company's best known products are medications that help regulate the central nervous system. Paxil, a selective serotonin re-uptake inhibitor (SSRI), treats depression, panic attacks, posttraumatic stress disorder, obsessive-compulsive disorder and anxiety disorders. Other Glaxo CNS medications include the antidepressant Wellbutrin and the migraine headache treatment Imitrex.

Two of Glaxo's other blockbusters are the respiratory medications Advair and Flovent, among the most commonly prescribed for asthma patients. The company has also been at the forefront in the development of antiviral drugs to treat HIV, currently producing three different antiviral medications: Retrovir, Epivir and Ziagen. Glaxo also manufactures a number of drugs related to these core antivirals: Combivir (a dosage formula that contains Retrovir and Epivir), Epzicom (a combination of Epivir and Ziagen) and Trizivir (which combines all three substances).

GlaxoSmithKline also boasts consumer products and over-the-counter medications, such as the antacid Tums, Citrucel laxatives and Contac cold medicine. For smokers looking to kick the habit, Glaxo offers Nicorette gum and the Nicoderm patch. Its oral care products include the Aquafresh, Sensodyne, Polident and Poligrip brands.

In September 2005, Glaxo added another big name to its stash—Canadian vaccine maker ID Biomedical. Valued at a whopping $1.4 billion, the acquisition increases Glaxo's flu vaccine line and, perhaps more importantly, helps offset rival Novartis' entry into the flu market (the firm paid $5.1 billion for 58 percent of Chiron it did not already own in October 2005). In a transaction valued at approximately $566 million, Glaxo scooped up CNS in 2006. Minnesota-based CNS makes FiberChoice dietary fiber supplements and Breathe Right nasal strips.

Taking a hit ...

In 2004, many dire predictions about the effect generic drugs would have on Glaxo's bottom line began to come true. In the second quarter of 2004, the company's profits fell a full 13 percent due to a weak dollar and generic competition, the company announced in July. On the upside, Glaxo also announced that sales in its diabetes franchise, which includes Avandia and Avandamet, surged 59 percent to $556 million and sales of asthma medication Advair were also strong, rising 22 percent to $1 million.

Meanwhile, Glaxo was hard at work on developing a number of new products, including Vesicare, for overactive bladder; Rotarix, a vaccine for rotavirus, and Epivir/Ziagen, a combination of two existing AIDS drugs. The FDA approved Vesicare in 2004, and the drug became available across the U.S. in early 2005. The Epivir/Ziagen combo also won the FDA's approval in 2004 and is now sold under the name Epzicom. Glaxo is thinking even bigger with its Rotarix vaccine, which won approval from the World Health Organization in April 2007; this WHO ratification allowed U.N. agencies to purchase it in bulk.

And, in an OTC twist of its own, Glaxo announced in July 2004 that it had acquired the rights to market the popular obesity drug Xenical from rival Roche. In February 2007, the FDA approved the drug, which will be sold over-the-counter as Alli.

... and coming back swinging

In 2006, the company's revenue from pharmaceutical sales grew 9 percent, to more than $39 billion. Seretide/Advair brought in more than $6.4 billion in revenue, an 11 percent increase from 2005. And GSK's diabetes drugs continue to be among its best sellers. Sales of the Avandia group of products were $3.2 billion for the year, up 25 percent from 2005.

The company is actively engaged in researching new drugs to replace former blockbusters whose profits are waning or will largely disappear after losing patent protection. In the first half of 2005, Glaxo received FDA approval for two new drugs, the first of which was Boniva, a once-monthly pill designed for women battling osteoporosis to be jointly promoted by its makers, Glaxo and Roche.

The other new drug approved in 2005 was Requip, Glaxo's treatment for restless leg syndrome and Parkinson's disease. In Boniva's first full year, the company's share of co-promotion income for the drug was around $423 million. Requip also performed strongly in the U.S., where its sales in 2006 grew 74 percent, to $525 million.

Other products in the pipeline are combinations of current hits, such as Avandaryl, launched in the U.S. in February 2006, which combines two oral diabetes medications. Glaxo expects to launch other new drugs in 2007, including migraine medication Trexima, a combination of current hit Imitrex (which goes off patent in 2009) and naproxen sodium. The firm has also filed for FDA approval of two follow-on products for Requip— Requip XL 24-hour Requip CR—which it expects will boost the drug's sales further.

Disappointing development

One new drug that will not be hitting the market is Entereg, a drug to treat postsurgical patients with gastrointestinal ailments, for which Glaxo had once had high hopes. The drug, which Glaxo developed with Adolor Corp., was moving through the FDA approval process when Glaxo entered phase III trials in September 2005. However, GSK and Adolor suspended trials of Entereg in April 2007 after it was linked to heart problems, skin cancers and bone fractures.

In-flu-ential deals

Other new business revolves around the flu vaccine market. Glaxo has taken strides to gain firm footing in this arena through two major acquisitions: a $300 million deal for Corixa Corporation, a Seattle-based biopharmaceutical company, in April 2005; and a whopping $1.4 billion for the Canadian flu-vaccine maker ID Biomedical Corp. in September of that year.

In August 2005, Glaxo received FDA approval for its flu vaccine, Fluarix, and also purchased rival Wyeth's vaccine production and research operations in Marietta, Penn., for an undisclosed amount. Glaxo predicted that by 2015, the global market for vaccines would be between $31 billion and $44 billion.

In March 2007, Glaxo announced that trial data from two new studies indicated that the company's pre-pandemic influenza vaccine could protect against different strains of H5N1 (Avian Influenza A). The following month, Glaxo received a $63.3 million contract from the U.S. Department of Health and Human Services to develop pandemic flu vaccines.

Glaxo's ventures into vaccines go beyond flu shots into the "mine is better than yours" area. The company initiated a clinical study about human papillomavirus

(HPV) vaccines in January 2007, comparing Glaxo's Cervarix head-to-head with Merck's Gardasil, the leading vaccine in the field. With the study, Glaxo hopes to show that its vaccine provides protection against different strains of the virus for the longest period of time. The firm launched Cervarix in September.

The firm's overall vaccine sales increased 23 percent in 2006, and soared in the U.S., increasing by 40 percent.

Levitra vs. Viagra vs. Cialis

Hindered by generic competition, Glaxo was looking for a successful new product in 2003. It believed it had found the solution with the erectile dysfunction treatment Levitra, co-developed with Bayer to compete with Viagra, Pfizer's earth-shaking blockbuster. The drug, having already received approval from inspectors in the European Union in March, was approved by the FDA for sale in the U.S. in August 2003—which cleared it for sale in more than 50 countries.

Glaxo tapped former NFL coach Mike Ditka as its spokesman, a move that mimicked the method used by Pfizer, which made Viagra a household name with former senator and presidential candidate Bob Dole as its voice. The field is a crowded one, though, as Eli Lilly (with help from the biotech firm ICOS) released its own ED drug, Cialis, in late 2003.

And Levitra didn't quite live up to Glaxo's expectations; it pulled in sales of $248 million in 2004, while Viagra's sales topped $1 billion in the same year. Bayer paid GSK $272 million the next year, regaining a great measure of Levitra's marketing rights. The two companies continue to co-market the impotence pill in the United States, but Glaxo's share of Levitra sales in 2006 was only about $84 million.

Paxil problems

Paxil, GlaxoSmithKline's popular antidepressant, pulled in $1.9 billion in U.S. sales overall in the calendar year 2003. And these figures would have been even greater that year if not for the Canadian generic drug firm Apotex and a negative appellate court ruling.

In March 2003, a U.S. Court of Appeals for the Federal Circuit ruled that Glaxo's patent for Paxil was invalid since the invention was publicly used for over a year before patent application. The next September, Apotex released a generic version of the drug and GSK's sales for the drug plummeted by 39 percent over the course of 2004.

Meanwhile, in February 2005, Glaxo was forced to pull some batches of Paxil CR, a timed-release version of the antidepressant, due to some pills splitting apart. Two months later, Glaxo announced it had identified and addressed the cause of the defects and instituted an independent observer at the factory where the drugs were produced. Analysts guess that it wouldn't be back on the market until 2006, but Glaxo was selling it by July 2005.

In 2006, total sales of Paxil grew 4 percent from 2005, bringing in more than $1.2 billion. This increase was in part due to strong growth of Paxil CR in the U.S.

Let's settle this

In August 2006, GSK reached an agreement to settle claims by over 40 states alleging the company had inflated prices on drugs used to treat cancer patients. The suit, brought by hard-charging, steamrolling (and later governorship-winning) New York Attorney General Eliot Spitzer, charged that the company had inflated the average price of wholesale antiemitic drugs used to combat nausea in patients undergoing chemotherapy.

The $41 million settlement included more than $1.5 million to New York state's Medicaid program for cancer treatments and $940,000 for overpriced antibiotics. At the same time, Glaxo announced a $40 million restitution fund for Medicaid recipients nationwide.

The following month, GSK agreed to pay $3.1 billion to settle another dispute in which the IRS charged the company with engaging in "transfer pricing," a maneuver designed to reduce taxable U.S. profits by overpaying international subsidiaries for product supplies. The IRS' beef with GSK extended all the way back to an audit first begun in 1992 by the tax authority of GSK's corporate predecessor, Glaxo Wellcome. The settlement reached in 2006 concerned activity from 1989 to 2000 (set to go to trial in 2007) as well as from 2001 to 2005 (which had not yet received a trial date).

Taking legal arms to protect its patents

But Glaxo has been the aggressor in lawsuits, as well. In October 2007, the company sued the U.S. Patent and Trademark Office, taking issue with new rules set to take effect the following November 1st. The new rules attempt to tackle the PTO's growing backlog of patent applications, especially as large drug firms tinker with their drugs to extend their shelf-life and protection from generic competition. If

Glaxo's lawsuit is unsuccessful, the firm won't be able to apply for as many patents or for as many reasons.

Avast, ye Avandia!

The company received some bad new—or a bad news report—in May 2007, when the *New England Journal of Medicine* reported a 43 percent increase in the risk of heart attacks from the use of Avandia, its top-selling diabetes treatment. The American government then immediately launched a congressional inquiry, and regulatory agencies worldwide began to reevaluate the drug.

Later that May, the FDA stated that Glaxo had expressed similar concerns about Avandia in August 2006, and that the two were working on contrasting studies. The FDA also advised people using Avandia to check with their doctors about cardiovascular risks and is considering restricting its use somewhat.

The other shoe dropped in July—sort of. That month, the government's report confirmed the risk of heart attacks with the drug and the FDA convened an extraordinary meeting to assess whether to remove it from the market. A number of officials came out strongly against the drug—one estimated it causes 1,600 to 2,200 heart attacks and strokes per month—but the panel voted overwhelmingly not to take drastic regulatory action (22 to 1 against regulating its marketing and 20 to 3 against heart attack risk). The panel did recommend a more explicit warning on its label.

In October, the European Medicines Agency took a similar course, revising its labeling of the drug while still approving Avandia for widespread use. In the meantime, sales have dropped dramatically for the drug that grossed over $3 billion in 2006; *The New York Times* estimated that the drug's sales had dropped by as much as 60 percent from May to October 2007. Over a similar period, from March to October 2007, Glaxo's stock price tumbled by 12 percent.

The drug is also losing some major clients, such as the U.S. Department of Veterans Affairs, which decided to severely limit its prescription of the drug, also in October. Finally, as if October wasn't momentous enough for Avandia, Glaxo settled a lawsuit with generic drug manufacturer Teva Pharmaceutical later in the month—Teva will now market three generic versions of Glaxo drugs in the U.S., one of which is Avandia.

In search of the next big boss

Also perhaps related to Glaxo's current ups-and-downs is the long (and "unusual," according to *The Wall Street Journal*) process to settle on the firm's next CEO. Since 2005, the firm has been focused on replacing the retiring CEO Jean-Pierre Garnier. And three internal candidates have been the front-runners all along—Chris Viehbacher, president of U.S. pharmaceuticals; David Stout, president of pharmaceutical operations; and Andrew Witty, president of European pharmaceuticals.

But management might have been distracted by their two-year vetting, which has gone through many channels and directions. Glaxo Chairman Christopher Gent has discussed hiring options with major shareholders and hired outside consultants to evaluate each candidate's "leadership capabilities." For quite some time, these executives were focused not only on steering the firm, but on competing with each other. Retiring CEO Garnier told the *Journal* that it's "unusual" for a company to have more than one qualified CEO prospect, and that's necessitated this "fair process."

And what has the process been like? Actually, it sounds like a Vault survey, as these external consultants have interviewed each executive's staff for details of their management style, personality, etc. The process has also shed different light on company events where each of the three CEOs-to-be have essentially campaigned for the job, such as when Stout, Witty and Viehbacher each addressed the company at Glaxo's biennial retreat in late 2005. According to the *Journal*, onlookers dubbed the event "the beauty contest." In October 2007, the winner was announced: the youngest CEO in Glaxo history, 43-year-old Andrew Witty. He will take the top post in May 2008.

In search of the next big thing

GSK moved into the realm of biotech with its 2006 purchase of Domantis, a U.K.-based firm that has been researching antibody-based treatments for various illnesses. The deal went down for $454 million, and is quite the fashionable pharmaceutical purchase, as it follows on the heels of similar moves by Merck and AstraZeneca. Domantis' medicines are based around antibodies designed to attack cancer cells, although the company is investigating a similar mechanism to come up with treatments for asthma, chronic obstructive pulmonary disease and rheumatoid arthritis.

The main innovation that Domantis brings to the table is its method of creating small antibody molecules that can enter the body orally. (Current antibody medications must be injected because the molecules are too large to be absorbed through the digestive tract.) That said, don't expect to see any blockbuster drugs from this venture any time soon: analysts do not expect a viable treatment to come out of Domantis for another five to 10 years.

One cancer treatment that could make a difference immediately for GSK's bottom line is Tykerb, used to treat certain types of advanced breast cancer that haven't responded to treatment. Prescribed for use in conjunction with Roche Holding's Xeloda, Tykerb enters cancer cells to inhibit the production of HER2 or EGFR proteins, which control cancer growth. Scientists estimate that 20 to 25 percent of all breast cancer cases could be responsive to the treatment.

As a sign of their confidence in Tykerb, Glaxo asked the FDA to fast-track their review of the product. When the FDA did indeed approve the drug in March 2007, Glaxo said it would begin production within a month. Furthermore, the company said Tykerb— $2,900 for a month's supply —would be part of an expanded access program, available free for those without health insurance or below certain income levels.

But in the meantime ...

Andrew Witty's ideas are already being put into practice; ideas to cut costs and apportion layoffs, that is. In November 2007, the firm responded to the rapidly falling sales of Avandia and a less profitable third quarter than expected by announcing job cuts in sales and R&D. Some of Witty's ideas will be put to use to overhaul the sales force on a global level, transforming it into a more efficient unit. The firm will also close some manufacturing plants, outsourcing the difference in production. which will result in a $1.5 billion charge for the company's fiscal year.

A good place to be

Free Tykerb is just one example of Glaxo's good deeds. The company is known for its philanthropic efforts. The firm received the Committee Encouraging Corporate Philanthropy's excellence in corporate philanthropy award in 2007. GSK's donations for all of 2006 were valued at $558 million.

One disease the company has tried to eradicate is lymphatic filariasis (LF), a tropical infection that can cause permanent disability. Glaxo is a founding member of the Global Alliance to Eliminate Lymphatic Filariasis. The company also supported HIV/AIDS programs in 17 countries in 2006. The GSK African Malaria Partnership fights that disease.

In addition, GSK supports underserved communities worldwide with education, donations and funding. Employees in the U.S. are encouraged to donate time to good causes through Days of Caring, a United Way program that connects volunteers with nonprofit organizations for short-term community service projects. In many countries, the company matches employees' cash donations to charities.

GETTING HIRED

21 ways to join Glaxo

Open positions in the U.S. and in Europe are listed on the careers section of Glaxo's web site (www.gsk.com/careers). Job seekers can search for opportunities in one of 21 departments: administrative, business development, clinical, corporate/public affairs, engineering, environmental health and safety, facilities, finance, human resources, information technology, legal, logistics, managed care, manufacturing, marketing, procurement, project management, quality and validation, regulatory affairs, sales and scientific.

In 2006, the U.S.-based Human Rights Campaign Foundation gave Glaxo a perfect score for corporate equity in an annual report card. And *Working Mother* magazine loves GSK—naming the company to is Hall of Fame in 2006. Later, in September 2007, *Working Mother* named Glaxo one of the 100-best companies in the U.S., the 16th consecutive occurrence of this recognition.

Rounds and rounds

Most GSK insiders say they had several rounds of interviews during the hiring process. A GSK salesperson says there are typically three or more rounds of interviews. Another GSK employee "had to meet with five different people for an hour each," and a scientist says the "interview process involved seven interviews and a presentation."

Most sources say interviews were fairly standard. The scientist explains, "Overall, questions centered around my experience as relevant to the position." This insider adds that "no line of questioning seemed out of the ordinary, and any standard interview prep would suffice to answer the majority of questions." An respondent in sales however, says, "The interview is very difficult, takes a great deal of preparation and interview performance."

OUR SURVEY SAYS

A great employer

Sources describe GSK as "the best employer I have had thus far" and say that working for the company is "very enjoyable." One source says, "The benefit and vacation package—which starts immediately from your first day of work—is excellent, and the staff is just wonderful." A sales manager adds, "The people are great and the company encourages diversity in thought. The corporate climate is realistic, candid and positive."

Many insiders at GSK say their standard work week is 35 or 40 hours a week. One source says, "The corporate culture is outstanding. They really value diversity, professionalism and employee satisfaction. The employee benefits—paid time off, company car, pay—are unmatched." One big perk is a business casual dress code.

Moving on up?

Sources generally say there are opportunities for career growth at GSK and a director says there are opportunities for advancement. An insider in sales adds, "GlaxoSmithKline is a very large company and the opportunities for advancement are almost limitless." But one insider feels that "opportunities for advancement seem to be limited within R&D, unless one is a PhD," and a pharmaceutical rep also says it can be difficult to move up in the ranks at GSK.

GSK should do okay

Overall, GSK staffers are optimistic about the company's future. One respondent says growth is expected to be between 20 and 40 percent over next few years. Someone in sales adds, "The company should continue to do very on Wall Street." Another source says, "GSK arguably has the strongest pipeline in the industry with around 90 to 100 drugs in development. The financials are also very strong and indications from the employment side are strong since the company is actively hiring 1,200 to 1,500 per year."

Visit Vault at **www.vault.com** for insider company profiles, expert advice, career message boards, expert resume reviews, the Vault Job Board and more.

VAULT CAREER LIBRARY   **191**

Hospira, Inc.

275 North Field Drive
Lake Forest, IL 60045
Phone: (224) 212-2000
Fax: (224) 212-3350
www.hospira.com

LOCATIONS

Lake Forest, IL (HQ)
Aguadilla, PR • Ashland, OH •
Atlanta, GA • Austin, TX • Buffalo,
NY • Clayton, NC • Dallas, TX •
King of Prussia, PA • Los Angeles,
CA • McPherson, KS • Morgan Hill,
CA • Pleasant Prairie, WI • Rocky
Mount, NC • San Diego, CA •
Adelaide, Australia • Finisklin,
Ireland • La Aurora, Costa Rica •
Liscate, Italy • Montreal • San
Cristobal, Dominican Republic

THE STATS

Employer Type: Public Company
Stock Symbol: HSP
Stock Exchange: NYSE
Chairman & CEO: Christopher B.
 Begley
2006 Employees: 13,000
2006 Revenue ($mil.): $2,689
2006 Net Income ($mil.): $238

DEPARTMENTS

Accounting & Finance
Administrative
Engineering
Human Resources
Information Technology
Legal
Manufacturing & Operations
Medical Affairs
Public/Investor Relations
Quality Assurance & Regulatory
 Affairs
Sales & Marketing
Science
Technical Support

KEY COMPETITORS

Abraxis BioScience
Baxter International
Becton Dickinson

EMPLOYMENT CONTACT

careers.hospira.com

THE SCOOP

How about Hospira?

Although it doesn't sound like it, Hospira has been a leader in the hospital products business for over 70 years. For the great span of that time, Hospira was the hospital products division of pharmaceutical giant Abbott Laboratories, and the Hospira name was created in 2004, when Abbott spun its hospital assets into a publicly traded company. With the goal of "advancing wellness," the company develops, manufactures and markets a wide range of products for hospitals, clinics, home healthcare providers and long-term care facilities.

The company's products span several areas: medication management systems; IV sets, solutions and irrigation; drug delivery systems; pharmaceuticals; invasive monitoring systems and suction systems. In 2006, Hospira's revenue reached nearly $2.7 billion, about a 2 percent increase from 2005. The bulk of the company's 2006 sales, some 83 percent, were in the United States.

In 2007, Hospira ranked 697th on *Fortune*'s list of America's largest companies, a slight drop from 2006, when the company's rank was No. 660.

Hospira history

As the hospital products business of Abbott Laboratories, Hospira discovered and launched Pentothal, one of the most widely used induction anesthetics, in the 1930s. Later, the company introduced the first fully disposable IV administration set and the first patient-controlled analgesia device. In the 1990s, the company debuted premixed solutions, prefilled syringes and needleless products. In the 2000s, Hospira introduced bar coding on IV solutions and injectable drugs. The firm also created Hospira MedNet, a drug-dose safety software that helps reduce medication error.

Hospira became an independent public company when Abbott Laboratories spun off its hospital products business in April 2004. Why did the two part ways? Because, said Abbott, hospital products were no longer a primary focus. Abbott's shareholders received one Hospira share for every 10 shares of Abbott that they held and Hospira successfully completed its separation from Abbott in 2006.

Visit Vault at **www.vault.com** for insider company profiles, expert advice, career message boards, expert resume reviews, the Vault Job Board and more.

VAULT CAREER LIBRARY   **193**

Following suit

After gaining independence, Hospira cut off medical and dental retirement benefits for its nonunion U.S. employees, saving itself about $40 million in the process. A group of these workers—about 10,000 of them—filed a class-action lawsuit against Abbott and Hospira. They claimed that Abbott had misled them about what would happen to their pension benefits if they joined Hospira.

Hospira and Abbott are linked to another lawsuit, in which Abbott is one of many pharmaceutical companies facing charges of engaging in improper marketing and pricing. Allegedly, Abbott and these other firms reported misleading or false pricing information in connection with federal, state and private reimbursement for certain drugs—many of which are made by Hospira.

These lawsuits and investigations could have an adverse effect on Hospira's business and could lead to changes in pricing polices or business practices, penalties or fines, or the exclusion of Hospira products from federal or state programs. For now, Hospira is cooperating with authorities.

Transitioning away from Abbott

Hospira completed a self-imposed "transition period" in April 2006, during which time it wrapped up 70 years of functioning as part of Abbott Laboratories and adapted to life as a solo firm. The company was saddled with a bunch of debt after the spin-off, some of which was due to its agreement to purchase the net operating assets of Abbott's hospital products division for $300 million between 2004 and 2006. Hospira finalized this transaction in late 2006, after accruing charges of around $100 million.

The transition to independence also meant the shuttering of many of Hospira's facilities. In 2006 the company sold its Salt Lake City plant and closed another in Ireland. Examination of the company's annual reports shows that it has since closed other locations in Atlanta, Dallas and Los Angeles, among others. In the near future, the planned closings of Hospira's Ashland, Ohio, and Montreal locations in 2008 will affect 1,100 jobs, while creating the opportunity for 400 full-time positions elsewhere.

Aussie addition

By February 2007, Hospira was positioned to start spending in a big way. That month, it purchased Australian company Mayne Pharma Limited for around $2 billion. Mayne, which has a direct commercial presence in some 20 countries and indirect distribution in more than 45 nations, makes generic injectable drugs, mostly for the treatment of cancer.

The deal made Hospira a leader in injectable pharmaceuticals, which will represent approximately half of the firm's sales. The company had already moved in this direction the previous year, purchasing both LifeCare PCA and BresaGen Ltd., both makers of biogeneric pharmaceuticals. Hospira's overall sales outside of the United States, following the Mayne acquisition, doubled to more than 30 percent of the company's total. The company is clearly betting on biogenerics, a risky and fledgling sector of the pharmaceutical industry—it entails the manufacturing of generic drugs, but for biologics, which are constructed from living cells. If such generics gain acceptance, important medications could reach the market in much cheaper forms.

Hospira has a renewed focus on research and development, and the firm has brought several new products to market over the past year. One such product is a wireless security platform for the company's medication infusion devices. The platform, launched in April 2007, features authentication standards and encryption protocols to help hospitals securely transfer data and comply with patient confidentiality regulations. In the future, Hospira plans to continue to aggressively pursue developing new products.

Helping communities in need

The Hospira Foundation, launched in 2005, focuses on improving health and wellness in communities around the world. Since Hospira became an independent company in 2004, the foundation and Hospira's employees have given more than $30 million in monetary and product donations to those in need.

One example of an organization Hospira has supported is the Starlight Starbright Children's Foundation, which helps seriously ill children and their families cope with sickness by providing them with entertainment, education and family activities.

GETTING HIRED

Hospira extends its hospitality to you

Applicants can search for openings and apply for positions on the company's career web site (careers.hospira.com). The company suggests that applicants apply for only one position at a time. Hospira is particularly interested in high-caliber candidates in operations, sales and marketing, science and engineering, information technology, global regulatory and global medical affairs, finance, accounting and taxation and administration. The company recruits at universities including Perdue, Stanford, Howard and a number of state universities.

Benefits at Hospira are similar to those at other biotech and pharmaceutical companies. They include choice of several medical plans, dental, vision, flexible spending accounts, paid vacation, a 401(k) plan with matching, life insurance, long- and short-term disability, optional long-term care insurance, adoption assistance and tuition assistance.

Hospira's career web site also includes employee testimonials. For example, an account manager says: "The culture is casual, but intense in terms of expectations of performance. It's very business-focused and much less bureaucratic than most places." A medication management specialist describes the company's employees as "hardworking people who like a challenge. Who see a need and take action. Who believe that what we are doing is important."

Human Genome Sciences, Inc.

14200 Shady Grove Road
Rockville, MD 20850
Phone: (301) 309-8504
Fax: (301) 309-8512
www.hgsi.com

LOCATION

Rockville, MD (HQ)

THE STATS

Employer Type: Public Company
Stock Symbol: HGSI
Stock Exchange: Nasdaq
Chairman: Argeris N. Karabelas
President & CEO: H. Thomas Watkins
2006 Employees: 880
2006 Revenue ($mil.): $25.8
2006 Net Income ($mil.): -$251

DEPARTMENTS

Accounting • Administration • Analytical Development • Animal Facility • Antibody Discovery & Development • Bioanalytical Sciences • Biostatistics • Clinical Data Management • Clinical Operations • Clinical Research • Corporate Communications • Corporate Development • Corporate Security • Drug Development • Drug Formulation & Delivery • Drug Safety • Engineering • Facilities • Finance • General & Administrative • High Throughput Screening • Human Resources • Information Technology • Investor Relations • Legal • Manufacturing • Materials Management • Media Preparation • Medical Writing • Pharmaceutical Operations • Preclinical Development • Preclinical Discovery • Process Development • Project Management • Protein Development • Purchasing • Quality • Quality Systems • Regulatory Affairs • Research • Research & Development • Safety • Strategic Marketing • Validation

KEY COMPETITORS

Amgen
GlaxoSmithKline
Johnson & Johnson

EMPLOYMENT CONTACT

www.hgsi.com/jobs

THE SCOOP

HGS 101

Biopharmaceutical company Human Genome Sciences' mission is to discover, develop, manufacture and market innovative drugs that serve patients with unmet medical needs. The Maryland-headquartered firm's primary focus is on protein and antibody drugs.

The company's pipeline of novel compounds in clinical development includes drugs to treat hepatitis C, lupus, anthrax disease, cancer, rheumatoid arthritis and HIV/AIDS. In 2006, the company's revenue reached more than $25 million, a nearly 35 percent increase from 2005. Yet the firm also has very high costs, and in 2006 the company saw net losses of more than $250 million.

Finding genetic therapies

In 1992, William A. Haseltine, a Harvard University professor and AIDS researcher, founded HGS. At the time, Haseltine talked about finding the "the fountain of youth" in genetic therapies and his firm, under his leadership, developed a genomics-based pipeline of drugs. The company went public in 1993 and delved into developmental projects.

Several of HGS' drugs failed in subsequent clinical trials, despite massive investments. For example, in 2003 the firm ceased development of repifermin, a drug to intended treat chronic leg ulcers. During trials of the drug, it was no better than a placebo in closing up leg wounds.

Haseltine retired from the company in 2004, the same year that the firm laid off 20 percent of its workforce. In November 2004, the company announced the hiring of H. Thomas Watkins, formerly head of Tap Pharmaceutical Products, as its new chief. Unlike Haseltine, Watkins had experience in late-stage product development, manufacturing, and pharmaceutical sales and marketing. The company's board hoped Watkins could help the firm transition from genomic research to drug development.

No profits yet, but possible products

Currently, Human Genome Sciences is unprofitable and has no approved products on the market. However, three of the company's products are advancing into late-stage clinical development. These are Albuferon for chronic hepatitis C, ABthrax for anthrax disease and LymphoStat-B for systemic lupus erythematosus.

In March 2006, Human Genome Sciences released trial data showing that Albuferon couldn't be administered on a monthly basis with efficacy. However, the phase IIb trial showed effectiveness and safety in the drug in combination with ribavirin. In addition, the hepatitis C treatment showed promise of efficacy at relatively high doses and at two-week intervals. In September, the company received $40 million in funding from Novartis for this successful phase II trial.

In October 2005, Human Genome Sciences announced that the company had been awarded a two-phase contract to supply ABthrax to the U.S. government for treating anthrax disease. The first installment of the contract came in June 2006, when the U.S. Department of Health and Human Services placed a $165 million order for about 20,000 doses of ABthrax. Human Genome Sciences expects to receive this $165 million upon full delivery of the drug in 2008. The government hopes to put the drug—which neutralizes the deadly toxin that anthrax bacteria produce—in a biodefense stockpile, starting in 2009.

Making deals

Since its inception, HGS has relied on strategic partnerships for the funding of all of the company's many R&D endeavors (and all of its endeavors, actually, since it has not yet turned a profit). Between 1993 and 1997, the firm entered into major collaborations with GlaxoSmithKline, Schering-Plough, Sanofi-Synthelabo, Takeda and Merck KGaA.

The company even consolidated these collaborations into a 1993 to 2001 project called the Human Gene Therapeutic Consortium, which aimed at producing a high number of drug candidates. Upon the consortium agreement's expiration, the company issued a press release, stating that HGS would "seek near-, intermediate- and long-term revenue from up-front payments and product development milestones, as well as the right to sell the products with our partners, royalties on sales, or both."

In October 2004, the company announced another agreement with GlaxoSmithKline, under which GSK acquired exclusive worldwide rights to develop and commercialize GSK716155, formerly Albugon. HGS' researchers created and brought this novel, long-acting form of glucagon-like peptide-1 (GLP-1) to late-stage pre-clinical development for the treatment of diabetes.

Visit Vault at **www.vault.com** for insider company profiles, expert advice, career message boards, expert resume reviews, the Vault Job Board and more.

VAULT CAREER LIBRARY **199**

The company entered into a license agreement with GlaxoSmithKline two years later, for the development and commercialization of lupus treatment LymphoStat-B. In June 2006, Novartis AG agreed to license rights to HGS' hepatitis C treatment Albuferon.

Looking ahead

In February 2007, Human Genome Sciences and GSK announced the initiation of dosing in one of two phase III clinical trials of LymphoStat-B in patients with active systemic lupus erythematosus. The company expects the second phase III trial to begin in the first half of 2007 and anticipates completion of enrollment in 2008.

GETTING HIRED

Join up with HGSI

The careers section of the Human Genome Science's's web site (www.hgsi.com/jobs) allows applicants to search for opportunities in dozens of areas such as administration, clinical operations, finance, manufacturing and quality. In addition, each year the firm hosts summer interns from high schools and colleges. Interns gain work experience and learn about the biopharmaceutical business in departments such as IT, engineering and pharmaceutical services.

The firm prefers for job applicants to submit resumes online. However, you can also fax a resume to (301) 309-1845 or mail it to the attention of the Human Resources Department at 14200 Shady Grove Road, Rockville, MD 20850.

Full- and part-time employees who work at least 24 hours per week have medical, dental and vision benefits. Other benefits include flexible spending accounts, life insurance, tuition reimbursement, a 401(k) plan with company match, stock options and education assistance.

Human Genome Sciences has been a recipient of the Maryland's Workplace Excellence seal of approval since 2002. The company sponsors events such as monthly happy hours, coffees where employees can meet with senior managers and ask questions, leadership development seminars and a Take Your Kids to Work day. Another unique feature of the firm is its "wellness rooms," where staff can pray, nurse babies or rest.

ImClone Systems Incorporated

180 Varick Street
New York, NY 10014
Phone: (212) 645-1405
Fax: (212) 645-2054
www.imclone.com

LOCATIONS

New York, NY (HQ)
Branchburg, NJ

THE STATS

Employer Type: Public Company
Stock Symbol: IMCL
Stock Exchange: Nasdaq
Chairman: Carl Icahn
CEO: John Johnson
2006 Employees: 993
2006 Revenue ($mil.): $678
2006 Net Income ($mil.): $371

Visit Vault at **www.vault.com** for insider company profiles, expert advice, career message boards, expert resume reviews, the Vault Job Board and more.

VAULT CAREER LIBRARY   201

THE SCOOP

One of a kind

Although best known as the biotech whose founder (Sam Waksal) and most notorious investor (Martha Stewart) were both jailed on corruption charges, there's more to ImClone than the inside of a courtroom. ImClone Systems Incorporated is a biopharmaceutical pioneering biologic medicines in oncology. By combining molecular biology, oncology, genomics and antibody engineering, the company built a unique pipeline of product candidates concentrated on the specific genetic mechanisms that cause tumor growth and development. ImClone posted a total 2006 revenue of nearly $678 million.

The company runs out of two locations—a corporate and scientific headquarters in New York City (home of the company's research and executive offices) and a complex in Branchburg, N.J., which houses its manufacturing, product development, finance, clinical, regulatory and quality assurance, and commercial departments.

Diagnostic beginnings

ImClone, founded in 1984, opened its current headquarters in 1986. At first the company concentrated on immunology-based diagnostics and infectious disease vaccines, resulting in two FDA-approved diagnostics and several vaccine research programs, which were subsequently licensed to pharmaceutical companies. In the early 1990s, ImClone shifted course from diagnostics and infectious diseases to the creation of oncology treatments.

Sam's big adventure

ImClone founder Samuel Waksal went from Wall Street golden boy to courtroom defendant in June 2003, when a federal judge sentenced him to more than seven years in prison and $4.3 million in fines for insider trading. Prior to forming the company with his brother Harlan in 1984, Waksal worked as a researcher at Stanford, Tufts and Mount Sinai School of Medicine. In 1993, ImClone acquired molecule C225 (discovered by Dr. John Mendelsohn at the University of California, San Diego), which would later be dubbed with the brand name Erbitux.

After years of clinical trials, Waksal presented the case of Shannon Kellum to the American Society of Clinical Oncology. After other treatments had failed, Erbitux had shrunk Kellum's two grapefruit-sized tumors to the size of peas, enabling doctors to surgically remove them. In September 2001, Bristol-Myers Squibb stepped in to pay ImClone up to $2 billion for a 20 percent stake in the company and sales rights in the U.S. and Canada. The deal valued ImClone at $70 per share and reaped a financial windfall for the Waksal brothers' company.

In December 2001, ImClone and Bristol-Myers met with the FDA regarding Erbitux, the last meeting before the companies officially learned that the FDA was not ready to review the drug due to insufficient data. (Prosecutors would later allege that Waksal knew that the FDA had concerns about the drug prior to the meeting.) At the end of the month, Harlan told Sam that the FDA was going to reject Erbitux's FDA application, prompting Sam to attempt selling 79,797 shares of ImClone. Two different brokerages refused to execute the order.

The next day, family members and close friends of Sam, including his daughter Aliza and friend Martha Stewart (who ended up serving five months after she was convicted of misleading investigators), sold close to $3 million of stock on a day when the stock closed at $58.30. The day after the sales, ImClone announced that the FDA had rejected its application and the stock spiraled down to the high teens.

Waksal submitted a partial guilty plea to insider trading and obstruction of justice in October 2002. In June 2003, Waksal was sentenced to 87 months of prison and ordered to pay $4.3 million in fines for tax evasion and insider trading.

Big bux from Erbitux

While the company now has a number of drugs in testing and research phases, its only drug currently on the market is Erbitux, which the FDA did eventually approve in February 2004 as a treatment for colorectal cancer. ImClone promoted the drug in collaboration with Bristol-Myers Squibb in the U.S. and Canada and with Merck KGaA outside those regions. The company earns royalties from BMS and Merck KGaA's sales of Erbitux.

Bristol-Myers Squibb currently owns a 16.58 percent interest in ImClone. In 2006, total royalty revenue increased by more than $113 million, or 64 percent, from 2005. This jump was primarily due to an increase in net sales of Erbitux and the change in royalties earned under the Merck KGaA agreement. Erbitux's 2006 sales came in at $652.2 million in the U.S., compared to $413.1 million the year prior. Much of this increase was due to expanded use for the drug, as the FDA had approved Erbitux— in combination with radiation therapy—for the treatment of certain types of head and neck cancer back in March 2006.

Visit Vault at **www.vault.com** for insider company profiles, expert advice, career message boards, expert resume reviews, the Vault Job Board and more.

V/\ULT CAREER LIBRARY　203

Erbitux binds specifically to the epidermal growth factor receptor on normal and tumor cells, entirely inhibiting the binding of the epidermal growth factor and other ligands. Erbitux is recommended for patients with colorectal cancer that has spread into other parts of the body and whose tumors express an EGFR. Treatment can be administered two ways: in combination with another chemotherapy drug (Camptosar) for patients who have seen tumor growth after Camptosar chemotherapy, or by itself for patients who can't tolerate Camptosar.

Currently, Erbitux's efficacy is based on clinical studies that have shown a reduction in tumor size. ImClone revealed a colon-cancer clinical study's results in early 2007, comparing effects of chemotherapy drug Folfiri and those of both Erbitux and Folfiri together: patients showed a longer duration of "progression-free survival" when given both drugs.

I think Icahn, I know Icahn ...

In January 2006, ImClone announced that investment bank Lazard Ltd. would help it explore a possible sale; the company was faced with a likely strong competitor to Erbitux and experiencing declining stock prices. Industry analysts fingered Bristol-Myers Squibb as a potential buyer, since the two companies already co-marketed Erbitux and BMS already owned 17 percent of the company. ImClone also announced that Joseph Fischer, a member of its board of directors, would take over as interim CEO, succeeding Philip Frost, interim CEO since November 2005.

But the company scrapped plans for the sale, and investor extraordinaire Carl Icahn increased his stake in ImClone to 11.68 percent after purchasing 1.13 million shares in August 2006. For the foreseeable future, the company would remain independent.

In October 2006, ImClone's chairman David Kies and director William W. Crouse resigned; this pleased Icahn, who'd criticized the company as being poorly run. Evidently Icahn believes that if he wants a job done well, he has to do it himself. Later in October 2006, having already filled five of the 11 seats on the board with his supporters, Icahn became the board's chairman.

Soon after Joseph L. Fischer, former chairman and CEO, stepped down and a newly formed executive committee of the board, chaired by Alexander J. Denner, replaced him. This committee gave way to a more conventional CEO figure in August 2007, when former Johnson & Johnson executive John Johnson (no kidding) took the reins.

What's next?

In late 2006, the FDA approved Amgen's drug Vectibix, which competes with Erbitux. However, in March 2007, Vectibix failed an experiment to treat a wider population of patients with earlier stages of colon cancer. Some analysts said the test results blew Vectibix's chances at becoming a more competitive drug in a larger market, and ImClone's stock price went up.

Until its research drugs (such as IMC-1121B, an investigational antibody currently in phase I trials) are ready to hit the market, ImClone's priority begins and ends with Erbitux, and whether it can expand the drug's market share and approved usage. Erbitux proved effective in treating head and neck cancers, but not all studies have been successful. In April 2007, the firm said the drug failed to help pancreatic cancer patients live longer. ImClone and its Erbitux partners BMS and Merck KGaA are charging ahead with clinical trials on the drug's effectiveness in treating other cancers: of the brain, stomach, rectum, esophagus, cervix, endometrium, ovary, bladder, prostate and breast, plus pediatric malignancies.

The product's all-important stock price keeps alternately ebbing and flowing, most recently rising in September 2007 on news from a three-year study that the drug could help treat lung cancer—rising 18 percent in one day. Imclone doesn't know the full story, though; Merck KGaA commissioned the research and hasn't yet released all of the data. The preliminary hype suggested Erbitux could be in for over $1 billion in annual lung cancer sales by 2012; but a few days later a contrary report quoted oncologists as saying they wouldn't prescribe the drug, and the stock tumbled down by 6 percent (sigh).

This stock news didn't go unnoticed by one very prominent Imclone figure—new CEO Johnson. Apparently, he had purchased $500,000 worth of company stock days before the positive study results emerged, after which the stock appreciated by roughly $90,000. The company released a statement that this was "pure coincidence," as Johnson's contract from the previous month stipulated he buy the stock.

Meanwhile, the ImClone boardroom continues to weather buyout talk linking the firm to Bristol-Myers Squibb. Analysts eager for gossip must have loved the July 2007 announcement between the two firms to expand Erbitux's clinical development plan by "several hundred million dollars."

Visit Vault at **www.vault.com** for insider company profiles, expert advice, career message boards, expert resume reviews, the Vault Job Board and more.

VAULT CAREER LIBRARY   **205**

GETTING HIRED

Making ImClone your home

ImClone's web site (sh.webhire.com/public/149/) enables interested candidates to search available job openings individually by location (New York, N.Y., and Branchburg, N.J.) as well as by department. Instructions for applying vary per position.

Job categories include accounting, antibody technology, bioanalytical science, biostatistics, business development, cell engineering and expression, clinical affairs, clinical QA, commercial manufacturing, corporate communications, environmental health and safety, experimental therapeutics, facilities, field operations, human resources, IT, legal, manufacturing, marketing, medical writing, metrology, operations planning, product development, project management, protein science, QA compliance, quality control, regulatory affairs, toxicology and tumor biology.

ImmunoGen, Inc.

128 Sidney Street
Cambridge, MA 02139
Phone: (617) 995-2500
Fax: (617) 995-2510
www.immunogen.com

LOCATIONS

Waltham, MA (HQ)
Norwood, MA

THE STATS

Employer Type: Public Company
Stock Symbol: IMGN
Stock Exchange: Nasdaq
Chairman, President & CEO: Mitchel
 Sayare, PhD
2007 Employees: 213
2007 Revenue ($mil.): $38
2007 Net Income ($mil.): $19

DEPARTMENTS

Antibody Development
Cell Biology
Chemistry
Biochemistry
Finance
Manufacturing
Regulatory
Quality Systems (Quality
 Assurance/Quality Control)

KEY COMPETITORS

Delcath
Immunomedics
Seattle Genetics
SuperGen
Vion Pharmaceuticals

EMPLOYMENT CONTACT

www.immunogen.com/wt/page/jobs

Visit Vault at **www.vault.com** for insider company profiles, expert advice,
career message boards, expert resume reviews, the Vault Job Board and more.

VAULT CAREER LIBRARY   207

THE SCOOP

The ImmunoGeneration

A cancer-focused research firm, ImmunoGen specializes in targeted anticancer biopharmaceuticals. The company works mostly with TAPs, or tumor-activated prodrugs, that combine cancer-killing medicines with monoclonal antibodies and attach exclusively to tumor cells.

ImmunoGen has five TAP compounds in clinical testing—huN901-DM1 and huC424-DM4 (targeting small-cell lung cancer and colorectal/pancreatic cancers respectively, both wholly-owned by ImmunoGen), AVE1642 and AVE9633 (in development with sanofi-aventis), and trastuzumab-DM1 (in development with Genentech). In 2007, ImmunoGen's total revenue was over $38 million, an increase from around $33 million in 2006. Over $25 million of this sum came from funding provided by ImmunoGen's research partners.

The company employs about 190 employees in research and development, clinical research, manufacturing and administrative functions. In addition to its new Waltham headquarters, ImmunoGen runs a GMP manufacturing facility in Norwood, Mass.

ImmunoGen's genesis

In 1981, the venture capital firm T.A. Associates was hot off the success of Biogen SA, which it had founded in 1978 for $150,000 and (according to *The New York Times*) was already worth over $9 million. Interested in more biotech pursuits, the firm settled on gene-splicing as a worthy investment, but couldn't find anything worthwhile. So, T.A. raised about $3.5 million and founded an entirely new company in Cambridge, Mass., with a roster of distinguished scientists from nearby Yale, Harvard and (of course) M.I.T.

Since 1986, the company's history has been tied to Mitchel Sayare, who joined the company as CEO that year and has served in that role ever since. He was president of the company from 1986 until 1992, and when the company hit a rough patch in 1994, laying off 100 of its 180 employees, he returned to the position. He became chairman of the company's board in 1989, the same year it went public.

Prior to joining ImmunoGen, Sayare was VP of development at Xenogen, a biotech specializing in antibody-based cancer treatments. Before getting into the commercial realm, Sayare was an assistant biophysics and biochemistry professor at the University of Connecticut and holds a PhD in biochemistry from the Temple University School of Medicine.

TAPping into a big idea

ImmunoGen's TAP attaches a proprietary cancer-killing agent to antibodies, which then deliver the agent directly to cancerous cells. Theoretically, the targeted approach makes ImmunoGen's cancer-killing treatments more effective than typical oncology chemotherapies, which also damage healthy cells while targeting malignant cells. The "payload" in the lead TAP products is DM1, a derivative of maytansine.

TAP product candidates have many advantages over traditional cancer treatments, claims ImmunoGen, since their design brings with it a number of improvements. These compounds have high specificity, targeting treatment only to malignant cells, and high potency, at least 100 to 1,000 times more cytotoxic than traditional chemotherapeutics.

They are also more stable for the patient, as the treatment "payload" is released and active only after the TAP product is inside his or her cell. Also, they are non-immunogenic (contrary to the company's name!), which means that TAP products use only humanized antibodies and non-protein-based small-molecule effector drugs. This reduced toxicity improved the quality of life for patients and produced fewer side effects.

The buddy system

ImmunoGen has partnered with a number of larger biotech firms that are looking to benefit from this TAP technology. The company signed a large deal in August 2003 with sanofi-aventis, which promised as much as $99 million over the next three years for the rights to develop and market three cancer treatments in the ImmunoGen pipeline.

This deal came after two major stumbling blocks for ImmunoGen the year before. Two former partners, GlaxoSmithKline and Genentech Inc., changed their plans for developing ImmunoGen drugs. Genentech chose to run additional tests before it began clinical trials of an oncology treatment and Glaxo ceased developing an ImmunoGen cancer drug it was working on altogether.

Recently, sanofi-aventis exercised options to extend the research part of its collaboration with ImmunoGen. In doing so, sanofi committed to provide

ImmunoGen with significant research support funding through August 31, 2008. After that time, ImmunoGen will be entitled to receive milestone payments, manufacturing payments and royalties on the sales of collaboration products, as well as retaining certain co-promotion rights.

The lots-of-buddies system

In December 2004, ImmunoGen licensed its cancer-fighting technology for $1 million to the Johnson & Johnson biotech subsidiary Centocor. These licensing fees will increase to $42.5 million if experimental cancer applications reach certain goals in patient trials. ImmunoGen would also then receive royalties from any drugs that are approved for market. In October of the same year, ImmunoGen inked a deal with Biogen Idec with an identical financial structure.

In December 2005, ImmunoGen announced that it sold Genentech exclusive rights to use TAP technology with therapeutic antibodies to attack an undisclosed tumor target. The license was the fourth such agreement with Genentech.

ImmunoGen has three types of out-license collaborations focused on TAP technology. These single-target licenses give other companies the right to develop and market products that use TAP to attack specific targets, which benefits ImmunoGen as well, developing TAP product candidates with antibodies on which the company doesn't focus. In 2006 the company maintained single-target collaborations with Genentech, Centocor, Biogen Idec, Millennium and Boehringer Ingelheim.

ImmunoGen also offers multi-target agreements that give other companies the right to test TAP treatments with a predetermined number of their own antibodies at any time. In 2006, ImmunoGen had multi-target collaborations with Genentech, Millennium and Amgen.

A new deal

ImmunoGen gained a new partner in July 2006. Biotest AG, which specializes in innovative immunology and hematology products, licensed the exclusive right to the company's TAP technology for use with a specific target. Like ImmunoGen's other single-target licenses, this one allows ImmunoGen to receive potentially significant milestone payments, manufacturing payments and royalties on product sales.

But the collaboration differs from ImmunoGen's other deals, as it also provides ImmunoGen with the right to opt in on the U.S. development and commercialization of resulting product candidates, so ImmunoGen will share in any profits from the products' U.S. commercialization.

A new position

The company will have help thinking up more collaborative agreements, having created the new position of vice president, general counsel and secretary in October 2007 and immediately hiring Craig Barrows for the gig. Barrows previously worked as a chief corporate legal officer for 13 years, with a strong background in transactions and corporate deals, and with ImmunoGen's collaborative research business taking off, he was an ideal fit.

CEO Sayare stated at the time that ImmunoGen was very interested in his "experience in the development of contacts with a wide range of partners, suppliers and other third parties, (because ImmunoGen's) needs in this area have increased substantially with … expanding collaborations and the advancement of TAP compounds."

Off and then on again

In January 2006, Millennium Pharmaceuticals decided to discontinue development of MLN2704, a compound that targets the prostate-specific membrane antigen. Millennium expressed concerns about certain economic challenges and the drug's tolerability; it also wanted a compound with a broader therapeutic window. However, in March 2006, Millennium extended the agreement with ImmunoGen for an additional year.

Good news

In November 2006, ImmunoGen reported promising results from trials of one of the company's drug candidates. During the early-stage human clinical trial of huN901-DM1, a potential treatment for small cell lung cancer and multiple myeloma, patients tolerated the compound well. In the phase-1 trials, huN901-DM1 also demonstrated solid anticancer activity.

There's also been positive news about trastuzumab-DM1, a drug candidate in development with Genentech. In a March 2007 meeting, Genentech disclosed that 18 patients with HER2-positive metastatic breast cancer had received trastuzumab-DM1 in a phase I study. The patients received trastuzumab-DM1 (under the brand name Herceptin) once every three weeks.

Genentech reported sustained antitumor activity in many of the patients treated with the compound. The company is conducting a second study with the compound to evaluate a weekly dosing regimen, and in August 2007 the California biotech company took the compound into phase II testing, triggering a $5 million payment from Genentech.

Down the road

In mid-2007, ImmunoGen intends to begin a phase II study that will evaluate huC242-DM4 for the treatment of gastric cancer. Looking even farther ahead, ImmunoGen expects two to three more compounds to enter clinical trials during the firm's 2008 fiscal year.

The company will move into new territory in April 2008—literally. In July 2007, the company signed a lease on a new corporate headquarters down the road from Cambridge in the sunny suburbs of Waltham, Mass. ImmunoGen's new digs will be located at 830 Winter Street, with 88,930 square feet of space, quite a step up from its 50,000-odd square feet in Cambridge.

The move represents maturity, both of ImmunoGen as a company and as the Cambridge-Boston area as a hotbed of biotechnology. The Massachusetts Biotechnology Council has estimated that 7 percent of all pharmaceutical developments derive from Massachusetts and *Commercial Property News* wrote in October 2007 that "The demand for biotech and lab space in Cambridge is also generating investment and development beyond the city's borders." Among the companies to join ImmunoGen in expanding beyond or away from Cambridge are Shire plc, Altus Pharmaceuticals and Biogen Idec.

GETTING HIRED

Finding an in at ImmunoGen

The careers section of ImmunoGen's web site lists available opportunities; information about positions as well as how to apply can be found at www.immunogen.com/wt/page/jobs. The company has also been known to post jobs on Boston Craigslist. Applicants can reach the firm's human resources office by e-mail at resumes@immunogen.com or fax resumes to (617) 995-2510.

Jobs offered have included research associates in cell biology, chemistry and assay development, research scientists in discovery research, manufacturing associates, quality control analysts and pharmacology scientists. The company's departments are cell biology, chemistry, biochemistry, process development, antibody development, manufacturing (pharmaceutical), regulatory, quality systems (QA/QC) and finance.

ImmunoGen offers a benefits package that includes 100 percent-paid health and dental insurance, a 401(k) plan and tuition assistance.

Visit Vault at **www.vault.com** for insider company profiles, expert advice, career message boards, expert resume reviews, the Vault Job Board and more.

VAULT CAREER LIBRARY 213

Incyte Corporation

Experimental Station
Route 141 & Henry Clay Road
Building E336
Wilmington, DE 19880
Phone: (302) 498-6944
Fax: (302) 425-2707
www.incyte.com

LOCATION

Wilmington, DE (HQ)

THE STATS

Employer Type: Public Company
Stock Symbol: INCY
Stock Exchange: Nasdaq
Chairman: Richard U. De Schutter
President & CEO: Paul A. Friedman
2006 Employees: 186
2006 Revenue ($mil.): $27.6
2006 Net Income ($mil.): -$74.2

KEY COMPETITORS

Applera Corporation
Bristol-Myers Squibb
CuraGen
Gilead Sciences
GlaxoSmithKline

EMPLOYMENT CONTACT

www.incyte.com/about_careers.html

THE SCOOP

It's all about the passion

Based in the corporate hamlet of Wilmington, Delaware, Incyte Corporation is uninhibited about its passion for inhibitors. The biotech firm, once known as Incyte Genomics, now concentrates on discovering and developing novel small molecule drugs to treat serious unmet medical needs. The firm's pipeline includes programs for HIV, cancer, diabetes and inflammatory diseases such as rheumatoid arthritis, multiple sclerosis and asthma. It has shifted its focus from its former practice of offering access to its genomic database and patent library.

A couple of Incyteful fellows

One storied day in the labs of a now-defunct biotech firm, British investor Roy Whitfield and researcher Randal Scott crossed paths. Two years later, in 1991, they founded Incyte Pharmaceuticals to research, develop and sell genomic database products, software applications and related services.

The company went public in 1993 and landed its first gene expression database subscriber a year later, with Pfizer. Two years after that, Incyte acquired the gene-mapping firms Genome Systems and Combion, then opened an office in Cambridge, England, and formed diaDexus with GlaxoSmithKline. Incyte added microarray developer Synteni in 1998 and its GSK venture diaDexus submitted an IPO two years later.

Suddenly bereft of pharmaceuticals operations, the firm renamed itself Incyte Genomics to signal its new concentration. The decision to change names backfired when the company announced plans to develop drugs in 2001, teaming with former competitor Agilent to share DNA microarray technologies. Another name change came in 2003, when the firm dubbed itself Incyte Corporation to refocus its business on drug production.

Keeping a grip

With the February 2004 closing of its Palo Alto plant, Incyte finalized its transition from genomic research to drug research, where its business solely lies now. The move eliminated $50 million in annual operating expenses and cut 257 jobs (57 percent of headcount) off the company payroll. Currently, Incyte has 186 employees, about 100 of whom are scientists, equally divided between chemistry and biology.

Visit Vault at **www.vault.com** for insider company profiles, expert advice, career message boards, expert resume reviews, the Vault Job Board and more.

V/\ULT CAREER LIBRARY   **215**

In January 2006, Incyte entered into a collaboration agreement with Pfizer for developing and commercializing CCR2 antagonists to treat multiple sclerosis, a deal that could net the company up to $803 million in payments, including a $40 million up-front payment. That December, Incyte filed an IND for the company's lead CCR2 antagonist, INCB8696. The company plans to initiate development of the compound as a treatment for multiple sclerosis (MS), beginning with a phase I trial in healthy volunteers.

During 2006, the company filed Investigational New Drug (IND) applications with the FDA for four novel compounds. HIV treatment INCB9471 is now in phase IIa clinical development, as is INCB13739 for type 2 diabetes. The firm plans to enter into phase IIb trials of INCB9471 in 2007. In addition, it has drugs for cancer, inflammatory disease and other diseases in clinical and preclinical trials. In 2007, the company plans to file additional INDs for a new program targeting Janus-associated kinases (JAKs). Incyte believes JAK inhibitors have the potential to treat certain cancers, chronic inflammatory conditions and other illnesses.

The company has suffered net losses since 2004, with losses clocking in at $74.2 million in 2006. The firm expects to incur losses for the next several years as it expands drug R&D programs. Investors seem pleased with the company's long-term prospects, however, as a bevy of clinical trials have yielded promising results in 2007, prompting company stock to rise by over 40 percent from September 2006 to September 2007.

GETTING HIRED

Finding an in

The careers section of Incyte's web cyte (www.incyte.com/about_careers.html) offers information about working life at the company and lists available job opportunities. Among the types of jobs listed there are VP of the oncology drug department, senior statistician/director of biomedical and statistical programming, research investigator in pre-clinical biology and staff scientist in drug metabolism and biopharmaceutics. Interested candidates should submit a resume by e-mail to careers@inctye.com. Job seekers should include the requisition number of the position for which they are applying in the subject line of the e-mail.

Infinity Pharmaceuticals, Inc.

780 Memorial Drive
Cambridge, MA 02139
Phone: (617) 453-1000
Fax: (617) 453-1001
www.ipi.com

LOCATION

Cambridge, MA (HQ)

THE STATS

Employer Type: Public Company
Stock Symbol: INFI
Stock Exchange: Nasdaq
Chairman & CEO: Steven H. Holtzman
2006 Employees: 115
2006 Revenue ($mil.): $18.5
2006 Net Income ($mil.): -$28.4

KEY COMPETITORS

AstraZeneca
Bristol-Myers Squibb
Pfizer

EMPLOYMENT CONTACT

www.ipi.com/careers.html

Visit Vault at **www.vault.com** for insider company profiles, expert advice,
career message boards, expert resume reviews, the Vault Job Board and more.

VAULT CAREER LIBRARY 217

THE SCOOP

Infinite discoveries

Infinity Pharmaceuticals' mission is to discover, develop and deliver the best-in-class medicines for the treatment of cancer and related conditions. Formerly known as Discovery Partners International, the Cambridge, Mass.-based firm uses its expertise in small molecule drug technologies to build a pipeline of innovative product candidates for multiple cancer indications. In 2006, Infinity Pharmaceuticals' revenue reached $18.5 million.

A finite history of Infinity

The company was incorporated in California in 1995 under the name IRORI Quantum Microchemistry. But after two straight unprofitable years, the firm replaced its corporate leadership in 1998 and renamed itself Discovery Partners International (DPI). The company signed a number of major collaborative deals with firms such as Pfizer and Bristol-Myers Squibb and went public in June 2000, raising over $100 million. But it was still unprofitable; its stock price stagnated and funds ran dry by 2006.

In a rare corporate feat, the firm completed a reverse merger on September 12, 2006 with another small, unprofitable, (although scientifically trailblazing) firm—Infinity Pharmaceuticals Inc. (IPI). In the deal, IPI became a wholly owned subsidiary of DPI, which then divested all of DPI's former operations and changed its name to Infinity Pharmaceuticals. The transition was complete later that month, when the new company named Infinity founder and CEO Stephen Holtzman as its new chief executive and began trading publicly on the Nasdaq exchange. All the reshuffling did the job: newly-branded Infinity Pharmaceuticals ended the year with more than $100 million in cash.

A few promising products in the pipeline

Infinity's lead product, IPI-504, is currently in phase I clinical trials for a variety of tumors. In 2006, the company expanded IPI-504's phase I trials to include patients with gastrointestinal stromal tumors. Infinity also designed and submitted a protocol for a new trial of IPI-504 to treat patients with non-small cell lung cancer, starting enrollment for the new trial in February 2007. More recently, Infinity entered IPI-504 in phase Ib trials for patients with a number of solid tumor cancers.

Another product in the pipeline is directed against the Hedgehog cell signaling pathway, which is implicated in cancer cell proliferation and survival in some of the most lethal cancers. Infinity is developing systemic inhibitors that would interfere with its effects. Another ongoing Infinity program focuses on discovering inhibitors of the Bcl-2 family of proteins, key regulators of cancer cell survival.

Let's make a deal (or two or three)

In August 2006, Infinity generated a bunch of cash by entering into a major alliance with Maryland-based MedImmune, centering on Infinity's Hsp90 and Hedgehog pathway programs. MedImmune agreed to shell out $70 million for a share in developmental costs in the two products, as well as a 50-50 share of all profits. Infinity could end up receiving $430 million in milestone payments, provided the company meets certain late-stage development and sales objectives for products resulting from the collaboration.

AstraZeneca Plc purchased MedImmune in 2007, but the collaboration will continue in accordance with Infinity and MedImmune's pre-existing agreement, regardless of the latter's new ownership. However, AstraZeneca's emergence into the agreement may delay Infinity's development programs or cause other, unforeseen problems.

Infinity entered into another alliance in 2006, partnering with Novartis to develop and commercialize compounds that inhibit the Bcl-2 family of proteins. Under the terms of the agreement, Novartis paid Infinity a $15 million up-front licensing fee and committed to funding roughly $10 million worth of Infinity's R&D over the initial two-year research term. Novartis could also end up paying Infinity milestone payments exceeding $400 million for discovery, development and commercialization, as well as royalties on sales.

On top of these product alliances, Infinity has several ongoing technology alliances with Amgen, Novartis' Institute for BioMedical Research and Johnson & Johnson's pharmaceutical research and development division.

Coming next

In 2008, the company expects its partnership with MedImmune to start bearing fruit, hoping to see new clinical data in phase 1 clinical trials of IPI-504 for the treatment of non-small cell lung cancer and gastrointestinal stromal tumors. Both companies received promising news in September 2007, when the FDA granted the drug orphan status—recognition that it can be used to treat rare diseases. Infinity and

MedImmune also begin a phase II trial of the drug in November 2007, in combination with other approved therapies and clinical development for the oral formulation of the drug. In addition, Infinity anticipates continued progress in both its Hedgehog and Bcl-2 programs.

GETTING HIRED

Finding an in at Infinity

Through the careers section of the firm's website (www.ipi.com/careers.html), applicants can view a list of job openings such as senior accountant, medical director, oncology and senior clinical research associate. The site also allows job hunters to create an online profile and submit a resume.

Infinity "seeks the most talented and dedicated scientific, business, and technology professionals in the world." The company is especially interested in hearing from post-doctoral candidates in Chemistry and Biology, as well as from folks with a Ph.D. or M.S. in chemistry, Ph.D. or M.S. in biology, or M.S. in computer science.

The company offers a nearly infinite array of benefits. These include stock options, a 401(k) plan, a first time homebuyer assistance program, health insurance, dental insurance, pre-tax flexible spending accounts, basic life, accidental death and dismemberment, and short- and long-term disability insurance, 15 paid vacation days, 12 scheduled paid holidays and discounted home and auto insurance. In addition, after five years of regular full-time employment, workers may be eligible for paid sabbatical leave.

Inspire Pharmaceuticals, Inc.

4222 Emperor Boulevard, Suite 200
Durham, NC 27703-8466
Phone: (919) 941-9777
Fax: (919)-941-9797
www.inspirepharm.com

LOCATIONS

Durham, NC (HQ)

THE STATS

Employer Type: Public Company
Stock Symbol: ISPH
Stock Exchange: Nasdaq
Chairman: Kenneth B. Lee Jr.
President & CEO: Christy L. Shaffer
2006 Employees: 170
2006 Revenue ($mil.): $37.1
2006 Net Income (loss) ($mil.): -$42

DEPARTMENTS

Clinical Research
Commercial Operations
Corporate-Manager
Drug Evaluation
Finance
Managed Markets
Molecular Pharmacology
Pharmaceutical Sales
Pharmaceutical Sciences
Regulatory Affairs
Sales & Marketing
Technical Operations

KEY COMPETITORS

Allergan
Bausch & Lomb
Schering-Plough

EMPLOYMENT CONTACT

www.inspirepharm.com/careers.html

THE SCOOP

A rundown on Inspir-ation

Biopharmaceutical company Inspire focuses on discovering, developing and commercializing new treatments for diseases in the respiratory/allergy and ophthalmic areas. The firm's products include AzaSite for bacterial conjunctivitis; Elestat for allergic conjunctivitis; and Restasis, currently the only approved prescription product for dry eye disease. Inspire co-promotes Elestat and Restasis under agreements with California-headquartered health care company Allergan.

In 2006, Inspire's total revenue reached more than $37 million, a 59 percent increase from approximately $23 million in 2005. The increase in was primarily due to increased co-promotion revenue from net sales of Elestat and Restasis.

Inspire's initial days

Inspire, incorporated in October 1993, started operations in March 1995. The company completed an Initial Public Offering of common stock in August 2000, with follow-on common stock offerings in March 2003, July 2004 and November 2004.

During the firm's early years, Inspire scientists—together with University of North Carolina researchers—made and patented many discoveries relating to P2Y2 receptors, protein molecules expressed on the surface of cells. These discoveries had potential importance in the treatment of diseases involving deficiencies in the body's mechanisms for protecting mucosal surfaces such as the lungs and sinuses, but also (most importantly for the company's future direction) the eyes.

From making discoveries to making friends

Since its early discoveries, Inspire has discovered and developed potential drug candidates for treating dry eye and retinal disease, as well as cystic fibrosis, cardiovascular disease and more. As early as 2001, the company was eyeing the ocular health market, signing a collaborative deal with competitor—and fellow eye-pharmaceuticals firm—Allergan, in which Inspire's INS365 developmental project would combine with Allergan's successful Restasis product.

By 2004, this collaboration led Inspire to venture beyond its customary R&D activities, as it created a commercial alliance with Allergan to co-promote Restasis and Elestat (the market name for INC365) in the United States. Each firm will primarily market their own products, but it would be Inspire's first foray into sales and marketing. The co-promotion agreement, therefore, gave Inspire a share of Allergan's net sales to cover for any lapses or cost overruns in Inspire's fledgling sales operations. Inspire's sales and marketing organization calls on optometrists, ophthalmologists and allergists in the United States.

But the success of the agreement has emboldened—inspired, even—the firm to enter into other, similar agreements. In February 2006, the company entered into a development and license agreement with Boehringer Ingelheim, which gives Inspire certain exclusive rights to develop and market an epinastine nasal spray for the treatment or prevention of rhinitis, the irritation and inflammation of the nose. Then, in October 2006, Inspire entered into an agreement with FAES for the U.S. and Canadian development and commercialization of bilastine, an oral antihistamine compound for eye allergies and irritation.

InSite-ful agreement

In February 2007, the company signed an exclusive licensing agreement with InSite Vision to commercialize AzaSite in the U.S. and Canada. The two firms co-developed AzaSite, a drug to treat bacterial conjunctivitis, an eye infection common in children. In April 2007, the Food and Drug Administration approved AzaSite for the treatment of bacterial conjunctivitis and Inspire launched it stateside in August. No longer the junior partner in such a collaboration, Inspire will do most of the sales and marketing, and InSite will get a cut of the proceeds.

Promise in the pipeline?

Inspire is focused on strengthening the company's product pipeline to position the business for 2007 and beyond. Products that are currently in clinical trials include treatments for allergies, cystic fibrosis, glaucoma and dry eye.

As in the past, the firm has its eye on dryness: ophthalmology, to be exact, better known as "dry eye." The firm estimates that over nine million North Americans have dry eye disease, and the FDA is currently reviewing Inspire's Prolacria treatment for dry eye. But the drug won't be commercially available for some time, as the FDA recently asked for more proof of its effectiveness.

Inspire is also evaluating a series of compounds for the treatment of glaucoma, and the company began phase I clinical testing of the first drug in the series in 2007. Also, Inspire is still focusing on allergy treatments (the annual U.S. market for

Visit Vault at **www.vault.com** for insider company profiles, expert advice, career message boards, expert resume reviews, the Vault Job Board and more.

VAULT CAREER LIBRARY   **223**

prescription nasal allergy products is estimated at $2.7 billion). Its respiratory and allergy pipeline includes bilastine, an oral antihistamine candidate, which is in late phase III development; cystic fibrosis drug denufosol terasodium, which is in a two-year inhalation carcinogenicity study in rodents; and epinastine nasal spray for seasonal allergic rhinitis.

In May 2007, Inspire reported good and bad news from mid-stage trials of its nasal allergy spray with epinastine. The phase II trial tested two versions of the spray, each version containing a different dose of epinastine. The spray with the larger dose of the drug showed statistically significant results in treating allergies, but the spray with the smaller dose didn't.

The following July, however, Inspire demonstrated that it is not shrinking from its emergence into the business side of the pharmaceutical industry, as it announced a $75 million round of financing from private equity firm Warburg Pincus. The Jonathan Leff, Warburg's leading biotech investment director, will join Inspire's board, and his firm will receive a great deal of company stock. In a press release, Inspire stated that it would use the funds to further its phase III development programs but also—perhaps more importantly—continue with the commercialization of AzaSite.

GETTING HIRED

Getting inside Inspire

Applicants can search for jobs on the careers section of Inspweb site (www.inspirepharm.com/careers.html). Job seekers can search opening by location or by category such as commercial operations, corporate, drug evaluation, finance, molecular pharmacology, pharmaceutical sales, pharmaceutical sciences, regulatory affairs, sales and marketing, and technical operations.

In addition, Inspire Pharmaceuticals has an internship program designed to give students hands-on experience. Interns usually work within the company's scientific research and development areas and sometimes in the firm's business areas. Undergraduate students must have completed their sophomore year at an accredited college or university and need at least a 3.2 GPA. The majority of Inspire's internship opportunities are for braniacs who major in the physical or life sciences. Students must be from colleges or universities within commuting distance to the firm's

Durham, N.C., headquarters. For more information on how to apply for Inspire's internships, visit www.inspirepharm.com/interns.html.

Inspire is committed to "providing a fun, collegial environment that allows you to be creative, to get to know your colleagues and to celebrate a project, week or a year well done." Examples of activities the company organizes include "potluck" luncheon cookouts, new hire luncheons, monthly small-group employee meetings with the CEO and a winter holiday celebration. In addition, there are corporate golf, softball and bike teams, monthly on-site massage therapists to ease employees' sore muscles and weekly on-site yoga or pilates classes.

The company's comprehensive benefits include medical, dental, vision, short- and long-term disability, a 401(k) plan, flexible spending account programs, employee stock options, an employee assistance program, a wellness benefits program and life insurance. Inspire also gives employees generous vacation packages, paid holidays and personal days.

Visit Vault at **www.vault.com** for insider company profiles, expert advice, career message boards, expert resume reviews, the Vault Job Board and more.

VAULT CAREER LIBRARY   225

Invitrogen Corporation

1600 Faraday Avenue
Carlsbad, CA 92008
Phone: (760) 603-7200
Fax: (760) 602-6500
www.invitrogen.com

LOCATIONS

Carlsbad, CA (HQ)
Branford, CT
Brown Deer, WI
Camarillo, CA
Eugene, OR
Fredrick, MD
Grand Island, NY
Madison, WI
Rockville, MD

International locations in 75
countries.

THE STATS

Employer Type: Public Company
Stock Symbol: IVGN
Stock Exchange: Nasdaq
Chairman & CEO: Gregory T. Lucier
2006 Employees: 4,835
2006 Revenue ($mil.): $1,263.5
2006 Net Income ($mil.): -$191

DEPARTMENTS

Administration
Corporate Development
Executive
Finance/Accounting
Human Resources
Information Technologies
Legal
Operations/Manufacturing
Research and Development
Sales & Marketing

KEY COMPETITORS

Affymetrix
Applera
BD Biosciences

EMPLOYMENT CONTACT

invitrogen.recruitmax.com/
MAIN/careerportal/

THE SCOOP

From the garage to the globe

Since its humble beginnings in founder Lyle Turner's California garage in 1987, Invitrogen Corp. has evolved into a leading supplier in global genetic research tools, with annual revenue over $1 billion and subsidiaries around the globe. Invitrogen markets products and services to pharmaceutical and biotech companies as well as academic and government research foundations.

Invitrogen is headquartered in Carlsbad, Calif., with distribution offices and laboratories dotting the U.S. The company also has facilities in Asia, South America, Oceania and Europe. In 2006 the firm had 1,435 sales and marketing personnel, an increase from 1,330 in 2005. About 560 people work in research and development. In comparison, 550 people worked in R&D in 2005 and 440 in 2004.

In 2007, Invitrogen won awards in six categories, the most of any company, in *The Scientist*'s annual Life Science Industry Awards. These categories included Cell Biology Kits and Reagents, Cell Culture Media and Reagents, Most Responsive Customer Service, Most Knowledgeable Technical Support, Most Useful Web Site and Most Memorable Print Advertisement. In 2006, Invitrogen was on *Bio-IT World*'s top 50 list. That same year, *Business 2.0* named Invitrogen as one of the 100 Fastest-Growing Technology Companies.

Genetic makeup

Invitrogen is made up of two principal sectors, BioDiscovery and Cell Culture Systems. The BioDiscovery segment's name is pretty self-explanatory: it's an R&D outfit with an emphasis on molecular biology, the stuff of genes and genomes (where the "gen" comes from in the company's name). It contains the functional genomics, cell biology and drug discovery product lines.

Functional genomics includes products ranging from the cloning and manipulation of DNA, to the examination of RNA levels and the regulation of cellular gene expression, to the analysis of proteins through capture and separation. The BioDiscovery sector also designs software dedicated to improving the efficiency and accuracy of genomic, proteomic and other biomolecular analyses for use in pharmaceutical, therapeutic and diagnostic development.

Visit Vault at **www.vault.com** for insider company profiles, expert advice, career message boards, expert resume reviews, the Vault Job Board and more.

VAULT CAREER LIBRARY   227

Invitrogen's other sector, Cell Culture Systems, is the reason for the in vitro of the company's name—it contains the company's services and products that help scientists isolate cells in biochemical experiments. Its products include sera, cell and tissue culture media, reagents used in life sciences research and in the growth of cells in the laboratory, and other materials made through cultured cells. This sector also manufactures biologics for clients to use in clinical trials as well as for the worldwide commercial market.

BioDiscovery and Cell Culture Systems' products are made for research purposes, which generally places its products and business outside the realm of FDA (or any analogous international body) regulation.

A successful experiment in public funding

The company's BioDiscovery sector was responsible for much of its success in its first decade of operations. The ongoing Human Genome Project looked headed for the success it would achieve after the turn of the 21st century, and Invitrogen's business model—experimenting with genetic cloning and searching for new drugs through gene analysis—was sort of a hot biotech growth prospect. Company founder Lyle Turner had no problem securing funding and Invitrogen grew from a firm generating $4 million annually in 1990 to one that grossed $55.3 revenue in 1997.

Just two years later, Invitrogen spent nearly all of its 1997 revenue as, over the course of 1999, it both went public and merged with San Diego-based NOVEX for $52 million. With the company's first acquisition under its belt, it struck again in December 1999, purchasing Research Genetics. Both firms possessed a similar focus on genetic research, and each added something new to Invitrogen's portfolio: the budding field of proteonics, or protein analysis, a more precise way to guide DNA research, often using web-based software.

Invitrogen's cells multiply ...

The company's size and revenue increased dramatically after its IPO, a fact demonstrated by its audacious $1.9 billion (!) bid for Dexter Corporation in July 2000. This merger brought Invitrogen a company that had earned $409 million in 1999 and swelled its ranks by 2,300 employees; analysts crowed that it would make Invitrogen the leader in its field of supplies for molecular biology research.

The deal also gave Invitrogen an ever-lasting historical footnote, as Dexter was the oldest company listed on the New York Stock Exchange, founded by Seth Dexter II as a sawmill outfit in 1767. Of course, Dexter had evolved since then, and the apple of Invitrogen's eye was its Life Technologies subsidiary, a developer of scientific research products since 1983.

... and divide

In 2001, Invitrogen pulled in $630 million in sales, more than six times its pre-IPO revenue. But incorporating Life Technologies understandably proved to require some reshuffling and in May 2002, Invitrogen began adjusting to its newfound girth, shutting down the Huntsville, Alabama, facility it had gained in the Research Genetics purchase two years prior.

It also began restructuring European operations, closing both Invitrogen's and Life Technologies' Dutch properties and generally consolidating its business. Part of the streamlining was the discontinuance of a number of product lines, estimated as worth $55 million annually.

Leadership from outside, leadership from within

In June 2003, the Invitrogen board replaced company founder Turner with Gregory Lucier, then the 39-year-old chief executive of GE's medical systems information technologies unit. Despite Lucier's young age, no one could argue with his past, as sales at his GE unit more than doubled in three years under his watch.

The decision to hire someone from outside the biotech industry reflected Invitrogen's quest to take the company even further, with talk of creating a "multibillion-dollar" firm. Lucier increased R&D spending and expanded the chemical tool sets offered to customers and providing more cell-growth tools. Perhaps more importantly, Lucier's demanding style drastically altered Invitrogen's laid-back atmosphere, as the young Jack Welsh protégé favored administrative and leadership talents over executives with biotech experience.

Invitrogen invites other companies to join

Along with greater financial commitment to R&D and CEO Lucier's commitment to executive leadership, the firm continued its acquisitive streak, picking up a number of smaller firms (and the lucrative patents and research therein) in related fields. In January 2005, the company acquired Zymed Laboratories, which produced pathology products, cell and cancer biology reagents, and general immunochemical reagents used in life sciences research and clinical diagnostics.

Visit Vault at **www.vault.com** for insider company profiles, expert advice, career message boards, expert resume reviews, the Vault Job Board and more.

VAULT CAREER LIBRARY

229

In February 2005, Invitrogen bolstered its genetic testing products by snapping up Norwegian firm Dynal Biotech, maker of pathology products, cancer and cell reagents, and biomarkers. The acquisition also enabled Invitrogen to expand its budget for research and development from 7 percent to 10 percent.

Next to join were Caltag Laboratories and the package of Quantum Dot Corporation and the BioPixels unit of BioCrystal Ltd., in May and October 2005, respectively. The privately held Caltag expanded Invitrogen's opportunities in the BioDiscovery sector, as it developed and manufactured antibodies and reagents for biotech and pharmaceutical companies. The Quantum purchase augmented Invitrogen's molecular probes division, a department focused on advanced labeling and detection technologies through nanotechnology.

A global presence

Invitrogen had also started to aggressively target international markets during this period, although it had established an office in China way back in 1989. Days before the new World Trade Organization guidelines came into effect in December 2004, effectively opening Chinese biotech firms to foreign companies, the company acquired Shanghai-based BioAsia, a manufacturer and provider of sequencing reagents and custom R&D services to research institutions in China.

The acquisition brought the total number of Invitrogen China employees to more than 170, and the firm looks set to stay there for a long time. Around the same time, it committed more than $20 million dollars to its Chinese operation through 2010.

In July 2005, Invitrogen opened a research facility in New South Wales, Australia, focused on developing safe, consistent bovine sera products and reagents used in producing vaccines and biotherapeutic drugs for world markets.

As two of the few countries regarded as Bovine Spongiform Encephalopathy (BSE)-free (mad cow disease), Australia and New Zealand have become strong interests of Invitrogen, a pioneer among global pharmaceutical companies seeking secure supplies of locally produced biotech products. In addition to laboratories in Europe, Oceania and Asia, the company maintains distribution centers around the world.

Without a debt?

While Invitrogen's aggressive acquisitions bolstered technological and market growth, the price of such rapid expansion didn't come cheap. By the end of July 2005, Invitrogen's debt had grown to $1.5 billion, the company's highest to date.

Company leaders pointed to Invitrogen's large cash flow as an adequate buffer, and argued that the company's debt-to-equity ratio was in line with fellow biotech tool companies.

But in 2006, the firm faced a cyclical downturn in sera and bioproduction media and its share price declined by 15 percent over the course of the year. Invitrogen was quick to respond. It sold off two subsidiaries in February 2007: BioReliance, acquired in early 2004, which went to Avista Capital Partners for approximately $210 million; and BioSource Europe, S.A., a diagnostic business in Belgium, trundled off to a Belgian private investor group. Invitrogen also saved millions of dollars by consolidating satellite facilities into larger locations during 2006.

In 2007, the company stated that it would continue efforts to integrate its products, systems, and personnel into one company. The firm also announced a new capital structure plan, which will return excess cash to shareholders through a $500 million share repurchase program. In February 2007, after a JPMorgan analyst said Invitrogen's restructuring plan would not pay off until 2008, the company's stock dipped again.

Invitrogen investments

The firm continues to believe that a strong research and product development effort is essential for the company's future growth. In 2006, Invitrogen spent $107.6 million on R&D, an increase from $99.3 million in 2005 and $73.1 million in 2004. Over the course of 2006, the company's R&D staff worked with other institutions to identify hundreds of new biomarkers, which may improve lung cancer and prostate cancer screening.

Also in 2006, Invitrogen developed genomics-based pathogen detection kits for possible bioterrorism threats, such as anthrax, hemorrhagic fevers, plague and smallpox. In the field of transplantation diagnostics, the company developed genetic tests to match recipients to donors. The company's R&D is getting industry props: one of its new products—the Quibit platform for DNA, RNA and protein quantitation—won an award in 2007 from *R&D* magazine, which named it one of the year's most significant developments on its R&D 100.

The research supply juggernaut shows no signs of slowing down, either. As of October 2007, its stock shares were up 43 percent from the previous year. Seemingly every other month, it strikes a new partnership deal with other research firms. In August 2007, it announced the start of work with IDEXX Laboratories on the development and distribution of products for the water testing industry. Invitrogen will put this work to use in China in 2008, as the Beijing Summer Olympic Games have contracted the company to provide water testing services for the event. The following October, Invitrogen was expanding its genetic offerings, licensing a number of MicroRNA sequences from Natural Selection, which would give Invitrogen the "most comprehensive human and mouse MicroRNA arrays on the market."

The firm is increasingly investing in stem cell technology. It announced a new partnership in May 2007 with San Diego-based Cytori Therapeutics, which will expand its stem cell products, and it started rolling them out a few months later. In August, it debuted a new disposable device to simplify the process of dividing human stem cells. This product was complemented by Invitrogen's new "Multiplex Kit" in October, which promises better storage for stem cells in the midst of research.

GETTING HIRED

Goin' back to Cali

Job openings are listed on Invitrogen's web site (invitrogen.recruitmax.com/MAIN/careerportal); the database is searchable by geographic location or department, including international positions. Categories include administration, corporate development, executive, finance/accounting, human resources, information technologies, legal, operations/manufacturing, sales and marketing, and research and development. Applicants should submit a resume online.

Day of interviews, standard questions

Most Invitrogen insiders say there was a single round of interviews, during which they met with a variety of people. A scientist in California says interviews were with "the team leader and other teammates." One business development manager says there was a single day of interviews which included meetings with HR, the SVP of sales, a hiring manager (director of the division), the director of specialist groups, the VP of finance and others. Another employee says there was "one interview with the VP of sales and director of bioproduction, both of whom I had known previously."

Sources say interview questions are fairly traditional. One says there were "standard interview questions" that included the reason the individual wanted the position, qualifications, potential limitations and concerns. Another, "I recall the interview was heavily focused towards aspects of my work and life of which I was particularly proud." The respondent adds that the interviewer also asked about times where the applicant "had made a distinct difference to the success of collaborations, licensing deals and partnerships."

OUR SURVEY SAYS

International and in flux

Sources say that Invitrogen has a "very exciting culture" with "a bit of a Microsoft feel to it." One insider adds that Invitrogen's culture is "very West Coast," and a manager describes the company's people as "smart, good-looking, professional team players." The company's environment is very diverse, "with many Asian, South Asian and former Soviet bloc scientists on staff," and it's "not uncommon to hear multiple languages being spoken in the hallways." A source who works for the company in Europe feels that, although Invitrogen is a "global company," the firm's "decision-making process, vision and strategy" are "very much U.S. focused."

Sources say most scientists and business people at Invitrogen work 40 hours a week. One insider adds, "Lots of lower level nonscience jobs are outsourced, so these workers also tend to work 40 hours." A scientist reports that the biotech company has "good benefits." According to another insider, these include a "discounted stock purchase plan, three weeks vacation after first year and great medical insurance (company pays a lot of the plan costs)." Additional perks mentioned are a car allowance, laptop and cell phone.

One insider feels the company has been in "a state of flux" due to "many acquisitions in a short period of time." The source says the amount of change at Invitrogen "makes organization and communication difficult and incomplete." The source feels this many be one reason the company has relatively high turnover.

Upbeat about its outlook

Overall, people at Invitrogen are positive about the company and its future. A scientist says, "It's among the top biotech companies in the U.S.," and a business development manager describes the firm's business outlook as "positive." Another business development manager says, "Invitrogen has one of the best and most

Visit Vault at **www.vault.com** for insider company profiles, expert advice,
career message boards, expert resume reviews, the Vault Job Board and more.
V/\ULT CAREER LIBRARY 233

comprehensive product portfolios [in the life sciences field]." One contact adds that Invitrogen is "either No. 1 or 2 for each product line in the field."

Johnson & Johnson

1 Johnson & Johnson Plaza
New Brunswick, NJ 08933
Phone: (732) 524-0400
Fax: (732) 524-3300
www.jnj.com

LOCATIONS

New Brunswick, NJ (HQ)

Offices in 57 countries worldwide.

THE STATS

Employer Type: Public Company
Stock Symbol: JNJ
Stock Exchange: NYSE
Chairman and CEO: William C.
Weldon
2006 Employees: 116,200
2006 Revenue ($mil.): $50,514

DEPARTMENTS

Administrative Support Services
Aviation
Corporate Affairs
Consumer
Engineering
Environmental Health & Safety
Finance
Health Care Compliance
HR
IT
Legal
Marketing
Medical Affairs
Medical Devices & Diagnostics
Operations
Pharmaceutical
Process Excellence
Quality
Regulatory Affairs
Research & Development
Sales

KEY COMPETITORS

Novartis
Pfizer
Procter & Gamble

EMPLOYMENT CONTACT

www.jnj.com/careers

Visit Vault at **www.vault.com** for insider company profiles, expert advice,
career message boards, expert resume reviews, the Vault Job Board and more.

VAULT CAREER LIBRARY   235

THE SCOOP

To your health

Johnson & Johnson just wants you to feel better. One of the largest, most diverse companies in the world, Johnson & Johnson, founded in 1886, is made up of three primary sectors—consumer products, medical devices and pharmaceuticals (its largest division)—within which there are over 230 autonomous companies. J&J's consumer products, in addition to "No More Tears" shampoo and baby powder for the under-one set, include Splenda sweetener, Benecol spreads, Band-Aids, Rembrandt whitening toothpaste, Listerine mouthwash, and Aveeno, Clean and Clear and Neutrogena skin products. Johnson & Johnson also manufactures Tylenol, Motrin and OneTouch blood glucose monitors. Innovation has long been J&J's specialty, and the company's past is filled with significant creations, including the aforementioned Band-Aids, the PAP smear, the first tri-phasic birth control pill and, more prosaically, baby powder. The world's largest drug distributors are also J&J's biggest customers, with McKesson and Cardinal Health each responsible for 10 percent of sales, and AmerisourceBergen accounting for 8 percent.

The brothers Johnson

James and Edward Johnson opened a medical products company in New Brunswick, New Jersey, in 1885; they were joined a year later by their brother Robert to make the antiseptic surgical dressings he invented. In the banner year of 1921, J&J introduced to the world two of its most famous products: the Band-Aid and Johnson's Baby Cream. In 1932, Robert Jr. became chairman, a post he held until 1963. Products rolled out during his tenure included Ortho (birth control items) and Ethicon (sutures) in the 1940s. The company went public in 1944. In 1959, J&J added McNeil Labs, which released Tylenol the following year. During the 1970s, J&J concentrated on consumer products, cornering a significant portion of the feminine hygiene market and making Tylenol the best-selling pain reliever.

In 1989, J&J began a joint venture with Merck to sell Mylanta and other drugs purchased from ICI Americas. The firm focused on diversification during the 1990s and early 2000s, picking up companies ranging from skin products firm Neutrogena to two major pharmaceutical acquisitions: OraPharma, a boutique firm focused on developing and commercializing unique therapeutics, and Scios, a biopharm company concentrated on cardiovascular and inflammatory disease. In 2005,

Johnson & Johnson bought insulin pump maker Animas for $518 million, as a complement to its glucose monitoring unit.

Guidant light

From December 2004 through January 2006, J&J found itself in a bidding war with Boston Scientific over the purchase of Guidant Corporation, which makes pacemakers, implantable defibrillators, stents and other heart-related products. At the beginning of that period, J&J announced plans to acquire Guidant for $76 a share, at a total cost of $25.4 billion, a deal OK'd by Guidant stockholders in April. Then, a few months later, in July 2005, Guidant put out a warning on nine types of pacemakers it had issued from 1997 to 2000, causing J&J to express concern that the problems could affect the acquisition, a statement it backed up in November when it forewarned that it might kibosh the deal due to regulatory and legal liabilities. In response, Guidant sued to force J&J to complete the deal, and after a week, the two companies announced a compromised purchase price of $63 a share (or $21.5 billion). That December, smelling a bargain, Boston Scientific submitted a $25 billion bid, and J&J responded, but declined to raise its bid higher than $24.2 billion. In late January 2006, as the midnight deadline for a counteroffer came and went, Guidant inked a $27 billion offer from Boston Scientific. J&J accepted a $675 million breakup fee and took its leave—or so everyone thought.

In September 2006 J&J filed suit against Boston Scientific, Guidant and Abbott Labs (which ended up purchasing a portion of Guidant) for $5.5 billion, stating that the companies had illegally shared information in their acquisition of the pacemaker company. J&J contended that Guidant violated a clause that prevented solicitation of competing offers and that Boston Scientific should not have shared information with Abbott. Johnson & Johnson also stated that Boston Scientific would have faced a long antitrust review of uncertain outcome had it not been able to sell Guidant's stent and vascular products to Abbott. Naturally, both Abbott Labs and Boston Scientific responded that the suit was without merit.

Stent superiority

In August 2005, two major studies revealed that J&J's heart stent functions better than a rival device by Boston Scientific. The studies both found that the J&J stent did a better job of keeping blood flowing in weakened coronary arteries. Doctors had compared J&J's sirolimus-coated Cypher stent with the paclitaxel-coated Boston Scientific model; the drug coatings are meant to prevent the stents, which are tiny wire mesh tubes, from becoming clogged after they are inserted into coronary disease-damaged arteries. While the risk of heart attack and death was equivalent for each product, the J&J device thwarted scar tissue buildup in arteries treated with stents. The Cypher has about 40 percent of the $2.8 billion market in the U.S. Researchers noted, however, that stent-makers were still subject to manufacturing limitations—and sales worldwide decreased after a 2006 revelation that receiving stents with any coating increased the risk of death.

A year after the two studies, J&J made a further move to solidify its position in stents with the purchase of Conor Medsystems, a manufacturer of the wire devices, for $1.4 billion. J&J was especially keen on Conor's CoStar stent, which has the ability to deliver several drugs simultaneously.

Buyer's remorse

Also in May 2007, J&J's stent division encountered some problems when its CoStar stent was found to deliver an ineffective dose of the medicine with which it was coated, thus leaving patients implanted with the device more likely to develop scar tissue and a narrowing of the artery at the implantation site. J&J opted to recall its CoStar stents that had been in use in other countries, and not seek FDA approval for the device. The firm plans to test a new version of the stent coated with a more powerful drug. Assuming it passes all the regulatory hurdles, the device will be ready for sale in about three years. The recall will affect J&J's earnings by about $100 million, according to analysts.

A many Splenda'd thing

The president of the National Sugar Association joined the executive director of the Center for Science in Public Interest—the Association's nemesis—in February 2005 to argue that J&J company McNeil Nutritionals should stop advertising Splenda as a natural product. The Sugar Association and Merisant Worldwide, maker of rival sweetener Equal (a/k/a the blue one), sued to stop Splenda (the yellow one) from claiming that the product is natural and using the tagline "made from sugar, so it tastes like sugar." The suit claims that the phrase misleads consumers into thinking Splenda is natural, when, according to the two plaintiffs, it is actually "a highly processed chemical compound." The sweetener industry has good reason to fear Splenda—since its introduction in 2000, it had built up a 51 percent market share by the time of the suit in 2005. McNeil hit back that the suit was a "malicious smear campaign" meant to besmirch Splenda's reputation.

O, T can you C?

In February 2006, Pfizer announced a desire to sell off its consumer health care unit, home to such famous over-the-counter treatments as Listerine, Rolaids, Lubriderm and Rogaine, catching the ear of J&J CEO William C. Weldon. His interest was piqued by the strength of the brands in the offering, and in June 2006 J&J announced that it would buy the Pfizer segment for $16.6 billion, becoming the world's biggest consumer health care company in the process. Industry experts surmised that the deal, which added to J&J's smallest unit, might be part of a strategy to put the company's consumer goods holdings at a level comparable to its medical device and pharmaceutical market share.

Community chest

J&J has been a supporter of disaster relief since the 1906 San Francisco earthquake, having in the century since set aside cash and products for relief efforts as well as social responsibility programs. The company's Contributions Annual Report outlines J&J's worldwide initiatives through five programs—Access to Care, Advancing Health Care Knowledge, Community Responsibility, Global Public Health (which focuses on HIV/AIDS work) and Women's and Children's Health. In 2005, the company collaborated with hundreds of American and international organizations—including the Elizabeth Glaser Pediatric AIDS Foundation and UNICEF—to give some $592 million in money and products for the global good.

GETTING HIRED

Join the J&J family

Johnson & Johnson's careers web site (www.jnj.com/careers) offers a searchable database of job opportunities, both for students and experienced professionals. The data is searchable by location, J&J organization and job department. Areas that hire undergrads for co-ops or internships include engineering, finance/accounting, information management, HR, logistics, operations, quality assurance, research and development, and sales. Leadership development programs are also available in finance, information systems and global operations. Finally, there is also career information for experienced hires on the web site, as well as info on benefits, diversity and work/life programs.

Get ready to talk in interviews

"In general J&J wants professional, creative and energetic people who are highly motivated," says one source—and here's how the company goes about finding such gems: most respondents reported at least two rounds of interviews, with one college hire 'fessing up to six. While some employees admitted to some grilling on the expertise front, J&J's powers that hire seem to be very fond of behavioral questions, so job seekers should be prepared to answer involved questions like "Tell me a time you were a leader"; "When you have worked on a team and a teammate was not pulling his weight, what did you do to address the problem?"; and "Describe a situation when you helped turn around a project that was heading off the deep end." Interviewees may have a big audience for their tales of fearless leadership—one source warns of "panel interviews." Fear not, though, as another enthusiastic contact put it, "The interview process was very pleasant and the people I spoke to were great."

OUR SURVEY SAYS

Luck of the draw

Culture at Johnson & Johnson generally seems to reflect the pleasantness of the people, with certain regional variations. "Different affiliates are drastically different in culture," muses one source. "I found the culture of the Los Angeles affiliates to be more quirky and laid-back than that of the affiliates I worked with out in New Jersey. Corporate HQ has a very strong, old corporate culture." His co-worker adds, "Overall the environment is quite friendly, people seem to be helping each other and there is a robust young crowd." An insider from Puerto Rico is less impressed, describing his office's work environment as "intimidating … with long extended working hours."

On the other side of the globe, says a respondent in Russia, the "atmosphere in the office is very friendly," though, "it is often difficult to make changes happen, due to extensive bureaucracy," moans another. His colleague chimes in, adding that he's irked by "the amount of alignment that goes on" before decisions are made. Another agrees, adding that there's "too much training for too many procedures." Ultimately, one's experience at J&J will depend on whom one gets thrown in with: "The head of the department/affiliate you are in sets the culture of that affiliate, so it's very touch and go. Some affiliates are great to be at, others not so great."

Dress, in its infinite varieties

Along with culture, the dress of the natives varies from region to region. "At HQ," one well-traveled female source reports, "hosiery is a must," while "at some California affiliates, jeans are acceptable every day." A member of the Russian office observes, "Dress code: not strict, business casual is accepted on most occasions. Jeans and T-shirts are accepted on Fridays. Many women wear minis." New staffers should be prepared to invest in their wardrobes as they climb the corporate ladder. One notes "men wear button-down shirts (no tie), dress pants (khakis, slacks) and dressy shoes." He goes on to add that dress becomes "more formal when upper management visits."

Work/life mix

As might be imagined in such a large organization, opinions of work/life balance vary. One member of the finance department reports that "Most people like to get in very early in the morning (7 or 7:30 a.m.), and out by about 5 or 6 p.m.—however, there are many nights that last until 10 or 11 p.m." Another source reports that he works "normally from 9 a.m. till 6 p.m., overtime not compensated. Overtime [happens] often." One intern reports that "the hours usually range from 40 to 50 hours a week." A colleague helpfully adds, "For students looking for jobs [at J&J] but [who] are worried about the death of their social life, it's very close to Princeton University, Rutgers University, TCNJ and Ride."

Opportunities are bound

A member of the pharmaceutical sales team remarks, "The opportunities for advancement are not as plentiful as they were in the heady days of the 1990s. Those opportunities that do exist are in management and sales training; pursuing these opportunities today means waiting in a very long line, playing politics with your superiors and being able to relocate immediately." His colleague adds, "opportunities and environment vary from franchise to franchise, and are the best in the pharmaceutical franchise." A member of the finance department notes, "There is opportunity for advancement to senior analyst positions, but the jump to manager is a difficult (but imperative) one. Those that make it go far in the organization."

Johnson & Johnson & friends

Diversity at J&J is one of the company's high points. "There are plenty of women," notes one insider, though her colleague would like J&J to institute some "women's

Visit Vault at **www.vault.com** for insider company profiles, expert advice, career message boards, expert resume reviews, the Vault Job Board and more.

VAULT CAREER LIBRARY   **241**

leadership initiatives" and a "diversity team." Minorities' representation at the company gets good marks as well.

King Pharmaceuticals, Inc.

501 Fifth Street
Bristol, TN 37620
Phone: (423) 989-8000
Fax: (423) 274-8677
www.kingpharm.com

LOCATIONS

Bristol, TN (HQ)
Bridgewater, NJ
Cary, NC
Columbia, MD
Middleton, WI
Rochester, MN
St. Louis, MO
St. Petersburg, FL

THE STATS

Employer Type: Public Company
Stock Symbol: KG
Stock Exchange: NYSE
President & CEO: Brian Markison
2006 Employees: 2,700
2006 Revenue ($mil.): $1,989
2006 Net Income ($mil.): $289

DEPARTMENTS

Accounting
Business Development
Clerical/Admininstrative
Corporate Affairs
Corporate Compliance
Customer Service
Engineering
Finance
Human Resources
Information Technology
Legal Affairs
Manufacturing & Distribution
Professional Information Services
Public Relations
Quality Management
Regulatory Affairs
Research & Development
Sales & Marketing

KEY COMPETITORS

Biovail Corp.
Forest Laboratories
Shire Plc

EMPLOYMENT CONTACT

www.kingpharm.com/kingpharm/
Careers

THE SCOOP

King of the mountains

With headquarters in the scenic Blue Ridge Mountains, King Pharmaceuticals develops, manufactures, markets and sells branded pharmaceutical products. This vertically integrated company, a relative newcomer to the pharmaceutical scene, focuses its efforts on three therapeutic areas: cardiovascular and metabolics, neuroscience, and hospital and acute care.

King's top-selling product is the heart drug Altace, which the company acquired from Hoechst Marion Roussel (now part of sanofi-aventis) for $363 million in 1998, along with two other products. Altace racked up $653 million in 2006 sales, an almost 18 percent increase from 2005. Another top seller is muscle relaxant Skelaxin, whose 2006 sales were $415 million, a 20 percent increase from the previous year.

A King is born

King kicked off operations in January 1994, when the Gregory family purchased a pharmaceuticals plant in Bristol, Tenn. The company has grown by leaps and bounds since then, with annual revenue increasing more than tenfold from 1994 to 2006, from $13 million to almost $2 billion. The company's number of employees, initially 145, now stands at around 2,800. King had 24 sales professionals in 1994, and now employs more 1,100.

During its early years, King assumed contracts to make prescription pharmaceuticals for companies like SmithKline Beecham and Novartis. It then focused mostly on manufacturing, acquiring and marketing previously approved products until 2004, when Bristol-Myers Squibb veteran Brian Markison became the company's CEO. Under Markison, King started to develop its own drugs and acquired a number of novel pharmaceutical products in the later stages of development.

Preparing for generics

The first patent on top-selling Altace is due to expire in 2008 and King is taking steps to protect its best-selling drug. In February 2006, the company entered into an agreement with Arrow International Limited and some of its affiliates to commercialize one or more novel formulations Altace's active ingredient, ramipil. Also, King has developed a combination of Altace and a diuretic called hydrochlorothiazide, and stated in April 2007 that a late-stage study evaluating the product yielded positive initial results. The company plans to file for FDA approval of the drug during early 2008.

But King's plans to extend its Altace-based success received a heavy blow in September 2007, when an appeals court ruled that the Indian generic firm Lupin Ltd. could start marketing a generic version of ramipil, Altace's active ingredient. A lower court had ruled in favor of King but a subsequent Supreme Court decisions subsequently found that the obviousness of this product is cause for invalidating its patent. King has another appeal pending.

Our pain is their gain

King is pouring more money into in-house research and development, too. In 2006, the firm's research and development expenses increased to $143.6 million, nearly twice what it spent the previous year. The company spent $74 million on R&D in 2005, and about $68 million in 2004. One drug the firm is developing is T-62, a novel treatment for neuropathic pain. King continues to purchase some promising medications from other companies, recently complementing its R&D efforts by acquiring pain medications. In 2005, the company acquired worldwide commercial rights to Pain Therapeutics' Remoxy and other abuse-deterrent opioid drugs, and in February 2007, it acquired Avinza—an extended release formulation of morphine— from Ligand Pharmaceuticals.

Oddly, King's executives trumpeted further R&D investment in September 2007, when the company sold a manufacturing facility in Rochester, Mich. That month, King closed on a $93 million sale of the facility—and some of the products it had developed for King—to the fledgling firm JHP Pharmaceuticals. Eric Bruce, King's chief technical operations officer, stated that the sale "will enable (King) to redeploy our current investments [into] our ongoing R&D and business development initiatives."

GETTING HIRED

King me!

The careers section of King's web site, at kingpharm.com/kingpharm/Careers, includes a searchable database of available positions. Departments include accounting, business development, clerical/administrative, corporate affairs, corporate compliance, customer

Visit Vault at **www.vault.com** for insider company profiles, expert advice, career message boards, expert resume reviews, the Vault Job Board and more.

VAULT CAREER LIBRARY   **245**

service, engineering, finance, human resources, information technology, legal affairs, manufacturing and distribution, professional information services, public relations, quality management, regulatory affairs, research and development and sales and marketing.

Benefits at King Pharmaceuticals include medical insurance, vision, dental, disability plans, life insurance, flexible spending accounts, a retirement plan, an adoption benefit and tuition reimbursement. Under the company's prescription coverage plan, employees don't have a co-payment for King's drugs.

In January 2006, *Fortune* named King Pharmaceuticals one of the nine best-managed drug companies. The company ranked No. 862 on *Fortune*'s 2007 ranking of America's largest companies, a slight jump from 2006, when it was No. 865.

Lexicon Pharmaceuticals, Inc.

8800 Technology Forest Place
The Woodlands, TX 77381-1160
Phone: (281) 863-3000
Fax: (281) 863-8088
www.lexpharma.com

LOCATIONS

The Woodlands, TX (HQ)
Princeton, NJ

THE STATS

Employer Type: Public Company
Stock Symbol: LEXG
Stock Exchange: Nasdaq
President & CEO: Arthur T. Sands
Chairman: Samuel Barker
2006 Employees: 585
2006 Revenue ($mil.): $73
2006 Net Income ($mil.): -$54

DEPARTMENTS

Administration & Finance
Clinical Development
DMPK
Expression Analysis & Cloning
Human Resources
Legal & Intellectual Property
Pharmaceutical Discovery
Process Chemistry
Vivarium Operations

KEY COMPETITORS

Exelixis, Inc.
Human Genome Sciences
Millennium Pharmaceuticals

EMPLOYMENT CONTACT

www.lexpharma.com/careers

Visit Vault at **www.vault.com** for insider company profiles, expert advice, career message boards, expert resume reviews, the Vault Job Board and more.

VAULT CAREER LIBRARY   247

THE SCOOP

Tex.-Lex

Nestled in the forests of The Woodlands, Texas, Lexicon Pharmaceuticals focuses on the discovery and development of breakthrough treatments for human disease. To date, the company has used a proprietary gene knockout technology to discover more than 100 promising drug targets in the areas of diabetes and obesity, cancer, cardiovascular disease, psychiatric and neurological disorders, immune system disorders and ophthalmic disease. The firm's 2006 revenue was approximately $73 million.

From mice to drugs ...

Lexicon Pharmaceuticals started out as Lexicon Genetics in 1995; it tendered an IPO in 2000. The firm is still under the leadership of Arthur Sands, the PhD who co-founded Lexicon with Brian Zambrowicz.

Lexicon uses a patented technology to knock out, or disrupt, the function of genes in mice. The company's researchers then use advanced medical technologies to systematically discover the physiological and behavioral functions and pharmaceutical utility of the genes they've knocked out and the potential drug targets encoded by the corresponding human genes.

In simpler terms, Lexicon scientists create genetically engineered mice that are missing particular genes (with stem-cell technology). The researchers then use physiological and behavioral tests to compare these super-mice to normal ones that still have the gene in question. Some of the "knockout" mice might then be able to fight tumors more effectively or age more quickly; some may get fat while others are exceptionally smart. In one specific example, one type of mice, the LG-617s, scored twice as well on learning and memory tests than normal mice after having a specific neurological gene knocked out.

Lexicon lacks the resources to develop drugs for all of the gene targets it identifies, so the firm has struck several collaboration agreements with large pharmaceutical companies. The company has drug discovery alliances with Genentech (to discover novel therapeutic proteins and antibody targets), N.V. Organon (to discover, develop and commercialize novel biotherapeutic drugs), Takeda (to discover new drugs for the treatment of high blood pressure); Bristol-Myers Squibb (to discover, develop and commercialize new small molecule neuroscience drugs). In addition, the firm has established collaborations with academic institutions and research institutes such as Texas A&M and the NIH.

... and drugs to men

In 2006, Lexicon initiated its first human clinical trials. Two drugs are currently in clinical development. LX6171 is the company's oral drug candidate for the treatment of cognitive impairment associated with disorders such as schizophrenia, Alzheimer's disease and vascular dementia. The company started a phase Ib clinical trial for LX6171 in January 2007.

Another drug in clinical trials is LX1031, a product for the treatment of irritable bowel syndrome and other gastrointestinal disorders. In April 2007, Lexicon advanced LX1031 into phase Ib clinical trials. Additional drug programs are in preclinical development and research.

Lexicon Genetics Incorporated changed its name to Lexicon Pharmaceuticals in April 2007. CEO Sands stated that the name change reflected Lexicon's transition from a research stage company to an integrated biopharmaceutical firm that has "an exciting pipeline of product candidates." For just this reason, the company secured $205 million in financing from Invus LP and entered into a $60 million product development deal with Symphony Capital Partners in June 2007.

Developing a success

In 2006, the company's R&D expenses for company-sponsored as well as collaborative R&D activities topped $106 million. In comparison, Lexicon spent about $94 million on R&D in 2005 and $91 million in 2004. The firm's target discovery work over the past decade has provided Lexicon with a large portfolio of new drug programs that will fuel the company's product pipeline.

The goal of Lexicon's so-called "10 to 10" initiative is to advance 10 drug candidates into human clinical trials by the end of 2010. The company plans to advance at least two drug programs per year into clinical development. Lexicon expects to increase its alliance activity in 2007 to accelerate the clinical and commercial development of the company's discoveries.

Visit Vault at **www.vault.com** for insider company profiles, expert advice, career message boards, expert resume reviews, the Vault Job Board and more.

VAULT CAREER LIBRARY   **249**

GETTING HIRED

Lex respects its employees

Prospective applicants can search Lexicon's online database of open jobs to view current employment opportunities (www.lexpharma.com/careers). Departments at the company include administration and finance, clinical development, DMPK, expression analysis and cloning, human resources, legal and intellectual property, pharmaceutical discovery, process chemistry and vivarium operations. Each job posting has a link at the bottom that allows applicants to express interest in the job using an online response form. After job hunters complete the form and hit the "Submit" button, resumes are submitted to Lexicon for review. The firm's web site stresses that submitting a resume more than once will not increase an applicant's chances of being hired, and the company prefers not to get follow-up phone calls.

Lexicon views employees as a key to the company's success, and the firm offers highly competitive starting salaries based on prospective employees' experiences and qualifications. Comprehensive benefits at Lexicon include medical, prescription drug, dental and vision coverage; company-paid life and AD&D insurance and the option to purchase additional insurance at group rates; company-paid disability insurance, flexible spending accounts, a traditional or Roth 401(k) plan with a company match, stock options, a 529 college investing plan; an educational assistance plan and corporate training programs. Employees are eligible for most benefits on their first day of employment at Lexicon. Exceptions are the 401(k) plan (first of the month after hire date) and the educational assistance plan (six months). The company offers relocation assistance for some positions.

In 2007, *The Scientist* named Lexicon Pharmaceuticals one of the Best Places To Work in Industry for the fourth year in a row.

Merck & Co., Inc.

1 Merck Drive
P.O. Box 100
Whitehouse Station, NJ 08889-0100
Phone: (908) 423-1000
Fax: (908) 735-1253
www.merck.com

LOCATIONS

Whitehouse Station, NJ (HQ)
Albany, GA • Atlanta, GA • Blue Bell, PA • Boca Raton, FL • Boston, MA • Branchburg, NJ • Burlingame, CA • Cary, NC • Cokesbury, NJ • Costa Mesa, CA • Dublin, OH • Elkton, VA • Fulton, MO • Glen Allen, VA • Indianapolis, IN • Irving, TX • Kirkland, WA • Miami Lakes, FL • Minnetonka, MN • Norcross, GA • Overland Park, KS • Rahway, NJ • Reno, NV • Rockville, MD • Roswell, GA • Scottsdale, AZ • Somerset, NJ • West Point, PA • Westchester, IL • Westwood, MA • Wilson, NC • Woodbridge, NJ

International locations in more than 140 countries.

THE STATS

Employer Type: Public Company
Stock Symbol: MRK
Stock Exchange: NYSE
Chairman, President & CEO: Richard T. Clark
2006 Employees: 60,000
2006 Revenue ($mil.): $22,636
2006 Net Income ($mil.): $4,434

DEPARTMENTS

Corporate
Finance
Human Resources
Legal
Public Affairs
Information Services
Manufacturing & Supply
Research
Sales & Marketing

KEY COMPETITORS

Bristol-Myers Squibb
Pfizer Inc.
sanofi-aventis

EMPLOYMENT CONTACT

www.merck.com/careers

Visit Vault at **www.vault.com** for insider company profiles, expert advice, career message boards, expert resume reviews, the Vault Job Board and more.

VAULT CAREER LIBRARY   251

THE SCOOP

Snapshot

Founded in New York in 1891, Merck & Co. discovers, develops, produces and markets vaccines and medicines to treat a variety of conditions. Driven by its research, the company sells its products mainly to pharmaceutical wholesalers and retailers, hospitals, clinics, government agencies and managed health care providers, and its product line contains vaccines and medicines in more than 20 therapeutic categories.

The company employs about 60,000 people in about 140 countries around the globe. One of the largest pharmaceutical companies in the world, Merck's 2006 revenue was $22.6 billion, compared to $22 billion from 2005.

Tracing it all back

Though officially founded in 1891, Merck's history actually begins much earlier—in 1668, actually, when Frederic Jacon Merck opened a chemistry business in Darmstadt, Germany. One of his descendants, George Merck, took the business to the U.S. in 1891, offering its chemical products to stateside shoppers.

In the early 1930s, Merck started its foray into the fairly new pharmaceutical business with its research. Among the breakthroughs Merck helped bring about was the groundbreaking predecessor to all modern antibiotics: penicillin. The company merged with Sharp & Dohme in 1953, creating the pharmaceutical firm Merck Sharp & Dohme.

Merck and the "me decade"

The firm lost its leading status after an attempt at diversification in the 1960s, but CEO John Honran steered it back to dominance, starting in the late 1970s. For every year between 1981 and 1985, the company's revenue grew by at least 9 percent; and Honran claimed in 1984 that Merck was the largest American pharmaceutical in the markets of Europe, Japan and the U.S.

The ascent only continued after Honran stepped down mid-decade—Vasotec became its first billion-dollar drug in 1988 and at one point, *BusinessWeek* ranked it as the world's leading drug company and a top-10 most valuable company overall. All told, from 1980 to 1989 the firm's revenue doubled and its profits tripled.

Modern Merck

Merck had less blockbuster products in the 1990s, with the notable exception of billion-dollar baby Zocor. There was a blockbuster merger, though, for $6.6 billion in 1993 with medical distributor Medco. But soon other companies' mergers made this one look paltry—especially Pfizer and Warner Lambert's $90 billion marriage in 2000—and Merck lost its world-leading status.

The company responded by investing in new drugs, releasing a record eight new medications in the 18 months after new chief Raymond Gilmartin took over in 1994. Merck then augmented the bottom line by divesting some assets—selling its crop protection unit to Novartis for $910 million in 1997; selling its half-interest in a joint venture to partner DuPont for $2.6 billion in 1998; restructuring a joint venture with Astra and receiving $1.8 billion in royalty fees from the AstraZeneca merger in 1999. Also in 1999, the company released the drug that, for better and for worse, has come to be synonymous with Merck: Vioxx.

Coming through a Mercky period

In late September 2004, Merck announced it would withdraw Vioxx from the market, causing the company's stock to fall 40 percent and its market value to correspondingly fall by $50 billion. A long-term clinical trial had revealed that some patients developed certain types of cardiovascular events after 18 months of taking the product. The FDA later concluded that long-term use of Vioxx, and all similar COX-2 inhibitors, were associated with an increased risk of certain types of cardiovascular events.

After learning about Vioxx's health risks, over 30,000 people sued the company for products liability. Of the 29 lawsuits that have been scheduled for trial as of February 2007, seven were withdrawn from the trial calendar by plaintiffs, seven more were dismissed (for various reason), and juries have decided in Merck's favor nine times. Four plaintiffs have been successful at trial. During 2006, Merck spent $500 million in Vioxx legal defense costs. As of December 2006, the company had set aside $858 million for potential Vioxx-related legal expenses through the end of 2008.

Let's get to the bottom of this!

Besides spending money on Vioxx-related lawsuits, Merck's board commissioned its own $21 million, 20 monthlong investigation on whether the company tried to hide potential risks associated with Vioxx. In September 2006, the investigator, former federal judge John Martin Jr., delivered his verdict. "The report is essentially a very positive one," Martin said at a press conference, adding that Merck took "reasonable steps" to research Vioxx's possible health risks, and that it was impossible for the company to know how dangerous the drug was prior to withdrawing the drug in 2004 after a clinical trial revealed its risks.

The report echoed much of the Merck defense team's rebuttals of criticisms leveled by scientists and plaintiffs' attorneys, and answered the main concern of the Merck board, which was, according to Martin, "Did senior management ... knowingly put people at risk?" The ultimate finding of the 180-page report (with an additional 1,500 pages of appendices) was, in short, no.

In April 2007 the FDA rejected Merck's request to market Arcoxia, a Vioxx-like drug, in the United States. The agency was concerned that Arcoxia—another painkiller in the COX-2 class of drugs—would raise the risk of strokes and heart attacks. Merck sells Arcoxia in 63 other countries and plans to continue marketing it outside of the U.S.

Settle down, there!

And then, in November 2007, Merck attempted to end its legal involvement with Vioxx once and for all, committing $4.85 billion to settle up to 50,000 different Vioxx-related claims. At the time, about 47,000 plaintiffs were claiming damages in 27,000 pending lawsuits. The deal will be studied and discussed for years to come by lawyers and law students everywhere as it is a landmark, complex 70-pages-long document. One of its clauses, called "unusual" by both *The Wall Street Journal* and the *Los Angeles Times*, stipulates that lawyers either recommend accepting the settlement to all of their clients or none of them; and that lawyers must stop representing any clients who refuse the settlement. Needless to say, this provision raised the eyebrows of legal experts everywhere.

The settlement also requires that 85 percent of claimants agree to it by a March 1, 2008 deadline, or else it will become void. Legal analysts have already calculated that if the settlement is approved—which would require about 40,000 people accepting Merck's offer—the average payout would be between $100,000 and $200,000, before the 30 or 50 percent that a lawyer would charge, of course. Merck has received good press for the gambit, as the settlement would bring its legal costs to around $7 billion, below projected costs of $10 billion. In November 2007 *The New York Times* quoted Peter Schuck, a Yale law professor: "[Merck] played hardball, and the nature of the settlement that was reached reflects that. The predicted liabilities for [the company] were much, much higher."

Merck's remaining all-stars

Even prior to the company's September 2004 decision to immediately cease all sales of Vioxx, Merck had lagged behind industry leader Pfizer. Vioxx contributed $2.5 billion to Merck's coffers the previous year, some 11 percent of the company's total revenue. But the company's flagship drugs continued to rank either first or second in class, in terms of worldwide sales, and held unblemished safety and efficacy results.

Worldwide sales of Singulair, a once-daily medication that treats asthma and relieves symptoms of allergic rhinitis, reached sales of nearly $3.6 billion in 2006, an increase from $3 billion the year prior. In August 2005, the FDA approved Singular for perennial allergic rhinitis (indoor allergies) in adults and children aged six and older. At the end of 2006, Singulair continued to be the No. 1 prescribed product in the U.S. respiratory market.

Global sales of Merck's antihypertensive drugs Cozaar and Hyzaar remained strong in 2006, hitting $3.1 billion, compared to $3 billion the year before. In 2006, Cozaar/Hyzaar were the No. 2 branded medications for the treatment of high blood pressure in Europe and the United States.

Merck has also reaped the continued success of Fosamax, the world's most prescribed treatment for postmenopausal symptoms and glucocortoid-induced osteoporosis. The company celebrated the 2005 release of Fosamax Plus D, a new drug that continued Fosamax's ability to reduce the risk of hip and spine fractures, and added vitamin D consistent with recommended guidelines.

In 2006 sales of Fosamax came in at $3.1 billion, a slight decrease from 2005, when the drug had $3.2 billion in sales. The availability of a generic version of the drug in some key markets, including Germany, Canada and the United Kingdom, had a negative impact on Fosamax sales outside of the United States. In February 2008, Fosamax will lose market exclusivity in the U.S.

Hitting the Merck

In 2006, Merck launched five new medicines and vaccines. The FDA approved RotaTeq in February 2006. RotaTeq is a pediatric vaccine for gastroenteritis as well as severe diarrhea and dehydration, which lead to 500,000 deaths annually. Zostavax, a vaccine to reduce the incidence of and pain associated with shingles, won the FDA's approval in May 2006.

Visit Vault at **www.vault.com** for insider company profiles, expert advice, career message boards, expert resume reviews, the Vault Job Board and more.

VAULT CAREER LIBRARY   255

In October 2006, the FDA approved Zolinza to advanced cases of cutaneous T-cell lymphoma, a rare cancer. Also that month, Merck introduced Januvia, a new once-a-day pill for controlling type 2 diabetes, the most common form of that disease.

Analysts predict this could mean big bucks for Merck, as the market for diabetes treatments is expected to expand, in step with the national waistline. Already 7 percent of the American population—some 21 million people—is affected by the malady. The chief advantage of the new medication is that it has fewer side effects than other therapies, which can include weight gain and fluid retention.

A fracas over Gardasil

One new product that's sparked controversy is Gardasil, a vaccine against certain types of human papillomavirus (HPV). Certain types of HPV can cause cervical cancer. In June 2006, the FDA approved Gardasil for use against HPV in women aged nine to 26. Texas Governor Rick Perry liked the idea, issuing an executive order in February 2007, requiring girls be vaccinated against HPV prior to admission to the sixth grade.

But the order proved to be a political hot potato, and in March 2007 Texas' House of Representatives voted 119 to 21 to overturn the governor's orders. In other states, legislators said they would sign bills mandating vaccination against HPV. In April 2007, the Washington D.C. Council approved a requirement that girls entering the sixth grade be vaccinated against HPV; parents will be allowed to have their children opt out.

The opinions about Gardasil are still coming. In May 2007, two members of the obstetrics and gynecology department at the University of California-San Francisco, published an editorial in *The New England Journal of Medicine* that raised questions about Gardasil's overall effectiveness. The authors of the editorial suggested that policymakers, parents and doctors adopt "a cautious approach" toward vaccination. Also in May 2007, Judicial Watch, a conservative watchdog group, disseminated new reports of serious adverse events linked to Gardasil.

Free Vaccines

In 2006 Merck created a new Vaccine Patient Assistance Program. The program will provide Merck's adult vaccines, such as Gardasil, at no charge to uninsured U.S. adults who cannot afford them. In addition, a partnership with the Nicaraguan government will provide RotaTeq for free to every newborn baby in Nicaragua for the next three years.

Next on the Merck-et

Approximately 11,400 people are employed in research at Merck. In 2006 the company spent $4.8 billion on R&D programs, an increase from $3.8 billion the year before and $4 billion in 2004.

In 2007, Merck expects to file three new drug applications with the FDA. These new drugs are raltegravir for HIV, gaboxadol for insomnia, and MK-0524A, which decreases LDL, increases HDL and lowers triglycerides. In addition, three products are already under review. These drugs are Janumet for type 2 diabetes; Emend, to treat nausea and vomiting experienced by chemotherapy patients; and the aforementioned Arcoxia, for reducing osteoarthritis pain.

To complement internal R&D efforts, the company has cultivated external resources, either through collaborative alliances or through strategic acquisitions of other companies. Merck acquired three biotechnology companies in 2006, the first being privately held biopharmaceutical company Abrnaxis for approximately $80 million in May. The following month, Merck spent about $373 million on GlycoFi, a leader in the field of yeast glycoengineering and the optimization of biologic drug molecules. Finally, in December 2006, Merck acquired research-based pharmaceutical company Sirna for approximately $1.1 billion.

Merck is divesting assets these days, as well. In May 2007, the firm sold off its generics unit for €4.9 billion ($6.7 billion) to Mylan Laboratories, which then changed its name to Mylan Inc. The purchase makes Mylan the world's third-largest generics firm.

GETTING HIRED

Work for Merck

The careers section of Merck's corporate web site (www.merck.com/careers) lists job opportunities in five departments including research, sales and marketing, manufacturing and supply, information services, and corporate (which includes human resources, legal, finance and public affairs). Merck has a university recruiting section (www.merck.com/careers/university/index.html) where students can post their resumes and look for internships. Merck's internships are paid, and the firm offers subsidized housing for interns. There is a searchable database at www.merck.com/careers/search_jobs/index.html.

In 2005, Merck announced global restructuring plans that would eliminate 7,000 positions by the end of 2008, close five manufacturing facilities, two pre clinical sites and one basic research site. The company also said it planned to save $4.5 to $5 billion and reach double-digit compound annual growth by 2010. By the end of 2006, Merck reached $1 billion of its goal to save $1.2 billion in procurement by 2008. The firm had closed, sold or ceased operations at three of the five manufacturing facilities, and the company is in the process of doing the same to the other two. Merck has eliminated 4,800 positions.

Lots of interviews and a long wait

An insider who has been involved in hiring says, "Merck believes in having multiple hiring managers meet with the prospective employee, and frequently includes lower-level team members to gather opinions regarding the 'fit' of the prospect with the rest of the team." A programmer says an hourlong phone interview was followed by a "full day of interviewing," which included eating with a junior-level employee at the on-site cafeteria as well as meeting with three managers for about an hour an a half each. A source in Germany reports "two rounds of interviews" with "40 participants." One Merck scientist says that although there was only one round of interviews, "it was a full day, and I met with about five to six different people for about an hour each." The respondent adds, "You meet both peers and upper management during the interviews." The source says interview questions were "the expected ones." However, the contact adds, "I've heard other interviewers sometimes ask technical questions."

Sources say Merck can be slow getting back to applicants. One insider in the quality assurance department, who was hired internally from another position says, "What was particularly interesting was the delay between the interview and the offer—364 days, to be exact!" Another says, "The hiring process at Merck is notoriously very slow, so don't expect to actually start work for at least three months after you complete your interview, even if all goes smoothly." The same respondent has heard that "Merck likes to hire people with 3.5-plus GPAs" and says the company "definitely prefers big name schools."

OUR SURVEY SAYS

Times are changing

Sources describe Merck as "great" and "a good, solid company." An insider says, "The company is really very committed to developing quality products that will improve patient quality of life and values product safety over profits." The contact adds, "Overall, I love working here and I feel like the company values my contributions and treats employees well." One insider, who says Merck "prides itself on its diversity," adds that "walking through the halls of the corporate headquarters that diversity is very evident. There are times when one could mistake the place for a branch office of the United Nations!"

One longtime staffer says that, over the years, Merck has evolved from being "very traditional" to a company that is "becoming less conservative, and more flexible and agile." The source says a business casual dress code is a sign of changing times. Over the years, Merck has made some other changes. A New Jersey insider says the company rolled year end bonuses into the regular salary more than a decade ago. Another says that, in late 2006, Merck increased vacation time for new hires from two weeks to three weeks.

A good time to join?

A source in Germany thinks the company's outlook is "very good for the next five years." Some say morale has been low in certain departments due to layoffs and reorganization during recent years. However, one project manager says that, although Merck has been going through layoffs, "it may be an ideal time to join on." The respondent explains that if an applicant has, "the right set of competencies that match those that the company is currently lacking," Merck "may provide the right person with a true career launching pad."

Visit Vault at **www.vault.com** for insider company profiles, expert advice, career message boards, expert resume reviews, the Vault Job Board and more.

V/\ULT CAREER LIBRARY   259

Millennium Pharmaceuticals, Inc.

40 Landsdown Street
Cambridge, MA 02139
Phone: (617) 676-7000
Fax: (617) 374-7788
www.mlnm.com

LOCATIONS

Cambridge, MA (HQ)
Washington, DC
Chiswick Park, UK

THE STATS

Employer Type: Public Company
Stock Symbol: MLNM
Stock Exchange: Nasdaq
President & CEO: Deborah Dunsire
2006 Employees: 947
2006 Revenue ($mil.): $487
2006 Net Income ($mil.): -$44

KEY COMPETITORS

Celgene Corp.
Genzyme
Pharmion

EMPLOYMENT CONTACT

www.mlnm.com/careers

DEPARTMENTS

Administration • Analytical Chemistry • Animal Services • Bioanalytical Services • Biology • Biostatistics • Business Development • Cell Culture • Chemical Engineering • Cheminformatics • Chemistry • Clinical Data Management • Clinical Research • Computational Chemistry • Corporate Communications • Document Control • Drug Safety • Engineering • Environmental Health & Safety • Facilities • Finance • Formulation • Genomics • Human Resources • Informatics • Investor Relations • Information Technology • Legal • Manufacturing/Production • Marketing • Materials/Inventory Control • Medical Affairs • Medical Communications • Microbiology • Molecular Biology • Operations • Pharmacokinetics • Pharmacology • Postdoctoral • Preclinical Development • Process Development • Production Planning • Project Management • Protein Chemistry • Proteomics • Public Relations • Purchasing • Quality Assurance • Quality Control • Regulatory Compliance • Research & Development • Sales • Shipping/Receiving • Software Engineering • Statistics • Strategy Planning • Technical Services • Technicians • Toxicology • Training • Validation • Virology

THE SCOOP

Behind the Millennium

Millennium, a biopharmaceutical firm in the Boston area, focuses on discovering, developing and marketing drugs to treat patients with inflammatory diseases and cancer. In 2006, the company's total sales were around $467 million, a more than 12 percent decrease from approximately $558 million in 2005.

The company currently markets Velcade, an injected novel therapeutic that's used to treat patients with multiple myeloma, a cancer of the plasma cell. In December 2006 the FDA approved Velcade to treat of an aggressive form of non-Hodgkin's lymphoma. Currently, the product is approved in more than 75 countries worldwide, including the United States, the European Union and a number of countries within Southeast Asia and Latin America.

Millennium's milestones

In 1993, Millennium was born with the grandiose goal to develop breakthrough products that would fundamentally change the practice of medicine. During the company's early years, Millennium focused on building top-notch business and science teams to help achieve this objective.

The company entered into more than 20 strategic alliances with biotech and pharmaceutical companies, starting in 1994. Millennium brought its first drug, Campath, close to market in 1999 when the firm merged with Leukosite, also acquiring other investigational drugs in clinical trials. (The company later sold Campath to Genzyme.) In 2000, a merger with Cambridge Discovery Chemistry gave Millennium a strong presence in the U.K., adding more than 100 scientists with expertise in chemistry to the organization.

A merger with COR Therapeutics in February 2002 created a strong pipeline of novel therapeutics and also added cardiovascular research and drug development to the company's key therapeutic areas. COR also brought Millennium a product called Integrilin, which was an intravenous anti-platelet drug for patients with severe cardiovascular diseases. Millennium sold the rights to this drug to Schering-Plough in 2005.

In May 2003 the company launched Velcade to treat relapsed and refractory multiple myeloma. The drug has since won the FDA's approval for other indications. In

Visit Vault at **www.vault.com** for insider company profiles, expert advice, career message boards, expert resume reviews, the Vault Job Board and more.

VAULT CAREER LIBRARY   **261**

October 2006, Millennium announced a two-year agreement with Ortho Biotech to jointly promote the product in the United States. That year, Velcade's total revenue, including net sales of the product in the United States and strategic alliance revenue and royalties, was approximately $327 million, an increase from around $249 million in 2005.

Coming competition

Millennium expects traditional chemotherapy treatments and other therapies new to the market and in development to compete with Velcade. In December 2005, Celgene Corporation gained approval for Revlimid to treat a subset of patients with myelodysplastic syndromes, a group of related blood disorders.

In June 2006 Celgene's drug won FDA approval for the treatment of patients with multiple myeloma who have received at least one prior therapy. The FDA also approved Celgene's Thalomid for the treatment of newly diagnosed multiple myeloma in May 2006. Other potentially competitive therapies are in late-stage clinical development for multiple myeloma and could harm Velcade's harm future sales. Millennium (and Velcade) received a boost in October 2007, when the FDA approved it for use in cancer patients with impaired kidney function.

A new Millennium

The company isn't taking threats lying down. In June 2000, Millennium Pharmaceuticals entered into a broad agreement with Aventis (now sanofi-aventis). The agreement includes joint discovery, development and commercialization of small molecule drugs for the treatment of inflammatory diseases. One of the ways the agreement benefits Millennium is that it gives the firm potential access to sanofi-aventis' large promotional infrastructure to commercialize jointly developed products.

In June 2005, Mark J. Levin, who had been at the helm of Millennium since its inception, stepped down as chief executive. Around the same time, Millennium, which was one of the first firms to systematically search for genes linked to disease, shifted its focus to developing new drugs. Dr. Deborah Dunsire, a native of South Africa, medical doctor and former head of Novartis' U.S. oncology business, became president and CEO of this new Millennium in July 2005.

Merger meltdown

In September 2006, Millennium agreed to acquire Canadian biotechnology company AnorMED for $515 million, topping the terms of a hostile bid from Genzyme, another Cambridge biotech firm. AnorMED was in late-stage clinical trials of Mozobil, an experimental blood-cancer treatment, and Millennium hoped to expand its product offerings through the purchase. The following month, however, Genzyme raised its offer to $580 million. Millennium said it would not raise its price and was entitled to receive a $19.5 million termination fee from AnorMed.

In the next Millennium

Millennium's research and development expenses totaled $318.2 million in 2006. The company is building a pipeline of innovative new treatments for cancer and inflammatory diseases. Together with Johnson & Johnson Pharmaceutical Research & Development, the firm is investigating Velcade to treat hematologic and solid tumors in trials throughout Europe and the United States.

Millennium also has nine preclinical and clinical product candidates in the pipeline. These include MLN1202, a humanized monoclonal antibody that's in phase II trials for the treatment of multiple sclerosis and atherosclerosis, as well as potential medications for Crohn's disease, ulcerative colitis, rheumatoid arthritis, cancer and other malignancies.

GETTING HIRED

Applicants can search openings through Millenium's BrassRing site (www.mlnm.com/careers/search). The company hires in a slew of job categories including administration, analytical chemistry, animal services, biology, biostatistics, business development, chemistry, clinical research, corporate communications, drug safety, engineering, environmental health and safety, finance, human resources, IT, investor relations, legal, manufacturing/production, marketing, medical affairs, operations, pharmacology, preclinical development, project management, public relations, quality assurance, research and development, sales and technical services.

Benefits at Millennium include medical, dental and fitness insurance, pretax reimbursement accounts, fitness benefits, a 401(k) plan with company match and transportation and parking assistance. The company's tuition reimbursement program pays 100 percent of tuition, textbook and educational fees (up to $5,000 per year) for passing grades in career-related courses at accredited institutions.

The firm also attends career fairs, expos and conferences. A listing of career events is at www.millennium.com/careers/receptions.

Mylan Inc.

1500 Corporate Drive
Suite 400
Canonsburg, PA 15317
Phone: (724) 514-1800
Fax: (724) 514-1870
www.mylan.com

LOCATIONS

Canonsburg, PA (HQ)
Caguas, PR
Greensboro, NC
Morgantown, WV
Pittsburgh, PA
Rockford, IL
St. Alban's, VT
Sugar Land, TX
Washington, DC
Woodbridge, NJ

THE STATS

Employer Type: Public Company
Stock Symbol: MYL
Stock Exchange: NYSE
Chairman: Milan Puskar
Vice Chairman & CEO: Robert J. Coury
2007 Employees: 6,400
2007 Revenue ($mil.): $1,611
2007 Net Income ($mil.): $217

DEPARTMENTS

Administration
Ancillary Services
Business Development
Finance & Accounting
Flight Operations
Government/Public/Investor Affairs
Human Resources
Information Technology
Legal & Intellectual Property
Logistics
Maintenance & Engineering
Manufacturing
Manufacturing Technical Support
Marketing
Packaging
Pricing & Contracts
Project & Program Management
Sales/Customer Service
Security & Environment

KEY COMPETITORS

Barr Pharmaceuticals
Teva Pharmaceutical Industries
Watson Pharmaceuticals

EMPLOYMENT CONTACT

www.mylancareers.com

THE SCOOP

Mylan at-a-glance

Headquartered just outside of Pittsburgh, Mylan Laboratories develops, licenses, manufactures, markets and distributes generic, branded and branded generic pharmaceuticals. The company operates through three primary subsidiaries: Mylan Pharmaceuticals, UDL Laboratories and Mylan Technologies.

The firm also owns controlling interest in Matrix Laboratories, a supplier of active pharmaceutical ingredients. Matrix subsidiary Docpharma, a marketer of branded generics in Europe, offers Mylan a European platform. Mylan Laboratories makes and sells 160 generic products covering 46 therapeutic categories; it raked in about $1.6 billion in 2007, up from $1.25 billion in 2006.

Milan and Don (and Roy) create Mylan

Milan Puskar and Don Panoz, two army buddies in their 20s, founded Milan Pharmaceuticals in West Virginia, all the way back in 1961. The company started out as a distributor, but soon became a pharmaceutical manufacturer. After some management disagreements, Puskar left the company in 1972; the next year, it went public and changed its name to Mylan Laboratories.

Just two years later, Roy McKnight, president of a manufacturing company allied with Mylan, joined the company's board of directors. He discovered that it was "facing imminent bankruptcy," and took the reins as CEO himself, firing Mylan's president and bringing back alienated co-founder Milan Pusker in his place. The new leadership trimmed headcount by one third and refocused on developing generic drugs. Mylan turned a profit again in 1977 and became the first generic drug manufacturer to patent a new drug when it developed antihypertensive Maxide in the 1980s.

Mylan graduated to the realm of acquisition in the late 1980s and 1990s, purchasing innovative companies such as Dow B. Hickman, Bertek and Penderm. These acquisitions helped the firm become even more established in the pharmaceutical industry. By 1995, Mylan was the most dispensed line of pharmaceuticals—branded or generic—in the United States. When CEO McKnight suddenly died of a heart attack in 1993, Puskar became the company's chairman and CEO. Puskar stepped down as CEO in 2002, but he remains chairman of the board.

Legal woes

In 2000, Mylan agreed to pay a $147 million settlement in a price-fixing case. The FTC, 33 states and drug purchasers accused the company of improperly cornering the market on raw materials for two antianxiety drugs, lorazepam and clorazepate, and then raising the price of those drugs. (Mylan had raised the price of clorazepate by more than 3000 percent and lorezepam by more than 2,000 percent.)

Puskar, both chairman and CEO at the time, said it was the first time in the company's history that a government agency had accused the firm of improper conduct. The company's executives insisted that Mylan had done nothing wrong, but that the company had settled because of the continuing costs and uncertainties of the lawsuits.

Mylan actually has a history on the other side of such lawsuits—exposing corruption. The company actually hired private investigators to look into the FDA's practices in 1987, as it suspected illegal kickbacks and bribes were preventing the approval of Mylan products. The move was one of desperation after drastic and unexpected drops in Mylan's revenue, but it resulted in a Congressional investigation. The findings: three FDA employees admitted to taking bribes, at least five generic competitors engaged in improper activities and the FDA overhauled its approval process (a similar 1980s investigation was provoked by similarly suffering generics firm Barr Pharmaceuticals).

A patchy period

In July 2004, Mylan entered into an agreement to acquire King Pharmaceuticals but the two firms reneged in February 2005.

Then, in July 2005, the FDA issued a public health advisory warning that skin patches containing narcotic painkiller fentanyl could cause drug overdoses—Mylan markets a generic version of the patch. The FDA said it was investigating reports of serious side effects and possibly 120 deaths from the patches. An FDA spokeswoman said the agency was still investigating whether the patches had caused the deaths and other problems.

After news of the FDA investigation, financier Carl C. Icahn offered to sell his stock in Mylan, a decision he said was based partly on the news of the investigations (he owned 26.3 million shares). The company's stock fell 5 percent after Icahn's announcement. In fall 2006, Mylan announced that the company did not expect additional generic transdermal fentanyl approvals during the 2007 fiscal year.

In 2006, the FDA approved Emsam, the first and only transdermal MAOI for treating depression in patients with major depressive disorder. Mylan co-developed the depression patch with Somerset Pharmaceuticals, and the Bristol-Myers Squibb commercialized and launched the drug. However, at a 2007 Bristol-Myers Squibb annual meeting, an executive admitted that Emsam was a flop.

A robust pipeline

A large number of branded pharmaceutical products are scheduled to come off patent in the next few years, which could benefit Mylan and other generic drug companies. Over the past several years, Mylan has invested heavily in the company's generic product pipeline. The company's research and development expenses were $103 million in 2007, $102 million in 2006 and $88 million in 2005.

Mylan's pipeline is currently the most robust in the firm's 45-year history. The company also submitted a record number of product applications to the FDA in 2006, including 23 original Abbreviated New Drug Applications. Mylan anticipates that it will obtain FDA approval for more than 100 new products over the next five years. The company plans to continue to focus development efforts on products that require advanced manufacturing technology and technically difficult-to-formulate products.

In May 2007, Mylan agreed to buy the generics unit of German drug company Merck for €4.9 billion ($6.7 billion). Completed in October, the purchase made Mylan the world's third-largest generic drug company, following Novartis and Teva. Also with the purchase, Mylan took the opportunity to drop "Laboratories" from its name, recasting itself as Mylan Inc.

GETTING HIRED

Make it Mylan yours

Mylan "actively recruits graduates who are driven to succeed in the industry and eager for a challenge." The company also encourages recent graduates to search for openings on the company's career web site (www.mylancareers.com).

Job categories at Mylan include administration, ancillary services, business development,finance and accounting, flight operations, government/public/investor affairs, human resources, information technology, legal and intellectual property, logistics, maintenance and engineering, manufacturing, manufacturing technical support, marketing, packaging, pricing and contracts, project and program management, and sales/customer service.

The firm also has a summer internship program for undergraduate students. Applicants, who need to be at least 18 years old, must have completed their freshman year and must be enrolled for the following semester. Internship positions are available in a variety of departments.

Visit Vault at **www.vault.com** for insider company profiles, expert advice, career message boards, expert resume reviews, the Vault Job Board and more.

VAULT CAREER LIBRARY   269

Novartis AG

Lichtstrasse 35
Basel CH-4002
Switzerland
Phone: +41-61-324-1111
Fax: +41-61-324-8001
www.novartis.com

LOCATIONS

Basel, Switzerland (HQ)
Broomfield, CO • Cambridge, MA •
Carolina, PR • Des Plaines, IL •
Duluth, MN • East Hanover, NJ •
Emeryville, CA • Fort Smith, AK •
Freemont, MI • Humaco, PR • La
Jolla, CA • Larchwood, IA •
Laurelton, NY • Lincoln, NE • New
York, NY • Parsippany, NJ •
Princeton, NJ • Reedsburg, WI • St.
Louis Park, MN • Suffern, NY •
White Plains, NY • Wilson, NC

International locations in more than
140 countries.

THE STATS

Employer Type: Public Company
Stock Symbol: NVS; NOVZn
Stock Exchange: NYSE; Swiss
Chairman & CEO: Daniel Vasella
2006 Employees: 98,788
2006 Revenue ($mil.): $37,020
2006 Net Income ($mil.): $7,202

DEPARTMENTS

Consumer Health
Animal Health
CIBA Vision
Over-the-Counter
Pharmaceuticals
Research
Sandoz
Vaccines & Diagnostics

KEY COMPETITORS

Bayer AG
Merck
Pfizer Inc.

EMPLOYMENT CONTACT

www.novartis.com/careers

THE SCOOP

Swiss peak

The Swiss may be famous for their neutrality in world politics, but they've also developed a hearty pharmaceutical industry, and Novartis, headquartered in Basel, leads the pack. Business is booming at the $37 billion company. It has launched 15 new medicines in the U.S. since 2000, and maintains independent affiliates in more than 140 countries around the globe. Also, beginning in 2003, Novartis started reporting its financial statements in dollars so that investors and observers could more easily compare results with its rivals across the ocean in the U.S., Novartis' biggest pharmaceutical market.

What's what at Novartis

Novartis Pharmaceuticals is the main branch of the company, bringing in nearly $22.6 billion in sales in 2006. The unit includes a wide range of products for several disease areas, in particular products for treating cardiovascular diseases and central nervous system disorders as well as dermatological and gastrointestinal disorders. Novartis is also one of the top-five players in oncology due to the rapid development and success of leukemia drug Gleevec.

Novartis Consumer Health, the company's second division, is made up of additional business units that include over-the-counter (OTC), animal health and CIBA Vision. Until recently, this division also included medical nutrition and Gerber, both of which it sold to Nestlé.

Sandoz is the company's generics division. Based on sales, and aided by strong growth and two major acquisitions in 2005, Sandoz is currently the second-largest generics company in the world. Sandoz, whose global headquarters are in Germany, employs more than 21,000 associates in 110 countries.

Novartis is one of the only major pharmaceutical companies to have garnered global leadership positions in both patented and generic pharmaceuticals. It should be noted that Novartis entered the generic market recently, with its 2005 acquisition of Eon Labs and Hexal AG (more on which below). Generic firms have become increasingly profitable and influential, cutting into major firms' revenue and pipelines, and Novartis is buying in before most of its peers.

Visit Vault at **www.vault.com** for insider company profiles, expert advice, career message boards, expert resume reviews, the Vault Job Board and more.

V/\ULT CAREER LIBRARY   **271**

A new day

Novartis was born when two big Swiss chemical and life sciences companies—Sandoz and Ciba-Geigy—merged in 1996. It's been steadily growing since then, with a particular penchant for opening new research centers. In 1998, it set up the Novartis Institute for Functional Genomics. The company then opened the Novartis Respiratory Research Centre, the largest of its kind in the world, in 2001 in the southeastern English town of Horsham.

Later, Novartis reorganized its global research network, creating the Novartis Institutes for BioMedical Research (NIBR) in the process. After settling on the biotech hub of Cambridge, Mass., for a location, Novartis poured $760 million into renovating the city's old NECCO candy factory, creating 500,000 square feet of laboratory space as well as a ton of new jobs. Novartis opened the research facility in April 2004, and more than 1,300 technology experts and scientists now work in the region.

In July 2004, Novartis expanded its presence in Singapore, where it opened the Novartis Institute for Tropical Disease, which concentrates on discovering better treatments for dengue fever and drug-resistant tuberculosis (TB). The firm is constructing a new R&D center in Shanghai, which will focus on diseases prevalent in Asia. Additional company research sites are based in Switzerland, Austria, Japan and various U.S. locations.

Allegiances

Despite a couple of rounds of layoffs after sales of subsidiaries in 2003—the company cut 172 ophthalmics jobs in Duluth and 87 workers in Maryland—Novartis continued to strike up strategic partnerships. In 2003, it worked with Cell Genesys to develop and market oncolytic virus therapies; with Britannia Pharmaceuticals Limited to speed up work on an advanced nasal powder to treat migraines; with Sankyo of Japan to produce a treatment for gastroesophageal reflux and peptic ulcers; and with Momenta Pharmaceuticals to develop technology that utilizes complex sugars in drug discovery.

Novartis has also grown the old-fashioned way: by buying up parts of other businesses. In December 2003, the company spent $385 million to acquire an adult nutritional business from Bristol-Myers Squibb, a subsidiary of Mead Johnson & Company. In 2005, it also acquired BMS' OTC business in North America.

Generic approval

In February 2005, Novartis purchased U.S.-based Eon Labs and Germany-based Hexal AG for a total of $8.3 billion as part of a strategic plan to capitalize on the U.S. and German generic drug markets. Novartis is integrating the two companies into its Sandoz division, thus creating one of the world's largest generic drug companies.

The acquisition built on previous Novartis acquisitions that beefed up the firm's generic drug offerings: purchases from BASF AG in 2000, Lek in 2002, and Sabex Holdings Ltd. and Durasacan A/S in 2004. By 2010, Novartis hopes to claim 10 percent of the global generic-drugs market, expected to be worth roughly $100 billion by then.

Buying up business

Novartis picked up the rights to a portfolio of OTC products from Bristol-Myers Squibb for $660 million in July 2005—including Excedrin, Keri, No-Doz, Bufferin and Mineral Ice. As part of the deal, Novartis gained the rights to produce and market Bristol-Myers' North American OTC brand portfolio, including the related sales of brands in Latin America, Europe, the Middle East and Africa.

Also in 2005, the company attempted to broker its biggest deal yet—$5 billion for the 58 percent of Chiron, a biotech firm noted for its strong vaccine business, it did not already own. By October 2005, Novartis upped the bid to $5.4 billion and Chiron's board approved the better offer. The Chiron acquisition was finalized in April 2006, creating Novartis' new vaccines and diagnostics division. After the deal closed, Novartis laid off 111 workers at Chiron's Emeryville, Calif., site.

In July 2006, Novartis purchased British biopharmaceutical company NeuTec Pharma, which specializes in developing genetically recombinant antibodies. The $569 million acquisition gave the Swiss drugmaker entry into the rapidly growing market for anti-infectives.

Selling mushy peas

Although Novartis has been buying up businesses and products, it's also refined its emphasis on health care, selling off "non-core" assets to give the company funding to broaden its strategic options. Medical nutrition is (or was) one of these assets. As constituted under Novartis, the medical nutrition division made food for hospital patients and people who, due to an illness, may require foods with special textures or properties.

Visit Vault at **www.vault.com** for insider company profiles, expert advice, career message boards, expert resume reviews, the Vault Job Board and more.

VAULT CAREER LIBRARY   **273**

In February 2006, in a deal worth $260 million, the company completed the divestment of nutrition and Santé to ABN Amro Capital France, first begun in November 2005. Later in 2006, Novartis sold the rest of its medical nutrition business to Nestlé for $2.5 billion. The deal is expected to close officially in the second half of 2007.

Nestlé later agreed (in April 2007) to purchase Novartis' Gerber division as well, for $5.5 billion in cash. After the sale, contact lens maker CIBA Vision is left as the only remaining non-pharmaceutical division that Novartis still holds. The company estimates that almost all of its sales will now derive from drugs. This is a big change from 1996, when just 45 percent of the firm's sales were from drugs.

WHO cares

As the company has moved more explicitly to a drug-based business model, it has committed itself to using its drugmaking capacities for good, as with its many agreements with the World Health Organization. In 2003, Novartis inked a five-year deal with the WHO to make tablets to treat tuberculosis in developing countries. The WHO and Novartis also signed an agreement in 2001 to provide its drug Coartem at cost to malaria-endemic countries.

In addition, Novartis has provided free treatment for leprosy patients through a partnership with WHO since 2000. In November 2005, the Novartis Foundation for Sustainable Development extended this particular partnership with WHO through 2010. Such partnerships keep disadvantaged patients healthier while bumping up the company's brand loyalty and socially responsible image among investors and advocacy groups.

Developmental progression

The firm pledged up to $375 million in early 2005 for AD 237, an experimental treatment for chronic smokers' lung under development by the British companies Arakis and Vectura Group. The purchase was one of the largest deals ever in European biotechnology, but it was just one of more than 75 developmental projects that Novartis announced earlier that year. Officials said these new projects would address a number of conditions including oncology, diabetes, cardiovascular disease and pulmonary disease (expected to build a $10 billion market by 2010).

Up to one-tenth of that figure could be from new blood pressure medicine Tekturna, which the FDA approved in March 2007. Novartis produced the brand-new drug in partnership with small Swiss pharmaceutical Speedel Holding AG (who simplified the formula and made it cheaper to produce). Tekturna is expected to eventually replace Diovan, Novartis' current blood pressure blockbuster.

Novartis charts its new course

The suddenly all-drugs-all-the-time Novartis is adjusting to life as a pharmaceuticals-heavy company. Although it is on pace for record revenue and profits in 2007, the company drastically reshuffled its management after sales of several drugs in the U.S. severely affected quarterly results. In October 2007 the company announced that it would reassign the heads of its prescription drug and consumer health care divisions—to each other's jobs. Joe Jimenez will move from consumer to prescription and Thomas Ebeling will move in the opposite direction.

The company will emphasize getting all of its developmental drugs to market in a reorganization that will also wipe out 1,260 jobs in the U.S., 750 more jobs elsewhere at the company and the discontinuance of using 510 sales reps from outside the company. All of these changes should save the company about $230 million. Novartis also announced the creation of a new division—Novartis Biologics—to tackle that hot property within the industry, biotechnology.

Ad-MIT one

In September 2007 Novartis continued with its research funding, pledging $65 million over the following decade to MIT. Although a comparatively meager investment, the project should be interesting, as it seeks to revolutionize the way drugs are manufactured. MIT officials believe this is the largest research project of its kind, and has the potential to be "industry transforming."

As drugs are now made with many interruptions over a long period of time, this project's goal is to streamline the manufacturing process, making it continuous. This will be challenging, as it will necessitate inventing technology that doesn't yet exist. If or when the project concludes, Novartis and MIT will share equally in its results.

More restructuring

In December 2007 Novartis announced a further round of job cuts, affecting 2,500 employees worldwide, about 2.5 percent of the workforce. CEO Daniel Vasella remarked that it was an ideal time for the restrucuring, "given [a] short-term down-cycle in our pharmaceuticals business." Vasella also said that the company will

Visit Vault at **www.vault.com** for insider company profiles, expert advice, career message boards, expert resume reviews, the Vault Job Board and more.

VAULT CAREER LIBRARY   275

"simplify" and "redesign" its operations through 2008 and 2009, hopefully achieving annual savings of $1.6 billion by 2010. It's not all layoffs and reorganizing, though; the firm also announced intentions to expand in emerging markets like Northern and sub-Saharan Africa, Central Asia and Southeast Asia.

GETTING HIRED

Don't call us; we can't call you

As long as a position is listed on the career section (www.novartis.com/careers) of Novartis' web site, consider it available. Posting open spots externally is company policy. Novartis has more than 6,000 sales representatives in the U.S. and it is constantly seeking qualified candidates. Typical areas of employment include pharmaceuticals, consumer health, Sandoz, research, marketing, administrative, manufacturing and global support functions.

In addition, job seekers can find a link on the company's site to its BrassRing service (www.novartis.com/careers/en/job-search/brassring/index.shtml), through which applicants can create a profile, upload a resume and create search agents that automatically report back with positions as they become available. The company notes that applications submitted through BrassRing are reviewed faster by HR employees.

In 2007, Novartis ranked as the top company in the pharmaceuticals industry in the peer group results of *Forbes*' Most Admired Companies survey. The firm has risen steadily on the list since 2003. Because Novartis is a large international company, benefits vary depending on location, but generally include medical plans, group life insurance and pension plans

Novo Nordisk A/S

Novo Allé
2880 Bagsværd
Denmark
Phone: +45-4444-8888
Fax: +45-4449-0555

LOCATIONS

Bagsværd, Denmark (HQ)
Clayton, NC
Hayward, CA
Princeton, NJ

International locations in 78
countries.

THE STATS

Employer Type: Public Company
Stock Symbol: NVO
Stock Exchange: NYSE
Chairman: Sten Scheibye
President & CEO: Lars Rebien
 Sørensen
2006 Employees: 23,600
2006 Revenue ($mil.): $6,855
2006 Net Income: $1,142

DEPARTMENTS

Account Management
Administration
Finance
Human Resources
Information Technology
Legal
Marketing
Medical
Regulatory Affairs
Sales

KEY COMPETITORS

Eli Lilly
Pfizer
sanofi-aventis
Wyeth

EMPLOYMENT CONTACT

www.novonordisk.com/jobs

THE SCOOP

Novo Nordisk, a health care company headquartered in Denmark, is a world leader in diabetes care. The firm operates in two business segments: biopharmaceuticals and diabetes care—one of the broadest diabetes product portfolios in the industry. Key products in this segment include Novolog, a rapid-acting insulin analog; Levemir, a long-acting basal insulin; and insulin delivery systems. In biopharmaceuticals, Novo Nordisk specializes in haemostasis management, growth hormone therapy and hormone replacement therapy.

The company, which employs more than 23,600 people in 80 countries, markets its products in approximately 180 nations. The majority of the company's workers are in Denmark, but since 2000, it has grown significantly and expanded internationally, particularly in the United States. In 2006, the company's revenue hit more than $6.8 billion, a 15 percent increase over the previous year.

Insulin lab to industry giant

In 1922 August Krogh, Danish Nobel laureate in physiology, and his wife, Marie, a diabetic doctor, visited Professor J.J.R. Macleod in Canada, who was head of the Toronto institute that produced the world's first insulin extract. Macleod gave Krogh permission to make insulin, and—the following year—Krogh set up a company called Nordisk Insulin Laboratorium.

In 1925, brothers Harold and Thorvald Pedersen, who used to work for Krogh, set up a competing insulin company called Novo Terapeutisk Laboratorium. Over the next 65 years, both companies grew rapidly and began to develop other products. In 1989, the two Danish companies merged to become Novo Nordisk A/S.

In 2000, Novo Nordisk de-merged its enzyme business and gave it the name Novozymes A/S. Today these two businesses—health care and enzymes—have more operational freedom. Investment and holding company Novo Nordisk A/S manages both Novo Nordisk and Novozymes.

Growth in diabetes drugs

Novo Nordisk's goal is to become the world's leading diabetes care company. It already leads the world in insulin sales, with a 52 percent market share. In 2006, sales in the firm's diabetes care segment reached nearly $5 billion (28 billion Danish kroner), a 16 percent increase from 2005. In particular, the company's sales of diabetes drugs in the United States have surged in recent years. Novo Nordisk launched long-acting insulin Levemir in the United States in 2006 and toward the end of that year, the firm announced plans to expand its U.S. diabetes drug field sales force from 1,200 to 1,900 people.

The International Diabetes Federation projects an increase from 246 million people with diabetes to about 380 million in 2025. Many of these people will be in the developing world. As a result, the company is also focusing on emerging markets such as China, India and Brazil.

In 200, the company established the World Diabetes Foundation to improve diabetes care in developing countries. Novo Nordisk also makes efforts to increase public awareness about diabetes. For example, in 2003 the company founded the Novo Nordisk Media Prize for excellence in writing on diabetes. The award is given to a TV feature or article on diabetes in general, with an independent international jury selecting the winner.

Banking on biopharmaceuticals

The biopharmaceuticals segment of the company had sales of nearly $2 billion (11 billion Danish kroner) in 2006, an increase of 12 percent over 2005. When it comes to human growth hormone products, the company holds the No. 2 position worldwide, with market share of approximately 22 percent.

In addition, this segment of the company discovers, develops, manufactures and sells hormone replacement therapy and products in haemostasis management. In 2006, the FDA approved Novo Nordisk's NovoSeven to treat bleeding episodes as well as to prevent bleeding in invasive procedures and surgical procedures, in patients with acquired hemophilia, with inhibitors.

Copycat insulin?

In the United States, people with diabetes, as well as private insurers and the government, spend a combined $3.3 billion annually on insulin. If generic versions of insulin became available, the treatment's price might fall by 25 percent. This is why American politicians have started to pressure the FDA to allow generic insulin.

Typically, generic versions of conventional drugs hit the market shortly after patents have expired on brand-name pharmaceuticals. Generic drug companies simply need to show that the generic contains the same active ingredients, purity and quality as the brand-name version, and that the copycat version provides "bioequivalence" (the same level of the drug in the blood over time as the original).

Biologics, however, are made from cultures of living material rather than chemical recipes; and brand-name drugmakers and many scientists have urged caution in the development of generic biologics, insisting that biologic drugs are inherently variable and difficult to duplicate, and that patients could develop dangerous allergic reactions.

Insulin—created by extracting the gene for insulin from a human cell—is considered a biologic drug. Novo Nordisk and its competitor, Eli Lilly & Co., have stated opposition any FDA action that would approve generic insulin without clinical studies. Availability of generic insulin would put price pressure on branded insulin. The approval of generic insulin could also open the door to the development of generic versions of other biologics.

Future focus

Novo Nordisk started increasing its focus on pharmaceuticals based on therapeutic proteins in 2002. Now the company's pipeline in protein-based pharmaceuticals for haemostasis, growth disorders and diabetes is larger than ever.

At the end of 2006, the company initiated a global phase III study of Liraglutide in people with type 2 diabetes. Liraglutide, the first human compound in a new class of type 2 therapies, is a modification of a natural hormone produced in the gut. The firm expects to launch the product in the U.S. in 2009. In 2006, Novo Nordisk's AERx, an inhalable insulin, entered phase III clinical trials.

Some analysts have warned that the firm may be lagging behind competitors in developing new diabetes products, especially as Eli Lilly has stumbled upon the fastest-growing new diabetes drug on the market—Byetta, an oral treatment developed with Amylin Pharmaceuticals.

In January 2007, Novo Nordisk responded, announcing a decision to focus all its R&D resources on the company's growing pipeline of protein-based pharmaceuticals. Because of this, the firm is discontinuing R&D activities within its oral diabetic segment. Perhaps it is banking on its dominance in making insulin and other biologics to compete with rivals such as Lilly, which are more traditional drug manufacturers.

In biopharmaceuticals, the company's strategy is to expand its portfolio within haemostasis management, growth deficiency and hormone replacement therapy as well as to build a presence in immunotherapies. The company has also signaled that it will be focusing less on biopharmaceuticals in the future. It hinted in August 2007 that it would sell its subsidiary NNE Pharmaplan, a biopharmaceutical engineering and consultancy company that employs over 1,500 people in 22 locations worldwide.

An environmental leader

Novo Nordisk was the first company in Denmark to print an environmental report. In 1994, it is still a leader in environmental issues. Recently, Novo Nordisk has jumped on the global warming bandwagon. In January 2006, the firm became a member of the World Wildlife Fund's Climate Savers program. The company sponsored employee screenings of Al Gore's documentary *An Inconvenient Truth* in fall 2006. Novo Nordisk is aiming to reduce its CO_2 emissions by 10 percent by 2014 (as compared with emissions in 2004).

GETTING HIRED

Nominate yourself to Novo now!

In the United States, applicants can search and apply for openings at nov.hrdpt.com/cgi-bin/c/jobsearch.cgi. Job categories include account management, administration, finance, human resources, information technology, legal, marketing, medical, regulatory affairs and sales. The firm also has internships as well as a management associate program. The 24-month Novo Nordisk Residency Program, established in 2005, provides pharmacy professionals with hands-on experience in the pharmaceutical industry.

Novo Nordisk tries to keep employees happy and healthy with a wide range of benefits. On their first day of work, employees can choose from three types of medical plans. If they pick the HMO or PPO, Novo Nordisk pays 97 percent of the cost of the monthly premium for employees and eligible dependents. A traditional indemnity option is also available. The company automatically contributes 8 percent of an employee's annual pay and bonus to the 401(k) plan, even if the employee doesn't save through the plan. Novo Nordisk also offers a comprehensive health plan for retirees. Other perks include dental, short- and long-term disability insurance, a prescription drug plan and group rates on auto and homeowners' insurance.

Visit Vault at **www.vault.com** for insider company profiles, expert advice, career message boards, expert resume reviews, the Vault Job Board and more.

VAULT CAREER LIBRARY   **281**

Nuvelo, Inc.

201 Industrial Road
Suite 310
San Carlos, CA 94070-6211
Phone: (650) 517-8000
Fax: (650) 517-8001
www.nuvelo.com

LOCATION
San Carlos, CA (HQ)

THE STATS
Employer Type: Public Company
Stock Symbol: NUVO
Stock Exchange: Nasdaq
Chairman & CEO: Ted W. Love
2006 Employees: 146
2006 Revenue ($mil.): $3.9
2006 Net Income ($mil.): -$130.6

DEPARTMENTS
Clinical Development
Finance & Accounting
Research & Development

KEY COMPETITORS
Genentech
PDL BioPharma Inc.
sanofi-aventis

EMPLOYMENT CONTACT
www.nuvelo.com/join

THE SCOOP

The tiny, California-based Nuvelo, with just 146 employees, is investing big bucks in research and development. In 2006, the firm's R&D expenditures reached $89.4 million. By comparison, the company's year-end revenue totaled about $3.9 million and the company recorded year-end losses of more than $130 million. These R&D expenditures were also a dramatic increase from 2005 and 2004, when Nuvelo expended $57.8 million and $40 million, respectively

The firm is dedicated to discovering, developing and commercializing novel drugs for acute cardiovascular cancer and other debilitating diseases, and boasts a portfolio of oncology and acute cardiovascular drugs. These include alfimeprase, a direct acting thrombolytic in phase III clinical development for the treatment of thrombotic-related disorders like acute ischemic stroke and catheter occlusion. The company also has two preclinical candidates, NU206 and NU172, for inflammatory bowel disease and chemotherapy/radiation therapy-induced mucositis, and for use as a short-acting anticoagulant during medical procedures. The firm currently has research and development collaborations with Amgen, Dendreon, Archemix and the pharmaceutical division of Kirin Brewery.

From Yugoslavia to California

Two Yugoslavian scientists, Radoje Drmanac and Radomir Crkvenjakov, formed Nuvelo in 1992, initially calling the venture Hyseq. While working at Belgrade's Institute of Molecular Genetics, the duo had discovered a new and more sensitive way to detect rare genes. Drmanac came to the United States, where he partnered with Lewis Gruber, a patent attorney who helped raise venture capital to fund the firm's launch.

Hyseq completed its IPO in August 1997. The company used its signature-by-hybridization technology platform to start building a proprietary collection of novel and rarely expressed genes. In July 2002, the firm began its first human clinical trial with its lead product candidate, alfimeprase. But earlier that year, the company ended its collaboration with BASF Plant Science ahead of schedule and lost a large amount of funding. Nearly 80 employees (about 40 percent of total headcount) quit the company in ensuing months.

Enter Variagenics, a Cambridge, Mass.-based genetic company with lots of cash but no products to develop. In April 2002, Variagenics' CEO Taylor Crouch left the company, and the company laid off 44 employees the next month. Variagenics then revised its business model, moving to become a molecular diagnostics company that aimed to predict patients' reactions to certain drugs. In November 2002, Variagenics and Hyseq announced plans to merge.

After a deal worth $50.2 million, the new entity emerged under the name Nuvelo in January 2003. The company started trading on the Nasdaq the following month and its executives proudly announced that Nuvelo could conduct R&D until 2004 without any outside funding. The firm moved all of its operations to California and now employs more than 140 people.

All about Alfimeprase

Alfimeprase is a blood clot dissolver for the potential treatment of thrombotic-related disorders. In January 2006, Nuvelo entered into a collaborative agreement with Bayer, which committed to pay as much as $385 million for the rights to commercialize alfimeprase. But Bayer and Nuvelo both announced in December 2006 that the product failed to meet targets in two phase III trials and Nuvelo's stock took a hit. The companies halted enrollment in two other phase III trials of the drug and began working on a comprehensive review of data from the two completed trials. Bayer terminated its end of the agreement in June 2007. Nuvelo is plowing ahead, however. By August 2007, Nuvelo re-initiated alfimeprase's phase III trial for catheter occlusion, and in December 2007 it commenced phase II trials for acute ischemic stroke.

On February 9 2007, a securities class action lawsuit filed in a New York federal court named Nuvelo and some of its former and current officers and directors as defendants. The lawsuit alleges that the firm misled investors about both alfimeprase's efficacy and the likelihood of its success and seeks damages on behalf of people who purchased Nuvelo's stock between January 5, 2006 and December 8, 2006. Investors filed a second class-action lawsuit on February 16, 2007.

What's new at Nuvelo

Nuvelo expects to complete alfimeprase's phase III trial for catheter occlusion and report its top-line data in the first half of 2008. The company also plans to advance some of its other drug candidates into phase I trials early 2008. These include NU172, a candidate in the cardiovascular pipeline, as well as NU206, for inflammatory bowel disease as well as cancer therapy. Nuvelo also expects to continue its research programs in leukemia therapeutic antibodies, expand its pipeline, and create additional partnering and licensing opportunities.

GETTING HIRED

Could you be the new fellow at Nuvelo?

Job seekers can check job postings, and other employment-related information, at Nuvelo's careers site, www.nuvelo.com/join. At press time, there were openings in clinical development, regulatory and R&D.

The company prefers for applicants to apply electronically. Job hunters should e-mail a resume as a Microsoft Word attachment to: hr@nuvelo.com, and the company advises including the position's job code in the e-mail's "subject" line. Individuals interested in more than one open position should include the job code for the position in which they are most interested in the "subject" line. In the body of the e-mail, applicants should indicate the job code for any other open position for which they would like to be considered.

Benefits at Nuvelo include health benefits, dental, company-paid basic life insurance, a 401(k) plan, an employee stock purchase plan, an educational assistance program, employee assistance program and paid time off and holidays. Other perks are events such as monthly parties and a company picnic. The firm also maintains an on-site fitness center, as well as break rooms stocked with free coffee, a wide selection of teas, hot chocolate, soups, instant oatmeal and popcorn.

Visit Vault at **www.vault.com** for insider company profiles, expert advice,
career message boards, expert resume reviews, the Vault Job Board and more.

VAULT CAREER LIBRARY   285

Perrigo Company

515 Eastern Avenue
Allegan, MI 49010
Phone: (269) 673-8451
Fax: (269) 673-9128
www.perrigo.com

LOCATIONS

Allegan, MI (HQ)
Bronx, NY
Greenville, SC
Piscataway, NJ
Bnei Brak, Israel
Hyderabad
Petach Tikva, Israel
Ramos Arizpe, Mexico
Shandong
Wiesbaden, Germany
Wrafton, UK

THE STATS

Employer Type: Public Company
Stock Symbol: PRGO
Stock Exchange: Nasdaq
Chairman: David T. Gibbons
President & CEO: Joseph C. Papa
2006 Employees: 6,200
2007 Revenue ($mil.): $1,447
2007 Net Income ($mil.): $74

DEPARTMENTS

Accounting/Financial
Administrative/Clerical
Art Department
Customer Service
Engineering
Facilities/Maintenance
Human Resources
IT/MIS/Computers
Manufacturing/Operations
Marketing
Quality
R&D/Analytical Chemistry
Regulatory Affairs/Clinical Affairs
Sales/New Business Development
Supply Chain
Technical Support

KEY COMPETITORS

Alpharma Inc.
Chattem Inc.
Leiner Health Products Inc.

EMPLOYMENT CONTACT

www.perrigo.com/careers

THE SCOOP

Perrigo primer

The Perrigo Company is a leading global health care supplier. The company is also the world's largest manufacturer of nutritional products and over-the-counter pharmaceuticals for the store-brand market. Perrigo supplies stores with products that include analgesics, cough and cold remedies, gastrointestinal and feminine hygiene products, vitamins, dietary supplements and nutritional drinks. Currently, Perrigo sells approximately 1,150 store-brand products to roughly 130 retail stores. The company's largest customer is Wal-Mart, which comprises some 22 percent of its total net sales.

In addition, Perrigo develops and manufactures active pharmaceutical ingredients, generic prescription drugs and consumer products. The firm had nearly $1.5 billion in revenue in 2007, an increase from $1.3 billion in 2006.

From general store to a whole lot more

Luther Perrigo, who owned his own general store and apple-drying business, founded a company to package and distribute household items and medicines for other country stores in 1887. The business grew steadily, and—by the early 1920s—Perrigo's salesmen called on rural stores throughout the Midwest. As a way to build customer loyalty, the company developed the "private label" concept, through which it would imprint the individual stores' names on the labels for items such as bay rum and Epsom salts.

The Perrigo company first started to diversify in the 1930s, as its first major private-label customer, the K&W Group (later the People's Drug Store) spurred the firm into manufacturing its own generic drugs. As chain stores and mass-market retailers have multiplied over the following decades, Perrigo has kept ahead of the game.

Other retailers have attempted to build customer loyalty with products sold under store-brand labels, and Perrigo has diversified its operations accordingly. In 2005, Perrigo acquired Israeli company Agis Industries for about $818 million, expanding its generic drug offerings—Agis had generated sales of $376 million the year before. Currently, the company sells about 150 generic prescription products to roughly 100 customers. And more than two-thirds of its revenue—$1 billion out of $1.4 billion total in 2007—derives from its consumer health care segment.

Visit Vault at **www.vault.com** for insider company profiles, expert advice, career message boards, expert resume reviews, the Vault Job Board and more.

VAULT CAREER LIBRARY   287

Getting settled

In 1996, Perrigo and generic drug manufacturer Alpharma each filed applications with the FDA for approval to sell the same drug—a generic version of children's liquid ibuprofen. Two years later, however, a change in FDA regulations set up a scenario: the FDA would approve Alpharma's drug, then wait 180 days before approving Perrigo's, thus giving virtual market exclusivity to Alpharma.

In 2004, the matter became major news when the Federal Trade Commission filed a lawsuit against both companies. The FTC claimed that after the 180-day mix-up with the FDA, Perrigo had approached Alpharma and paid it a flat rate not to sell its drug at all. In a "naked restraint on competition," the two companies worked out a deal where Perrigo would sell the drug at a higher price and the two companies would share the profits.

What was the result of all this legal activity? Later in 2004, both Perrigo and Alpharma settled the charges for a grand total of $6.25 million. The FTC settlement also prohibited Alpharma and Perrigo from entering into similar agreements in the future.

Pseudoephedrine sales slumps

On September 30, 2006, a new federal law called the Combat Methamphetamine Epidemic Act took effect. The law requires retailers to sell products containing pseudoephedrine, such as the decongestant Sudafed, from behind the counter or from a locked display case.

It also stipulates that all customers, including law-abiding ones with runny noses, sign a logbook upon purchase of the substance. Finally, as of April 2006, the law limits the amount of pseudoephedrine that consumers can buy. The law came with all of these precautions because, in large amounts, pseudoephedrine and some other decongestants can be used to make the illegal drug methamphetamine.

These legislative and marketing changes have impacted Perrigo. The firm responded to the new federal law by developing new cold medicines without pseudoephedrine, a costly process. For the 2007 fiscal year, the company expects its sales of pseudoephedrine products total about a third of what they were in 2006, and roughly a fifth of what they were in 2005.

New developments

Perrigo's strategy for the future is to invest in R&D. The numbers don't lie, as the firm's R&D spending in 2006 was nearly double that of its 2004 expenditures. Perrigo launched a number of new products during 2006, including a type of nicotine lozenge for smoking cessation and several acetaminophen products. In addition, the FDA approved six of Perrigo's over-the-counter drug applications. By the end of the 2006 fiscal year, the firm had 90 new prescription and OTC products under development.

In addition to researching drugs in house, Perrigo has also continued to buy other companies and new products. In March 2007, the company announced an agreement to acquire the Qualis, a privately held manufacturer of OTC lice removal products (the transaction was completed in July). The same month, Perrigo agreed buy nine generic skin products and three pipeline products from Glades Products for $54 million.

GETTING HIRED

Go Perrigo

Applicants can search for job openings, by location or by category, on the careers section of Perrigo's web site (www.perrigo.com/careers). Job categories at the company include accounting/financial, administrative/clerical, art department, customer service, engineering, facilities/maintenance, human resources, IT/MIS/computers, manufacturing/operations, marketing, quality, R&D/analytical, chemistry, regulatory affairs/clinical affairs, sales/new business development, supply chain and technical support. The company also offers internships. One recent example of these is an IT security internship located in the company's Michigan offices.

Visit Vault at **www.vault.com** for insider company profiles, expert advice, career message boards, expert resume reviews, the Vault Job Board and more.

VAULT CAREER LIBRARY   289

Pfizer Inc.

235 East 42nd Street
New York, NY 10017-5755
Phone: (212) 573-2323
Fax: (212) 573-7851
www.pfizer.com

LOCATIONS

New York, NY (HQ)
Ann Arbor, MI • Cambridge, MA •
Groton, CT • Henrietta, MI •
Kalamazoo, MI • La Jolla, CA •
Lincoln, NE • New London, CT •
Peapack, NJ • Richland, MI • South
San Francisco, CA • St. Louis, MO
• Melbourne • Amboise, France •
Nagoya, Japan • Sandwich, UK •
Shanghai • Tokyo

Additional manufacturing locations
in Belgium, Brazil, China, France,
Germany, Ireland, Italy, Japan,
Mexico, Singapore, Sweden, the UK
and the US.

THE STATS

Employer Type: Public Company
Stock Symbol: PFE
Stock Exchange: NYSE
Chairman & CEO: Jeffrey B. Kindler
2006 Employees: 98,000
2006 Revenue ($mil.): $48,371
2006 Income ($mil.): $19,337

DEPARTMENTS

Animal Health
Corporate Functions
Global Manufacturing
Global Research & Development
Pharmaceuticals
Pharmaceutical Sales

KEY COMPETITORS

Bayer
Merck
Novartis

EMPLOYMENT CONTACT

www.pfizer.com/careers

THE SCOOP

Pharmaceutical giant

Pfizer is the world's largest pharmaceutical company in terms of sales. Its biggest selling prescription drug is cholesterol-lowering Lipitor, which Pfizer gained when it acquired Warner-Lambert in 2000 for a whopping $90 billion. Its other drugs include hypertension drug Norvasc, popular antidepressant Zoloft and impotence treatment Viagra.

The New York-based firm's medicines help some 150 million people a year around the world. It also offers health care products for animals ranging from cats to cattle. For fiscal 2006, the company racked up more than $48 billion in revenue, up from about $47 billion in 2005. (In 2004, however, Pfizer's revenue came in at close to $49 billion.)

A long history

Cousins and German immigrants Charles Pfizer and Charles Erhart founded Pfizer in 1849 in Brooklyn, N.Y. For decades, citric acid was the company's most popular product, but when the ingredients needed to make the product became scarce during World War I, Pfizer was forced to find new supply sources. It did so after years of experiments with fermentation, a process that eventually enabled Pfizer to produce vitamins and penicillin on a large-scale basis, as it did during WWII.

Pfizer specialized in the development of vitamins and antibiotics after the war. Then, over the next several decades, Pfizer diversified into animal health care and expanded its pharmaceutical business overseas. Revenue passed the billion-dollar mark in 1972; when Pfizer celebrated its sesquicentennial in 1999 it was the fourth-largest pharmaceutical company in the U.S.; revenue topped $16 billion and the company spent $4 billion that year on research and development.

Warner-Lambert, for its part, began as a mom-and-pop pharmacy owned by William Warner in Philadelphia in 1856; the Warner family closed the pharmacy 30 years later, and opened a drug manufacturing plant. The firm grew through a series of partnerships, ventures and acquisitions, merging with Lambert Pharmacal (which developed Listerine mouthwash) in 1955.

Warner-Lambert bought the American Chicle Company, producer of Adams gum and mint products, as well as Trident gum and Certs mints, in 1962, and Parke-Davis in

1970. Parke-Davis was the first pharmaceutical firm to standardize drug dosages and commercially develop vaccines (the company sold various forms of cocaine until the U.S. government classified it as an illegal narcotic in 1914) and it had a strong stable of workhorse drugs, such as antihistamine Benadryl, developed in 1949. The Parke-Davis division of Pfizer is still one of the largest producers of vaccines in the world.

A merger of titanic proportions

The firm later purchased Wilkinson Sword shaving products in 1993 to augment its Schick line of razors—but the real gem in Warner-Lambert's crown was cholesterol drug Lipitor, which hit the market in 1997. By 1999, immediately prior to the merger with Pfizer, Warner-Lambert was among the world's top-10 producers of over-the-counter medicines (including heartburn remedy Zantac) and the leading producer of fish food and aquarium products.

Pfizer made an unsolicited $82.4 billion offer for Warner-Lambert just a few hours after the rival drug firm agreed to merge with American Home Products (now Wyeth). Pfizer's offer was significantly sweeter than AHP's, but Warner-Lambert seemed not to be interested.

After upping its bid to $90 billion, Pfizer eventually won the battle for Warner-Lambert, and the two companies merged in June 2000, creating a nearly $30 billion dollar company, rivaled only by Merck. The combined company kept Pfizer's name and New York headquarters, and Warner-Lambert's New Jersey home base became the site for the company's consumer products division.

The arithmetic of pharmaceutical mergers

Since the merger with Warner Lambert, Pfizer has racked up even more billion-dollar acquisitions, bringing in a bunch of companies with new drugs nearing approval, while continuing its own in-house research and development initiatives. In April 2003, Pfizer acquired big pharmaceutical peer Pharmacia, in a deal worth $60 billion.

The merger added Pharmacia's popular Celebrex arthritis drug to Pfizer's offerings—Celebrex, and its follow-up drug, Bextra, had sales of $2.4 billion in 2003. When does 60 plus 90 equal 48? When a $90 billion merger (Warner Lambert), followed by a $60 billion one (Pharmacia) results in the current Pfizer, an industry juggernaut with more than $48 billion in annual revenue.

After the deal closed, Pfizer discovered that two subsidiaries of Pharmacia were involved in off-label marketing of a human growth hormone medicine and inappropriate use of a vendor contract. Pfizer reported these improper activities to the Department of Justice and the subsidiaries in question reached a $34 million settlement with the FDA in 2007.

Insatiable appetite for drugs (and drug firms)

During recent years, the firm has acquired, purchased drugs from and entered into licensing agreements with smaller pharmaceutical and biotech companies. In February 2004, Pfizer spent (the relatively paltry) $1.3 billion to acquire Esperion Therapeutics, which focused on the developing "good cholesterol" therapies to treat cardiovascular disease. That summer, Pfizer purchased Campto, a treatment for advanced colorectal cancer from Paris-based Sanofi-Synthelabo, for about $620 million. Pfizer now sells it under the name Camptosar.

Pfizer bought private biopharmaceutical company Idun Pharmaceuticals in 2005 (for an undisclosed sum). Idun focused on developing therapies to control apoptosis, a type of cell death. The same year, Pfizer bought Vicuron, a company that developed anti-infective drugs, for $1.9 billion.

2006 was also a big year for Pfizer, with more acquisitions. In February, the company completed its acquisition of sanofi-aventis' rights to market inhaled insulin Exubera, a drug the two firms developed together. Pfizer also acquired Rinat Neuroscience Corp., a biologics company developing treatments for central nervous system diseases and disorders, in May 2006. That September, Pfizer entered into licensing agreements with Transtech Pharma, to develop and sell compounds to treat Alzheimer's disease and diabetes, and Quark Biotech, which is working on a new treatment for age-related macular degeneration. Pfizer purchased PowerMed, a British company working on DNA-based vaccines, in October 2006.

Not all winners

Inspira, a medicine for the treatment of heart failure, was one of the biggest disappointments to come out of the company's purchase of Pharmacia. Before the merger, analysts had forecasted Inspira as a potential billion-dollar pill, but its 2005 sales were an anemic $49 million. Inspira remains a challenge for Pfizer, in part because many doctors feel the drug provides little extra benefit compared with an existing heart failure drug, spironolactone, but at a higher cost. Pfizer may let this failure slip into generic oblivion in 2008, when its initial patents expire.

In 2004, new research found that patients taking painkiller Celebrex had an increased risk of heart problems. The company's stock dropped on the news, and there was an industrywide call to reexamine the negative effects of similar COX-2 inhibitor drugs, such as Merck's Vioxx. The following year, the FDA forced Pfizer to pull Bextra, another member of the same drug class, from the market. But the FDA decided Celebrex's benefits outweighed the risks and allowed Pfizer to keep selling it, although the agency did put its most serious warning—known as a "black box"—on the drug.

The public still has concerns about Celebrex's health effects, and, in April 2007, Pfizer launched a lengthy television commercial for the drug, which discusses the risks and benefits of Celebrex. Public Citizen, a consumer advocacy group, called on the FDA to order Pfizer to pull the commercial. The group said the ad contained misleading statements that could lead viewers to underestimate the drug's gastrointestinal and cardiovascular risks.

Celebrex may increase the chance of heart disease and strokes, and it also increases the chance of stomach and intestinal problems and serious conditions. However, it relieves arthritis pain, inflammation, and stiffness—and recent studies have also shown that the drug may help prevent colon cancer in some people. Revenue from Celebrex is down from 2004, but the drug sells well, in part because similar medications have been taken off the market and it enjoys a near monopoly on its sector. The drug's sales continued to increase in 2007.

Selling off

To help fund its acquisitive streak, Pfizer has sold off non-core assets over the past several years. In December 2002, the company sold its Tetra aquarium and pond supply business to the Triton Fund for $238 million. In March 2003, Pfizer successfully sold Warner-Lambert's old Schick-Wilkinson razor business for a cool $930 million in cash to U.S. battery maker Energizer Holdings. The same month, it closed a deal to sell Adams, its little-known candy division, to Cadbury Schweppes for $4.2 billion.

Also in 2003, the company sold oral contraceptive lines Loestrin and Estrostep to Galen Holdings, the Northern Irish pharmaceuticals business, in a deal valued at €309.2 million ($484 million). Pfizer also sold rights to its hormone replacement therapy, femhrt, to Galen later that year. In January 2004, Pfizer agreed to sell its in-vitro allergy and autoimmune diagnostic testing business for $575 million, again tapping the Triton Group to take an unwanted business off its hands.

In December 2006, Pfizer sold its entire consumer health care business, which included products such as Visine and Listerine, to Johnson & Johnson for $16.6 billion. Other bidders for the consumer health unit included British company Reckitt Benckiser and GlaxoSmithKline. At the time, Pfizer said it wanted to divest the consumer health unit to focus on selling prescription drugs, but the deal also enriched company coffers, potentially fueling more acquisitions of smaller companies with drugs close to gaining FDA approval.

The little blue pill that could

Aside from this lengthy recent history of acquisitions, Pfizer has had an internal blockbuster in impotence drug Viagra, launched in 1998. In its first month on the market, the "little blue pill" generated over $100 million in sales, making it the fastest-selling new drug at that time. But Viagra hasn't been without its faults. Dozens of people claimed to have suffered heart attacks caused by the pills, and several lawsuits (later dismissed) were brought against the drugmaker.

Due to Viagra's popularity, Pfizer was soon fighting off efforts to develop similar products by other drug companies. After winning a U.S. patent for Viagra as a treatment for erectile dysfunction in October 2002, the company immediately turned to the court system to keep two joint ventures led by Eli Lilly and Bayer from getting a piece of the $2 billion impotence market that Viagra dominated.

Despite the legal action, major rivals Bayer and Glaxo won FDA approval for impotence drug Levitra, which hit the U.S. market in September 2003. Lilly and Icos also received federal clearance for impotence drug Cialis shortly after Levitra hit the market. Regardless, Viagra continues to be the leading treatment for erectile dysfunction. In 2005, worldwide sales of Viagra reached $1.6 billion; however, revenue increased only slightly in 2006.

Patent woes

Although prescription drugs have been the firm's most profitable division, basic product patents on some of Pfizer's most popular drugs have expired or are about to expire. In 2006, Pfizer sold just three of the world's 25 best-selling medicines. This is a decline from 2003, when Pfizer sold 14 of the world's top-selling medicines, more than any other company.

In June 2006, Pfizer lost patent protection on antidepressant Zoloft. The company will suffer another round of patent losses in 2007; these include Norvasac, an antihypertensive that's the company's No. 2 product, and allergy medicine Zyrtec.

Cholesterol-lowering Lipitor, Pfizer's best-selling drug, began to lose significant market share in 2006. The slide actually wasn't triggered by the expiration of a Pfizer patent, but by one of rival Merck's—the blockbuster cholesterol drug Zocor lost protection in June of that year. This was influential, since generic versions of cholesterol drugs customarily receive large discounts from health insurers, like WellPoint, and Zocor hitting the generic market proved no exception.

To try to reduce declines in Lipitor's sales, the company is working on an ad campaign about the benefits of the drug, which include reducing the risk of nonfatal heart attacks, certain types of heart surgery, nonfatal and fatal strokes; hospitalization for heart failure and chest pain in heart disease patients. Sales of Lipitor in 2006 totaled around $12.9 billion, up a little from $12.2 billion in 2005; they accounted for more than 28 percent of the company's total pharmaceutical revenue. But as of October 2007, the drug was on pace for its first year of declining profits ever.

Trials and tribulations with torcetrapib

One big disappointment for Pfizer involved the development of torcetrapib, a drug which increases the body's production of "good cholesterol." Pfizer had hoped the drug would be a blockbuster and spent over $800 million alone to develop it. In late 2006, Pfizer announced it was ditching the experimental drug, as clinical trials had revealed that the medicine caused an increase in heart problems and death.

In May 2007, John LaMattina, head of research and a major booster of torcetrapib, announced that he was leaving the company by the end of the year. LaMattina said he decided to leave the firm because he'd put a foundation for future drug development in place.

Investing in R&D

Pfizer's drug development will be crucial in the coming years, as the company is racing to get new drugs on the market before generic drugs affect the rest of its products coming off patent protection. More and more, the firm's strategy has involved buying or working with other companies that are developing new drugs.

Previously, the company was devoted to investing heavily in research and development efforts in house. Pfizer employs more than 13,000 people at its research and development centers around the world. In 2006, Pfizer invested $7.6 billion in R&D, more than any other firm in the industry, and now has more than 200 projects in its drug development pipeline. A new web site (www.pfizer.com/pipeline), launched in 2006, will be updated twice yearly with a timeline for drug delivery.

However, recent restructuring efforts have led to cuts across the company, including R&D. In January 2007, Pfizer announced that it will close its research and development facilities in Ann Arbor, Mich., by the end of 2008, cutting more than 2,400 jobs. Later that year, in October, Pfizer recommitted to R&D, but of a different sort. When LaMattina retired in May 2007, the company hired Martin McKay as his replacement and simultaneously launched a new R&D center in the bay area, focused on biotechnology. Corey Goodman, co-founder of the biotech firms Exelixis and Renovis, heads up the new division's research and report directly to CEO Jeffrey Kindler, himself a newcomer to the firm in 2006.

New products

One newer drug that seems to be doing well is Lyrica, approved by the FDA in December 2004. This product treats epilepsy and also neuropathic pain. Pfizer introduced Lyrica to the market in 2005. The company expected about $900 million in sales for Lyrica for 2006, and the drug's sales ended up surpassing $1 billion. Some analysts have estimated that global sales could reach $2.7 billion in 2010.

In January 2005, Pfizer and Eyetech Pharmaceuticals launched Macugen, a drug to treat wet age-related macular degeneration, the leading cause of elderly blindness in the developed world. Doctors treated 40,000 patients with Macugen in the year of its release.

Pfizer was part of an industrywide drug development slump in 2005. The FDA only gave the thumbs up to 20 new drugs in the U.S. over the course of the entire year. Pfizer failed to win FDA approval for a single new drug invented in its own labs. Other big companies, such as Eli Lilly and Johnson & Johnson, also experienced a drought in new drugs.

Pfizer seemed to bounce back a bit in 2006, introducing a handful of new and notable drugs. In January, the FDA approved Sutent for advanced renal cell carcinoma. Sutent boasted $219 million in sales in 2006. In addition, Americans and Europeans who are trying to quit smoking gained access to Chantix/Champix, the first new prescription treatment for smoking cessation in almost 10 years.

Not so Exubera-nt

Later in 2006, the FDA and the European Commission gave the green light for Exubera, the first inhaled insulin therapy for adults with type 1 and type 2 diabetes, developed with sanofi-aventis. Some analysts predicted that Exubera could someday top $1 billion annually in sales but it only moved units worth about $5 million in 2006. By the third quarter of 2007, Pfizer pulled the plug on Exubera—the company took a $2.8 billion charge in the process, leading to a 77 percent decline in profits from the previous quarter.

The decision also directly affected the Terre Haute, Ind., plant that handled nearly all of Exubera's manufacturing needs. In October, the company placed 600 of the factory's 750 workers on paid leave, as it simply had no work for them without more orders for the drug. Neither Pfizer nor the city want the facility to close—it has been a major employer in the area for over 50 years and, since the turn of the 21st century, Pfizer has invested roughly $300 million in the plant. The company is now weighing plans for its future in Terre Haute.

However, Pfizer has been cutting down on its manufacturing all throughout 2007. Early in the year, as part of its restructuring it announced plans to close manufacturing sites in Brooklyn, N.Y., and Omaha, Neb., and sell a plant in Feucht, Germany. By August 2007, it announced it would also close its Augusta, Ga., plant after failing to find a buyer. And then, in December 2007, the firm announced it was considering doubling its level of manufacturing outsourcing to 30 percent, with most of the new business going to Asia. All of the plant closures and sales should occur in 2008.

Currently in the pipeline

A forthcoming drug with promise is maraviroc, a new AIDS treatment that works by blocking a human protein that HIV uses to enter and infect cells. Pfizer has applied for approval to sell maraviroc, which would expand treatment options for HIV/AIDS patients. In particular, it may help people who have forms of HIV that are resistant to other drugs. The drug is currently in human clinical trials. In phase III trials, more than 40 percent of patients who took it had undetectable levels of HIV after 24 weeks, roughly twice the rate of those on placebos.

Pfizer is also focusing on new cancer treatments. One such drug in the pipeline is ticilimumab, which is for the treatment of metastatic melanoma, a serious type of skin cancer where the cancer cells have spread to other parts of the body. Analysts expect the drug to hit the market in late 2007 or 2008 and predict that Ticilimumab could have annual sales of $325 million by 2010.

In addition, Pfizer is working with Coley Pharmaceutical Group on an experimental lung cancer medication called ProMune. Initial clinical studies by Coley showed that ProMune, injected under the skin, had promising anticancer activity. One analyst thinks the drug, which is likely to launch in 2008, could have annual sales of $700 million by 2010.

Lending a helping hand

Pfizer's web site says its purpose is "helping people live longer, healthier, happier lives." Certainly, the company carries out this mission through developing new drugs, such as maraviroc. However, the firm also tries to make the world a healthier place through donations to individuals and organizations.

Pfizer started its first charitable drug program, Sharing the Care, in the early 1990s, and it has provided over one billion free or low-priced prescriptions to low-income patients. In August 2004, Sharing the Care became part of a new program called Pfizer Helpful Answers, which helps the uninsured get Pfizer medicines for free or at significant savings in community clinics and doctors' offices.

The company has set up a web site and a toll-free number for uninsured people to call to find out how to enroll in the program. A prescription discount card called Pfizer Pfriends offers savings on Pfizer prescription medicines to Americans without prescription drug coverage.

In early 2005, the company joined Together Rx Access, along with nine other pharmaceutical companies. The program gives savings on more than 275 medicines to Medicare-ineligible, uninsured individuals under 65. Program participants must fall below a certain income level to qualify for Together Rx Access.

Recently, Pfizer and the Pfizer Foundation announced a new three-year HIV/AIDS initiative. The program targets midsized AIDS service organizations that provide innovative, comprehensive health care services in the U.S. communities most affected by the disease. The Pfizer Foundation supports approximately 20 community-based organizations with grants up to $100,000 each. The foundation funds these programs in the 10 states with the greatest number of reported AIDS cases: California, Florida, New York, Texas, New Jersey, Illinois, Georgia, Pennsylvania, North Carolina and Maryland.

Visit Vault at **www.vault.com** for insider company profiles, expert advice,
career message boards, expert resume reviews, the Vault Job Board and more.

VAULT CAREER LIBRARY   **299**

Shake-up at the top

In 2006, Jeffrey Kindler took the place of Henry "Hank" McKinnell as CEO of Pfizer. Kindler, a former McDonald's executive, was Pfizer's general counsel before he became CEO. After Pfizer announced the change in leadership, the media noted that picking a lawyer for the post was logical in an age when pharmaceutical companies have to deal with loads of lawsuits.

Investors hoped Kindler would rekindle growth and bring new ideas to the company. But not all of the new CEO's changes have been popular with employees. For starters, Kindler reshuffled most of his senior team and cut the company's U.S. sales force by 20 percent. Then, in January 2007, Kindler announced a strategic plan to reduce the company's worldwide workforce by about 10 percent (10,000 jobs) over the next two years, in hopes that would save the company over $2 billion in costs.

At the same time, Kindler received total compensation valued at more than $11 million in 2006. Anonymous posters on an industry message board suggested that "Jeff Kindler should change his name to Jeff Swindler."

Kindler also wants to see the company triple the number of drugs in its development pipeline by 2009, leading Pfizer to release at least four new drugs every year beginning in 2011; the company also plans to launch two new drugs gained via acquisitions of smaller companies per year, beginning in 2009. Kindler has also predicted that 2009 will be the next year that Pfizer will record a growth in revenue.

GETTING HIRED

How to apply

The company's careers site, www.pfizer.com/careers, provides information on a wide range of openings, as well as links to other Pfizer job pages. Interested applicants can apply online for specific positions and submit a resume to the company database. Pfizer actively recruits on a number of undergraduate and graduate campuses across the country, including Harvard, Columbia, Northwestern and the Massachusetts Institute of Technology.

Positions are available in the six divisions of the company: animal health; corporate functions, which includes human resources, information technology and finance; global manufacturing; global research and development; pharmaceuticals; and pharmaceutical sales. Requirements vary according to position, and the company looks for candidates with degrees ranging from BS to MBA to PhD. Check the web site for detailed descriptions and contact information, which vary with each operating group.

Another way in

In his 2005 tell-all book *Hard Sell: The Evolution of a Viagra Salesman*, Jamie Reidy described his life as a drug sales rep for Pfizer. He worked for the firm from 1995 to 1999, the company's golden age. Reidy, a former U.S. Army officer, discussed the training program for new salespeople: "Curiously, boot camp and Pfizer training each lasted six weeks; an ominous parallel," he writes. "In both places, I was told when to eat, and my dining options were severely limited." Later in the book, Reidy describes how he worked as little as possible during his years as a sales rep; he did things like falsify signatures on sample sheets when he wanted time off.

Sensational tales aside, salespeople at Pfizer now have it hard, no matter how you slice it. The company completed a 20 percent reduction of its U.S. sales force in December 2006. The downsizing didn't end in sales. In early 2007, Pfizer announced a plan to eliminate roughly 10,000 positions. This hemorrhaging of jobs is supposed to take place by the end of 2008. Due to the looming layoffs, it might be more difficult to get a job at Pfizer than it's been in the past.

In part, it's who you know

Pfizer employees say the number of interview rounds varies depending on position. One applicant for a sales job, who never made it to a face-to-face interview, says there were "two phone interviews conducted by their HR department," which were each "20 to 30 minutes long." An assistant scientist says, "You will end up interviewing for a whole day" with "the group you will be hired into" as well as "the sister groups or clients of the group, [into] which you will be hired." The scientist adds, "They will ask you anything under the sun."

If you know someone or have been temping at the company, expect a less intensive interview process. One source who temped at Pfizer before interviewing for a permanent position says, "I had one round of interviews with two separate people. First I met with my current supervisor and then I met with the department head. It was very informal with very few technical questions."

Visit Vault at **www.vault.com** for insider company profiles, expert advice, career message boards, expert resume reviews, the Vault Job Board and more.

VAULT CAREER LIBRARY   **301**

Getting in through internships

As at many companies, a summer internship can help you get a foot in the door at Pfizer. One insider, who started out in Pfizer's summer MBA finance internship program says, most internship applicants had "two rounds of interviews, first at their respective universities then at the New York headquarters." The source says the internship led to a "full-time offer based on my relative ranking within the summer class."

Growing or shrinking?

One department where the number of jobs actually increased during the past couple of years was research and development. However, this probably won't be the case in the future. As noted above, the company is closing some of its R&D facilities.

Pifzer's business has a reputation for treating its employees well. In recent years, Pfizer has earned accolades from numerous publications, including *Working Mother*, which named the firm one of the 100 best companies for working mothers in 2005 and 2006, and *Fortune*, which listed it as one of the 100 Best Companies to Work for in America in 2005.

OUR SURVEY SAYS

Pay and perks

Sources at Pfizer say benefits are fairly standard. One manager says, "Vacation is a standard three weeks for all staff employees with a fourth week after 10 years of service. An additional week is given for each 10 years of service after that." The company's compensation system is "based on grades," but "You are not supposed to know what your grade is or the grades of others." The insider adds, "When you interview, you are only told whether the position is a grade above, below or lateral—which you have to take the interviewer's word on." Folks at Pfizer also say raises have been low in recent years. Employees "do not receive bonuses or stock options."

Difficult times

Insiders say the past few years at Pfizer, once a "wildly successful" company, have been difficult. One source reports that, due to organizational changes, there's been "a mass exodus of talent, which management is now seeking to replace." The respondent adds, "You may be able to come into the organization and be part of a turnaround and as one of the few remaining have a chance at a senior position."

Another says that, following recent mergers, there's been "a great deal of uncertainty" at the company. The source adds, "Be it job security or the mission for a specific group, no one seems to know what is going on at Pfizer." The insider says the company has been downsizing, but the firm "steadfastly refuses to give numbers as to the number of positions eliminated." The contact adds that Pfizer is a high-pressure environment with a "lot of pushing and shoving."

Looking up?

One associate scientist says, "The business outlook for big pharma and consumer products companies is almost always strong despite public sentiment." However, most sources at Pfizer are pessimistic about the company's future. One insider points out that Lipitor and other blockbusters will go off patent in the coming years. The respondent feels that Pfizer "is quick to point to the numerous product launches it is anticipating, but the hard reality is that none of the drugs coming on line can be expected to generate even remotely the amount of revenue the current product portfolio does."

Another source says, "The industry is now at a crossroads due the expiration of numerous blockbuster drugs and thin pipelines," adding that Pfizer is "only now coming to grips with its size" after swallowing up other companies. The insider concludes, "It is now in the middle of a restructuring, and I cannot say that I see the company as great place to start one's career."

Visit Vault at **www.vault.com** for insider company profiles, expert advice, career message boards, expert resume reviews, the Vault Job Board and more.

VAULT CAREER LIBRARY

303

Promega Corporation

2800 Woods Hollow Road
Madison, WI 53711
Phone: (608) 274-4330
Fax: (608) 277-2601
www.promega.com

LOCATIONS

Madison, WI (HQ)
Pittsburgh, PA
San Luis Obispo, CA
West Chester, PA

International locations in Austria,
Belgium, China, Germany, Italy,
Latin America, Luxembourg, The
Netherlands and the UK.

THE STATS

Employer Type: Private Company
Chairman & CEO: William A. Linton
2006 Employees: 911

DEPARTMENTS

Administration
Operations
Research & Development
Sales & Marketing

KEY COMPETITORS

Bayer AG
Roche Holding Ltd.
Sigma-Aldrich Corporation

EMPLOYMENT CONTACT

www.promega.com/hr

THE SCOOP

Alpha and Promega

Think Wisconsin is all about cheese? Think again. In the form of Promega, the state also produces science and technology. Besides adding more than dairy to Wisconsin's state economy, the privately held Promega Corporation serves as a sort of hardware store for scientists everywhere. The company describes itself as "a leader in providing innovative solutions and technical support to the life sciences industry." It holds about 200 patents and sells more than 1,450 products that help life scientists conduct research, especially in genomics, proteomics and cellular analysis. Promega's main customers are laboratories, most of which are associated with universities, medical research centers and government and research institutions. Promega has branches in about a dozen countries and more than 50 distributors worldwide.

Promega's progress

In 1978, William A. Linton founded a company called Biotec in his garage. By 1981 the company had 15 employees and was already oriented eastwards in its business philosophy, gaining the first Asian distributor for its products, SKK Japan, late in the year. In 1984 the firm, then known as Promega Biotec, launched a joint venture to set up China's first genetic biochemical manufacturing facility. Three years later, in 1987, it dropped the "Biotec" from its name and made *Inc.* magazine's list of fastest-growing American companies.

The company continued to grow, opening Promega France in 1993 and acquiring San Luis Obispo-based JBL Scientific Inc. in 1999. (After the acquisition, the division changed its name to Promega Biosciences.) Along the way, the firm kept cranking out biotechnological advancements, often basking in the appreciation of *R&D* magazine. To name two examples, its TNT coupled reticulocyte lysate made the magazine's list of 1993's 100 Most Technologically Significant Products, and its DNA IQ System and AluQuant System both made 2002's list of the year's Top 100 Technologies.

Being Zen

Promega's employees conduct research, but some of them have also been research subjects. In July 1997, Richard Davidson, a Harvard-trained neuroscientist, recruited

Visit Vault at **www.vault.com** for insider company profiles, expert advice, career message boards, expert resume reviews, the Vault Job Board and more.

VAULT CAREER LIBRARY **305**

human subjects at Promega. Davidson's goal was to study the effects of Buddhist-style meditation on ordinary office workers' neural and immunological activity. Some employees were reluctant to volunteer, but eventually Davidson got about four dozen Promega staff members to participate in the study.

Dr. Jon Kabat-Zinn, an emeritus professor of medicine at the University of Massachusetts Medical School, led the study. Once a week for eight weeks, he arrived at Promega with a boom box, meditation tape cassettes and Tibetan chimes; and Promega employees, whose brains were wired and measured before they began the course in meditation training, sat on a conference room floor and practiced mindfulness for three hours.

After eight weeks, the researchers tested brain and immune markers to evaluate the effects of meditation. In July 2003, the experiment's results appeared in a journal called *Psychosomatic Medicine*. The research showed that Promega employees who practiced meditation for two months experienced significant activity increases in several areas of the left prefrontal cortex. When the subjects were tested again four months after the experiment, this heightened activity persisted. Meditation also seemed to help some participants' immune systems, as a few employees claimed to demonstrate a more robust ability to produce antibodies after receiving a flu vaccine.

West meets East

Promega's encounters with Asia go beyond experiments with Buddhist-style meditation in the conference room. In 2003, CEO Linton met with Michio Oshio, director of Kazusa DNA Research Institute, at a lunch arranged as part of Wisconsin's sister-state relationship with Japan's Chiba prefecture. A rural section of Japan, Chiba wasn't on Linton's radar screen before the lunch but it led to a deal for Promega two years later. In 2005, Promega agreed to work with the Kazusa Institute, using Promega's gene expression technology to commercialize Kazusa's libraries of human DNA.

In April 2007, West met East again, when Promega announced a collaboration agreement with China's Guangzhou Institute of Biomedicine and Health (GIBH). Together, Promega and GIBH will develop compound profiling solutions for small molecule and traditional Chinese medicine drug screening.

Promega put pen to paper again in October 2007, announcing a collaboration with the German firm Amaxa. The two companies will exchange technology to develop solutions for monitoring hard-to-reach cells that are important for research, such as stem cells, cancer cells and primary cells.

GETTING HIRED

Browse Promega's employment prose

The firm's careers web site (www.promega.com/hr) allows applicants to search for openings at its offices in Madison, Wisc., and San Luis Obispo, Calif. Applicants can also browse for opportunities in international offices in Austria, Switzerland, Latin America, Germany, China, Italy, the U.K., Belgium, Luxembourg and The Netherlands. Departments at the firm include administration, marketing, operations, Promega biosciences, research and development and sales. Promega prefers for job seekers to apply for positions online. Applicants who don't have access to a computer can send a resume to: Promega Corporation—Human Resources, 2800 Woods Hollow Road, Madison, WI 53711.

Award time!

In October 2004, Promega received a top 100 award from *R&D* magazine for one of its products, the P450-Glo CYP450 Assay System. The firm has also won awards for the way it treats employees. In 1996, *Working Mother* magazine named Promega one of its 100 Best Companies for Working Mothers, giving the firm good scores for child care and scheduling flexibility. Benefits at Promega include health and dental insurance, a 401(k) plan, flexible spending accounts, term life insurance, short- and long-term disability insurance, tuition assistance and more.

Practice wellness at Promega

At Promega's Madison headquarters, employees enjoy a "campus-like environment" with casual dress and architecture inspired by Wisconsin's prairies, wetlands, woods and ridges. Employees can walk, jog, bike or ski across wooded trails on the company's grounds. The headquarters also has a wellness center, an on-site cafeteria, a new mother's room, a seasonal farmer's market and quarterly art shows.

Promega's corporate culture is as enlightened and forward-thinking as one would expect of a firm located in the renowned college-town of Madison, with a wellness center and "campus-like" atmosphere. "The Science of Cool," a 2006 profile of the company by *Madison Magazine*, revealed Promega's abundance of, well, cool company culture. The piece detailed an annual ethnic food potluck ("The taste of Promega"), a farmer's market near the company driveway, on-site dry cleaning and massage services, computer subsidies after the first year of employment up to $1,200 and even CEO Linton refereeing a company soccer game.

And these innovations aren't a top-down attempt to be hip. The company has a "Social Committee" of workers, often composed of HR employees, that organically invents these "Promega Perks." And they are often funny. For example, on every employee's birthday, he or she visits with CEO Linton for two hours at the "periodic table." Linton still sets much of the tone at the company, walking around "in jeans and a golf shirt, lingering at desks and striking up conversations."

Quintiles Transnational Corp.

4709 Creekstone Drive, Suite 200
Durham, NC 27703
Phone: (919) 998-2000
Fax: (919) 998-9113
www.qtrn.com

LOCATIONS

Durham, NC (HQ)
Atlanta, GA
Austin, TX
Cambridge, MA
Falls Church, VA
Morrisville, NC
Overland Park, KS
Rockville, MD
San Diego, CA
San Francisco, CA
Smyrna, GA
Thousand Oaks, CA
Vernon Hills, IL
Williamston, NC

International locations in more than
50 countries.

THE STATS

Employer Type: Private Company
Chairman & CEO: Dennis Gillings
2007 Employees: 19,000
2005 Revenue ($mil.): $2,399
2005 Net Income ($mil.): -$5

DEPARTMENTS

Administrative Services •
Biostatistics • Business Development
• Clinical Data Management • Clinical
Project Management • Clinical
Research & Monitoring •
Communications • Contracts •
Corporate & Executive • Customer
Relationship Management •
Customer Service/Call Center • Drug
Safety/Pharmacovigilance • Event
Planning • Executive • Facilities •
Finance & Procurement • Graphic
Arts/Publishing • Healthcare/Human
Services Consulting • Human
Resources • Information Technology
• Laboratory/Research • Learning &
Development • Legal • Library •
Marketing • Materials & Distribution
• Medical & Scientific Services •
Medical Communications &
Education • Medical Writing •
Nursing/Nurse Education •
Pharmaceutical/Medical Sales •
Phamacokinetics • Pharmacy •
Proposal Development • Quality
Assurance • Regulatory • Site &
Patient Services

KEY COMPETITORS

Covance Inc.
IMS Health Incorporated
Parexel International Corporation

EMPLOYMENT CONTACT

www.qtrn.com/Careers

Visit Vault at **www.vault.com** for insider company profiles, expert advice,
career message boards, expert resume reviews, the Vault Job Board and more.

VAULT CAREER LIBRARY   **309**

THE SCOOP

Quintiles quickly

Quintiles Transnational—a global leader in pharmaceutical services—provides professional expertise, market intelligence and partnering solutions to the pharmaceutical, biotechnology and health care industries. The company has helped develop and/or commercialize the world's 30 best-selling drugs. Quintiles, whose headquartered near Research Triangle Park, North Carolina, has 16,000 employees and offices in about 50 countries.

The company is divided into three major groups: Quintiles product development services, Innovex commercialization and NovaQuest strategic partnering solutions. The product development services unit conducts clinical trials and offers preclinical research. Innovex deals with sales team recruitment and managing. The company's strategic partnering group, NovaQuest, provides funding, management services and strategic expertise to emerging biotechnology companies worldwide.

In 2005, the company's revenue was about $2.4 billion, an 11 percent increase from the previous year. All in all, the outlook is good for contract research organizations (CROs) like Quintiles, because the development and commercialization market for new medicines is booming.

Forbes ranked Quintiles No.135 on its list of the largest private companies in 2005 and 2006. *Fortune* ranked the company No. 781 on its annual ranking of America's largest corporations in 2006, up from No. 810 the year before.

See CRO grow

In January 1974, Dennis Gillings, a native of England and professor at the University of North Carolina, signed a consulting contract with a European pharmaceutical company to analyze a product's performance. Gillings and his staff provided contract services to various pharmaceutical firms between 1974 and 1982, and during this period the contract research organization industry developed.

In February 1982, Gillings' company was incorporated as Quintiles Inc. in North Carolina. The firm grew during the 1980s, when many pharmaceuticals companies started farming out testing on experimental drugs. The company's management decided to form Quintiles Transnational Corp., a holding company for all Quintiles subsidiaries, in 1990.

In 1996, Quintiles joined forces with Innovex Ltd., a U.K.-based international contract pharmaceutical company specializing in sales and marketing services for pharmaceutical companies. With the addition of Innovex, Quintiles became the world's largest full-service contract pharmaceutical and health care company. Quintiles went public in 1994, and completed a successful secondary stock offering in 1997. It then acquired several other companies in the late 1990s, and the firm joined the S&P 500 index in November 1999.

In the fall of 2002, founder and Chairman Dennis Gillings unsuccessfully bid $1.3 billion to take the company private. Then, in April 2003, Gillings raised his offer to $1.7 billion. The chairman made his offer through Pharma Services Holding, a company he created in 2002 for the buyout effort. This time, Gillings' offer was successful and the company bid farewell to the days of SEC filings.

Growing in private

Although analysts were wary of the company's future after it retreated behind the private veil, Quintiles had good growth during its first year as a private firm. In 2005, Quintiles completed a strategic partnership agreement with Aptuit, acquiring three business units in a deal worth approximately $125 million. They are presently known as preclinical services, pharmaceutical sciences and clinical trial supplies.

In April 2006, Quintiles launched its expanded strategic partnering group under the NovaQuest brand. The company also announced an alliance with TPG-Axon Capital, a global investment firm, to support significant co-development and co-promotion agreements. During 2006, NovaQuest invested in 16 emerging biotech companies, double the number it had invested in the previous year.

Quintiles announced the formation of a global biologics regulatory team in May 2007. The team, created in response to increasing requests for regulatory expertise in the growing field of biologics, will advise customers about development plans and strategy for regulatory submissions for biological products such as monoclonal antibodies, stem-cell based therapies and vaccines.

New locations

Also in May 2007, CEO Gillings dedicated a new Quintiles facility in Overland Park, Kansas. Gillings said the 236,000-square-foot building would give Quintiles' regional clinical development services, clinical pharmacology units and phase I clinical research unit the space necessary to expand.

The company also broke ground in September 2007 on what it plans to be its future headquarters in 2009: a 252,000-square-foot facility in Durham, North Carolina. Quintiles will be looking to fill its new offices, stating in June 2007 that it expects to hire 5,000 new workers around the world over the next five years. In Durham alone, Quintiles has stated it will probably be adding 1,000 (!) employees to its staff.

GETTING HIRED

Quintessentials for a Quintiles careers

Through Quintiles Transnational's careers web site (www.qtrn.com/Careers), applicants can submit a resume or complete an applicant profile. The company recommends that job seekers create a full profile, which helps the firm's recruiters match applicants to job opportunities as they become available.

Applicants can search for job openings at www.quintiles.com/Careers/USJobs.htm. An extensive list of job categories includes administrative services, biostatistics, business development, clinical data management, clinical project management, clinical research and monitoring, communications, contracts, corporate and executive, customer relationship management, customer service/call center, drug safety/pharmacovigilance, event planning, executive, facilities, finance and procurement, graphic arts/publishing, healthcare/human services consulting, human resources, information technology, laboratory/research, learning and development, legal, library, marketing, materials and distribution, medical and scientific services, medical communications and education, medical writing, nursing/nurse education, pharmaceutical/medical sales, pharmacokinetics, pharmacy, proposal development, quality assurance, regulatory, and site and patient services.

The firm also has a clinical research associates (CRA) program. Employees in this program often start out as clinical trial assistants who gain hands-on experience, join experienced CRAs on site, and receive general and specialized training. The company then assigns the associates to specific geographic regions.

Quintiles Transnational recruits at job fairs around the country, as well as in the United Kingdom and Bangalore, India. A schedule of career fairs the company attends can be found online at www.qtrn.com/Careers/CareerFairSchedule.htm.

Know thy resume, and be analytical

Insiders at Quintiles say applicants can expect multiple rounds of interviews. One researcher at Quintiles reports that there were five rounds of interviews, which included questions about education and work experience. There was also a case study, "which they tell you beforehand," plus analytical and behavioral questions.

An interviewee, who didn't get an offer in the end, says there was a 50-minute phone interview followed by a meeting with "HR and other team players within two weeks." Another insider says the interview process entailed three phone interviews and two face-to-face meetings. The respondent adds, "I met with colleagues/peers, executives in my business line and executives in other business lines." The insider says interview questions "were mostly behavioral based."

One source who has been involved on the hiring side says interviews "generally last about 30 minutes" and "decisions about hires are made immediately after candidates leave." The individual adds, "It's not about getting the correct answer, but instead mainly how you think through problems." In addition, the insider advises, "It's good to have a strong understanding of your resume, because they will ask about each position."

OUR SURVEY SAYS

Friendly and hardworking

One Quintiles source says the organization's culture "varies from site to site and country to country." Overall, however, insiders say the company is known for having "a people-friendly culture." One respondent says, "I thoroughly enjoy the working environment." The source, who describes co-workers as "very smart and hardworking," adds, "It's a very collaborative effort. Everyone is equally hardworking and offers equal input in the deliverables." One insider reports that, in addition to salaries, there are "minimal year-end bonuses." Other perks include a technology reimbursement fund, vacation days and sick days and "some corporate discounts."

A strong outlook

Sources at Quintiles are optimistic about the company's future. One, who observes that CROs are doing well now, says, Quintiles' business outlook "is extremely strong" and that the company "has a record backlog of new business and sales pipelines that are full."

The insider says the organization's strengths "lie in the depth of experience and size of Quintiles." The contact explains, "Those two ingredients coupled with the ability to hire nice people make the company both strong and pleasant." A researcher says Quintiles is "in a phase of growth" and is generally "doing very well." This source adds, however, that the CRO has high turnover, "which is partially due to the constantly changing business lines, and the fear of eliminating some groups." In addition, the insider says, some jobs have been outsourced to India and South Africa.

Roche Group

Grenzacherstrasse 124
CH-4070 Basel
Switzerland
Phone: +41-61-688-1111
Fax: +41-61-691-9391
www.roche.com

LOCATIONS

Basel, Switzerland (HQ)
Nutley, NJ (US HQ)
Alameda, CA
Boulder, CO
Branchburg, NJ
Florence, SC
Humacao, PR
Indianapolis, IN
Palo Alto, CA
Pleasanton, CA
Ponce, PR

International locations in over 150 countries.

THE STATS

Employer Type: Public Company
Stock Symbol: RHHBY [ADR]; ROG
Stock Exchange: OTC; Swiss
Chairman: Franz B. Humer
CEO: Severin Schwan
2006 Employees: 74,372
2006 Revenue ($mil.): $34,495
2006 Net Income ($mil.): $7,549

DEPARTMENTS

Administration & Support
Communications/PR
Customer & Product Support
Development
Engineering
Finance & Accounting
Government Affairs
Human Resources
Information Technology
Legal
Logistics
Procurement
Production/Manufacturing
Project Management
Quality Management
Research
Sales & Marketing
Technical Operations.

KEY COMPETITORS

Dade Behring
Pfizer Inc.
Schering-Plough Corporation

EMPLOYMENT CONTACT

careers.roche.com

Visit Vault at **www.vault.com** for insider company profiles, expert advice, career message boards, expert resume reviews, the Vault Job Board and more.

VAULT CAREER LIBRARY   315

THE SCOOP

Health care stalwart

When Fritz Hoffmann founded F. Hoffmann-La Roche & Co. near the Rhine in Switzerland in 1896, he wanted to produce medicines on an industrial scale outside of the pharmacy and sell them on the international market. One of the first products the young company introduced was Airol, a wound antiseptic that debuted in Germany. Today, Basel, Switzerland-based Roche has grown into a global health care player, with more than 150 subsidiaries around the world across two divisions (pharmaceuticals and diagnostics).

In 2006, Roche recorded pharmaceutical sales growth of 21 percent, more than three times as fast as the global market. Soon-to-be former CEO Humer noted that this increase was mostly driven by continued demand for Roche's cancer drugs, sales of osteoporosis drug Bonviva/Boniva and government stockpiling of Tamiflu (discussed below).

The Swiss company launched a hostile $3 billion bid for Ventana Medical Systems in June 2007. The offer underlines Roche's strategy of acquiring small and medium-sized companies whose diagnostic products permit the company to target medications to individual patients. The firm wants to purchase Ventana to broaden its portfolio of diagnostic tests.

Roche's strong growth and commitment to innovation has led to its pre-eminence as one of the industry's top employers. The company received a number of awards in 2006 and 2007 from publications including *Science*, which named it a top employer for a fifth consecutive year, and *Fortune*, which included Roche's U.S. affiliates on its Best Companies to Work For list.

Prescription for growth

The company opened European subsidiaries in the latter part of the 19th century and into the early 1900s. Roche then crossed the ocean to launch its first U.S. subsidiary, Hoffmann-La Roche Chemical Works Inc., in New York City in 1905.

A few years later (1909), Roche's longest-selling drug—Pantopon, a pain, anxiety and cough reliever—hit the market, where it remains today. A series of international events—including a German boycott of Roche products and the loss of a Russian operation as a result of the 1917 revolution—prompted Roche to become a limited company in 1919.

Entering new markets

Roche's entry into the vitamin market came in the 1930s, after scientist Tadeusz Reichstein offered the company a workable method of synthesizing vitamin C. During the late 1930s and into the subsequent decade, Roche began producing a variety of different vitamins and became a leading supplier. (In 2003, the company ended its long run in this sector with a deal to sell its vitamins division to Dutch company DSM.)

In the postwar years, Roche became a fully diversified pharmaceutical outfit. It increased its presence in the nonprescription drug segment with the 1958 acquisition of Geneva-based Laboratoires Sauter S.A., and debuted its first anticancer drug four years later—Fluoro-uracil Roche. In 1963, the very next year, Roche's R&D efforts paid off with the release of one of the most famous names in prescription drugs, the worldwide blockbuster Valium. In 1968, Roche created its diagnostics department as well as one of the first centers for biotech R&D, the Roche Institute for Molecular Biology.

The pharmaceutical 1970s

In the 1970s, whether fairly or not, Roche became a poster child for high drug costs. First, the U.K.'s Monopolies Commission ordered the company to lower its prices by 50 to 60 percent. Roche protested, running full-page newspaper ads about such costs being necessary, due to its expensive R&D efforts.

The company also made its financial records public for the first time in 1973, revealing that it had earned $500 million that year on the sales of Valium and related drug Librium alone (the equivalent of $2.2 billion in 2006). A host of other countries then began to examine Roche's pricing but the proceedings largely ended in 1980, when the company agreed to voluntary price restraints.

In 1976, Roche became associated with tragedy when an accidental chemical reaction in one of its plants led to the escape of a huge toxic cloud in Seveso, Italy, containing a dioxin found in Agent Orange. Thousands of animals died soon afterwards and about 700 human inhabitants of the area developed chloracne, a skin disease caused by overexposure to dioxins. On its company web site, Roche mentions that "from the beginning Roche and [its subsidiary] made every effort to

Visit Vault at **www.vault.com** for insider company profiles, expert advice, career message boards, expert resume reviews, the Vault Job Board and more.

V/\ULT CAREER LIBRARY   **317**

redress the damage done … directly assist[ing] the authorities in dealing with the after-effects of the disaster."

Corporate modernity

The firm first adopted standardized accounting practices for all of its divisions in the 1970s, and in the next decade it refined these divisions even further. The heads of every unit convened in 1986 and adopted a stricter "group structure" for the company. The groups were further refined in 1989, with the creation of a holding company that brought the firm into the realm of international finance.

Soon, the more corporate Roche would flex its muscles, acquiring a majority interest stake in genetics firm Genentech in 1990. The firm struck again in 1994, purchasing the U.S.-based pharmaceutical Syntex Corporation, which was renamed Roche Bioscience. As a result of its global reach, Roche now sells its products in more than 150 countries.

Roche Diagnostics: building an empire

These days, Roche is keen on diagnostic testing, which allows companies to develop drugs designed to target very specific disease variations. The way has been paved with more acquisitions, the largest of which was Roche's $11 billion purchase in 1997 of the then-second-largest diagnostics firm in the world, Boehringer Mannheim.

In July 2003, the company announced it would acquire Igen International, a Gaithersburg, Md.-based developer of blood testing equipment, used in industrial food and water processing. Roche spun off a new unit of Igen's auxiliary pursuits after completing the $1.4 billion acquisition in early 2004, calling it BioVeris. But by April 2007, Roche changed its mind and purchased 100 percent control of BioVeris for $600 million.

At the time, Roche stated that the acquisition "will allow Roche Diagnostics to expand its immunochemistry business from the human diagnostics field into new market segments such as life science research, life science development, patient self-testing, veterinary testing, drug discovery, drug development and clinical trials." Perhaps more importantly, the firm added, "The market for clinical trials is growing at approximately 10 percent per annum."

In March 2007, Roche and CuraGen signed an agreement under which Roche Diagnostics will pay as much as $154.9 million for CuraGen's Connecticut-based subsidiary, 454 Life Sciences. The new Roche holding brings a wealth of nanotechnology-based genome sequencing systems to the table; this is the stuff that analyzes the stuff of life—DNA and RNA.

Diagnosis: CEO

The diagnostics division is so entrenched as Roche's focal point that it is providing the entire company with its new CEO, effective March 2008. Dr. Franz Humer, the current chairman and CEO, will stay on as chairman of Roche holdings; and Dr. Severin Schwan, the 40 year-old CEO of Roche Diagnostics, will become CEO of the Roche Group. This management restructuring was announced in July 2007, when Dr. Humer explained that "in view of the increasing complexity of the tasks involved, the board has decided to separate the chairman and CEO roles."

Getting the flu bug

Roche has excelled in quickly providing governments around the world with a vaccine for avian influenza, or "bird flu," which has, in turn, boosted revenue—it increased by double-digits in the first half of 2005. This windfall in revenue has come from some major clients clamoring for Tamiflu, including the international body of record—the United Nations started building a stockpile of the drug in 2005, which may be delivered quickly to areas where early outbreaks of bird flu are detected.

Roche isn't just raking in Tamiflu dough, though; in 2005 the firm also agreed to donate millions of doses of the vaccine to the World Health Organization, which will count towards the UN's stockpile. WHO has called Tamiflu the "primary recommended antiviral of choice" for bird flu. UN officials have even started pressuring Roche about releasing it in generic form, although nothing has resulted in that direction so far.

The drug has been at the center of a legal fight that has slightly impacted Roche's earnings. Gilead Sciences invented Tamiflu, which Roche manufactures and sells, pursuant to a 1996 contract. In June 2005 Gilead accused Roche of violating the contract by not doing enough to manufacture and promote Tamiflu. The legal dispute ended in November 2005, when Roche agreed to pay Gilead between 14 and 22 percent of annual net sales of Tamiflu, depending on the volume of sales of the drug.

In March 2007, Japanese health officials questioned Tamiflu's safety, warning that the anti-influenza drug shouldn't be given to teenagers. Why such precautions? In Japan, some children who were taking Tamiflu died or were injured after they jumped from balconies or ran into traffic. Roche insists that the drug is safe. Europe has no such worries, apparently—the European Union approved child-sized doses of Tamiflu in September 2007.

The Tamiflu locomotive finally stalled in October 2007, when Roche quarterly earning reports revealed that sales of the drug had slid 60 percent over the course of the period. Apparently, government and international bodies were satisfied with their stockpiles of the stuff. Roche's stock fell slightly upon release of the earnings, but the company added that it had been expecting this drop-off in Tamiflu sales and was still on track to meet all of its revenue goals for 2007.

Looking forward

In 2006, the company filed 13 new drug applications and gained 14 regulatory approvals. The firm also has about 100 pharmaceutical projects in the clinical development stage and another 110 projects in the preclinical research stage. In its projection for fiscal 2007, Roche has said it again expects double-digit sales growth in pharmaceuticals.

The company is investing in new manufacturing facilities to meet the growing demand for biodiagnostics and biotherapeutics. Roche is building biotech facilities in Basel, Switzerland, and Penzberg, Germany, and the firm plans for the facilities to be fully operational by 2009. In addition, to deliver more products tailored to the needs of specific populations, Roche plans to intensify cooperation between the pharmaceuticals and diagnostics divisions.

Roche continues to develop other vaccines besides Tamiflu. In April 2007, for instance, the firm signed a deal with French biotech company Transgene to develop and sell a cervical cancer vaccine called TG-4001. The experimental vaccine differs from vaccines produced by competitors Merck and sanofi-aventis because it appears to be effective in treating established infections.

The recent October 2007 drop-off in sales of the Tamiflu vaccine has revealed how well Roche is positioned in its other areas of operation. The company's stock fell slightly, but analysts urged people to invest. *Forbes* quoted one who called Tamiflu a "red herring," noting that, "The company is going to deliver good top-line growth in pharmaceuticals over the next five years. [It has] a very strong franchise of oncology [cancer treatments], half a dozen key drugs in that area, and outside that [it] probably ha[s] the strongest pipeline of late stage drugs in that sector."

GETTING HIRED

You're hired!

Roche offers job seekers opportunities across its two divisions and in several countries. Start by searching in the careers section of the company's web site at careers.roche.com. Links to different locations, from the U.S. to Switzerland to Spain, will show sales and non-sales positions. The company has U.S. locations in New Jersey, California, Georgia, Indiana, South Carolina and Colorado, as well as facilities in Puerto Rico.

Standard and straightforward

Sources say the interview process at Roche typically involves multiple rounds of interviews. One insider in New Jersey, who "was interviewed by six people in daylong interview," says there was also a lunch with a larger group. Another in Switzerland reports that there were "two rounds of interviews," adding that the first interview was with "just the direct line manager recruiting" and the second was "with the line manager and members of the team."

One source, who describes interviewing with Roche as an "extremely pleasant experience," traveled from another European country to Switzerland for two rounds of interviews on the company's dime. The respondent adds, "Each interview lasted five to six hours, and I met an excellent representation of potential bosses and colleagues at each interview session." The insider says questions were straightforward, adding, "There were no trick questions. They were genuinely interested in learning who I was, why I wanted to work at Roche and why [I wanted] this particular position."

OUR SURVEY SAYS

Constructive and open (or rigid with red tape)?

People at Roche describe the company as "constructive," "open" and "personal." An insider in Switzerland says, "The company culture is one of the best in the business." Another insider, who works for Roche in the United States, says the firm makes "extensive efforts to embrace diverse groups" and says there are "opportunities to grow and advance." Sources say the dress code at Roche tends to be "business casual

Visit Vault at **www.vault.com** for insider company profiles, expert advice, career message boards, expert resume reviews, the Vault Job Board and more.

VAULT CAREER LIBRARY   321

with a trend towards formal." When dealing with customers, some say, they dress up more. Hours can be long, but "Roche has a cool system to track overtime, which allows you to have flexible work hours."

A few people feel the company's culture is rigid. One insider says, "This is a Swiss-based company. The Swiss are very Germanic and want things done their way only." Some respondents also say Roche is bureaucratic. Another source explains, "There's a tendency for many meetings and heavy use of internal computer systems to manage workflows, which adds many layers to tasks."

A strong pipeline and good morale

Roche insiders are positive about the company's future. One says the company "has been doing very well for the past few years" and expects that Roche "will continue to enjoy success for the next few years." Another says, "Roche has a very strong portfolio, strong pipeline. Roche will probably continue to establish itself as a leader in oncology." Because the company's outlook is good, another source says, morale at the company is "generally very good."

sanofi-aventis

174 Avenue de France
Paris 75013
France
Phone: +33-1-53-77-4000
Fax: +33-1-53-77-42-96
en.sanofi-aventis.com

US Headquarters:
55 Corporate Drive
Bridgewater, NJ 08807
Phone: (908) 981-5560
Fax: (908) 981-7870
Toll-free: (800) 981-2491
www.sanofi-aventis.us

LOCATIONS

Paris (HQ)
Bridgewater, NJ (US HQ)
Cambridge, MA • Decatur, GA • Des
Plaines, IL • Great Valley, PA •
Sparks, NV • St. Louis, MO •
Swiftwater, PA • Tucson, AZ •
Washington, DC

Locations in over 100 countries
worldwide.

THE STATS

Employer Type: Public Company
Stock Symbols: SAN; SNY
Stock Exchanges: Paris; NYSE
Chairman: Jean-François Dehecq
CEO: Gérard Le Fur
2006 Employees: 100,000
2006 Revenue ($mil.): €28,373
2006 Net Income ($mil.): €4,399

DEPARTMENTS

Administrative Support
Communications
Corporate Services
Discovery
Field Sales
Finance
Human resources
Industrial Operations
Information Technology
Legal
Managed Markets
Marketing/Sales Operations
Medical Affairs
Pharmacovigilance
Quality & Compliance
Regulatory Affairs
Research & Development
Supply Chain

KEY COMPETITORS

Bristol-Myers Squibb
GlaxoSmithKline
Merck

EMPLOYMENT CONTACT

www.sanofi-aventis-job.com

Visit Vault at **www.vault.com** for insider company profiles, expert advice,
career message boards, expert resume reviews, the Vault Job Board and more.

VAULT CAREER LIBRARY   323

THE SCOOP

Viva la France!

The Paris-headquartered sanofi-aventis is the world's third-largest pharmaceutical company, having formed out of the 2004 merger of Sanofi-Synthelabo and Aventis. The firm covers seven primary therapeutic areas: cardiovascular, thrombosis, oncology, metabolic disorders, central nervous system, internal medicine and vaccines. Its top sellers include Lovenox, Plavix, Ambien and Lantus.

Making a name for itself

The Sanofi group (and name) began in 1973 when French oil conglomerate Elf Aquitaine merged together several health care, cosmetics and animal nutrition companies. Over the next 25 years, Sanofi accumulated and divested a number of cosmetic and perfume subsidiaries, but by 1999, its entire beauty division had been sold off to prepare for its merger with Synthelabo.

Synthelabo also formed out of a merger, this one between the French drug firms Laboratoires Dausse and Laboratoires Robert et Carriere in 1970. Synthelabo became the No. 3 drug company in France in 1980 when it acquired the pharmaceutical company Metabio-Jouille. Throughout the 1980s and 1990s, the firm became a wheeler and dealer in mergers, acquisitions and collaborations, usually adding Asian partners and purchasing French rivals. By 1996, Synthelabo stated its goal: to garner 80 percent of its sales from Asia and the U.S. Also in 1996, it signed on with both Human Genome Sciences and SmithKline Beecham (now GlaxoSmithKline) to fund genetic research.

Sanofi merged with Synthelabo in 1999 and almost immediately made good on the latter's plans to target the U.S. market, significantly expanding its sales force there in 2000. Another merger, with Strasbourg-based Aventis, originated with Sanofi Synthelabo's hostile takeover bid worth €47.8 billion ($56.5 billion) in early 2004.

Aventis rejected the bid because of its low value (!), at least, it was low based on the company's share value. A three-month tête-à-tête concluded when Sanofi Synthelabo launched a bid of €54.5 billion ($64.4 billion), upon which Aventis smiled. The French government played an influential role by leaning on Sanofi Synthelabo to up its bid, once it became clear that Swiss pharmaceutical firm Novartis was snooping around for its own merger possibilities.

Researching priorities

Sanofi-aventis has among the largest research and development budgets worldwide, employing a research staff of more than 17,600 people, with 25 R&D centers spread out over three continents. The company spent €4.044 billion ($5.399 billion) on research in 2006 alone, some 15.6 percent of net sales, an increase from 2005's R&D spending by 14.8 percent. At the close of 2006, the company had 127 projects under development, including 56 at advanced stages (phases II and III).

Sanofi-aventis divides R&D efforts into two groups, each with its own organizational approach—the discovery research and international development departments. Discovery research identifies promising research targets for therapeutic innovation, using biological and chemical techniques. It annually puts out 15 to 20 compounds that are potentially capable of improving existing treatments or offering solutions to unmet needs. International development takes these compounds and turns them into medicines, also handling them at the marketing stage.

About a dozen trials in late stages of clinical observation came back with results for sanofi-aventis in 2006, in fields such as cardiovascular and disorders of the central nervous system. The firm has a number of new medicine applications it will soon be fielding with regulatory agencies, including dronearone, an atrial fibrillation treatment, saredutant for depression/anxiety, and a vaccine for dengue fever.

One potential blockbuster that's encountered some roadblocks is Acomplia (rimonabant), a drug designed to battle obesity and cardio-metabolic risk factors. In 2006, the European Commission granted marketing authorization in the EU to Acomplia for treatment of obese and overweight patients with associated risk factors such as diabetes. However, in the United States, the FDA delayed a decision on the drug in 2007.

A throbbing thrombosis sector

Lovenox/Clexane is sanofi-aventis' best selling drug, with €2.435 billion ($3.214 billion) in 2006 sales worldwide. The drug prevents venous thrombosis and prophylactic treatment for ischemic complications of unstable angina and non-Q wave myocardial infarction. Lovenox/Clexane is the leading low molecular weight heparin (LMWH) in the U.S., France, Germany, Italy, Spain and the U.K. Since its launch in 1987, medical professionals have used the drug to treat some 170 million patients in 96 countries.

Visit Vault at **www.vault.com** for insider company profiles, expert advice, career message boards, expert resume reviews, the Vault Job Board and more.

VAULT CAREER LIBRARY

325

Plavix is sanofi-aventis' second best selling drug and one of the world's 10-leading medicines, with over 52 million patients worldwide using it since its initial approval in 1997. In 2006 it racked up some €2.229 billion ($2.942 billion) in sales. A stroke preventative, Plavix works to prevent ischemic events caused by atherothrombosis and has become what scientists call the "foremost platelet antiaggregate agent."

Not so sleepy sales

The anti-insomnia pill Ambien (also known as Stilnox and Myslee) reached €2.026 billion ($2.674 billion) in sales in 2006. Chemically different from benzodiazepines, Ambien is distinguished by its selective binding to brain receptors mediating hypnotic activity, resulting in a type of sleep that is qualitatively close to natural sleep. The pills' effects last six to seven hours, and generally allow the patient to awake refreshed. The main drawback to this kind of hypnotic medicines is usually the risk of dependency, which is minimized in this case with recommended doses and treatment lengths. Ambien is the undisputed market leader in America, both by value and treatment nights, accounting for a prescriptions market share of 46.2 percent. It is also sanofi-aventis' leading prescription product, with 12 billion doses prescribed worldwide since the company introduced the drug in 1988.

In September 2005, sanofi-aventis received FDA approval for Ambien CR, an extended-release version of Ambien. The news came at just the right time for the product's hopes of continued success: it was losing market share to Sepracor's Lunesta and was scheduled to lose patent protection in October 2006. When that patent expiration arrived, the FDA gave it a six-month extension, ordering sanofi to study the drug for potential use in children.

Protecting its patents

In April 2007, just as the original Ambien came off its (extended) patent, New Jersey-based Barr Laboratories tried to take on Ambien CR, filing an application with the FDA for a generic version of the drug. On April 5, 2007, sanofi-aventis filed suit to prevent Barr from commercializing this generic version.

Meanwhile, sanofi is seeking to bar Barr, and other generic manufacturing firms, from impinging on its other products. In September 2005 sanofi-aventis' subsidiary Aventis Pharmaceuticals filed a motion for a preliminary injunction in federal court to prevent generic sales of Allegra. The motion would have prevented Barr and Teva Pharmaceuticals from selling Allegra's active ingredient, fexofenadine HCl and prevent Ranbaxy Laboratories and Amino Chemicals from commercial production of fexofenadine. But in January 2006, the court found for the generic firms. Sales of Allegra were affected. For instance, retail customers reported a 70 percent generic substitution rate for Allegra in the first full week following the September 2005 generic launch.

The company has also struggled to protect other drugs in its cabinet. In February 2007 sanofi-aventis lost a patent lawsuit related to its bestseller, Lovenox. The other parties in the lawsuit, Amphastar and Teva, received the go-ahead to start selling generic versions of the product and sanofi said it would investigate options for further legal recourse.

Apotex stress

In August, 2006, Canadian company Apotex began selling a generic version of Plavix. For several weeks, Plavix sales plummeted until sanofi reached a settlement with Apotex to stall sales of the generic Plavix—before taking the matter to court. The two companies did go to court over the strength of Plavix's patent, with the judge finding in October 2007 that Apotex could not sell a generic version and would owe sanofi significant damages.

There was one problem, though. Patent infringers, like Apotex, usually owe treble damages for violating a patent, but sanofi waived this right in the August 2006 settlement. Legal controversy has surrounded Bristol-Myers Squibb, sanofi's partner in marketing Plavix. (For more on the subject, please see the Bristol-Myers Squibb profile.)

Cancer concerns

Sanofi-aventis' leading oncology drug, Taxotere, brought in sales of €1.752 billion ($2.313 billion) in 2006. Taxotere is a chemotherapy agent that primarily battles breast cancer, non-small cell lung cancer and prostate cancer. In 2006, the drug won approval for two new indications: advanced stage gastric cancer in combination with the standard treatment, and head and neck cancer in combination with a classic regimen.

Vaccination domination

Sanofi-aventis was the largest supplier of flu vaccine to the U.S., selling some 55 million doses of Fluzone influenza during the 2005-2006 winter flu season. It was a decrease from the previous, record-setting season for the company's vaccination sales, when it had recorded about 60 million doses sold. Rival Chiron had been unable to deliver flu shots in 2004 and sanofi-aventis' sales skyrocketed some 70 percent compared to the same quarter a year earlier. For the 2007 season and beyond, sanofi is doubling the capacity of its American flu vaccine manufacturing unit; it expects to produce upwards of 100 million shots annually by 2009. With the help of a $97 million grant from the U.S. government, sanofi-aventis began construction of a U.S.-based plant capable of supplying up to 300 million monovalent flu vaccine doses annually.

In April 2006, though, the FDA slapped sanofi with a warning letter after an inspection of its Stillwater, Penn., facility turned up contaminations within the manufacturing process of monovalent vaccines. The warning alerted the public and the company alike, as the Stillwater plant is America's largest manufacturer of flu vaccine.

In July 2006 sanofi reported to the FDA that it had identified the source of the contamination and was still on track to product 50 million doses for the 2006-2007 flu season. Sanofi's vaccination business for the 2007-2008 flu season looks like it will be just as spry, as health officials are already pushing flu shots in the fall of 2007 in an attempt to redress past low immunization rates.

Not just for the birds

The federal government also tapped the company to produce a vaccine for a potential bird flu epidemic. Sanofi pasteur, the firm's vaccine subsidiary, received a $100 million contract in September 2005 to deliver a vaccine by the end of the year. The partnership with the American government began in 2004, when the U.S. paid sanofi-aventis $41 million to maintain a year-round supply of egg-laying hens and promised millions of dollars in investment to enhance the company's production capacity locally.

The two parties expanded the contract in February 2006, when sanofi shipped an additional $50 million worth of vaccine for stockpiling purposes. The FDA chose sanofi as the supplier for the first avian flu vaccine licensed stateside in April 2007, approving its H5N1 vaccine in April 2007.

A new boss

Sanofi-aventis is still adjusting to its new CEO, and also adjusting to a CEO who is not the chairman of its board. In January 2007, longtime Chairman and CEO Jean-François Dehecq—who had steered the company to enormous size through its various mergers—

stepped down as CEO, keeping the chairman's duties. His replacement was longtime right-hand man Gérard Le Fur. Company insiders said the transition was smooth, even though the firm has never before had a split chairman and CEO; Dehecq and Le Fur didn't even change offices.

Other sanofi executives have had to change offices, though, as Le Fur has put his stamp on the company and departed from the methods his predecessor maintained for over 30 years. In terms of decision-making, he shook up the close-knit four advisors of Dehecq, in favor of a "team" of 20. You can even see this team all laid out on the sanofi corporate web site, at en.sanofi-aventis.com/group/presentation/p_group_presentation_key execs.asp.

Looking forward

But life in the pressure cooker of sanofi-aventis is never totally smooth. In his first few months on the job, Le Fur had to deal with an FDA Advisory Committee suggesting that rimonabant, sanofi's new anti-smoking and anti-obesity drug, contains risks of major depression. The medication was designed to block the brain's cannabinoid receptors, which make one very hungry when activated, which usually occurs in smokers of cannabis (marijuana). Sanofi-aventis withdrew rimonabant's application in the U.S. and Le Fur announced that the company would resubmit the rimonabant file to the FDA at a future date.

Sanofi-aventis should continue to be one of the major forces in the pharmaceutical industry, especially if its oft-rumored acquisition of Plavix-partner Bristol-Myers Squibb ever happens. Such rumors have been floated for close to a year, though, with a merger never coming. And other rumors persist about sanofi joining with other pharmaceutical giants—Pfizer, perhaps?

In terms of the pipeline, sanofi revealed in September 2007 that it could have 31 candidates by the end of 2010, with 48 current projects currently in advanced preclinical testing (phases IIb and III). Investors didn't like what they saw, though, and company shares fell after the announcement. Whether sanofi's new drugs deliver or whether the firm merges its operations altogether, remains to be seen.

Visit Vault at **www.vault.com** for insider company profiles, expert advice, career message boards, expert resume reviews, the Vault Job Board and more.

VAULT CAREER LIBRARY   329

GETTING HIRED

Getting in

A searchable database of available positions worldwide can be found online at the sanofi-aventis corporate web site (www.sanofi-aventis-job.com, in French); interested U.S.-based applicants search site at careers.sanofi-aventis.us. . Job categories include pharmaceutical and medical affairs, research, scientific support, chemical and pharmaceutical development, logistics and distribution, production, administration, auditing, communications, finance, health/safety and environment, human resources, information systems, integrated health care markets, legal, medical marketing/sales, purchasing, quality, strategy and technical support.

Schering-Plough Corporation

2000 Galloping Hill Road
Kenilworth, NJ 07033
Phone: (908) 298-4000
Fax: (908) 298-7653
www.schering-plough.com

LOCATIONS

Kenilworth, NJ (HQ)
Atlanta, GA • Baton Rouge, LA •
Berkeley Heights, NJ • Branchburg,
NJ • Cambridge, MA • Chamblee,
GA • Chatsworth, GA • Cleveland,
TN • Cranford, NJ • Elkhorn, NE •
Lafayette, NJ • Madison, NJ •
Memphis, TN • Miami Lakes, FL •
Millsboro, DE • Omaha, NE • Palo
Alto, CA • Reno, NV • Rockville,
MD • Rogers, AR • San Diego, CA •
Sparks, NV • Springfield, NJ • St.
Louis, MO • Summit, NJ •
Suwanee, GA • Terre Haute, IN •
Union, NJ • Washington, DC
Williamsburg, KS

International locations in more than
125 countries.

THE STATS

Employer Type: Public Company
Stock Symbol: SGP
Stock Exchange: NYSE
Chairman & CEO: Fred Hassan
2006 Employees: 33,500
2006 Revenue ($mil.): $10,594
2006 Net Income ($mil.): $1,483

DEPARTMENTS

Consumer Healthcare
Global Animal Health
Global Functions
Global Pharmaceutical Business
Global Quality Operations
Global Supply Chain
Research & Development

KEY COMPETITORS

GlaxoSmith Kline
Johnson & Johnson
sanofi-aventis

EMPLOYMENT CONTACT

www.schering-plough.com/schering_
plough/careers

Visit Vault at **www.vault.com** for insider company profiles, expert advice,
career message boards, expert resume reviews, the Vault Job Board and more.

VAULT CAREER LIBRARY   331

THE SCOOP

Schering-Plough is one of the largest pharmaceutical manufacturers in the world, with major branded drugs such as Claritin (now off-patent and sold over-the-counter) and its current blockbuster, anti-cholesterol drug Vytorin. The company has long been known for its efforts in tackling allergies, boasting old favorites such as Clarinex and Nasonex, but it has made diversification a priority. By now, the firm is discovering, developing and manufacturing drugs for diseases such as hepatitis, cancer and more.

Pretty please ... with a Schering on top

Schering-Plough Corporation traces its roots back to mid-19th-century Berlin. It was there, in 1864, that chemist Ernst Schering began selling his wares to the city's pharmacists. He took the company public in 1871 as Chemische Fabrik auf Actien (Chemical Works with Stocks) and the company debuteded its first specialty drug, a gout medication, in 1890. By the 1920s, the company dealt extensively in all kinds of chemicals.

The firm renamed itself Schering AG following a 1937 merger with mining and chemical outfit Oberkoks, and the company grew to encompass chemicals for agricultural, industrial and laboratory purposes, as well as electroplating and the study of hormones. By the beginning of World War II, Schering had 30 foreign subsidiaries around the world—all of them were to disappear during wartime (Schering had dissolved an earlier American subsidiary, first founded 1876, during World War I).

In 1952, a group of investors headed by Merrill Lynch purchased the New York-based Schering Corporation, which the German parent company had first established in 1928 and the U.S. government had seized in 1942. The American-owned Schering Corp. quickly established itself as a leader in the American drug industry.

Meanwhile, Schering AG somehow muddle through and became the only surviving German multinational corporation to keep its headquarters in Berlin after the war. But from this point, the two companies led distinctly separate existences, as Schering Corp. quickly grew too large for its former owner to purchase. Just to clarify, the Bayer-Schering AG merger of 2006 had nothing to do with Schering-Plough.

Enter the Plough

Schering merged with Plough, Inc. in 1971 and took on its current name. Plough was an aged firm itself, beginning in 1908 when a 16-year-old entrepreneur named Abe Plough borrowed $125 to start a business in Memphis, Tennessee. He was a savvy young businessman, and grew the company both through innovations and acquisitions—purchasing the Maybelline and Coppertone brands, for example. He became chairman of Schering-Plough after the merger.

The enlarged Schering-Plough's sales increased fourfold within 10 years. The company became known for its pharmaceutical breakthroughs in the 1980s and 1990s (while engaging Schering AG in a copyright battle over the Schering name in the mid-1980s). In 1996, Richard Jay Kogan took over as president and CEO, and the firm's value skyrocketed—some analysts calculated its market value as increasing fivefold.

Schering-Plough turns over a new leaf

By 2001, however, Kogan's methods were provoking controversy. The FDA was warning Schering-Plough that its inspections had turned up serious problems in quality control at S-P's manufacturing plants, and Schering-Plough fell under the scrutiny of other authorities. The SEC opened an inquiry into its financial practices and the U.S. government started an investigation over alleged Medicaid fraud.

The next year, matters came to a head at Schering-Plough. First, the patent on its blockbuster drug Claritin expired, with no apparent replacement. But more importantly, the FDA and Schering-Plough signed a consent decree over the firm's drug manufacturing practices, with S-P agreeing to an FDA record $500 million fine. The decree wasn't just about the money—the FDA shut down Schering-Plough's Puerto Rican manufacturing plant (which produced roughly 90 percent of the firm's drugs) and suspended manufacturing on 73 products, while forcing S-P to overhaul its process for 125 others. Finally, the decree set a five-year timetable, during which the FDA monitored Schering-Plough's adherence to its standards and recommendations.

New CEO Fred Hassan arrived in 2003 and established an "Action Agenda"—a five-step plan to address the company's situation. Schering-Plough subsequently moved to stabilize and grow its primary business franchises, reinvest savings into productive areas, strengthen its operating systems, expand its product line and research portfolio. The company's revenue grew to $9.5 billion in 2005 and $10.6 billion in 2006.

Visit Vault at **www.vault.com** for insider company profiles, expert advice, career message boards, expert resume reviews, the Vault Job Board and more.

VAULT CAREER LIBRARY   333

In the medicine cabinet

Besides Claritin—now sold as an over-the-counter drug—Schering-Plough makes PEG-Intron and Rebetol, two of the leading Hepatitis C drugs on the market; Lotrimin, a leading antifungal; Afrin nasal decongestant and Nasonex nasal inhaled corticosteroid, for allergies; Temodar, a cancer drug; and a host of less well-known products. With Clarinex/Aerius, a patented second-generation form of Claritin (it works on indoor allergens as well as outdoor ones!), the company may have found a new, albeit smaller, cash cow. Clarinex had $722 million in sales in 2006, a 12 percent increase from 2005.

In other areas, Schering-Plough continues to earn profits from its numerous animal-related products, including growth hormone for cows and vaccines for chickens. The company also leads the U.S. sun care market, as sales for its Coppertone sunscreen line heat up every summer. The company leads with its feet, too—its foot care franchise, anchored by the Dr. Scholl's brand, surpasses all others in the market for North American podiatry products.

The doctor is in

Before taking over at Schering-Plough, new CEO Hassan had helmed fellow industry giant Pharmacia & Upjohn (now part of Pfizer). Before that, he was in charge of pharmaceuticals as an executive vice president at Wyeth, and before that he spent 17 years in top management positions at Sandoz Pharmaceuticals (now part of Novartis).

Hassan is known for weathering the type of storms Schering-Plough was facing—he turned around Pharmacia well enough to sell it Pfizer for $56 billion—industry insiders have been known to refer to his companies having "the Fred Factor." But in more literal and less mystical terms, the man knows his industry, and is acquainted with lots of its top brass.

In his first six months as CEO, Hassan put his rolodex to good use as he replaced almost every top Schering-Plough executive with a hand-picked successor. That was a key component in his five-step plan to unify what had become a fragmented (and politically troubled) company. By centralizing decision-making, merging supply lines and pushing an across-the-board cost-reduction plan, Hassan and his colleagues hoped to quickly stop the hemorrhaging of company funds and enter what they called the "turnaround" phase.

Then, Hassan and Schering-Plough convinced 900 employees to sign up for voluntary early retirement at the start of 2004. Later in the year, the company laid off 200 workers and temporarily froze hiring to cut payroll costs. Meanwhile,

Schering-Plough's factories were operating below full capacity due to the effects of the consent decree regulations, and a generic form of leading hepatitis drug Rebetol hit the market in April 2004, significantly cutting into company profits.

With a little help from his friends

Hassan turned to his list of contacts again, seeking to form "partnerships" with other pharmaceutical manufacturers, distributors and marketers—a strategy aimed at quickly increasing Schering-Plough's presence in the market without forcing the company to lay out major amounts of cash.

More than anything else, Schering-Plough's joint venture with Merck turned around its fortunes. Shortly after Hassan took over at S-P, the two firms agreed to work on an anti-cholesterol treatment Vytorin, combining Schering's Zetia and Merck's Zocor products.

The two firms won federal approval for Vytorin in July 2004, granting both companies an opportunity to compete with market leader Lipitor, a Pfizer product. That October, Schering-Plough posted its first profit in more than a year; a few years later, Schering's share of 2006 revenue from Vytorin and Zetia totaled $2 billion.

The arrangement worked well, with Bloomberg calling it "the fastest-growing brand-name cholesterol reducer [ever]." Soon, the drug giants decided to collaborate again, and in early 2007 Schering-Plough and Merck announced that once Lipitor goes off-patent in 2010, they plan to combine it with Zetia and produce a cholesterol-reducer even more effective than Vytorin.

What to do with all this money? Study!

Once Schering-Plough returned to profitability, the company increased its R&D investment by 17 percent in 2006—committing $2.2 billion. Areas of research include inflammatory diseases, oncology, infectious diseases, cardiovascular diseases, central nervous system disorders, cardiovascular and metabolic disease, and respiratory diseases

All of this R&D funding isn't a turn away from Hassan's strategy of partnering with other pharmaceutical firms, though. In fact, Schering-Plough's R&D has been an integral factor in a number of collaborative deals with other companies. In July 2005, for instance, Schering-Plough paid $35.5 million upfront (plus royalty fees of $170 million over 2006 and 2007) to the European firm Millennium Pharmaceuticals. In return, Schering received exclusive U.S. rights to develop and market Millennium's cardiovascular drug Integrilin; the product sold $329 million worldwide in 2006.

More recently, the firm exercised rights to co-develop and commercialize Remicade, an experimental arthritis treatment developed by Centocor. Designed for serious inflammation, Remicade is given through infusion. In October 2006, the FDA approved Remicade for the treatment of ulcerative colitis. Worldwide sales of Remicade were more than $1.2 billion in 2006, a 32 percent increase from 2005.

The ghost of Schering past

Schering-Plough continues to feel the effects of its past record of corporate mismanagement. In August 2006 the U.S. government's long-running investigation of the company's past marketing and pricing practices ended in a court of law, with a jury finding Schering-Plough both guilty and civilly liable for fraud.

The Department of Justice inquiry had looked at illegal sales and marketing of Schering-Plough's brain cancer drug Temodar and the medicine Intron A, used to treat bladder cancer and hepatitis A. It also covered fraud allegations connected to Medicaid pricing for the company's Claritin RediTabs allergy medicine and the drug K-Dur, used to treat stomach conditions. The jury ordered the company to pay $435 million in combined criminal fines ($180 million) and civil damages ($255 million). These payments would not affect earnings, as the company had apportioned financial reserves for the litigation.

Getting better

In early 2007, CEO Hassan said the "turnaround" phase had been completed. He added that the company was now embarking on the next phase of his five-step plan, "Build the Base," during which Schering-Plough will build on the company's strengths while extending its reach.

He wasn't kidding, either, as within a few months Schering-Plough announced a whopper of an acquisition. In March 2007, Schering announced the purchase of Organon BioSciences group from Akzo Nobel NV for $14.4 billion. Just before the purchase, Organon had actually been planning to go public on Amsterdam's stock exchange, as the division constitutes a large pharmaceutical company by itself.

Organon's addition will not only increase the number of women's health products in Schering-Plough's roster, but will provide an additional pipeline for new drugs, including vaccines. Organon's ongoing research includes the promising schizophrenia drug Asenapine, Esmirtazapine for insomnia, and oral contraceptive Nomac/E2. Akzo Nobel's animal-health concern, Intervet, will also be part of the package.

What's next?

All eyes will be on the Organon acquisition in coming months, as the merger has yet to pass the European Commission's all-important antitrust review. It was first scheduled for the end of September 2007, but the EC has delayed the deadline for a four-week study of the companies' "commitments," which usually translates to assets they will need to sell before such a large merger can proceed.

Analysts are eager for Schering to integrate its new purchase, as they still worry about the firm's reliance on a single blockbuster product—Vytorin seems to have replaced Claritin as Schering's blockbuster du jour. But even if the Organon deal doesn't go through, Schering's commitment to R&D has resulted in a number of new drugs set to come out of the pipeline.

The FDA has designated four Schering projects in phase II as "fast track," including a protease inhibitor compound for hepatitis C, viciviroc for HIV, a novel thrombin receptor antagonist for acute coronary syndrome and secondary prevention; and a new potential treatment for patients with Parkinson's disease.

And the company's facilities finally look to be recovering from a long period under the shackles of the FDA's consent decree, as plans have been made to expand research operations in Cambridge, Mass., and open a new science center in New Jersey.

Schering is caring

The Schering-Plough Foundation, established in 1955, makes grants in health, community initiatives and education. The company also has patient assistance and support programs. These programs help secure drug reimbursement and provide lifesaving drugs at no cost to low-income patients.

GETTING HIRED

Ploughing through HR

Schering-Plough posts job openings on its online job database, found at www.schering-plough.com/schering_plough/careers. The site also provides a search agent feature that automatically e-mails applicants when new positions open that meet their search criteria. Applicants can also submit a resume online for future job opportunities that may become available.

Visit Vault at **www.vault.com** for insider company profiles, expert advice,
career message boards, expert resume reviews, the Vault Job Board and more.

VAULT CAREER LIBRARY   337

Visit www.schering-plough.com/careers to see a listing of open positions. Job categories include compliance, corporate communications, engineering, finance, human resources, information technology, law, manufacturing, marketing, materials management, quality assurance/control, research and development, sales/customer solutions and secretarial/administrative.

If you want to work as a researcher for Schering-Plough, you'll need a PhD in a scientific field from a top university. (A quick survey of current Schering-Plough executives turns up PhDs from Colorado State University, Harvard University and the University of Cape Town, South Africa.) The company recruits heavily on such campuses, at least in the U.S. As a global company, Schering-Plough also needs people in the fields of law, public relations, manufacturing and quality control, materials science and engineering, information technology and finance; but candidates need to show consistent past performance in their fields.

Ploughing money into benefits

Schering-Plough offers the standard array of corporate benefits, including medical and dental insurance, a 401(k) plan, a profit-sharing plan and disability and life insurance. Not only that, but employees are 100 percent covered for drugs made by the company. (No co-pays!) Benefits are also extended to spouses and life partners. In addition, some Schering-Plough employees are eligible for relocation expenses and, depending on location, may have access to on-site health care facilities.

In September 2005, *Working Mother* magazine named Schering-Plough to its list of Top 10 Best Companies in the nation for working mothers, marking the ninth time Schering-Plough has received applause from the magazine, which rates firms on flexibility, opportunities for advancement, compensation, family leave, child care and work/life culture. In 2006 and 2007, the company didn't make it into *Working Mother*'s top 10, but the magazine recognized Schering-Plough as one of the 100 Best Companies in the country for working mothers in both years.

Shire PLC

World Headquarters:
Hampshire International Business Park
Chineham, Basingstoke
Hampshire RG24 8EP
United Kingdom
Phone: +44-1256-894-000
Fax: +44-1256-894-708

US Headquarters:
725 Chesterbrook Boulevard
Wayne, PA 19087
Phone: (484) 595-8800
Fax: (484) 595-8200
www.shire.com

LOCATIONS

Basingstoke, United Kingdom (HQ)
Wayne, PA (US HQ)
Cambridge, MA
Florence, KY
Owing Mills, MD

Additional locations in Canada,
France, Germany, Ireland, Italy,
Singapore and Spain.

THE STATS

Employer Type: Public Company
Stock Symbol: SHP; SHPGY
Stock Exchange: LSE; Nasdaq
Chairman: James Cavanaugh
CEO: Matthew Emmens
2006 Employees: 2,868
2006 Revenue ($mil.): $1,797
2006 Net Income ($mil.): $278

DEPARTMENTS

Administrative
Biometrics
Biosciences
Business Development
Clinical/Medical Affairs
Commercial Operations
Corporate Accounts & Managed Care
Corporate Communications
Engineering
Facilities
Finance
Human Resources
Information Technology
Legal/Intellectual Property
Investor Relations
Manufacturing
Pharmaceutical Technology
Pharmacovigilance & Drug Safety
Planning & Materials Management
Program Management
Quality Supply Chain
Regulatory/Regulatory Affairs
Research & Development
Sales & Marketing

KEY COMPETITORS

Celgene Corporation
Eli Lilly and Company
Novartis AG

EMPLOYMENT CONTACT

careers.shire.com

THE SCOOP

Not such a little Shire

Shire has swelled from a tiny business into one of the world's fastest growing specialty pharmaceutical companies. Over a 12-year period between 1994 and 2006, Shire grew through acquisition, merging with or acquiring seven other companies to become the third-largest pharmaceutical company in the United Kingdom.

The company focuses its business on a few key areas: attention deficit and hyperactivity disorder, human genetic therapies, and gastrointestinal and renal diseases. Shire's most popular pharmaceuticals include ADHD drug Adderall XR—which boasted nearly $731 million in sales in 2005—and ulcerative colitis medicine Pentasa.

Humble beginnings

In 1986, four entrepreneurs—Dennis Stephens, Harry Stratford, Peter Moriarty and Geoff Hall—founded and funded Shire Pharmaceuticals. (It wasn't originally called Shire, though; its initial appellation was AimCane.) The company started in a small office above a shop in Hampshire, a county on the south coast of the United Kingdom. Its founders soon changed its name to Shire, after the building that housed the company during its early days.

Shire initially launched and sold calcium products designed to treat osteoporosis. After 1988, it expanded its product line by adding hormone replacement therapy (HRT) and treatments for Alzheimer's disease. Around 1992, the company set foot on the mergers and acquisitions path, gaining the rights to galantamine, a drug used to treat the symptoms of Alzheimer's. It also entered into a partnership with Janssen to develop this product into what's now known as Reminyl, Shire's lucrative Alzheimer's drug.

Admire the acquiring Shire

In 1995, Shire made its first acquisition, purchasing Imperial Pharmaceutical Services, another business in Hampshire. Imperial brought with it a range of product licenses and capital, which allowed Shire to expand and make a series of additional acquisitions.

Over a six-year period, the company made six acquisitions. Shire purchased two U.S. companies—Pharmavene and Richwood—in 1997, in the process gaining the rights to Richwood's ADHD product Adderall XR. The company expanded its global presence further when it scooped up Fuiz and Roberts in 1999 and merged with Canadian company Biochem Pharma in 2001. Shire acquired Transkaryotic Therapies, a company focused on curing diseases through gene therapy, in July 2005.

ADHD deal

Most recently, in April 2007, Shire bought New River Pharmaceuticals for $2.6 billion. Through the purchase, Shire gained a new ADHD drug, Vyvanse, which it hopes will be the next generation product to succeed Adderall. This is a matter of import, as Adderall is the company's best-selling drug and will soon lose patent protection. The opportunists are already circling: Shire settled patent litigation over Adderall with generic manufacturer Barr Pharmaceuticals in 2006. Under the terms of the settlement, Barr will be able to market a generic version of the drug as soon as April 2009.

Until 2007, Shire had yet to receive the green light from the U.S. Drug Enforcement Administration and Food and Drug Administration to market Vyvanse in America. Historically, the DEA has classified all ADHD stimulant medications, such as Vyvanse, as schedule II controlled substances. This classification is exactly what the FDA recommended for Vyvanse, and the DEA followed its recommendation in May 2007, granting it schedule II status and clearing the way for its launch in the United States.

Shire shares

Like many pharmaceutical companies, Shire supports the communities in which its offices and manufacturing facilities are located. Shire makes cash and in-kind contributions to local, national and international organizations. In addition, the firm gives all employees one paid day off per year to volunteer with a not-for-profit organization.

In the United States, the company has a patient assistance program, through which Shire gives free products to patients who lack adequate health insurance coverage to pay for treatments.

Visit Vault at **www.vault.com** for insider company profiles, expert advice,
career message boards, expert resume reviews, the Vault Job Board and more.

VAULT CAREER LIBRARY   **341**

In the pipeline

Since January 2004, the FDA has approved eight of Shire's products. In 2006 the agency approved Daytrana, a patch for ADHD, and Elaprase, a drug for Hunter's disease. In early 2007, in addition to ADHD drug Vyvanse, the FDA approved Lialda, an oral treatment for patients with ulcerative colitis. Shire has two other products, SPD 503, a non-stimulant ADHD drug, and SPD 465, for ulcerative colitis, in registration in the United States.

Shire is focused on developing new drugs in the company's core areas of human genetic therapies, attention deficit and hyperactivity disorder, and gastrointestinal and renal diseases. The firm has a total of 14 projects in full development. Of these projects, four are in phase II or beyond.

In fact, Shire is so focused on these core areas that it's selling off its drugs outside of them. In October 2007 the firm raised $213 million in the sale of eight products to Almirall, including the dermatology products Solaraze and Vaniqa. This doesn't signal that the company is becoming smaller, though. The same month as it sold off these medications, it sent out requests to contractors in the Lexington, Mass. area for cost estimates concerning a new manufacturing facility, estimated at $390 million and 370,000 square feet. The firm is planning to build on Raytheon Co.'s old campus. Shire hasn't settled on tax incentives with the town or the commonwealth, but it looks certain to become yet another biotech firm leaving the cluttered biotech climes of Cambridge for the suburbs of eastern Massachusetts.

GETTING HIRED

Shire hires

The company is looking for talented, team-oriented individuals. Shire's career web site divides job openings into U.S. and non-U.S. opportunities. Applicants can search open positions and save a profile at careers.shire.com.

In the United States, departments include administrative, biometrics, biosciences, business development, clinical/medical affairs, commercial operations, corporate accounts and managed care, corporate communications, engineering, facilities, finance, human resources, information technology, legal/intellectual property, investor relations, manufacturing, pharmaceutical technology, pharmacovigilance and drug safety, planning and materials management, program management, quality supply chain, regulatory/regulatory affairs, research and development and sales and marketing.

Shire's benefits include health coverage (medical, dental and vision), life and accidental death and dismemberment insurance, disability insurance, business travel accident insurance, flexible spending account arrangements, a health and fitness subsidy, adoption assistance, educational assistance, flexible work hours and a business casual dress code. The company also offers competitive compensation programs. In the United States, these include performance-based incentives, a 401(k) with company match, a share purchase plan and a stock-option program.

Visit Vault at **www.vault.com** for insider company profiles, expert advice, career message boards, expert resume reviews, the Vault Job Board and more.

V/\ULT CAREER LIBRARY   **343**

Takeda Pharmaceutical Company Limited

1-1, Doshomachi 4-chome
Chuo-ku, Osaka 540-8645
Japan
Phone: +81-6-6204-2111
Fax: +81-6-6204-2880
www.takeda.com

US Headquarters:
1 Takeda Parkway
Deerfield, IL 60015
Phone: (847) 383-3000

LOCATIONS

Osaka, Japan (HQ)
Deerfield, IL (U.S. HQ)
Lake Forest, IL • New York, NY •
Palo Alto, CA • San Diego, CA •
Aachen • Amsterdam • Bangkok •
Cambridge • Dublin • High
Wycombe, UK • Jakarta •
Kilruddery, Ireland • Lachen,
Switzerland • London • Makati City,
The Phillipines • Puteaux Cedex,
France • Rome • Singapore • Taipei
• Tianjin, China • Vienna

THE STATS

Employer Type: Public Company
Stock Symbol: 4502
Stock Exchanges: Tokyo
Chairman & CEO: Kunio Takeda
President & COO: Yasuchika
 Hasegawa
2006 Employees: 15,069
2006 Revenue ($mil.): $11,100
2006 Net Income ($mil.): $2,849

DEPARTMENTS

Administration & Clerical
Business Development
Ethics & Compliance
Executive
Facilities
Finance & Accounting
Government Affairs
Human Resources
Information Technology
Internship
Legal
Managed Markets
Marketing
Medical Affairs
Operations
Public Relations
Purchasing & Outsourcing
Quality Assurance
R&D
Regulatory;
Sales
Security

KEY COMPETITORS

Astellas
Daiichi Sankyo
Shionogi & Co.

EMPLOYMENT CONTACT

www.tpna.com/jointheteam.asp

THE SCOOP

The nuts and bolts

Takeda, the largest pharmaceutical company in Japan, has been around since 1781. A research-based, global pharmaceutical firm, its medicines are now used around the world. The official company philosophy, called "Takeda-ism," commits to "contributing to society by producing medicine through integrity (fairness, honesty and perseverance) in corporate activities."

Pharmaceuticals, the company's core business, make up about 81.5 percent of its net sales. Takeda's hypertension treatment, Blopress, is the No. 1-selling product of all prescription drugs available in Japan. The firm, which has six operating bases in the U.S., also sells prescription medications in America, including Actos for type 2 diabetes (one of the company's mainstay drugs) and Prevacid for ulcers. In 2005, sales of Actos were nearly $1.8 billion, a 17 percent increase from the previous year.

In addition, Takeda manufactures over-the-counter drugs including vitamins, cold remedies and gastrointestinal treatments, that are sold in Japan and other Asian countries. In April 2006, the company transferred its Takeda Food Products business to House Wellness Foods Corporation.

From traditional medicine to modern times

More than 200 years ago, 32-year-old Chobei Takeda started a business in Osaka, selling traditional Chinese and Japanese medicines. In 1871, his descendent Chobei Takeda IV began importing Western medicines such as the anti-cholera drug phenol and the antimalaria drug quinine.

The company established its own factory in Osaka in 1895, producing branded pharmaceutical products such as quinine hydrochloride. In 1915, the firm established its own research division; 10 years later, it completed the long journey from individually-owned business to a modern corporate organization when it was incorporated as Chobei Takeda & Co., Ltd.

After World War II, vitamins and antibiotics became big sellers. The company converted the bombed-out ruins of a naval arsenal in Hikari into a factory in 1946. The creation of this plant—which primarily manufactured vaccines—was the first private use of publicly owned Japanese land after World War II. Takeda began expanding into overseas markets in 1962 by establishing manufacturing and marketing companies throughout Southeast Asia. The company forged a marketing joint venture in France in 1978.

The rise of TPNA

In May 1998, Takeda Chemical Industries established Takeda Pharmaceuticals North America. The wholly owned U.S. subsidiary, based in Deerfield, Ill., had just three employees in 1998 but has grown rapidly since then. By April 1999, TPNA had 192 employees, which grew to 680 in July of the same year. The firm surpassed the 1,000 employee mark the next year.

The firm expanded across the country in November 2001, opening Takeda Research Investment in Palo Alto, California, for biotechnology ventures as well as R&D. The success of Actos continued to propel the company forward—TPNA expanded its sales force in March and June 2003, adding over 300 new employees. By the end of the year, the firm was employing over 2,000 people in the Unites States.

In October 2006, TPNA opened its brand new headquarters in Deerfield, Illinois, housing some 1,100 employees. The following June 2007, the facility won Gold LEED (Leadership in Energy and Environmental Design) certification, then one of only five buildings in Illinois to receive the distinction.

Playing TAPs for Abbott's lawsuit

Not all of its partnerships have been happy ones. Chicago-based Abbott Laboratories and Takeda have shared a joint venture in TAP Pharmaceutical Partners since 1985. Abbott filed a lawsuit against its partner in 2005, claiming that Takeda was overcharging TAP by some $200 million annually in manufacturing an ingredient for the ulcer drug Prevacid; this would, if true, cut into TAP's revenue by about $100 million per year.

In February 2006, a U.S. district court judge dismissed the case, finding that, pursuant to an Abbott and Takeda agreement back in 1985, any legal action needed to take place in Japan. An appeals court upheld the decision in 2007; Abbott will have to take to the air if it's serious about the case.

This wasn't the first time that a legal dispute has arisen over TAP Pharmaceutical. In October 2001, Takeda and Abbott agreed to pay $875 million to the U.S. government to settle a case involving cancer drug Lupron. Governmental prosecutors contended that TAP gave doctors free samples of the drug, then helped them get hefty government reimbursements from Medicare and Medicaid.

Just two years earlier, Takeda was involved in a similar price-fixing settlement over vitamins, along with seven other vitamin manufacturers. Under the terms of the agreement, reached in 1999, Takeda agreed to pay approximately $100 million to the purchasers of its bulk vitamins (food companies such as Kellogg, Kraft and Tyson). The full settlement, including fines levied to other firms, amounted to $1.1 billion.

Activated by Actos

The main product that drove the growth of Takeda's North American arm was Actos, a drug for those with type 2 diabetes. After gaining FDA approval for Actos in July 1999, the firm co-promoted the product with Eli Lilly and attained over one million prescriptions by May 2000. Within another two years, Actos was leading its sector of TZDs, or drugs that reduce insulin resistance, in terms of both overall and new prescriptions.

But Actos has not been a perfect medication, as it has fallen prey to the same faults as similar diabetes medications—cardiovascular risk. In June 2007, the FDA revised its labeling of Actos, warning of the potential for congestive heart failure among users. Such concerns arrived amid a flurry of controversy over GlaxoSmithKline's Avandia, a type 2 diabetes drug that can increase risk of heart attacks, strokes and other cardiovascular events. Secondary studies of Actos have actually shown that it can lower the risk of heart attacks and stroke but increase that of heart failure. Takeda has released statements that it stands by the safety of its product, backed up by multiple studies.

Research

In 2006, Takeda spent close to $1.5 billion on research and development costs, nearly 20 percent more than its R&D expenditures in 2005. But these figures don't convey the full picture of Takeda's commitment to research—the firm has pursued a number of alliances with biotechnology companies, other pharmaceutical manufacturers, research institutions and universities, both in Japan and overseas.

For example, in July 2006 Takeda acquired an exclusive worldwide right from California-based Galaxy Biotech to develop, manufacture and market Hul2G7, an investigational antibody to treat cancer. Later that year, Takeda and another California company, XOMA, initiated a collaboration to discover and develop therapeutic antibodies; in April 2007, XOMA and Takeda expanded this collaboration.

Contributing to society

Takeda believes in giving something back to society. The Takeda Foundation gives an annual international award to researchers and engineers who are working on leading-edge R&D projects "that will have a substantial benefit for mankind in the future." In the United States, Takeda Pharmaceuticals North America awards five scholarships to students pursuing science degrees at Chicago-area universities. The company also has a patient assistance program to provide the company's products to uninsured or underinsured patients.

GETTING HIRED

Talk to Takeda

Individuals interested in working for Takeda should contact the individual company's personnel department. Takeda Pharmaceuticals North America has a careers web site at www.tpna.com/jointheteam.asp. Job categories include administration and clerical, business development, ethics and compliance, executive, facilities, finance and accounting, government affairs, human resources, information technology, internship, legal, managed markets, marketing, medical affairs, operations, public relations, purchasing and outsourcing, quality assurance, R&D, regulatory, sales and security. In early 2007, the company announced that, in response to its increasing portfolio of products, it is expanding its pharmaceutical sales force in North America.

Benefits at Takeda Pharmaceuticals North America include 401(k) with matching; medical, dental and vision insurance; a prescription drug program; life insurance; health care flexible spending account; short- and long-term disability coverage; business-casual dress code; tuition reimbursement; adoption assistance; home office lactation rooms; and flexible schedule. Vacation benefits start at three weeks. In April 2007, the company announced that it was starting a groupwide leadership training program.

Internships and openings

Takeda Pharmaceuticals North America has a summer internship program that "blends real-world experience with an extensive overview of the pharmaceutical industry." The 12-week internships have competitive pay, and temporary financed housing may be available. Applicants should be enrolled at an accredited U.S. university as first- or second-year PharmD student, a third- or fourth-year student pursuing a Bachelor of Science, a master's and/or PhD student in the sciences, or an MBA with a science background.

Individuals who are interested in working for Takeda San Diego, which is Takeda's global center for structure-based drug discovery, should search posts at www.takedasd.com/career; some of the job openings that office was hoping to fill recently included a computational scientist, research associates and an IP counsel. Those applying to Takeda San Diego should mail resumes to Takeda San Diego, Attn: Human Resources, 10410 Science Center Drive, San Diego, CA 92121, or e-mail them to HR@takedasd.com.

Visit Vault at **www.vault.com** for insider company profiles, expert advice, career message boards, expert resume reviews, the Vault Job Board and more.

VAULT CAREER LIBRARY   349

Teva Pharmaceutical Industries Limited

5 Basel Street
Petach, Tikva 49131
Israel
Phone: +972-3-9267267
Fax: +972-3-9234050
www.tevapharm.com

LOCATIONS

Petach Tikva, Israel (HQ)
Fort Dodge, IA
Guayama, PR
Hackensack, NJ
Irvine, CA
Kansas City, MO
Miami, FL
Mexico, MO
North Wales, PA
Sellersville, PA

International locations in about 50 other countries.

THE STATS

Employer Type: Public Company
Stock Symbol: TEVA
Stock Exchange: Nasdaq
Chairman: Eli Hurvitz
President & CEO: Shlomo Yanai
2006 Employees: 26,000
2006 Revenue ($mil.): $8,408
2006 Net Income ($mil.): $1,867

DEPARTMENTS

Accounting/Finance
Administrative/Clerical
Business Development
Customer Service/Support
Engineering
Human Resources
Information Technology
Legal
Manufacturing/Warehouse
Marketing
Operations
Public Relations
Purchasing
Quality
Regulatory Affairs
Research & Development
Retail
Sales
Scientific
Supply Chain
Transportation

KEY COMPETITORS

Alpharma
Barr Pharmaceuticals
Sandoz International GmbH

EMPLOYMENT CONTACT

www.tevausa.com/default.aspx?page
id = 42

THE SCOOP

When you hear "Teva," you probably think of sandals. In this case, however, Teva is a global pharmaceutical company that focuses on generic and branded pharmaceuticals, active pharmaceutical ingredients and biogenerics. This Israel-headquartered firm is one of the 20-largest pharmaceutical companies in the world and one of the largest generic drug manufacturers. Teva develops, produces and markets all of its own products, while operating in more than 50 countries and employing some 26,000 people.

In 2006, Teva's revenue totaled about $8.4 billion, an increase of more than 60 percent over 2005. The company attributes this explosion in sales to major launches of several generic products in the United States as well as the 2006 acquisition of Ivax Corporation. The majority of Teva's sales are in Europe and North America.

In September 2007, *BusinessWeek* evaluated Teva as the largest pharmaceutical company in the U.S. "on a total prescription basis," as its drugs accounted for 11.4 percent of all branded and generic drug prescriptions. The publication also credited Teva with the largest generic drug pipeline in the U.S., with an even bigger market share—18.4 percent of all generic prescriptions in 2006. Although more limited, its offerings in branded drugs grant the company a diversified portfolio and level of legitimacy.

Growing up with the country

Salomon, Levin and Elstein Ltd. is Teva's present-day marketing arm. But it is also the name of the company's earliest historical forebear, a small wholesale drug business that imported medicines through Jerusalem—often on the backs of camels and donkeys—that was established in 1901. At that point, Israel didn't exist and Jerusalem was but one outpost of the far-flung Ottoman Empire; in fact, Jews were a minority in the city.

After World War I ended in 1917, British forces occupied and controlled Jerusalem and the surrounding lands, including Jerusalem and the rest of modern-day Israel. The British partitioned the territory into Jewish and Arab sections and Jews soon started emigrating to the Jewish section. This trend increased during the 1930s as the Nazis rose to power in Germany and central Europe. Germany's pharmaceutical industry was a world leader at that point, and many of these emigrants were scientists. Soon, a number of pharmaceutical firms started up in the 1930s, including

Visit Vault at **www.vault.com** for insider company profiles, expert advice, career message boards, expert resume reviews, the Vault Job Board and more.

VAULT CAREER LIBRARY   **351**

Assia and Zori. During the same period, Salomon, Levin and Elstein established a manufacturing arm, known as Teva (the Hebrew word for "nature").

After Israel was officially established as a state in 1948, the country's pharmaceutical industry grew by leaps and bounds. During World War II, drug firms took on new importance as the only source of treatments for the local market. Teva went public on the Tel Aviv Stock Exchange in 1951. The industry grew even larger in the 1960s and 1970s, a period when Assia and Zori merged together (1964), and then merged with Teva (in 1976) to form Teva Pharmaceutical Industries, Israel's largest drugmaker. The new company grew larger in 1980 with the acquisition of Israel's second-largest drug firm, Ikapharm, and continued to acquire other companies throughout the 1980s and 1990s.

From camels to Copaxone

In the late 1990s, Teva launched one of its first major branded products: the multiple sclerosis treatment Copaxone. It was the first innovative drug developed in Israel that won FDA approval and ranks as one of Teva's current best sellers, with record global sales in 2006 of more than $1.4 billion, an increase of 20 percent over 2005. Still, the drug has been leading its sector in the U.S. since 2005.

Azilect, Teva's once-daily oral treatment for Parkinson's disease and the company's second innovative drug, became available in the U.S. in July 2006. Its first year on the market, Azilect boasted $44 million in sales worldwide. Azilect is unique because it was the first once-daily treatment for Parkinson's disease.

Pains and gains

Like most generic pharmaceutical companies, Teva faces strong competition from big brand-name companies, who have often entered into licensing agreements or strategic alliances with generic pharmaceutical companies to neutralize the competition. Also, some of these companies have sued generic drug companies, including Teva, for manufacturing copycat versions of pharmaceuticals. For instance, Pfizer won a court ruling in early 2007 that blocked Teva from marketing a generic version of top-selling arthritis drug Celebrex until 2015. Teva plans to appeal the ruling.

In early 2006, Teva acquired the Miami-based Ivax Corporation in early 2006. Also a developer and manufacturer of generic and branded pharmaceuticals (as well as veterinary products), Ivax added to the company's core strengths and deepened its pipeline, while further entrenching its American presence. In particular, Ivax offers a number of inhaled respiratory drugs for asthma and pulmonary diseases, which accounted for $374 million in sales over the first half of 2007.

In the pipeline

In 2006, Teva's R&D expenses were $495 million, a 34 percent increase from 2005. Two drugs in the pipeline—Laquinimod, a treatment for relapsing MS, and Stem Ex, a cell therapy product—are in phase III development. The firm had hopes for its lupus drug edratide, but in September 2007 it failed expectations in mid-stage clinical trials.

It's likely that Teva, with its extensive offerings in generic drugs and its handful of successful branded pharmaceuticals, will continue to do well in the future. In early 2007, the firm said that it expects its net sales to surpass $9 billion in 2007 and to exceed $10 billion in 2008. Over this two year period, Teva has indicated it will launch anywhere from 70 to 80 products. Between January and June 2007, it had brought 19 generic products to market.

GETTING HIRED

Joining the Teva team

Applicants can search for open positions at Teva USA's employment opportunities web site (tevausa.com/default.aspx?pageid=42). Job categories include accounting/finance, administrative/clerical, business development, customer service/support, engineering, human resources, information technology, legal, manufacturing/warehouse, marketing, operations, public relations, purchasing, quality, regulatory affairs, research and development, retail, sales, scientific, supply chain and transportation.

Teva Pharmaceuticals offers comprehensive benefits including full medical and dental coverage, which start the first of the month following an employee's date of hire. Benefits also include life insurance, short- and long-term disability, business travel accident coverage, and child and elder care referral. Other programs available to employees include a stock purchase plan, a 401(k) plan with employer contribution, supplemental life insurance, flexible spending accounts and tuition reimbursement.

Teva on campus

The company participates in career fairs at different locations across the United States. In 2007, these included the California Life Science Career Fair in San Diego and the Celebrate Diversity Career Fair in Philadelphia.

In addition, Teva Pharmaceuticals offers summer internships. Although the number of internships and departments vary from year to year, the company looks for "eager and intelligent students to share their skills and talents with the Teva team." Internships may be available for students with majors such as accounting, animal sciences, biology, chemical engineering, chemistry, criminal justice, human resources, information technology, law, marketing, pharmacy and nursing.

At Teva USA, the company encourages employees to participate in community events such as blood drives. The firm sponsors annual activities that include an Easter egg hunt, a company picnic and a Halloween pumpkin-carving contest. In addition, an activities committee plans trips to local sporting events and the theater. Teva employees can also join activity groups such as running and ski clubs.

UCB S.A.

60 Allée de la Recherche
B-1070, Brussels
Belgium
Phone: 32-2-559-9999
Fax: 32-2-559-9900
www.ucb-group.com

LOCATIONS

Brussels, Belgium (HQ)
Los Angeles, CA
New York, NY
Rochester, NY
Smyrna, GA
Wilmington, DE

International locations in over 40
countries worldwide.

THE STATS

Employer Type: Public Company
Stock Symbol: UCB
Stock Exchange: Euronext Brussels
Chairman of the Board: Baron Jacobs
**Chairman of the Executive
Committee & CEO:** Dr. Roch
 Doliveux
2006 Employees: 8,400
2006 Revenue ($mil.): $3,166
2006 Net Income ($mil.): $461

DEPARTMENTS

Business Development
Clinical Development
Engineering
Facilities
Finance
General Management
Health, Safety & Environment
Human Resources
Information Technology
Legal/Patents
Manufacturing
Marketing
Medical Affairs
Quality Assurance
Regulatory Affairs
Research
Sales
Supply Chain

KEY COMPETITORS

Bayer AG
Johnson & Johnson
Pfizer

EMPLOYMENT CONTACT

www.ucb-group.com/careers/

Visit Vault at **www.vault.com** for insider company profiles, expert advice,
career message boards, expert resume reviews, the Vault Job Board and more.

VAULT CAREER LIBRARY   355

THE SCOOP

Nuts and bolts

True to its name, the Union Chimique Belge (UCB) is a Belgium-based firm that has made a living through the years with chemicals and pharmaceuticals. The firm is just now adding a biological focus to its pharmaceutical research, joining the burgeoning field of biopharmaceuticals.

UCB has a global presence, with more than 10,000 employees in more than 40 different countries (composed of over 75 nationalities, to boot). Its mission is to research, develop and commercialize products for severe diseases, including central nervous system disorders, allergy/respiratory diseases, immune and inflammatory disorders, and cancer (e.g., Crohn's and Parkinson's). In 2006, the firm's revenue was $3.1 billion, an 8 percent increase from 2005.

From Brussels it sprouts

The Union Chimique Belge started out as exactly what it described—a union of Belgian chemical companies. They were 13 chemical manufacturing companies, to be exact, brought together into one entity in 1928 by Belgian businessman Emmanuel Janssen. Union's early work initially focused on industrial chemicals, although it had a small pharmaceutical division even then. UCB expanded into the U.S. in the next decade, and started manufacturing films for sterile packaging in the 1940s.

UCB set up a research center in the early 1950s, where it developed new medicines such as Atarax and a compound called piracetam, marketed in the 1970s as Nootropil. The success of the drug, used to treat memory and balance problems, enabled UCB to build a modern pharmaceutical site south of Brussels. Other drugs UCB has developed include the antihistamine Zyrtec and the blockbuster epilepsy treatment Keppra.

From the 1970s to the late 1990s, the firm focused on the core areas of chemicals, films and pharmaceuticals. As the company continued to find success in major pharmaceutical products, it decided to divest itself of non-pharmaceutical activities in the last decade of the 20th century. UCB merged its chemical and films sectors in 2002, then acquired the resins, additives and adhesives activities of Solutia. The company turned around and sold this reconstituted films sector to Innovia Films in September 2004.

During the same period, UCB has acquired other pharmaceutical companies. In May 2004 UCB swooped in for British biotech concern Celltech Group, shelling out €2.2 million for the privilege. In September 2006, UCB announced plans for a much larger deal—the purchase of German pharmaceutical firm Schwarz Pharma for €4.4 billion ($5.6 billion).

A few good deeds

UCB invites patients with severe diseases to talk to the company's employees about the social and physical impacts of their illnesses. The firm also runs an "epilepsy ambassadors" program, where people with epilepsy tell health care professionals about the illness. UCB also funds initiatives such as the Canine Assistance Programme, which trains dogs to look after patients with epilepsy.

The Internet isn't excluded from this vision, either; in March 2007 UCB launched a web site called crohnsandme.com. Exclusively dedicated to Crohn's disease, an inflammatory illness of the digestive track, the site allows people with Crohn's to share their experiences. Over 30,000 people have registered to the web site so far.

Best sellers

One of UCB's best selling drugs is the epilepsy treatment Keppra. In both Europe and the U.S., Keppra is the leading treatment in its field, grossing €761 million (almost $1 billion) in global sales for 2006, a rise of 36 percent from 2005. Allergy medicine Zyrtec continues to have strong sales. In 2006, Zyrtec sales in the U.S. grew by 15 percent to more than $1.5 billion.

Unfortunately, UCB faces patent expirations on both of these products, starting in 2007, when Zyrtec goes off-patent in the United States. Keppra goes off-patent in 2009. As a result, UCB has started to focus on investing in new products. In 2006, the firm spent €615 million (about $772 million) on research and development, a 20 percent increase from 2005.

What's next?

Antiepileptic brivaracetam, the hopeful successor to Keppra, is scheduled to enter phase III trials in 2007. Another drug UCB is banking on is Cimzia, the company's first biologic. This Crohn's disease drug is unique because it uses the smallest possible fragment of an antibody, called nanobodies. Cimzia is also the first Crohn's treatment that is administered by injection through the skin.

In 2006, the company submitted Cimzia for Crohn's for regulatory approval in the U.S. and Europe, but the drug's launch has faced delays thus far. UCB is still in discussions with the FDA, who may require the outcome of a study on Cimzia's effectiveness, which won't be completed until 2008, before it approves the drug. UCB is also looking at other possible uses for the drug. In 2006, Cimzia successfully completed phase II trials for psoriasis and phase III trials for rheumatoid arthritis.

Another of the firm's strategies is to partner with other companies with strengths in complementary fields. For example, in 2006 UCB entered into a new commercial partnership with sanofi-aventis to co-promote Zyertec's successor, Xyzal, in the U.S. (the drug became available for American prescription in October 2007). The company has also teamed up with Amgen to treat osteoporosis through the co-development of antibodies against sclerostin (a protein that UCB discovered and validated).

UCB strengthened its pipeline through the Schwarz Pharma acquisition, gaining three new products in late-stage development. One Schwarz-developed drug immediately ready to launch was Neupro, a patch for Parkinson's disease. UCB trumpeted Neupro's July 2007 launch as the first day when itself and Schwarz Pharma truly began to integrate, a process UCB hopes to complete within two to three years. The launch coincided with yet another good deed from the company: PD-Aware, a public education campaign across the U.S. to "raise the profile of Parkinson's disease" and "highlight the experiences and personal achievements of Parkinson's patients in order to increase understanding of the disease."

Regardless of the speed of this integration, the company now has a far-flung pipeline. It has 11 molecules in development, spanning 13 potential indications that include rheumatoid arthritis, Crohn's disease, osteoporosis and non-small cell lung cancer.

GETTING HIRED

UCB wants to see you!

UCB's employment web site (www.ucb-group.com/careers) allows applicants to search for openings around the world. Job categories include business development, clinical development, engineering, facilities, finance, general management, health, safety and environment; human resources, information technology, legal/patents, manufacturing, marketing, medical affairs, quality assurance, regulatory affairs, research, sales and supply chain. Job seekers can also create an applicant profile and upload a resume.

Vectura Group PLC

One Prospect West
Chippenham, Wiltshire SN14 6FH
United Kingdom
Phone: +44-12-4966-7700
Fax: +44-12-4966-7701
www.vectura.com

LOCATIONS

Wiltshire, UK (HQ)
Cambridge
Ruddington, UK (Innovata)

THE STATS

Employer Type: Public Company
Stock Symbol: VEC
Stock Exchange: London
CEO: Chris P. Blackwell
2007 Employees: 236
2007 Revenue ($mil.): $27.7
2007 Net Income ($mil.): $21.2

KEY COMPETITORS

Ark Therapeutics Group PLC
Oxford Biomedica PLC
Skyepharma PLC

EMPLOYMENT CONTACT

www.vectura.com/companyInfo/
careers.asp

Visit Vault at **www.vault.com** for insider company profiles, expert advice,
career message boards, expert resume reviews, the Vault Job Board and more.

VAULT CAREER LIBRARY   359

THE SCOOP

The Vectura sector

Vectura Group wants to help you breathe easier. Literally. This emerging pharmaceutical company is developing a variety of inhaled drugs for the treatment of lung diseases and other conditions. A number of these products are in clinical development, and some of them have been licensed to major pharmaceutical companies.

Vectura formed in 1997. Two years later, it acquired two centers of expertise—Co-ordinated Drug Development Limited and the Centre for Drug Formation Studies. Both had high pedigrees: a group of six eminent U.K. academic pharmaceutical scientists owned Co-ordinated Drug Development Limited, established in 1983; and The Centre for Drug Formulation Studies had been at the University of Bath since 1974. The acquisition of the two centers gave Vectura a broad base of formulation expertise (focused primarily on drugs for inhalation), an extensive intellectual property estate, an established development services business and a talented team of scientists.

The company acquired the Aspirair inhaler technology and the associated device engineering team from Cambridge Consultants in 2002. Vectura then floated an initial public offering of stock in 2004 and listed its shares on AIM, a section of the London Stock Exchange for small companies. Over recent years, the company has increasingly focused on developing its own pharmaceutical products using its proprietary inhaler device and formulation technologies. In January 2007 Vectura advanced its aim to be a principal player in the development of pulmonary pharmaceutical products when it acquired Innovata, a company that specialized in developing pulmonary products to treat respiratory diseases and other serious illnesses. Also in 2007, Vectura switched from AIM to the Main List of the London Stock Exchange.

In the pipeline

Courtesy of its acquisition of Innovata, Vectura has eight marketed products that are marketed by its pharmaceutical partners. The company also has several products, pulmonary and non-pulmonary, in the pipeline. Respiratory products that will be entering registration trials in 2008 include NVA237 (for chronic obstructive pulmonary disease, a/k/a COPD), QVA149 (also for COPD) and VR315 (for asthma).

Also in the respiratory area, the company has a collaboration with Boehringer Ingelheim. In the neurology area Vectura has VR040 (for Parkinson's disease) that has completed two phase II trials, as well as VR147 in phase I clinical trials for migraine.

The company is looking to license other programs, which fall outside of its respiratory and neurology focus. These include VR004, for erectile dysfunction, and VR776, for premature ejaculation, as well as its inhaled insulin program.

Partnerships with companies (some secret)

Over the past few years, Vectura has established collaborations with several large pharmaceutical companies. In April 2005, Vectura and Arakis, a Japanese-owned, British-based biotech firm, licensed an experimental drug for Chronic Obstructive Pulmonary Disease (COPD) to Novartis AG. Assuming the drug, NVA237, succeeds in late-stage clinical trials and makes it to market, the transaction could bring Vectura, Arakis and Sosei as much as $375 million. In addition, Novartis is developing QVA149, a combination therapy for COPD that includes the active ingredient in NVA237 coupled with a long-acting bronchodilator.

In addition to Novartis, other partners include Baxter, GlaxoSmithKline, Merck Generics (part of Mylan), UCB, Otsuka and others. The company's collaboration with Boehringer Ingelheim concerns development of a dry powder inhaler, which will then deliver a variety of Boehringer Ingelheim's respiratory products. More mysteriously, Vectura has licensed asthma treatment VR315 for Europe to an undisclosed leading international pharmaceutical company and has also signed a cost share/profit share agreement with another undisclosed leading international pharmaceutical company for the U.S. market.

Vectura's future

What's next for the company? CEO Chris Blackwell offered some hints in March 2007. "The next 12 months will see further advances in our product development as we continue to drive the value of our portfolio," said Blackwell. The company believes it will play a key role in the burgeoning respiratory market and is quickly approaching some significant growth catalysts.

GETTING HIRED

Hitch your wagon to Vectura

Applicants should take a look at Vectura's vacancies on the careers section of the firm's web site (www.vectura.com/companyInfo/careers.asp) and submit an application by e-mail. Job openings at Innovata are listed at www.innovata.co.uk/iov/about/careers/vacancies.

The firm frequently has vacancies for pharmaceutical scientists based at Vectura's Chippenham laboratories. The company's web site states that "applicants should have a positive, scientific approach towards challenges, and be able to organize and prioritize work in a flexible way." In addition, the ideal candidate "will be qualified to degree level or equivalent in a chemical, pharmaceutical or biological discipline" and will have experience working in a laboratory environment.

The company also has job openings at Cambridge-based Vectura Delivery Devices. There, the firm is looking for design engineers to help develop innovative drug delivery devices such as dry powder inhalers.

Verenium Corporation

55 Cambridge Parkway
Cambridge, MA 02142
Phone: (617) 674-5300
www.verenium.com

LOCATIONS

Cambridge, MA (HQ)
Alachua, FL
Jennings, LA
San Diego, CA

THE STATS

Employer Type: Public Company
Stock Symbol: VRNM
Stock Exchange: Nasdaq
Chairman: James H. Cavanaugh
President & CEO: Carlos A. Riva
2007 Employees: 240

DEPARTMENTS

Analytical Science • Bioinformatics •
Business Development • Cell
Engineering • Chemical Products •
Collaborations • Commercial Process
Development • Engineering
Technology • Environmental Health &
Safety • Enzyme Technology •
Facilities • Finance & Accounting •
Fungal Support • Gene Expression •
Gene Modification • Human
Resources • Imported • Industrial
Enzymes • Information Technology •
Intellectual Property • Internal
Development • Molecular Diversity •
Operations Management • Pharma •
Pre-Clinical • Protein Therapeutics •
Proteomics • Quality Assurance •
Scale-up & Manufacturing •
Scientific Affairs • Sequencing •
Small Molecule Discovery

KEY COMPETITORS

Aventine Renewable Energy
Genencor International
Mascoma Corp.

EMPLOYMENT CONTACT

www.verenium.com/Pages/Career/Ab
outUsCareersWhyVerenium.html

Visit Vault at **www.vault.com** for insider company profiles, expert advice,
career message boards, expert resume reviews, the Vault Job Board and more.

VAULT CAREER LIBRARY   363

THE SCOOP

Using enzymes to unleash energy

In the future, if cars run on renewable biofuels made from canes, cornstalks and grasses, you might have to thank Verenium Corporation. The Cambridge-headquartered company describes itself as a "leading developer of cellulosic ethanol technology and a pioneer in the development of high-performance specialty enzyme products which, in turn, provide access to even broader commercial biofuel opportunities." In other words, Verenium is trying to develop cutting-edge, commercially viable biofuels.

Verenium came into existence in 2007 with the merger of Diversa Corporation, a leader in industrial enzyme discovery and development, and Celunol Corporation, a pioneer in the creation of cellulosic ethanol. The firm has three business units: biofuels, specialty enzymes, and research and development. Verenium's headquarters are in Cambridge, Massachusetts. The company also has research and operations facilities in Jennings, Louisiana; Gainesville, Florida; and San Diego, California.

The biotech's beginnings

Verenium's predecessor, Diversa Corporation, started out in Delaware under the name Industrial Genome Sciences in December 1992. The company changed its name to Diversa Corporation in August 1997. After that, the firm entered into strategic alliances with a range of companies, including BASF, DMS, DuPont Bio-Based Materials, and Cargill Health and Food Technologies.

But not all of Diversa's partners were corporations. In 1997, for example, Yellowstone National Park signed an agreement with Diversa to share in profits generated by enzymes taken from the park. Some environmental groups contended that the agreement violated rules prohibiting the park's ban on the sale or commercial use of park property and filed a lawsuit, but a judge dismissed the case.

To develop high-performance specialty enzymes, the firm engaged in what is sometimes called "bio-prospecting," tapping into an array of extreme ecosystems, such as rain forests, volcanoes and deep sea hydrothermal vents, to collect small samples from the environment. (The company discovered one of its microbes in frozen cow manure from Siberia.)

Diversa then used proprietary and patented technologies to extract microbial DNA from the samples. After identifying a candidate enzyme, the firm used patented technologies to optimize it. The company customized enzymes for manufacturers in the industrial, and health and nutrition markets. In addition, the firm was applying its enzyme expertise to develop alternative fuels.

Reorganizing before a merger

Diversa announced a strategic reorganization in January 2006, the goal of which was to focus the company's resources on advancing the most promising products and product candidates in three key areas: alternative fuels, specialty industrial processes, and health and nutrition.

Through the course of 2006, the firm discontinued the development of less promising products and programs and reduced the company's workforce by 83 employees. In January 2007, in connection with an announcement of a refocused collaborative agreement with Syngenta, the company announced a new strategy of vertical integration within biofuels.

The following month, Diversa announced that the firm had signed a definitive agreement to merge with Celunol Corporation. Under the terms of the merger, Diversa would acquire the outstanding equity of Celunol and provide Celunol with up to $20 million in debt financing to fund its operations prior to the closing. James Cavanaugh, Diversa's chairman, said the merger would significantly accelerate both companies' strategic plans, creating "a new company capable of technical and commercial leadership in the emerging cellulosic ethanol industry."

Verenium is born

In June 2007, Diversa and Celunol merged, and the company was renamed Verenium. Carlos Riva, who had joined Celunol as its CEO in 2006, took the reins of the new entity. Prior to Celunol, he had directed the global construction and engineering company Amec; and from 1995 to 2003, Riva served as CEO of Boston-based InterGen, a joint venture between engineering and construction company Bechtel and oil and gas group Shell.

Riva addressed the merger in a company press release: "Verenium is now positioned to be a vertically-integrated leader in the rapidly-evolving worldwide biofuels industry through the unique combination of assets, technologies and personnel resulting from this merger. We believe that commercial success in this industry

Visit Vault at **www.vault.com** for insider company profiles, expert advice, career message boards, expert resume reviews, the Vault Job Board and more.

VAULT CAREER LIBRARY   **365**

requires broad R&D capabilities and asset development expertise, which we have now brought together within one, highly focused company, Verenium Corporation."

Notable developments at the new company

Since the merger, Verenium has enjoyed some big developments. In September 2007, the firm was added to Nasdaq's Clean Edge U.S. indexes, which are designed to follow the performance of publicly traded clean-energy companies. The same month, Verenium announced that the company had met a technical milestone in the development of a new food-related product that it's working on with Cargill.

Harnessing the power of ... termites?

In the next few years, the company would like to launch new products that use more efficient enzymes to convert biomass to ethanol, a biofuel alternative to gasoline. The firm is now researching enzymes that will break down biomass such as wood and wheat stalks to make ethanol.

The company's projects include exploring of the guts of wood-boring insects, such as termites and pine beetles, as these insects' innards are highly efficient at converting wood into energy. Verenium's researchers hope to harness these microbes to create ethanol more efficiently. Down the line, the company also hopes to apply genetic engineering more broadly to the process of producing biofuel. For instance, the firm has developed energy cane, a new type of sugarcane. This inedible plant has super-high quantities of cellulose.

By 2009, the company expects to have built the first of several biofuel production factories. Each of these plants is designed to convert biowaste materials into 25 to 30 million gallons of ethanol per year. However, even if Verenium masters the process of making biofuels and has the factories to make renewable fuels, barriers to success remain.

Although ethanol is mixed in small amounts into current gasoline, only a tiny percentage of cars sold in the United States today can use ethanol alone as fuel. Even those who drive "flex-fuel" cars, which can run on both gasoline and ethanol, are limited by the scarcity of stations that pump it.

GETTING HIRED

In Verenium veritas

Prospective hires can search job openings on Verenium's career web site at www.verenium.com/Pages/Career/AboutUsCareersJobs.html. The firm prefers that job seekers submit applications and resumes through its online career center.

One of the more unusual job categories at Verenium is fungal support. If supporting fungi isn't your thing, other categories include analytical science, bioinformatics, business development, engineering technology, environmental health and safety, finance and accounting, information technology and quality assurance.

Very good benefits

Verenium treats employees well. When it comes to health benefits, the firm offers medical, vision and dental coverage, which begins on the first day of hire. In addition to regular vacation and holidays, employees have 64 hours of sick leave; they can roll over 32 hours of unused sick time annually.

After eight years of service, Verenium's employees enjoy four-week sabbaticals with full pay and benefits. Other perks include a 401(k) plan with matching contributions, stock options, tuition reimbursement and more. Employees can join bike and surf clubs or attend company-sponsored events such as baseball games.

Visit Vault at **www.vault.com** for insider company profiles, expert advice, career message boards, expert resume reviews, the Vault Job Board and more.

VAULT CAREER LIBRARY   367

Watson Pharmaceuticals, Inc.

311 Bonnie Circle
Corona, CA 92880
Phone: (951) 493-5300
Fax: (973) 355-8301
www.watsonpharm.com

LOCATIONS

Corona, CA (HQ)
Brewster, NY • Carmel, NY •
Copiague, NY • Danbury, CT •
Davie, FL • Grand Island, NY •
Groveport, OH • Gurnee, IL •
Humacao, PR • Morristown, NJ •
Mt. Prospect, IL • Phoenix, AZ •
Salt Lake City, UT • Weston, FL

Changzhou, China • Coleraine, UK •
Goa, India • Mumbai • Shanghai

THE STATS

Employer Type: Public Company
Stock Symbol: WPI
Stock Exchange: NYSE
Chairman: Allen Chao
President & CEO: Paul Bisaro
2006 Employees: 5,830
2006 Revenue ($mil.): $1,979

DEPARTMENTS

Administrative/Clerical
Andrx/Anda (Product Distribution)
Business Development
Communications
Corporate Development
Distribution
Executive
Finance
Human Resources
Information Systems
International
Laboratory Operations
Laboratory Services
Legal Services
Operations
Quality Assurance
Research & Development
Regulatory Compliance
Sales & Marketing

KEY COMPETITORS

Barr
Johnson & Johnson
Merck
Novartis
Teva

EMPLOYMENT CONTACT

www.watsonpharm.com/career.asp

THE SCOOP

Elementary, my dear Watson

Watson Pharmaceuticals' mission is to create, manufacture and market innovative brand and generic pharmaceuticals in a cost-effective manner. The company sells more than 150 generic pharmaceutical and 25 brand pharmaceutical products. The company sells brand and generic pharmaceutical products primarily to drug wholesalers, retailers and distributors. Watson's customers include hospitals, clinics, government agencies, large chain drug stores and managed health care providers such as HMOS. Watson has three operating segments: generic, brand and distribution.

The company's top-selling branded drugs are the Trelstar franchise, for advanced prostate cancer, and Ferrlecit, for the treatment of iron deficiency anemia. The company also makes Androderm, a patch for men with low testosterone levels, and Oxytrol, the first and only skin patch to treat overactive bladder. In generics, the firm's oral contraceptive lines have strong sales.

From "Hwa's son" to Watson

Two scientists, Allen Chao and David Hsia, envisioned Watson Pharmaceuticals in 1984 in a small store in Libertyville, Illinois. They wanted to create a new type of pharmaceutical company that would combine innovative science with creative business acumen. Chao used his mother's name, Hwa, to form the company name. In an anglicized form, "Hwa's son" became Watson.

Watson received its first product approvals in 1985 and the firm acquired Zetachron, a drug delivery R&D company, in October 1991. Later that fall, Watson broke ground on the company's Corona, Calif., headquarters. The company had a successful IPO in 1993, which put it on Nasdaq. In 1995 Watson merged with New York-based Circa Pharmaceuticals, a developer and manufacturer of proprietary and generic pharmaceuticals. The newly enlarged Watson subsequently developed and received FDA approval for the first generic nicotine gum.

Over the years, Watson has continued to grow. Throughout the 1990s, the company acquired other pharmaceutical businesses including Royce Laboratories, Oclassen Pharmaceuticals, Nicobrand, the Rugby Group and TheraTech. In fall 1997, the company's common stock moved from Nasdaq to the New York Stock Exchange. By December 2000, Watson had $1 billion in revenue. In July 2005, the company

Visit Vault at www.vault.com for insider company profiles, expert advice, career message boards, expert resume reviews, the Vault Job Board and more.

VAULT CAREER LIBRARY   369

opened a new distribution operations facility in Illinois to meet the burgeoning demand for the company's brand and generic pharmaceuticals.

Andrx and other additions

In November 2006, Watson acquired Andrx Corporation for approximately $1.9 billion. The acquisition of Andrx, a leader in formulating difficult-to-replicate products, made Watson the third-largest generic pharmaceutical company in the U.S. Size and scale are becoming important requirements for continued success in the generic drug industry as margins get squeezed. The Andrx merger should help Watson in that regard, but the company may have to grow even larger if it wants to keep up with generic leaders like Barr and Teva.

Buddies abroad

The firm enacted a number of cost-saving measures in 2007, including the closing of its Puerto Rican manufacturing plant and the divesting of an Arizona manufacturing facility. At the same time, the company has been adding some facilities abroad to supply the U.S. market; it recently acquired a manufacturing facility in Goa, India, which will now partner in overseas production with its Chinese facility. In April 2007 the firm continued loading up, adding the Mumbai-based Sekhsaria Chemicals Ltd.

Future pharmaceuticals

Watson has three branded urology products in late-stage development. These include silodosin, a drug for benign prostatic hyperplasia, a noncancerous enlarged prostate that causes urinary problems. In early 2007, the company announced that it's had positive results in clinical studies of silodosin, and the firm expects to file a new drug application with the FDA in 2008.

The company's generic drug pipeline has also expanded significantly. In 2006, Watson submitted 27 new Abbreviated New Drug Applications (ANDAs), five more than in 2005. In early 2007, thanks to Watson's internal R&D efforts as well the acquisition of Andrx's pipeline, the company had more than 70 ANDAs on file with the FDA. And, in April 2007, the FDA gave the go-ahead to several generic pharmaceutical companies including Watson to market generic Ambien.

New fearless leader

Company co-founder—and Chairman, President and CEO—Allen Chao announced his retirement from active operations in August 2007 (although he will remain chairman of the company's board). He had been planning to step down for a few years, and credited his confidence in the company's direction as the main reasoning for his announcement's timing. He name-checked the company's expansion into China and India, as well as its acquisition of Andrx, as signs of the company's forward growth. His replacement is Paul Bisaro, a 15-year veteran (and former president) of Barr Pharmaceuticals, another leading generic drug firm.

GETTING HIRED

What's up at Watson

Applicants can search and apply for positions through the career section of Watson's web site (www.watsonpharm.com/career.asp). Job categories include administrative/clerical, Andrx/Anda, business development, communications, corporate development, distribution, executive, finance, human resources, information systems, international, laboratory operations, laboratory services, legal services, operations, quality assurance, research and development, regulatory compliance, and sales and marketing. Watson's web site also includes an employee opinions section, where current employees share their views on the company.

Watson describes itself as "a friendly place where creative approaches and new solutions are nurtured and encouraged." The company offers a slew of no-cost and optional benefits. These perks include medical, dental, vision, short- and long-term disability, long-term care insurance, domestic partner coverage, pet insurance, pre-paid legal, a 401(k) plan and tuition reimbursement.

The firm offers internships for college students. To apply for these internships, visit the company' career web site. In addition, Watson provides new college graduates with an orientation period. The goal of the orientation is to give recent grads a solid understanding of the company and how it works.

Visit Vault at **www.vault.com** for insider company profiles, expert advice, career message boards, expert resume reviews, the Vault Job Board and more.

VAULT CAREER LIBRARY   **371**

Wyeth

5 Giralda Farms
Madison, NJ 07940
Phone: (973) 660-5000
Fax: (973) 660-7026
www.wyeth.com

LOCATIONS

Madison, NJ (HQ)
Andover, MA • Bentonville, AR •
Cambridge, MA • Chazy, NY •
Collegeville, PA • Frazer, PA •
Georgia, VT • Guaynabo •
Indianapolis, IN • Monmouth
Junction, NJ • Oak Brook, IL •
Overland Park, KS • Pearl River, NY
• Princeton, NJ • Rancho Santa
Margarita, CA • Richmond, VA •
Rouses Point, NY • Sanford
(Raleigh/Durham), NC • Sparks, NV
• West Henrietta, NY

Additional locations throughout the
world.

THE STATS

Employer Type: Public Company
Stock Symbol: WYE
Stock Exchange: NYSE
Chairman & CEO: Robert A. Essner
2006 Employees: 52,000
2006 Revenue ($mil.): $20,351
2006 Net Income ($mil.): $4,197

DEPARTMENTS

Accounting & Finance
Administrative
Archives
Clinical Project Management
Clinical Science
Communications/PR
Customer Service
Engineering
Human Resources
Information Technology
Legal
Quality Assurance
Research & Development
Sales & Marketing
Laboratory Technicians
Training & Instructional
Veterinary

KEY COMPETITORS

Eli Lilly
Novartis
Pfizer

EMPLOYMENT CONTACT

www.wyeth.com/careers

THE SCOOP

A clear focus

Madison, New Jersey-based Wyeth (formerly known as American Home Products) is one of the largest pharmaceutical companies in the world. It produces a range of products, from the estrogen therapy medication Premarin—one of the most widely prescribed drugs in America—to top-selling, over-the-counter (OTC) medications such as Advil and Preparation H. The company also makes veterinary medicine. In April 2007, the company announced that it had purchased the final 20 percent stake in Wyeth K.K., headquartered in Tokyo, from Takeda Pharmaceutical Company.

Wyeth has more than 50,000 employees worldwide, and its products are sold in more than 145 countries. In October 2006, *Science* magazine named Wyeth as one of the top-20 biotech and pharmaceutical employers. Also in 2006, *Working Mother* magazine listed Wyeth as one of its 100 Best Companies for Working Mothers for the ninth year in a row.

What's in a name?

Wyeth began in Philadelphia in the 1860s as a small drugstore named John Wyeth & Brother Co. The drugstore eventually became the first American pharmaceutical manufacturer later in the 19th century, as its habit of prescribing specific, measured medicinal doses and its tablet press machine led to a professional drugmaking enterprise. The fledgling OTC business American Home Products (founded 1926) acquired Wyeth in 1931.

The combined entity retained the American Home Products name and experienced steady growth over the years as it made more acquisitions. Among these properties were Genetics Institute, A.H Robins (maker of Chap Stick, Dimetapp and Robitussin), Ayerst, Lederle Laboratories and American Cyanamid. By 1990, the company manufactured a wide variety of products, including household goods, food and medical supplies.

But since then, it has narrowed its focus to three health-related divisions: consumer health (OTCs such as Advil, Centrum and Dimetapp), pharmaceuticals and Fort Dodge Animal Health (veterinary products). In March 2002, the company changed its name from American Home Products to Wyeth, which had become its largest and most well-known

Visit Vault at **www.vault.com** for insider company profiles, expert advice, career message boards, expert resume reviews, the Vault Job Board and more.

VAULT CAREER LIBRARY

373

The names you know

Six of the company's core product franchises—Effexor, Enbrel, Premarin, Prevnar, Prempro, Wyeth Nutrition and Protonix—each exceeded $1 billion in annual sales in 2006. Antidepressants Effexor and Effexor XR reached sales of $3.7 billion, an increase of 8 percent over 2005.

Prevnar was also the No. 1-selling vaccine in the world in 2006, as Wyeth manufactured 42 million doses and net sales reached nearly $2 billion. Protonix, an inhibitor to treat gastroesophageal reflux disease, increased its 2005 sales by 7 percent, to $1.8 billion. Enbrel, the biopharmaceutical for rheumatoid arthritis, reached more than $4.4 billion in sales.

Wyeth has also started to manufacture a relatively new and effective breast cancer drug, called Herceptin (clinical name Trastuzumab). The drug, administered intravenously, is a targeted therapeutic antibody treatment for women with an aggressive form of breast cancer. In September 2004, Wyeth entered into an agreement with San Francisco-based Genentech (which co-developed Herceptin with ImmunoGen) to manufacture Herceptin. In November 2006, the FDA approved Herceptin as part of a treatment regimen for the adjuvant treatment of patients with HER2-positive, node-positive breast cancer. The FDA approved the manufacture of bulk Herceptin at the firm's Andover facility in 2006.

Prempro precautions

Two of Wyeth's $1 billion franchise products, the hormone replacement drugs Premarin and Prempro (for the treatment of menopausal symptoms, usually hot flashes), have been subject to some medical controversy since 2002. That year, the Women's Health Initiative, a federal study examining the health effects of Prempro, found that women taking the drug had an increased risk of heart disease. In addition, women taking Prempro had a higher incidence of breast cancer than those taking a placebo.

Sales of Prempro fell by 50 percent on the news, and sales continued to drop slightly in 2004. Also, Wyeth has faced numerous lawsuits from people claiming Premarin- and Prempro-related injuries (at least 5,000 were filed between 2002 and 2007, according to Bloomberg). Wyeth has adopted an aggressive legal strategy, fighting these claims in court. It is having mixed success, as four trials had concluded by February 2007, with even results—two returned verdicts in favor of Wyeth and the other two awarded damages to the plaintiffs.

And, unlike controversial drugs that were removed from the market (e.g., Vioxx), Premarin and Prempro are still available and still FDA-approved. Their availability, combined with Wyeth's decent track record in court, has resulted in rising Prempro sales, which increased to $909 million in 2005 and increased again in 2006, to a little more than $1 billion. In September 2006 CNN quoted an analyst who reasoned that "because Prempro is still on the market" and approved by the FDA, its links to breast cancer probably "[aren't] clear cut or severe."

However, in April 2007 a group of researchers published an article in *The New England Journal of Medicine*, suggesting that the 2003-2004 drop in breast cancer rates—at 10 percent, it was the biggest such decrease in over 25 years—occurred because many women stopped taking Prempro and Premarin. The researchers pointed out that cancer diagnoses decreased mostly in women 50 or older, precisely the Prempro demographic. This new health news may have an impact on Prempro's sales.

In 2005, Robert Ruffolo Jr., Wyeth's president of research and development, announced plans to file up to six new drug applications with the FDA by the end of 2007. In comparison, during the entirety of the 1990s, Wyeth had only three experimental compounds that entered the preclinical product development stage.

The firm spent $3.1 billion on research and development in fiscal 2006. The company's goal is to deliver two new drugs to patients and doctors every year. R&D is developing treatments in six general areas: cardiovascular/metabolic, inflammatory diseases, neuroscience, oncology/immunology/hemophailia, women's health and bone disease, and vaccines and infectious diseases.

Also, in June 2005, the company's BioPharma group announced plans to enter into a four-year research agreement with Dublin City University as part of a plan to promote and grow biopharmaceutical production, including a "deeper understanding of cell biology and its applications." At Dublin City University's National Institute for Cellular Biotechnology, Wyeth is currently collaborating on a project that involves Chinese hamsters' ovarian cells.

High rollers

Wyeth has high expectations for its new drugs in 2007—its products are so successful that it has large gaps to fill whenever blockbusters go off-patent. Nearly all of the drugs it has brought before the FDA in 2007 are projected to bring in about $2 billion in annual revenue. Among the debutantes were Viviant (for the prevention of bone loss, i.e., osteoporosis, projected $2 billion), Pristiq (a menopausal preventative, specifically for hot flashes and depression, projected $2 billion), bifeprunox (to treat schizophrenia,

Visit Vault at **www.vault.com** for insider company profiles, expert advice, career message boards, expert resume reviews, the Vault Job Board and more.

VAULT CAREER LIBRARY   **375**

projected $2 billion) and Torisel (to treat kidney cancer). Unfortunately for the firm, the FDA hasn't played along in bringing all of these products to market.

In April the FDA postponed review of Viviant and Pristiq, citing the need for more research and also held off on approving Pristiq for hot flashes in July, stating it needed more information before allowing the drug to go to market. The next month, bifeprunox was rejected by the same agency.

Torisel was the lone approved substance among the bunch, getting a thumbs-up in May after a delay in April. Upon all the news, Wyeth's shares fell to the lowest point in five years, representing a loss of $7.7 billion in market value. Wyeth has another new medication, though: Lybrel, the first contraceptive pill that's designed to eliminate a woman's menstrual periods for as long as she uses it.

The puissant Mr. Poussot

Wyeth announced a new CEO to go with its new drugs. Effective January 1, 2008, Bernard Poussot will ascend to the position from his current roles as president, vice chairman and COO of the company. Current Chairman and CEO Robert Essner will stay on through the end of the year, and afterwards remain interim chairman during the transitional period.

Just as Wyeth announced this management plan, however, a federal judge endangered the company's third-largest drug. Wyeth had taken Israel-based Teva Pharmaceutical to court for marketing a generic version of Protonix, its $1.8 billion, third-ranking drug. Teva countersued, claiming Wyeth's patent (which expires in 2010) is invalid. The judge made a preliminary ruling in September 2007 that Teva can go ahead with its marketing while the case proceeds to trial. While it hasn't yet, Teva could very possibly start selling the drug, and cut further into Wyeth's revenue.

GETTING HIRED

Wy at work

Wyeth's corporate headquarters, with a staff of about 600 employees, accepts resumes for the limited number of positions that open up each year. Wyeth's subsidiaries, however, conduct hiring autonomously to fit particular needs. Consult Wyeth's home page, located at www.wyeth.com/careers, for information about contacting these companies. The site features on online search tool where prospective employees can fill out an application for a specific job and submit a cover letter and resume. Some past openings have included research and development, sales and marketing, finance and administration, information systems and manufacturing and supply chain.

The site also lists the company's recruiting events at colleges and universities across the United States. Wyeth Consumer Healthcare recruits MBA students at universities that include NYU, Cornell, Darden, Columbia and the University of Michigan. The company also offers summer internships for college undergraduates at the firm's Madison, N.J., headquarters. In the past, internships have been offered in areas including medical sales, international, information systems and human resources. Wyeth Consumer Healthcare looks for "energetic, goal-oriented individuals who have solid records of achievement."

In June 2005, the firm announced plans to cut its sales force by up to 30 percent, affecting 750 full-time jobs, as part of a move to restructure the way the sales force operates. However, jobs are not expected to be cut everywhere, and the company is adding jobs in some locations. In June 2006, for example, Wyeth announced that it was adding 150 jobs at its Andover, Mass., biotech campus.

A long process and a long wait

Most insiders say getting hired at Wyeth involves a "very long, rigorous interview process." A senior researcher says that there was only "one day of interviews," which involved 30- to 45-minute "one-on-one interviews" with a future manager and peers. The respondent says, "questions were really about science and to assess cultural fit" and there were "no tough questions." A medical director recalls being asked "detailed questions on how I would structure my work and my department." Another contact recalls, "specific questions included how past experience influenced me, and how I could use that experience at Wyeth. In addition, I was asked why I would consider leaving my previous company."

An Illinois insider says there was "a very pleasant phone screen with the internal recruiter" followed by five or six interviews in Oak Brook with people in "various functions within the office." The respondent says that Wyeth now uses the STAR (situation, task, action, results) behavioral interviewing method. One source adds, "the decision process is notoriously slow."

Visit Vault at **www.vault.com** for insider company profiles, expert advice, career message boards, expert resume reviews, the Vault Job Board and more.

V/\ULT CAREER LIBRARY   **377**

Discounts on Advil!

A scientist says Wyeth has "great benefits overall." These include medical, dental, disability, tuition reimbursement, a pension plan and unlimited sick time. Sources say the company also has stock options and a couple of respondents say they have use of a company car. One individual in the company's Collegeville office says the location has a "great fitness center" as well as a store with "discounts on Advil and other company products." The employee adds that Benchmark Credit Union has a "very friendly staff." One source says the company's medical plans "are becoming more expensive."

OUR SURVEY SAYS

Why work at Wyeth?

Insiders at Wyeth describe the company's environment as "very fast-paced," "scientifically rigorous" and "collaborative." A source in Switzerland says the firm has an "excellent working atmosphere," adding that there is teamwork and "experience is valued." Not everyone, however, likes Wyeth's environment. One individual in Illinois feels it as a "very stuffy, starched-shirt culture." Another says Wyeth is "not perfect," but thinks it's a "good company" as a whole.

Getting more diverse

A source in Pennsylvania says that "Diversity is improving." Another says, "There is a diversity initiative underway in the company, but they have a long way to go in R&D. Most of the lower level people are female and most of the higher level people are male."

Moving up and looking forward

Some say it can be difficult to move up in the ranks at Wyeth. According to a researcher, "Opportunities for advancement vary greatly between departments and groups." A scientist comments that "it's pretty difficult to move into other positions within the company." Chances for promotions also vary depending on an employee's level within Wyeth. A more senior researcher says, "Opportunities for advancement at my level are limited, but available." One insider in Illinois feels, "there's simply no upper turnover." Another says, an inside joke at Wyeth "is that the best way to get a salary increase and a promotion is to quit your job and get rehired to do the same job!"

Most say Wyeth has an "excellent outlook" and a "great pipeline." One research scientist says, "The company's late-stage development pipeline is robust, and several new drug applications are planned for the next few years. Sales are increasing and there are no immediate dangers of patent expirations on top-selling products." Another source adds that Wyeth "is poised for success in the next few years" and says the company's R&D pipeline "is the envy of the industry." Not everyone agrees that Wyeth is going to do better, though. One source says that some of the firm's competitors—such as J&J, Novartis and Schering—"are much more geared to grow."

About the Editor

Michaela R. Drapes graduated from the University of Texas at Austin and has degrees in radio/TV/film and english. Before joining Vault, she was an editor at award-winning business publisher Hoover's Inc. and covered an array of industry sectors, including pharmaceuticals, amusement parks, real estate, and international banking and finance. Michaela is one of the founders of fashion startup Kindling & Tinder and is an irreverent music critic; she also occasionally DJ's at independent rock shows around New York City.

Nicholas R. Lichtenberg holds degrees from the University of Syracuse in drama and history. Before working at Vault, he covered and canvassed trial court bureaucracies in select states as an assignment editor at the legal publishing company ALM Media Inc. He lives in New York.